MW00861259

JOEL, OBADIAH, MALACHI

THE NIV
APPLICATION
COMMENTARY

From biblical text . . . to contemporary life

THE NIV APPLICATION COMMENTARY SERIES

EDITORIAL BOARD

General Editor
Terry Muck

Consulting Editors
Old Testament

Tremper Longman III
John H. Walton

Robert Hubbard
Andrew Dearman

Zondervan Editorial Advisors

Stanley N. Gundry
Vice President and Editor-in-Chief

Jack Kuhatschek
Executive Editor

Verlyn Verbrugge
Senior Editor

JOEL, OBADIAH, MALACHI

THE NIV APPLICATION COMMENTARY

From biblical text . . . to contemporary life

DAVID W. BAKER

ZONDERVAN®

ZONDERVAN.com/
AUTHORTRACKER
follow your favorite authors

ZONDERVAN®

The NIV Application Commentary: Joel, Obadiah, Malachi
Copyright © 2006 by David W. Baker

Requests for information should be addressed to:

Zondervan, *Grand Rapids, Michigan* 49530

Library of Congress Cataloging-in-Publication Data

Baker, David W. (David Weston), 1950–
    Joel, Obadiah, Malachi / David W. Baker.
        p. cm.—(The NIV application commentary)
    Includes bibliographical references and indexes.
    ISBN-10: 0-310-20723-1
    ISBN-13: 978-0-310-20723-8
    1. Bible. O.T. Joel—Commentaries. 2. Bible. O.T. Obadiah—Commentaries.
   3. Bible. O.T. Malachi—Commentaries. I. Title. II. Series.
    BS1575.53.B35 2005
    294'.707—dc22
                                      2005019363
                                                  CIP

All Scripture quotations, unless otherwise indicated, are taken from the *Holy Bible: New International Version*®. NIV®. Copyright © 1973, 1978, 1984 by International Bible Society. Used by permission of Zondervan. All rights reserved.

The website addresses recommended throughout this book are offered as a resource to you. These websites are not intended in any way to be or imply an endorsement on the part of Zondervan, nor do we vouch for their content for the life of this book.

All rights reserved. No part of this publication may be reproduced, stored in a retrieval system, or transmitted in any form or by any means—electronic, mechanical, photocopy, recording, or any other—except for brief quotations in printed reviews, without the prior permission of the publisher.

Printed in the United States of America

13 14 15 16 17 DCI 20 19 18 17 16 15 14 13 12 11 10 9 8 7 6 5

Table of Contents

The NIV Application Commentary Series

When complete, the NIV Application Commentary
will include the following volumes:

Old Testament Volumes

Genesis, John H. Walton
Exodus, Peter Enns
Leviticus/Numbers, Roy Gane
Deuteronomy, Daniel I. Block
Joshua, Robert L. Hubbard Jr.
Judges/Ruth, K. Lawson Younger
1-2 Samuel, Bill T. Arnold
1-2 Kings, Gus Konkel
1-2 Chronicles, Andrew E. Hill
Ezra/Nehemiah, Douglas J. Green
Esther, Karen H. Jobes
Job, Dennis R. Magary
Psalms Volume 1, Gerald H. Wilson
Psalms Volume 2, Jamie Grant
Proverbs, Paul Koptak
Ecclesiastes/Song of Songs, Iain Provan
Isaiah, John N. Oswalt
Jeremiah/Lamentations, J. Andrew Dearman
Ezekiel, Iain M. Duguid
Daniel, Tremper Longman III
Hosea/Amos/Micah, Gary V. Smith
Jonah/Nahum/Habakkuk/Zephaniah,
    James Bruckner
Joel/Obadiah/Malachi, David W. Baker
Haggai/Zechariah, Mark J. Boda

New Testament Volumes

Matthew, Michael J. Wilkins
Mark, David E. Garland
Luke, Darrell L. Bock
John, Gary M. Burge
Acts, Ajith Fernando
Romans, Douglas J. Moo
1 Corinthians, Craig Blomberg
2 Corinthians, Scott Hafemann
Galatians, Scot McKnight
Ephesians, Klyne Snodgrass
Philippians, Frank Thielman
Colossians/Philemon, David E. Garland
1-2 Thessalonians, Michael W. Holmes
1-2 Timothy/Titus, Walter L. Liefeld
Hebrews, George H. Guthrie
James, David P. Nystrom
1 Peter, Scot McKnight
2 Peter/Jude, Douglas J. Moo
Letters of John, Gary M. Burge
Revelation, Craig S. Keener

To see which titles are available,
visit our web site at www.zondervan.com

NIV Application Commentary
Series Introduction

THE NIV APPLICATION COMMENTARY SERIES is unique. Most commentaries help us make the journey from our world back to the world of the Bible. They enable us to cross the barriers of time, culture, language, and geography that separate us from the biblical world. Yet they only offer a one-way ticket to the past and assume that we can somehow make the return journey on our own. Once they have explained the *original meaning* of a book or passage, these commentaries give us little or no help in exploring its *contemporary significance*. The information they offer is valuable, but the job is only half done.

Recently, a few commentaries have included some contemporary application as *one* of their goals. Yet that application is often sketchy or moralistic, and some volumes sound more like printed sermons than commentaries.

The primary goal of the NIV Application Commentary Series is to help you with the difficult but vital task of bringing an ancient message into a modern context. The series not only focuses on application as a finished product but also helps you think through the *process* of moving from the original meaning of a passage to its contemporary significance. These are commentaries, not popular expositions. They are works of reference, not devotional literature.

The format of the series is designed to achieve the goals of the series. Each passage is treated in three sections: *Original Meaning, Bridging Contexts,* and *Contemporary Significance.*

 THIS SECTION HELPS you understand the meaning of the biblical text in its original context. All of the elements of traditional exegesis—in concise form—are discussed here. These include the historical, literary, and cultural context of the passage. The authors discuss matters related to grammar and syntax and the meaning of biblical words.[1] They also seek to explore the main ideas of the passage and how the biblical author develops those ideas.

---

1. Please note that in general, when the authors discuss words in the original biblical languages, the series uses a general rather than a scholarly method of transliteration.

After reading this section, you will understand the problems, questions, and concerns of the *original audience* and how the biblical author addressed those issues. This understanding is foundational to any legitimate application of the text today.

THIS SECTION BUILDS a bridge between the world of the Bible and the world of today, between the original context and the contemporary context, by focusing on both the timely and timeless aspects of the text.

God's Word is *timely*. The authors of Scripture spoke to specific situations, problems, and questions. The author of Joshua encouraged the faith of his original readers by narrating the destruction of Jericho, a seemingly impregnable city, at the hands of an angry warrior God (Josh. 6). Paul warned the Galatians about the consequences of circumcision and the dangers of trying to be justified by law (Gal. 5:2–5). The author of Hebrews tried to convince his readers that Christ is superior to Moses, the Aaronic priests, and the Old Testament sacrifices. John urged his readers to "test the spirits" of those who taught a form of incipient Gnosticism (1 John 4:1–6). In each of these cases, the timely nature of Scripture enables us to hear God's Word in situations that were *concrete* rather than abstract.

Yet the timely nature of Scripture also creates problems. Our situations, difficulties, and questions are not always directly related to those faced by the people in the Bible. Therefore, God's word to them does not always seem relevant to us. For example, when was the last time someone urged you to be circumcised, claiming that it was a necessary part of justification? How many people today care whether Christ is superior to the Aaronic priests? And how can a "test" designed to expose incipient Gnosticism be of any value in a modern culture?

Fortunately, Scripture is not only timely but *timeless*. Just as God spoke to the original audience, so he still speaks to us through the pages of Scripture. Because we share a common humanity with the people of the Bible, we discover a *universal dimension* in the problems they faced and the solutions God gave them. The timeless nature of Scripture enables it to speak with power in every time and in every culture.

Those who fail to recognize that Scripture is both timely and timeless run into a host of problems. For example, those who are intimidated by timely books such as Hebrews, Galatians, or Deuteronomy might avoid reading them because they seem meaningless today. At the other extreme, those who are convinced of the timeless nature of Scripture, but who fail to discern its timely element, may "wax eloquent" about the Melchizedekian priest-hood to a sleeping congregation, or worse still, try to apply the holy wars of the Old Testament in a physical way to God's enemies today.

The purpose of this section, therefore, is to help you discern what is time-less in the timely pages of the Bible—and what is not. For example, how do the holy wars of the Old Testament relate to the spiritual warfare of the New? If Paul's primary concern is not circumcision (as he tells us in Gal. 5:6), what *is* he concerned about? If discussions about the Aaronic priesthood or Melchizedek seem irrelevant today, what is of abiding value in these passages? If people try to "test the spirits" today with a test designed for a specific first-century heresy, what other biblical test might be more appropriate?

Yet this section does not merely uncover that which is timeless in a pas-sage but also helps you to see *how* it is uncovered. The authors of the com-mentaries seek to take what is implicit in the text and make it explicit, to take a process that normally is intuitive and explain it in a logical, orderly fash-ion. How do we know that circumcision is not Paul's primary concern? What clues in the text or its context help us realize that Paul's real concern is at a deeper level?

Of course, those passages in which the historical distance between us and the original readers is greatest require a longer treatment. Conversely, those passages in which the historical distance is smaller or seemingly nonex-istent require less attention.

One final clarification. Because this section prepares the way for dis-cussing the contemporary significance of the passage, there is not always a sharp distinction or a clear break between this section and the one that fol-lows. Yet when both sections are read together, you should have a strong sense of moving from the world of the Bible to the world of today.

THIS SECTION ALLOWS the biblical message to speak with as much power today as it did when it was first written. How can you apply what you learned about Jerusalem, Ephesus, or Corinth to our present-day needs in Chicago, Los Angeles, or London? How can you take a message originally spoken in Greek, Hebrew, and Aramaic and com-municate it clearly in our own language? How can you take the eternal truths originally spoken in a different time and culture and apply them to the sim-ilar-yet-different needs of our culture?

In order to achieve these goals, this section gives you help in several key areas.

(1) It helps you identify contemporary situations, problems, or questions that are truly comparable to those faced by the original audience. Because contemporary situations are seldom identical to those faced by the original audience, you must seek situations that are analogous if your applications are to be relevant.

(2) This section explores a variety of contexts in which the passage might be applied today. You will look at personal applications, but you will also be encouraged to think beyond private concerns to the society and culture at large.

(3) This section will alert you to any problems or difficulties you might encounter in seeking to apply the passage. And if there are several legitimate ways to apply a passage (areas in which Christians disagree), the author will bring these to your attention and help you think through the issues involved.

In seeking to achieve these goals, the contributors to this series attempt to avoid two extremes. They avoid making such specific applications that the commentary might quickly become dated. They also avoid discussing the significance of the passage in such a general way that it fails to engage contemporary life and culture.

Above all, contributors to this series have made a diligent effort not to sound moralistic or preachy. The NIV Application Commentary Series does not seek to provide ready-made sermon materials but rather tools, ideas, and insights that will help you communicate God's Word with power. If we help you to achieve that goal, then we have fulfilled the purpose for this series.

The Editors

General Editor's Preface

PROPHETS DIDN'T GET TO BE PROPHETS by being rays of sunshine. It is almost mandatory for prophets to be harbingers of doom. They sound dyspeptic, act morosely, and are generally irritable and cranky.

In the case of the biblical prophets, the context and nature of the doom that drove them to prophesy varies. Sometimes it is threats from outside Israel, sometimes internal dissention, and almost always a failure of holiness. The cause of the doom, however, never varies. It is always due to God's wrath falling on sin and sinner alike.

Joel, Obadiah, and Malachi are three concise examples of the prophetic genre. Judgment drips like blood from the pages of these three books. God's wrath challenges Israelites in almost every paragraph. None of these books is long, but they make up for their terseness with their pointed accusations and warnings.

We should not equate shortness with simplicity, however. It does not take much reading of this material to see that the judgment being communicated is a complicated affair. Each of the elements of the *orders peccatore*—sin leads to judgment leads to repentance leads to restoration—needs to be nuanced in order to have practical meaning. Joel, Obadiah, and Malachi are all about judgment, but three different settings for that judgment emerge. It is helpful to have David Baker deal with all three of these books in the NIV Application Commentary, because a great deal of understanding about prophecy and judgment comes from comparing and contrasting these three words from God.

Consider, for example, just one simple question: On whom does God's judgment fall? On Israel? On Israel's enemies? On us all? Joel likens God's judgment to an army of locusts that descends on us all. Like a winged AIDS infestation they destroy everything in their path. It is clear that for Joel, the locust invasion is a metaphor for what will happen on the Day of the Lord, when all righteousness accounts will be settled. To describe this judgment we are driven to metaphors of nature, the economy, or foreign armies, but Joel's point is that the scope of God's judgment exceeds them all. The scope is so wide that it drives us either to despair at ever measuring up or to submission to God's power.

Yet the second book of the trio, Obadiah, drives home the message that Israel's mortal enemy, Edom, will be brought low by God's consuming fire.

God's judgment, it becomes clear, inevitably falls on any and all of Israel's enemies. "The day of the LORD is near for all nations. As you have done, it will be done to you; your deeds will return upon your head" (v. 15). Obadiah's prediction that God will punish Edom for standing by as her kinsmen in Judah were overrun by Babylon could lead to a kind of nationalistic triumphalism ("We're number one and God will protect us") or to a humble recognition that God must not be trifled with.

The final book, Malachi, builds on this humble recognition theme because God's wrath is turned on Israel herself at a time when they have neglected the worship of God and failed to live according to God's will. Malachi pulls no punches. He calls the negligent priesthood to account, and he chastises the callous commoners who are ignoring their families.

The recognition that God's judgment falls on us all—on our enemies and on us—is a primary message of these three books taken together. Such a recognition helps us handle the more difficult questions those of us in the twenty-first century have about the ticklish questions of judgment:

- *Can a loving God at the same time be a judge?* The obvious answer for Joel, Obadiah, and Malachi is yes.
- *Are we God's instruments of judgment?* Only in the most indirect sense. Since we ourselves are often judged, we cannot really claim the authority of being God's judges. The collective effect of Joel's, Obadiah's, and Malachi's messages is to anticipate Matthew 7:1: "Do not judge, or you too will be judged." The most we can do is call attention to the fact that God hates sin and will judge sinners. The Day of the Lord will come. But we know neither the time nor the place—only imperfectly the method.
- *How clearly can we identify and differentiate between God's wrath and Satan's evil?* Not clearly at all. In biblical times it took God's specially anointed prophets to make those calls. Today we must recognize that we are equally ignorant of God's righteous ways and terribly short on true prophets (and not nearly short enough on prophet pretenders).

Joel, Obadiah, and Malachi tell us that God does judge righteousness. They tell us that God chooses the time, place, and method of judgment, but doesn't usually let us in on what he decides. And Joel, Obadiah, and Malachi do one more important thing. While discharging their messages of doom and destruction, they leave us all with a feeling not of hopelessness but of hopefulness. Joel does it with his promise of the outpouring of God's Holy Spirit on all people. "Return to the LORD your God, for he is gracious and compassionate, slow to anger and abounding in love, and he relents from sending calamity" (2:12–13).

Obadiah does it by describing restoration in concrete material terms: "But on Mount Zion will be deliverance; it will be holy and the house of Jacob will possess its inheritance" (v. 17).

Malachi does it in a way fitting for the last book of the Old Testament. He predicts the coming of a Messiah who will lead the people to the realization of all their dreams and hopes, a Messiah who would be announced by a prophet (who turned out to be John the Baptist).

Judgment for judgment's sake is not judgment but revenge. That is not what Joel, Obadiah, and Malachi are about. Theirs is a hard message, but it is a message that has repentance and restoration as its goal.

Terry C. Muck

Author's Preface

WAR, TERROR, PAIN, and sickness—signs of our times. It behooves us to remember that we are not alone in these situations. People from every generation have faced these challenges, and many have turned to God for help. Joel's audience faced a natural catastrophe in the form of a plague of locusts, which, with accompanying drought, threatened their agricultural livelihood. These events, along with overwhelming military forces, put their national existence in jeopardy, driving them to God. Obadiah's people faced attack from their neighbors, and Malachi had to contend with his own people showing antagonism and opposition to God. Each had to speak God's words of comfort or confrontation into their situation, just as the church must do in today's world.

I thank the faculty, administration, and students of Ashland Theological Seminary for providing a supportive environment in which to teach and write. It is interesting to see the truths of the prophets enfleshed, at times standing in faith before nature's onslaughts and at times exemplifying Malachi's experiences. I thank the institution for study leave support to pursue this project. I also thank those editors associated with this exciting and challenging commentary project: Terry Muck for the invitation, and Andy Dearman and Verlyn Verbrugge for their suggestions and improvements throughout the book.

Tyndale House in Cambridge, England, is a vibrant and supportive place in which to research and write, and I thank its staff and my fellow learners for the time I was able to spend there. I also thank the library staff and the interlibrary loan system at Ashland for its efficiency.

Most of all, I thank my wife, Morven, and my children, son Adam and his wife Jennifer, and daughter Emily, for their presence and support during the writing process. During this time, Morven completed her own doctoral studies in an area of counseling—sexual abuse and recovery—which receives mention in Malachi; she also took the time to read and comment on this work, which I deeply appreciate. My children are moving toward careers in education and counseling, for which we thank our God. The times spent apart for writing and research have been difficult, but I pray that God "will repay you for the years the locusts have eaten" (Joel 2:25).

Abbreviations

AB	Anchor Bible
ABD	*Anchor Bible Dictionary*
AHw	*Akkadisches Handwörterbuch*
ANEP	*Ancient Near Eastern Pictures*
ANET	*Ancient Near Eastern Texts*
AOAT	Alter Orient und Altes Testament
ASV	American Standard Version
ATJ	*Ashland Theological Journal*
BDB	Brown-Driver-Briggs, *Hebrew and English Lexicon of the Old Testament*
BEATAJ	Beiträge zur Erforschung des alten Testaments und des antiken Judentums
BJRL	*Bulletin of the John Rylands Library*
BST	Bible Speaks Today
BT	*The Bible Translator*
BZAW	Beihefte zum Zeitschrift für die alttestamentliche Wissenschaft
CAD	*Chicago Assyrian Dictionary*
CAT	Commentaire de l'Ancien Testament
CBQ	*Catholic Biblical Quarterly*
COS	*Context of Scripture*
CTR	*Criswell Theological Review*
DCH	*Dictionary of Classical Hebrew*
DDD	*Dictionary of Deities and Demons*
DOTP	*Dictionary of the Old Testament: Pentateuch*
DSB	Daily Study Bible
ESV	English Standard Version
GKC	Gesenius-Kautzsch-Cowley's *Hebrew Grammar*
GNB	Good News Bible
HALOT	*Hebrew and Aramaic Lexicon of the Old Testament*
HAR	*Hebrew Annual Review*
HCOT	Historical Commentary on the Old Testament
HSM	Harvard Semitic Monographs
ICC	International Critical Commentary
JB	Jerusalem Bible

Abbreviations

Joüon	P. Joüon, *A Grammar of Biblical Hebrew*
JSSR	*Journal for the Scientific Study of Religion*
KAT	Kommentar zum Alten Testament
KJV	King James Version
LXX	Septuagint
MT	Masoretic Text
NASB	New American Standard Bible
NBD	*New Bible Dictionary*
NCBC	New Century Bible Commentary
NCV	New Century Version
NEAEHL	*The New Encyclopedia of Archaeological Excavations in the Holy Land*
NIBC	New International Biblical Commentary
NIDOTTE	*New International Dictionary of Old Testament Theology and Exegesis*
NICOT	New International Commentary on the Old Testament
NIV	New International Version
NJPS	New Jewish Publication Society version
NJB	New Jerusalem Bible
NLT	New Living Translation
NRSV	New Revised Standard Version
NWT	New World Translation
OTL	Old Testament Library
REB	Revised English Bible
SBLDS	Society of Biblical Literature Dissertation Series
SAOT	Studies in Ancient Oriental Civilizations
TCS	Texts from Cuneiform Sources
TOTC	Tyndale Old Testament Commentaries
TUAT	*Texte aus der Umwelt des Alten Testaments*
UT	C. H. Gordon, *Ugaritic Textbook*
VTSup	Vetus Testamentum Supplements
Waltke-O'Connor	B. Waltke and M. O'Connor, *An Introduction to Biblical Hebrew Syntax*
WEC	Wycliffe Exegetical Commentary
Williams	Ronald J. Williams, *Hebrew Syntax: An Outline*
YNER	Yale Near Eastern Researches
ZAW	Zeitschrift für die alttestamentliche Wissenschaft

Introduction to Joel

WESTERN ECONOMIES, WHICH depend largely on manufacturing, service, and technology, react strongly to market fluctuations. The stock market plays a significant role by indicating the public face of economic health. Vacillations in it not only reflect but also affect the entire economy.

This is not the case in every society, however. For example, in more agriculturally based societies, such as in North America before the Industrial Revolution or in the ancient Near East during the period of the Old Testament, other factors play into economic fortune or failure. Events that affect crops or herds precipitate economic weal or woe. Timely, sufficient rainfall aid crop production, while blight or drought cripples it.

A disastrous event for agriculturalist and pastoralist alike is an infestation of locusts. When they hatch and swarm, they can be as dense as four to five thousand insects per square meter, and they strip all green foliage, destroying crops and trees.[1] This then depletes the next season's fodder for livestock as well as grain for the family larder. With no large-scale ability to stockpile supplies, such an event places nations in grave peril.

This is the situation driving Joel's prophecy. His hearers know and fear agricultural calamities. Such things also serve as the metaphorical vehicle to symbolize another rapacious catastrophe, an invading enemy army. The prophet plays off these two events in his prophecies. He likens the two events as both being catastrophic, but also as times in which Yahweh restores his people's fortunes.

This kind of hope in the face of catastrophe is not one that sits well with many Christians today. A "health and wealth gospel" understands blessing as flowing inevitably from a right relationship with God, while suffering indicates a breach in one's relationship with him. Joel gives a different take on this. He does not imply that blessing means elimination of obstacles and pain, but rather that God's presence, bringing one through these events, which are a natural concomitant to all human existence, is where blessing really resides.

---

1. For a sobering look at the number and power of such swarms, see the following website from the United Nations (http://www.fao.org/NEWS/GLOBAL/LOCUSTS/Locuhome.htm). See also J. A. Lockwood, *Locust: The Devastating Rise and Mysterious Disappearance of the Insect That Shaped the American Frontier* (New York: Basic, 2004).

Joel the Person

THE STATED WRITER of these prophecies is Joel, whose name means "Yah[weh] is God." While a ringing affirmation of faith at any time, it is an especially appropriate name during a period when Baalism was making inroads into Israel, evidence for which is suggested by some.[2] Since religious syncretism was a constant threat to God's people from the time of the Conquest to at least the time of Josiah (640–609 B.C.; 2 Kings 23:4–5) and possibly even until the postexilic period (Zech. 12:11), the name does not provide much interpretational help. It is used in the Old Testament during this entire time period.[3] The only other identifying feature of Joel is his father's name, Pethuel, which is otherwise unknown.

From internal evidence, Joel is a man of all the people. He announces suffering for all levels of society, from leader to common field laborer. All suffer, but also all will be blessed and restored. This extends not only throughout the various social strata, but also through divisions of age and sex (cf. 2:28–29). Joel's announcements are tinged more with empathy than with condemnation. He lays little blame for the situation on God's people (five times referring to them as "my people": 2:26–27); rather, he offers them the hope arising from judgment against their oppressors.

Geopolitical Context

THE PROPHECIES OF JOEL are directed toward Judah (3:1, 6, 8, 18, 19, 20) and Jerusalem (2:32; 3:1, 6, 16, 17, 20). "Israel" is mentioned only three times, once indicating the northern kingdom that has already been exiled (3:2) and twice referring to the entire nation, including and perhaps being coterminous with Judah (2:27; 3:16). Holy sites such as the temple ("the house of the LORD," 1:9, 14; cf. 2:17; "the house of your/our God," 1:13, 16); and "Zion" (2:1, 15, 23, 32; 3:16, 17, 21) are frequent, while there is no reference to any strictly northern Israelite sites. Unlike other prophets such as Amos, where both Israel and Judah find a place, Joel reserves his comments for Judah.

An unidentified army threatens Judah (2:1–11), while other peoples are explicitly identified in 3:4–8, raising the prophecies onto the world stage. The three enemies of Judah—Tyre, Sidon, and the "regions of Philistia" (3:4)—sell Judeans to the Ionians (Greeks, 3:6) and are themselves sold to the Sabaeans (3:8). Tyre is an island city on the Phoenician coast in what is now

---

2. J. L. Crenshaw, *Joel* (AB; New York: Doubleday, 1995), 46–47.

3. S. L. McKenzie, "Joel (PERSON)," *ABD*, 3:873.

Lebanon, about twenty-five miles south of Sidon. An ancient town, it is known from Egyptian, Assyrian, and Ugaritic sources as well as later, classical sources. It was connected to the mainland by a causeway under Alexander the Great in 332 B.C. In the tenth century B.C., its rulers befriended Israel (e.g., 2 Sam. 5:11; 1 Kings 5), but later the relationship degenerated (e.g., Amos 1:9–11), culminating with Tyrian celebration when Jerusalem fell to Babylon, and she was able to benefit from Judah's demise (Ezek. 26:1).

Sidon to the north is also an ancient coastal city mentioned in early extrabiblical sources, including some coins identifying it as the "mother of Tyre."[4] It experienced conflict with Israel as early as the judges period (Judg. 10:12) and was taken by Babylon at the same time that Jerusalem fell (cf. Jer. 25:22; 27:3; 47:4). The last reference indicates that Tyre and the Philistines would fall at the same time.

The five cities of Philistia (Gaza, Ashkelon, Ashdod, Ekron, and Gath) are situated further south on the Mediterranean coastline to the west of the Dead Sea. The settlers in the region apparently originated in the Aegean Sea area and arrived from the west and north at almost the same time as the Israelites moved into the land from the south and west. Conflict between the two peoples vying for the same territory was fierce, as reflected in Judges and throughout the life of David, who was able to subdue them (1 Sam. 17; 18:6–9, 25–27, 30; 19:8), though conflict was not eliminated (cf. 1 Kings 15:27; 16:15; 2 Chron. 21:16–17). Subdued by Assyria and Babylonia, the Philistines became a Persian colony, losing their own identity.[5]

The two other nations received exiles. Judeans and Jerusalemites ended up among the Ionians (3:6, "Greeks"; Heb. *yewānîm*). Mention is first made of the eponymous ancestor Javan (*yāwān*), a descendant of Japheth, in the Table of Nations (Gen. 10:2, 4; cf. 1 Chron. 1:5), but the nation itself is only mentioned in later biblical texts (Isa. 66:19; Ezek. 27:13, 19; Zech. 9:13; Dan. 8:21; 10:20; 11:2). Although it reached its greatest dominance over the region during the Hellenistic period (338–146 B.C.), Greece had contacts and influence in Israel from at least the seventh century B.C.[6] Nothing of this Greek human trade receives mention elsewhere in Scripture, but slavery formed a noticeable part of the Greek economy.[7]

---

4. Philip C. Schmitz, "Sidon (Place)," *ABD*, 6:18.

5. H. J. Katzenstein, "Philistines," *ABD*, 5:326–28. The only remaining legacy of the Philistines is in the name "Palestine."

6. John Bright, *A History of Israel*, 4th ed. (Louisville: Westminster John Knox, 2000), 322, n. 33.

7. Crenshaw, *Joel*, 25 and n. 25.

The nations exploiting Judah were themselves to be sold to the Sabaeans, "a nation far away" (3:8), whose eponymous ancestor is also first encountered in the Table of Nations as a descendant of Shem ("Sheba" in Gen. 10:28; cf. 1 Chron. 1:22). They are a south Arabian nation with diplomatic relations with Israel as early as the tenth century B.C., when their queen visited Solomon (1 Kings 10; 2 Chron. 9). Both the Greeks and the Sabaeans are far removed from the everyday life of Judah, so exile to these locations may be a way of saying that people end up in the back of beyond.

Finally, two nations, Egypt and Edom, suffer as a result of their violence against Judah (3:19). Egypt is one of the regional superpowers, gaining and losing control over Israel repeatedly.[8] Israel lies on the natural land routes between Egypt and her neighbors to the north and east, so military campaigns from or against Egypt naturally proceeded through Israel, with accompanying depredations from most who stormed through. A backward look at previous Egypt–Israel relationships could look to many periods, while reference to the future destruction could refer to that done by Assyria in the late eighth century B.C., Babylonia in the late seventh–early sixth centuries, or Persia in the mid-sixth century.

The history of interaction between Judah and her eastern neighbor Edom is riddled with animosity, perhaps culminating at the destruction of Jerusalem, but by no means only starting there (see the commentary on Obadiah in this volume). This animosity continued until at least 553 B.C., when Babylon captured Edom.[9] It may well have continued beyond this time among the remnants of the Edomites, but their history during the Persian and Hellenistic periods is not well known.[10]

Chronological Context

THERE IS NO direct evidence from the book itself to determine its historical setting conclusively, though circumstantial evidence has been mined for assistance. Its position toward the beginning of the Minor Prophets, between two prophets dated to the eighth century, has led some to place it early in the history of Israelite prophecy.[11] The LXX, however, associates Joel with the later Obadiah and Jonah, so chronology cannot be the deciding factor

---

8. See "Egypt, History of," esp. the section of A. Spalinger, "3rd Intermediate—Saite Period (Dyn. 21–26)," *ABD*, 2:356–67.

9. P.-A. Beaulieu, *The Reign of Nabonidus, King of Babylon, 556–539 B.C.* (YNER 10; New Haven, Conn.: Yale Univ. Press, 1989), 166.

10. J. R. Bartlett, "Edom," *ABD*, 2:293–94.

11. H. W. Wolff, *Joel and Amos* (Hermeneia; Philadelphia: Fortress, 1977), 3.

in both cases. The reasons for the relative position of books within the canon are unclear, so they provide no compelling proof. It is probable that matters of content rather than chronology (cf. the discussion of Joel 3:16, 18 and their ties to Amos 1:2; 9:13) led to Joel's placement before Amos.[12]

References to Judah (3:1, 6, 8, 18, 19) outnumber those to Israel (2:27; 3:2, 16). At least one reference to "Israel" (3:2) indicates that the northern nation of Israel was already exiled, placing the prophecies after the fall of Israel and its capital, Samaria, in 722 B.C. The term "Israel" can apply, however, to the entire nation, including Judah, as it seems to do in 2:27 and 3:16. If so, the prophecies concern either the period after the loss of territory and increased tribute to Assyria exacted in 701 B.C. (2 Kings 18:13–16), after the defeat and exile in 598/597 B.C. under the Neo-Babylonian Empire (2 Kings 24:10–16; 2 Chron. 36:6; Jer 36:30), or even after the destruction of Jerusalem and the temple in 587 B.C.

Weighing against the latter interpretation is reference to an existing "house of the LORD" or the temple where people minister before him (1:9, 13, 14, 16; 2:17). This rules out the period from 586–516/515 B.C., between its destruction and rebuilding under the leadership of Zerubbabel (cf. Haggai, Zechariah). A preexilic period might be preferred, since the temple destruction is anticipated and prayed against (2:17) rather than remembered, as it would have been after 587, though there are undoubtedly such prayers also brought for the Second Temple, rebuilt under Ezra.

Crenshaw suggests a later date since "the reference to the captivity (4:2 [3:2]) and deportation of Jewish children (3:3 [3:3]) exclude a time before the fall of Jerusalem. Furthermore, the animosity toward Edom (3:19 [3:19]) is best explained in connection with the events of 586, when fleeing Judeans were turned over to the Babylonians by neighboring Edomites."[13] Neither point is compelling for an exilic or postexilic date, though they do allow it. Capture and deportation were all too familiar to Judah from long experience, as already noted, and Edom's and Egypt's destruction is anticipated in 3:19 (see Obadiah, who also prophesies concerning Edom).

Joel looks back on Judah's mistreatment by several enemies: Tyre, Sidon, and Philistia (3:4), who sell captives to the Greeks (Ionians, 3:6) and themselves end up in the hands of the Sabaeans (3:8). No specific biblical reference is made to any of these events, so they do not help in determining the date of the events described. This is exacerbated since there is in each case a long history of animosity between Judah and these nations, and capture of prisoners for trade as slaves was a common element of ancient war.

---

12. Ibid., 3.
13. Crenshaw, *Joel*, 24.

The prophet makes frequent use of material from other prophets, and that might prove more useful in determining at least a relative date of the book. In some cases it is not clear in which way the borrowing went, but that is not the case in 2:32. There, in quoting Obadiah 17a, Joel uses the quotation formula "as the LORD has said." There are a number of other cases of prophetic allusion in the small book. These include the following (Joel references are listed first, without a book designation):

> 1:15–Isa. 13:6[2x]; Ezek. 30:2–3; Obad. 15; Zeph. 1:7
> 2:2–Zeph. 1:14–15
> 2:3–Isa. 51:3; Ezek. 36:35
> 2:6–Nah. 2:10
> 2:13–Ex. 34:6; Jonah 4:2
> 2:14–Jonah 3:9
> 2:17–Ps. 79:10; 115:2
> 2:20–21–Isa. 45:5, 6, 14, 18, 21, 22; 46:9
> 2:28–Ezek. 39:29
> 2:31–Mal. 4:5
> 2:32–Obad. 17
> 3:1–Jer. 33:15; 50:4, 20
> 3:2–Isa. 66:18; Zech. 14:2
> 3:5–Obad. 15
> 3:8–Isa. 1:2; 22:25; (24:3); 25:8; Jer. 13:15; Obad. 18
> 3:10–Isa. 2:4
> 3:16–Amos 1:2
> 3:16–Isa. 13:13
> 3:17–Ezek. 36:11 + nineteen other times in Ezekiel[14]
> 3:18–Amos 9:13

Meier makes the useful observation that "since much of the prophetic output is no longer available, it is difficult to determine just how many citations marked explicitly as divine speech are in fact quotations from anterior oracles."[15] In other words, there may well be additional citations in Joel that we cannot determine. From the existing allusions, however, a time period around 500 B.C. well fits the evidence.

---

14. Ezek. 6:7, 13; 7:4, 9; 11:10, 12; 13:14; 14:8; 15:7; 17:21; 20:38, 42, 44; 22:22; 25:5; 35:9; 37:6, 13, 14; cf. also Ex. 6:7; 10:2; 16:12; 1 Kings 20:28.

15. S. A. Meier, *Speaking of Speaking: Marking Direct Discourse in the Hebrew Bible* (VTSup 46; Leiden: Brill, 1992), 213. For the fullest treatment of this topic, see S. Bergler, *Joel als Schrift-interpret* (Frankfurt am Main: Peter Lang, 1988).

Prinsloo helpfully comments regarding the topic of dating of Joel:

It is virtually impossible to date it exactly purely on the basis of its contents. Without adopting an ahistorical approach or ignoring the problems, the sincere exegete should acknowledge this fact. And if it is conceded that it is all but impossible to date the book satisfactorily, he must adopt the only other course left open to him, namely to use the text of Joel itself to the utmost to try and discover its actual message and intention. Since the historical context cannot be accurately reconstructed, the book has to be expounded within its intrinsic literary context.[16]

Literary Art

JOEL IS WRITTEN mainly in poetry, as is the case for most prophecy. As such, it uses language carefully and for effect. Two literary devices used frequently in the book are simile and metaphor, figurative comparisons between things. Simile is evident through the twelve appearances of the comparative preposition "like" in Hebrew (see 1:8, 15; 2:2, 3, 4[2x], 5[3x], 7[2x], 9).

Metaphor is also plentiful in Joel. These include various types:

- personification: "nation" of locusts (1:6); ground mourns (1:10); land fears, is glad, rejoices (2:21); "innocent blood" (3:19)
- animal: Yahweh's roaring (3:16)
- plant: joy withers away (1:12)
- meaning extension: rend the heart (2:13); locusts as fire and flame (1:19; 2:3, possibly literal); locusts eating years (2:25); harvesting of sins (3:13); Yahweh as stronghold and fortress (3:16); pouring out Spirit (2:28–29); treading grapes as judgment (3:13, cf. Jer. 25:30; Lam. 1:15)

A central literary concern is the unity of the book, which is questioned because of the clear break between a description of a natural calamity that had befallen Judah (1–2:27) on the one hand, and a future international (eschatological?) judgment (2:28–3:21) on the other.[17] It must be noted, however, that much of the vocabulary in Joel is repeated within the book, often more than once, or else themes or motifs are reused. This emphasizes

---

16. Willem S. Prinsloo, *The Theology of the Book of Joel* (BZAW 163; Berlin: de Gruyter, 1985), 92.

17. Ronald Simkins, *Yahweh's Activity in History and Nature in the Book of Joel* (Lewiston, N.Y.: Mellen, 1991), 203–4; J. Barton, *Joel and Obadiah: A Commentary* (OTL; Louisville: Westminster John Knox, 2001), 5–7.

the seriousness of the message, but also the unity of the text.[18] One cannot with certainty say at what stage this unity is achieved, or whether it is the work of a single author[19] or of a redactor of originally separate units.[20] In its present form, however, the book functions well as a unit.

Theology

The Day of the Lord

THE DAY OF THE LORD plays a significant literary as well as theological role in the book. Five times Joel uses that phrase (1:15; 2:1, 11, 31; 3:14), while six times he describes days of God's intervention (1:15, "that day"; 2:2, "day of darkness and gloom," "day of clouds and blackness"; 2:29, "in those days" [pouring out God's Spirit]; 3:1, "in those days" [restore Judah's fortunes]; 3:18, "in that day" [abundance of wine, milk, and water]),[21] arranged in such a way throughout the book as to suggest that the writer saw it as a unifying theme.[22] The Day of the Lord plays a rich role in the prophets,[23] and two of its facets are brought out by Joel: the nature of this day and the time of its coming.

The Day is commonly held by Israel to be a day in which God blesses them, a day to be anticipated (e.g., Amos 5:18). This view is supported by numerous false prophets who present the same theological fallacy: If you are an Israelite, you only face hope and blessing (e.g., Jer. 14:13–15; 27:9–18; Ezek. 13:10–12; Mic. 3:5). It is thus easy for Joel's audience, and Israel from all periods in her history, to anticipate the wrong message when they hear about the coming of the Day of the Lord.

---

18. For a list of examples, see G. A. Mikre–Selassie, "Repetition and Synonyms in the Translation of Joel with Special Reference to the Amharic Language," *BT* 36 (1985): 230–37.

19. Wolff, *Joel*, 7–8.

20. B. S. Childs, *Introduction to the Old Testament as Scripture* (Philadelphia: Fortress, 1979), 389.

21. See J. D. Nogalski, "The Day(s) of YHWH in the Book of the Twelve," in *Thematic Threads in the Book of the Twelve*, ed. Paul L. Redditt and Aaron Schart (BZAW 325; Berlin, de Gruyter, 2003), 200.

22. L. F. Bliese, "Metrical Sequences and Climax in the Poetry of Joel, *Occasional Papers in Translation and Textlinguistics* 2.4 (1988): 74. There is also evidence that the concept unites the entirety of the twelve Minor Prophets; see Nogalski, "The Day(s)," 192–93 and bibliography.

23. See commentaries on Obadiah, 182–83, and Malachi, 271.

Three references to the Day of the Lord in Joel indicate that it is "near" or "at hand" (1:15; 2:1; 3:14), and another describes it as being already present (2:11). This is a common warning motif among the prophets, calling for attention to something before it might come (e.g., Isa. 13:6; Ezek. 30:3; Obad. 15; Zeph. 1:7, 14). The fifth occurrence of the Day, however, puts a different chronological slant on it, viewing it as distant (2:31), an event coming "afterward" (2:28). The two chronological vantage points also present different interpretations of its nature. All five occurrences in the book speak of a time of calamity, terror, destruction, and darkness. The first three have it happening to Israel and her people. The last two verses, however, direct the judgmental aspects of the Day against Israel's neighbors (3:12), or those even among Israel who are not responding appropriately to God (contrasted with those who do respond rightly in 2:32).

There is a distinction, therefore, between the near term "day," which is black indeed for everyone, and a more distant "day," which anticipates a time of hope for the faithful (cf. 2:29; 3:1, 18). In light of the despair facing everyone because of the current calamities, there needs to be a ray of future hope, but also a warning that there is no restoration without repentance.

There is also evidence that the blessings of the Day for a repentant people might not be that distant. Joel describes God's pity on his people (2:19), referring to the prophecy in Hosea 2:21–22. The immediate context of Joel does not mention the Day, but Hosea places it in that context.

This shows that the concept of the Day of the Lord is not monolithic, anticipating one event at a future time. While there is evidence for a future and cataclysmic event of judgment and of blessing, there are also other days, also of blessing and judgment, that are harbingers of that final event.[24] This can be compared with military events during World War II. There were numerous days of Allied offensive leading up to the main attack on *the* day of major assault, June 6, 1944, otherwise known as D-Day. The intermediary days of the Lord are in anticipation of the culminating D-Day of the Lord.

Zion

ZION ALSO PLAYS a theologically significant role in the book of Joel, explicitly mentioned seven times (2:1, 15, 23, 32; 3:16, 17, 21).[25] Its first occurrence

---

24. This has been referred to as Joel's multireferential nature (R. C. van Leeuwen, "Scribal Wisdom and Theodicy in the Book of the Twelve," *In Search of Wisdom: Essays in Honor of John G. Gammie*, ed. L. G. Perdue et al. (Louisville: Westminster John Knox, 1993), 40, n. 32.

25. It continues in importance in other prophetic books as well (e.g., Zech. 1:14, 17; 9:9, 13), and on into the New Testament (e.g., Heb. 12:22; Rev. 14:1).

is as the site of trumpet blasts, raising the alarm cry heralding the Day of the Lord (2:1) and calling the people to a solemn assembly (2:15). A summons to Zion is also mentioned in other biblical contexts, and the purpose for assembly is ambiguous. At times it has a negative connotation, being a warning of destruction or punishment (e.g., Isa. 3:6; 10:12, 24; 64:10; Jer. 4:6; 6:2). On other occasions, Zion will receive blessing (Isa. 52:1, 2, 7, 8), so the call does not of itself point unambiguously toward either good or ill.

Blessing bestowed anew on the land and its inhabitants is also the theme of the encounter with Zion in 2:23. It is often associated elsewhere with goodness, faithfulness, redemption, and even the law itself (e.g., Isa. 1:27; 2:3; 14:32; 33:20; 59:20; Mic. 4:2; Zeph. 3:14–17). These benefits come from its association with God. When the association is removed, so are the benefits (e.g., Jer. 14:19; 26:18; Mic. 3:12). A variation of this motif of blessing is Zion as the place of refuge and escape, picked up in its occurrence in Joel 2:32 as well as elsewhere (e.g., 2 Kings 19:31; Isa. 30:19; 35:10; 37:31; 51:3; Obad. 17; Mic. 4:7).

Noise is also associated with Zion in its next occurrence, this time in the form of a roar from God striking awe in enemies but being an encouraging sound for his people (3:16). This multivalent sound also occurs in other prophecies (e.g., Amos 1:2; cf. Isa. 31:4).

Zion as God's dwelling place is the subject of the final two Joel passages (3:17, 21). Its holiness is especially emphasized. This particular state is highlighted in other passages (e.g., Isa. 4:3–5), while the presence of God there is the focus of others (e.g., Isa. 8:18; 12:6; Jer. 31:6; 50:5). It will not only be the place of his presence but also of his sovereign rule (e.g., Isa. 24:23; Mic. 4:7; Zech. 9:9; cf. Isa. 16:1; 18:7), characterized by justice (e.g., Isa. 28:16–17; 33:5).

The prophecy thus shows a panoply of events related to Zion. As the residence of God in his temple, it is holy and therefore not welcoming of those who do not follow God. Those who turn to him, however, are welcome and provided rest and refreshment. It is the source of warning calls for those in opposition, but also a summons for those seeking succor. In a manner similar to that surrounding the Day of the Lord, Zion has two facets: a positive one for those desiring a positive relationship with God, and a negative one for those opposing his will and ways.

Outline of Joel

THERE ARE TWO TRADITIONS of verse and chapter divisions used today for Joel. Stephen Langton undertook the earliest division into chapters, using the Vulgate, in the early thirteenth century A.D. His division, used in the English Bible and this commentary, has three chapters, consisting of 1:1–20; 2:1–32; 3:1–21. From the sixteenth century, Jewish tradition divides the book into four sections (1:1–20; 2:1–27; 3:1–5; 4:1–21),[1] which are reflected in square brackets in this outline and in the headings, but not in the body of the commentary itself.

---

1. Barton, *Joel*, 5.

Annotated Bibliography on Joel

Ahlström, G. W. *Joel and the Temple Cult of Jerusalem*. VTSup 21. Leiden: Brill, 1971. A study of the setting and content of the book.

Barton, J. *Joel and Obadiah: A Commentary*. OTL. Louisville: Westminster John Knox Press, 2001. A useful mainline look at historical and linguistic backgrounds. Joel is pages xiii–xviii, 1–111.

Bergler, Siegfried. *Joel als Schriftinterpret*. BEATAJ 16. Frankfurt: Peter Lang, 1988. An important study of word and sound play, vocabulary, and inner biblical exegesis.

Bliese, L. F. "Metrical Sequences and Climax in the Poetry of Joel." *Occasional Papers in Translation and Textlinguistics* 2/4 (1988): 52–84. An analysis of the poetics of the prophecy.

Borowski, Oded. *Agriculture in Iron Age Israel*. Winona Lake, Ind.: Eisenbrauns, 1987. A useful illustrated study especially relevant for this prophecy.

Crenshaw, J. L. *Joel*. AB. New York: Doubleday, 1995. An important work of contemporary, mainline biblical scholarship.

Finley, Thomas J. "Joel." Pages 11–76 in *Joel, Amos, Obadiah*. WEC. Chicago: Moody Press, 1996. Useful in-depth analysis of Hebrew text. Mostly accessible to those without Hebrew.

Hubbard, D. A. "Joel." Pages 21–85 in *Joel and Amos: An Introduction and Commentary*. TOTC. Downers Grove, Ill.: InterVarsity Press, 1989.

Keller, C.-A. "Joël." Pages 99–155 in *Osée, Joël, Abdias, Jonas, Amos*. CAT 11a. Neuchatel: Delachaux & Niestlé, 1965. A French commentary especially helpful in its literary analysis.

Limburg, J. "The Book of Joel." Pages 55–77 in *Hosea–Micah*. Interpretation. Atlanta: John Knox, 1988. A brief commentary seeking to find application for the church.

Prinsloo, Willem S. *The Theology of the Book of Joel*. BZAW 163. Berlin: de Gruyter, 1985. An analysis of structure and inner-biblical exegesis as well as theology.

Prior, David. *The Message of Joel, Micah & Habakkuk*. Pages 17–102. BST. Downers Grove, Ill.: InterVarsity Press, 1998. While not a complete commentary per se, the volume provides useful exegetical and practical insights.

Redditt, Paul L., and Aaron Schart. *Thematic Threads in the Book of the Twelve*. BZAW 325; Berlin: de Gruyter, 2003. A helpful collection of essays on the Minor Prophets as a whole, with several aiding the interpretation of Joel.

Simkins, Ronald. *Yahweh's Activity in History and Nature in the Book of Joel*. Lewiston, N.Y.: Mellen, 1991. A detailed, often technical study especially useful in its discussion of nature and the Day of the Lord.

Stuart, Douglas. "Joel." Pages 221–71 in *Hosea–Jonah*. WBC. Waco, Tex.: Word, 1987. A useful commentary by a leading evangelical exegete.

Wolff, H. W. "Joel." Pages 3–86 in *Joel and Amos*. Hermeneia. Philadelphia: Fortress, 1977. A leading German scholar who provides a detailed exegesis of the book, which he holds is a literary unity.

Joel 1:1–20

T HE WORD OF the LORD that came to Joel son of
     Pethuel.

2 Hear this, you elders;
    listen, all who live in the land.
Has anything like this ever happened in your days
    or in the days of your forefathers?
3 Tell it to your children,
    and let your children tell it to their children,
    and their children to the next generation.
4 What the locust swarm has left
    the great locusts have eaten;
what the great locusts have left
    the young locusts have eaten;
what the young locusts have left
    other locusts have eaten.

5 Wake up, you drunkards, and weep!
    Wail, all you drinkers of wine;
wail because of the new wine,
    for it has been snatched from your lips.
6 A nation has invaded my land,
    powerful and without number;
it has the teeth of a lion,
    the fangs of a lioness.
7 It has laid waste my vines
    and ruined my fig trees.
It has stripped off their bark
    and thrown it away,
    leaving their branches white.

8 Mourn like a virgin in sackcloth
    grieving for the husband of her youth.
9 Grain offerings and drink offerings
    are cut off from the house of the LORD.
The priests are in mourning,
    those who minister before the LORD.

¹⁰ The fields are ruined,
   the ground is dried up;
 the grain is destroyed,
   the new wine is dried up,
   the oil fails.
¹¹ Despair, you farmers,
   wail, you vine growers;
 grieve for the wheat and the barley,
   because the harvest of the field is destroyed.
¹² The vine is dried up
   and the fig tree is withered;
 the pomegranate, the palm and the apple tree—
   all the trees of the field—are dried up.
 Surely the joy of mankind
   is withered away.

¹³ Put on sackcloth, O priests, and mourn;
   wail, you who minister before the altar.
 Come, spend the night in sackcloth,
   you who minister before my God;
 for the grain offerings and drink offerings
   are withheld from the house of your God.
¹⁴ Declare a holy fast;
   call a sacred assembly.
 Summon the elders
   and all who live in the land
 to the house of the LORD your God,
   and cry out to the LORD.

¹⁵ Alas for that day!
   For the day of the LORD is near;
   it will come like destruction from the Almighty.

¹⁶ Has not the food been cut off
   before our very eyes—
 joy and gladness
   from the house of our God?
¹⁷ The seeds are shriveled
   beneath the clods.
 The storehouses are in ruins,
   the granaries have been broken down,
   for the grain has dried up.

18 How the cattle moan!
　　The herds mill about
　because they have no pasture;
　　　even the flocks of sheep are suffering.

19 To you, O LORD, I call,
　　for fire has devoured the open pastures
　　and flames have burned up all the trees of the field.
20 Even the wild animals pant for you;
　　the streams of water have dried up
　　and fire has devoured the open pastures.

 GOD SPEAKS TO his people through his prophets, who are usually identified for the subsequent readers of the written prophecies. Since the intended audience of the written record is not present when God's words are initially given through the original oral medium, they need to be informed of some of the circumstances of that original delivery. Sometimes information such as date (cf. Hosea, Amos) or place (Ezekiel) is provided. In Joel this background information is meager: only the man's name and that of his father. The all-important source of his message, God himself, is identified.

Heading (1:1)

JOEL'S PROPHECIES ARE headed by two elements in addition to his name. First is the designation "the word of the LORD," which is frequent in all the prophetic books except Daniel, Obadiah, Nahum, and Habakkuk. It also heads Ezra (Ezra 1:1), which is not a prophetic book but a work of history. Therefore, the term should not be understood as indicating strictly literary genre. Rather, it indicates that the source of its contents is divine, deriving its authority from God rather than from either a king or another human being.

The Hebrew term lying behind "the LORD" is *yhwh*, the personal name of Israel's God. Technical studies refer to the name as *the Tetragrammaton*, that is, the four-letter word par excellence. Its pronunciation is not known, since between the Testaments it stopped being pronounced, being replaced by the Hebrew word for "Lord" (*ʾādôn*). From here it passed through Greek (*kyrios* = "Lord") to most of our English translations, which also use "Lord," though often done in small caps as "LORD." The New Jerusalem Bible is rare among English translations in presenting the form correctly as "Yahweh."

The difference between the "Yahweh" and the term "Lord" can at times be significant since Yahweh, a personal name, indicates an intimacy and covenant whereas "Lord" suggests a relationship of hierarchical and power differentiation. In other words, Israel is addressed by their God, with whom they are on a first-name basis, rather than by one who holds himself aloof because of his superior position. Yahweh plays the key role in the book, his name occurring more than any other word (thirty-three times). He is also the Author of the book, or at least the one inspiring its message. We know much more about him, not only from this book but also from the rest of Scripture, than we know about the book's human author.

"Joel" means "Yah[weh] is God." The name provides little help in dating the prophecy, since a dozen people in the Old Testament have this name, ranging between the tenth and fifth centuries B.C. Joel's father is Pethuel. His name means "a youth of/belonging to El," which reflects his parents' understanding of the divine source of offspring. He is unknown apart from this reference. The LXX (along with Syriac and Old Latin) read the name as "Bethuel" ("man of God"), replacing the voiceless "p" with the voiced "b." That name is used both for a person (the father of Rebekah and Laban, Gen. 22:22–23; 24:15, 24, 47, 50; 28:5) and an unidentified place (1 Chron. 4:30; cf. Josh. 19:4). The textual evidence for the switch is not compelling.

Warnings to Judah (1:2–14)

OFTEN PROPHETS NEEDED to confront people in positions of power (e.g., 2 Sam. 7:4–5; 1 Kings 22; Amos 7:9). Other times they explicitly addressed the nation as a whole (e.g., Isa. 6:9–10; Jer. 2:4; Amos 5). Joel's message is to the latter, to the nation represented by various strands in society, from religious and political leaders through production workers to inebriates. All society needs to hear God's warnings and join in national lament for the destruction facing them. This derives from a horrible plague, not of disease (e.g., Ex. 9:14; Num. 11:33) but of nature, in the form of locust swarms.

This section is set off from that 1:15–20 by form (the frequent use of imperatival forms—seventeen times vs. none in vv. 15–20); by vocatives, which frequently accompany imperativals (ten times vs. none in vv. 15–20); by frequent short, staccato clauses versus generally the longer, more discursive clauses in verses 15–20; and by subject (natural disaster vs. "the day of the LORD" in vv. 15–20).[1]

To the people (1:2–4). The first audience, the "elders" (v. 2; cf. 1:14; 2:16, 28), is ambiguous. This could mean those who traditionally held positions

---

1. Prinsloo, *Theology of Joel*, 12.

of rank or authority in a village/region (e.g., Num. 22:7; Judg. 8:14, 16; 1 Sam. 30:26–30)[2] or in clan life (e.g., Deut. 5:23; 31:28). They existed from the national captivity in Egypt (Ex. 3:16; 24:14) up through the time of Ezra (Ezra 10:8). One of their functions was judicial, making legal decisions on a local level for the people based on biblical law and practice (e.g., Deut. 21:19–20; 22:16). They represented the upper end of the societal spectrum. Scholars suggest that such a technical use of the term must be postexilic (cf. 2 Kings 23:1–2; Ezra 10:8), leading to such a date for Joel.[3] But the term enjoys this technical sense in preexilic texts as well (e.g., Num. 11:16–30; cf. Deut. 25:9), so any claim of the date of composition cannot hinge on it alone.

The term can also be literal, calling to the old folks.[4] This fits well in the context, providing a literary balance between this earlier generation and the future generations of the next verse. This is also supported by the juxtaposition with the young in 2:16 (cf. also 2:28). The elderly are respected not only as those preserving the tribal memory of such catastrophes as will soon be described, but also the wisdom about how to meet the challenges.

Both interpretations are problematic, however, when seen in light of the parallelism in the second line of verse 2. There, all of the land's inhabitants (cf. 1:14; 2:1, 28) are summoned, so the parallelism cannot be synonymous but complementary, with the elders representing part of the land's inhabitants. "The land" in Joel is Judah, since Israel is not mentioned. Both elderly and leaders are summoned to hear the dreadful news as part of all of the others who are affected.

The audience is commanded to pay attention. The two verbs used are synonymous, with the semantic duplication highlighting the seriousness of the following message. The first ("hear," *šm*ᶜ), is used over a thousand times in the Old Testament. "Listen" (*ʾzn*)—more precisely, "give ear"—is common in poetic texts, even from an early period, in literature as diverse as prophecy (e.g. Isa. 1:2, 10; Jer. 13:15; cf. Hos. 5:1; Mic. 1:2), wisdom (e.g., Job 33:1), and the Deuteronomist (e.g., Deut. 32:1; cf. Judg. 5:3). Often occurring in parallelism, the two verbs are a common summons to pay attention. The elders, in whichever capacity they function here, are the source of guidance and instruction, but now need instruction themselves, since they are facing a situation for which neither experience nor authority has an adequate

---

2. See K. Marti, *Das Dodekapropheton* (Tübingen: J. C. B. Mohr, 1904), 116.

3. Wolff, *Joel*, 25; cf. Barton, *Joel*, 41.

4. Crenshaw, *Joel*, 86; D. A. Hubbard, *Joel and Amos: An Introduction and Commentary* (TOTC; Downers Grove, Ill.: InterVarsity Press, 1989), 41; Barton, *Joel*, 41.

response. In fact, it is to become a precedent for future instruction (Joel 1:3).[5] God acknowledges a teachable moment.

The message starts with rhetorical questions (cf. 1:16; 3:4), which draw the audience into the message from the beginning, seeking a response rather than asking for actual information. When the audience's thinking is thus engaged, they are already invested in receiving the rest of the message. The questions concern an as yet unspecified "this" (cf. Judg. 19:30; 1 Sam. 4:7). This word also engages the attention, awaiting some indication about what is being talked about.

The second question makes the interrogative-plus-verb combination of the first part do double duty and raises the question up a notch: "Has this happened in your days? [Has this happened] even in the days of your fathers?"[6] Here is an event without parallel, either in the experience of the oldest among the audience or even their ancestors (2:2; cf. Ex. 10:6, 14). The term "forefathers" (lit., "fathers") points to generations beyond the biological father (e.g., Gen. 48:21; Ex. 3:15; Zech. 8:14; Mal. 3:7). This is our equivalent of saying that something has not happened since time immemorial, since this rhetorical question is most naturally answered in the negative.

One other event was unparalleled in previous generations: the plague of locusts God brought on Egypt when Pharaoh refused to free the Israelites. It is characterized as "something neither your fathers nor your forefathers have ever seen from the day they settled in this land [Egypt] till now" (Ex. 10:6, NIV). Both Exodus and Joel direct attention to past generations. In Joel the subject also is soon revealed as a locust swarm, though the rhetorical tension caused by the lack of indication of the nature of the unparalleled event has not yet been revealed here, so the tension continues to mount through this and the next verse.

The elusive, undefined "it" continues into verse 3, picking up the subject of verse 2 and slowing down the identification of what "it" is.[7] Hebrew word order heightens the impact: "concerning it to your children tell,"

---

5. Cf. David Prior, *The Message of Joel, Micah & Habakkuk* (BST; Downers Grove, Ill.: Inter-Varsity Press, 1998), 22–23.

6. The use of the disjunctive coordinator *wᵒim* between the two phrases (F. I. Andersen, *The Sentence in Biblical Hebrew* [The Hague: Mouton, 1974], 148) shows that more is involved here than simple conjunction, presenting options ("a or b"). Here there seems to be intensification ("a or even b"). Wolff (*Joel*, 17) suggests that the specific disjunctive interrogative form used here (*hᵃ–... wᵉîm*) is late. It is found in earlier documents as well, however (e.g., Gen. 18:21; 42:16; 2 Sam. 24:12; cf. G. W. Ahlström, *Joel and the Temple Cult of Jerusalem* [VTSup 21; Leiden: Brill, 1971], 3).

7. C.–A. Keller, "Joël," in *Osée, Joël, Abdias, Jonas, Amos* (CAT; Neuchatel: Delachaux & Niestlé, 1965), 109.

emphasizing the elements preceding the verb, which usually begins a Hebrew sentence. The command to "tell" is used elsewhere of narrating a story of interesting events (cf. Gen. 24:66; Num. 13:27; Isa. 43:26). This verb is implied in the next two lines (cf. Joel 1:2).

Verse 3 moves from two generations past (self and ancestors), who have not seen such a thing, to four generations yet to come (self, children, their children, and future generations), who are to be told of it. Other generations extending far into the future are significant in Joel, opening and closing the book (3:20; cf. 2:2). Joel says that it is not enough for his generation alone to learn about this event. It is a matter to teach to all who follow, like other mighty acts of God (e.g., Deut. 6:7–12; 11:19–20). It becomes part of the national lore, just as God's actions against a stubborn pharaoh became the lore of an earlier generation (Ex. 10:2).

Verse 4 finally reveals the subject of the message, the elusive "it": the devastation resulting from swarms of locusts. In each of the three clauses it has the same emphatic Hebrew structure: The direct object (NIV, "what X has left"; lit., "the remnant of X") precedes the verb, "it ate." Even here there is possible ambiguity, not resolving clearly whether the unparalleled event is positive or negative. The "remnant" often has a negative connotation, such as the dregs or the last remaining pittance when the majority or the best is gone (e.g., Ex. 23:11; Isa. 44:19). In Exodus 10:5, 12, 15 it occurs in the context of a locust swarm devouring the remainders after a hail shower (cf. Joel 2:25). This turns out also to be the context in our verse, but a first reading leaves another option open, since the word has another possible connotation. In several cases the same word is an adverb indicating excess or abundance (cf. Ps. 31:23; Isa. 56:12; Dan. 8:9), so it could be a pleasant surprise that will be revealed. It is only as the reader goes further into the clause that it is possible to ascertain that the state of affairs is not good.

Each clause designates a locust type that eats what is left by the other locust type in the clause. The three clauses yield four separate locust types (cf. also 2:25). In our translation they are rendered "locust swarm" (*gāzām*), "great locusts" (*ʾarbeh*), "young locusts" (*yeleq*), and "other locusts" (*ḥāsîl*), but the NIV marginal note accurately states that "the precise meaning of the four Hebrew words used here for locusts is unclear." There is debate over the meanings of the terms on both the etymological and entomological levels. Lack of clarity is evident from the various other English translations proposed for the words:

gāzām: palmer worm (KJV; ASV); gnawing locust (NASB; Keil); cutting locust
   (NCV; NRSV; NJPS; NLT; ESV); chewing locust (NKJV; Crenshaw); biter
   (Wolff); nearly full-grown locust (Stuart); shearer (Allen)

ʾarbeh: locust (KJV; ASV; NJPS; Wolff); swarming locust (NASB; NCV; NKJV; NRSV; NLT; ESV; Kapelrud; Allen; Crenshaw); adult locust (Stuart); multiplier (Keil)

yeleq: canker worm (KJV; ASV); creeping locust (NASB); hopping locust (NCV; NRSV; NLT; ESV; Wolff; Allen); crawling locust (NKJV); grub (NJPS); jumper (Kapelrud; Crenshaw); infant locust (Stuart); licker (Keil)

ḥāsîl: caterpillar (KJV, ASV); stripping locust (NASB; NLT); destroying locust (NCV; NRSV; ESV; Allen); consuming locust (NKJV); hopper (NJPS); finisher (Crenshaw); jumper (Wolff); young locust (Stuart); devourer (Keil)

The scarcity of several of the terms is one cause of the confusion. The second term (ʾarbeh), the most common word for locusts, occurs twenty-four times in the Old Testament. Exodus 10:1–20 contains seven occurrences, describing when they plagued Egypt (cf. also Ps. 78:46; 105:34), completely covering the land and eating all plants and tree fruit. The account claims to describe the ultimate of such plagues: "Never before had there been such a plague of locusts, nor will there ever be again" (Ex. 10:14). An etymological suggestion is that the term derives from the Hebrew root *rbh* ("to be many"), resulting in translations such as "swarms."[8]

The other terms used here are rarer. *Yeleq*, for which a derivation from a word for "lick" has been suggested,[9] occurs in six additional places (Ps. 105:34; Jer. 51:14, 27; Joel 2:25; Nah. 3:15–16). *Ḥāsîl*, related to an Aramaic verb for "come/bring to an end,"[10] occurs in five places (1 Kings 8:37; 2 Chron. 6:28; Ps. 78:46; Isa. 33:4; Joel 2:25). *Gāzām*, related to Aramaic, Ethiopic, and Arabic "to cut, clip,"[11] occurs in only two additional places (Joel 2:25; Amos 4:9). The main uses of the words are in contexts stressing their overwhelming numbers and greedy devouring, with several recalling the locust plagues in Egypt (Ps. 78:46; 105:34).

Some of the translations reflect a means of crop destruction, some a means of locomotion, and yet others a stage of development.[12] It is impossible to

---

8. See BDB. This is accentuated by the prefixed ʾ, which can strengthen the word (see Waltke-O'Connor, 91). For cognates in other Semitic languages, see *HALOT*.

9. See BDB.

10. BDB. *HALOT* suggests cognates in Syriac ("to stop"), Arabic ("to eat away"), and the Canaanite from the Amarna tablets ("to raid"); E. Klein, *A Comprehensive Etymological Dictionary of the Hebrew Language for Readers of English* (New York: Macmillan, 1987), 226.

11. See Hans Wehr, *A Dictionary of Modern Written Arabic* (Ithaca: Cornell Univ. Press, 1966), 124.

12. For a discussion of various identification options, see Wolff, *Joel*, 27–28; Simkins, *Yahweh's Activity*, 101–20; Edwin Firmage, "Zoology," *ABD*, 6:1151–59.

determine how the author understands the terms—whether as specific types or stages, or whether as serving a literary function, accentuating the overwhelming number of devouring creatures by overwhelming the reader with different words. The context supports the latter interpretation, since the surprising uniqueness of the event is not due to an unparalleled number of varieties present but their overpowering number. Similar references to numerous, consuming locusts are not rare in the literature of Israel's neighbors, who suffered under some of the same swarms as they cut a swath over a large geographical area.[13] Their arrival always means devastation and despair (cf. Amos 7:1–2).

Sound the alarm (1:5–14). Different people are addressed in this section, but its literary structure unites it internally. Each of the two subsections has two parts: prescription and description. The order of these alternates throughout in this manner:

A Prescription: v. 5
  B Description: vv. 6–7
    C Prescription: v. 8
      D Description: vv. 9–10
    C' Prescription: v. 11
  B' Description: v. 12
A' Prescription: vv. 13–14

Keller suggests that there is a chiasm based on prescription-description-description-prescription.[14] The above analysis shows that there is indeed a chiasm, but it is more complex than Keller proposes. It is significant that the central, pivot point of the chiasm is verses 9–10, the effect of the catastrophe on the Judean ritual practices, an element of life that is so central for the life of the people. Various elements of society are prepared to address how the catastrophe impacts them.

To drunkards (1:5–7). The second audience (after "elders" in v. 2) is the *šikkôrîm*, also identified as wine drinkers. Most English versions render the term as "drunkards/drunks," with the strong negative connotations of the word. Such folks are also viewed negatively in Hebrew society, since it is inappropriate behavior for those attending a divine sanctuary (1 Sam. 1:13) and results in loss of physical control and dignity (Job 12:25; Ps. 107:27; Isa. 19:14; 24:20). At other times, the connotation of the word is not as bleak, since the state can be a result of a good party (e.g., 1 Sam. 25:36; 1 Kings 16:9; 20:16). Crenshaw points out that in that culture, wine was a common

---

13. See Crenshaw, *Joel*, 91–94; Barton, *Joel*, 43–45.
14. Keller, "Joël," 109.

accompaniment of a meal, so a more neutral rendition such as "imbibers" better reflects what the audience heard from this text.[15] Joel's warnings thus are either directed to a small segment of the population (the town drunks, if you like) or to the population at large, all of whom feel the loss of a mainstay of sustenance, their drink soon to be taken from their lips.

The imperative verbs directed to these drinkers leave ambiguous the author's evaluation. While the verb "wake up" often denotes awakening from natural sleep (e.g., Ps. 3:6; Prov. 6:22; Isa. 29:8), it also is awakening from a drunken stupor (Gen. 9:24; Prov. 23:35). The second and third verbs describe lamenting, a natural response to a catastrophe. The first (*bkh*) regularly indicates weeping (2:17), the root occurring almost 150 times in the Old Testament. The other (*yll*; 1:11, 13) is rarer, indicating the loud, wailing cries of mourning, sounding like the shrieking desert winds (cf. Deut. 32:10). It appears to have been an onomatopoetic term and may be cognate, through Latin, of our English "ululation," the high, warbling cry of grief used in contexts of mourning in many societies.

The imbibers must lament for the wine that is newly pressed at this time of devastation (cf. Amos 9:13; Mal. 3:21). It is not yet bottled but still flows (Joel 3:18).[16] While not as potent as more aged wine (3:3), which would be in storage and thus not susceptible to the locusts, it can still lead to intoxication (Isa. 49:26). Not only are Israel's sustaining sources of nutrients, her grain foods and drink such as wine, devoured, the latter also serves to lessen the hardships of daily life (Ps. 104:15). As cleanly as a woodcutter severs a tree from its roots (1 Kings 5:20; Jer. 46:23), so nourishment will be cut off (Joel 1:9, 16) from mouths open to receive it.

In verse 6, a military metaphor expands on the impact of the locust swarms, anticipating an actualization of the metaphor in later verses. The insects are like a national army (cf. Prov. 30:27), having power through sheer numbers. They are a "nation,"[17] while in 2:2 they are called a "people."[18] The former term regularly describes foreign peoples (e.g., Deut. 7:1; Jer. 25:17–26), though it is also used of Israel (e.g., Deut. 32:28; Judg. 2:20). In one other case apart from Joel, it is used in conjunction with animals (Zeph. 2:14), but without this metaphorical power.[19] Animal metaphors more regularly occur

---

15. Crenshaw, *Joel*, 94.

16. Wine's occurrence here at both the start and end of the prophecy forms a chiasm; see Bliese, "Metrical Sequences," 56.

17. *Gôy*, used 10 times in the book.

18. *'am*, used 15 times in Joel; cf. also Prov. 30:25, 26.

19. *ḥaytô-gôy*, which the LXX takes as "beasts of the earth"; BHS suggests it might be a transliteration of Hebrew *gay'* ("valley").

with the synonym "people" used in Joel 2:2 and will be further discussed there. This "nation" is the subject of the next two verses.

This nation of locusts literally "goes up" (^ch), a verb commonly used for journeying toward Israel (e.g., Gen. 13:1; Ezra 2:1), but also frequent in military contexts, signifying attack (e.g., Joel 2:7, 9; 3:9; cf. 1 Kings 20:22; Isa. 7:1). The locust nation here moves against "my land" (cf. Ezek. 38:16). "My" occurs seventeen times in the book, and its use here is ambiguous. This could have been a rhetorical device of the author, showing that he identifies himself with his people (i.e., it is not just "your land" but mine as well; cf. Nehemiah's solidarity in Neh. 1:5–11; Joel 1:13), but it is more likely a reminder of the actual landowner, God himself, who is the speaker (Joel 2:1; cf. Isa. 14:25; Jer. 2:7; 16:18). Calvin notes that this claim to the land means that God, though its owner, chooses in this instance not to be its defender.

The attackers are devastating—"powerful" in strength and numbers (2:2, 5, 11; cf. Ex. 1:9; Zech. 8:22) and "without number" as they were in Egypt (Ps. 105:34; cf. 2 Chron. 12:3; Ps. 104:25; Jer. 46:23). Their ferocity is also accentuated, comparing their teeth to those of known killers, the lion (1 Kings 13:24; 20:36; cf. Job 4:10; Rev. 9:8) and lioness (Deut. 33:20; Hos. 13:8). The regular term for "tooth" (*šen*) is used first. The second, parallel term (*m^{e}tall^{ec}ôt*) is rarer, occurring only in conjunction with the former (Job 29:17; Prov. 30:14; cf. Ps. 58:7, with a reordering of two letters). A use of both terms in the Dead Sea material compares them with sword and spear (4QHa 13:10), sharp, offensive weapons of war.[20]

The result from this dental onslaught is devastating in an agricultural society (v. 7). The produce of the grape vine and fig tree are among the things that make life worth living (Num. 20:5; 2 Kings 18:31; Hab 3:17), but they are now totally destroyed. They represent the larger cultivated plants, occurring as a pair in Joel (Joel 1:12; 2:22). The resultant loss is horrible, like the devastation resulting from divine judgment (Isa. 13:9; Zech. 7:14; cf. words from the same root [*šmm*] in Joel 1:17; 2:3, 20; 3:7).

Five different verbs are used, not all easily distinguishable from each other. The term applying to figs (NIV "ruin") is unique in the Old Testament, with an appropriate use for the context being "break, splinter." They will be completely stripped of bark like one bares one's arm (Isa. 52:10; Ezek. 4:7),[21]

---

20. Bliese ("Metrical Sequences," 56, 72) suggests another chiasm with the roaring (lion) in 3:18. "Lion" is not explicit there, only its roaring. He notes the reversal from the destructive presence here and the saving presence there.

21. For the emphatic intensification of the form of infinitive absolute + perfect, see T. Muraoka, *Emphatic Words and Structures in Biblical* Hebrew (Jerusalem: Magnes, 1985), 87.

leaving even smaller branches (Gen. 40:10, 12) bare and white. In both cases, the speaker, most likely God (cf. Joel 1:6), claims the ruined plants as his own but makes no protective or restorative steps. Piling up the numerous verbs emphasizes the totality of destruction.[22]

To priests and producers (1:8—14). A new textual unit looks at other elements of society who also feel the locusts' destruction. First is an unidentified female.[23] From the context, she appears to be called to lament, though the verb does not occur elsewhere with this sense.[24] This feminine imperative has no near grammatically feminine object, though some suggest that Jerusalem and Israel, personified as feminine, can be implied in the context.[25]

The context of Joel as a whole suggests another referent, however, since the only other feminine singular verbal forms are addressed to the "land" (2:21), which here in 1:8 is bereft of produce.[26] She is called to identify with a young lady in a marriage arrangement of some kind, though its nature is unclear. The main terms are clear, but their combination is problematic. The object of comparison is a "virgin," a young woman without sexual experience (Gen. 24:16; Ex. 22:16; Deut. 22:28) who is wearing sackcloth. This course, black fabric (Isa. 50:3; Rev. 6:12) made from goats' hair[27] is worn against the skin (2 Kings 6:30) around the waist (1 Kings 20:32; Isa. 20:2) as a sign of mourning (e.g., 2 Sam. 3:31; Isa. 22:12; Lam. 2:10; Joel 1:13; Jon. 3:5), the pain of which the chafing cloth is a constant reminder.[28]

In this case mourning is due to the loss of her husband (Gen. 20:3; Ex. 21:3), whom she had taken while she was young (in "her youth"). The latter term is ambiguous since it can indicate a young, unmarried state, perhaps even prior to betrothal (e.g., Lev. 22:13; Num. 30:3, 16). This is difficult in this context since she does have a husband. The phrase can also refer simply to age, without any connotation of marriage, a "time of youth," an early age (Gen. 8:21; Zech. 13:5). This fits the context, but there is still the difficulty

---

22. Mikre–Selassie, "Repetition and Synonyms," 230.

23. Wolff (*Joel*, 29) suggests that the subject is "the daughter of my people," based on Jer. 6:6, though there is no evidence for the suggestion.

24. Ordinarily the root used here (ʾlh) means "curse" (*DCH*, 1:272, where a homonym "mourn" is suggested for this verse alone, apparently based on sense; see too *HALOT*), which is inappropriate for this context.

25. Crenshaw, *Joel*, 97.

26. Cf. L. J. Braaten, "God Sows: Hosea's Land Theme in the Book of the Twelve," in Redditt, *Thematic Threads*, 126.

27. Wolff, *Joel*, 29.

28. In Akkadian, *saqqu* is also listed among items of fine clothing, such as those included in a dowry (*CAD*, 15, 168–69), so it does not, at least in that context, have the negative connotation that English has derived from Hebrew.

of being a virgin while also having a husband. It seems best to view her as a young virgin, as yet unmarried but already betrothed to ("belonging to," Gen. 20:3; cf. Deut. 22:24, where an engaged "virgin" is called a "wife") a man. She has lost her fiancé.[29] The comparison of loss is clearer in the Hebrew, where the emotions called forth "because of" the husband are the same as those "because of" the new wine (Joel 1:5).

Agricultural loss affects other elements in society as well, some in ways that might not readily come to mind (1:9). What is mentioned here concerns the people's relationship with God in their religious rituals. Priests suffer partly because of the loss of regular daily foodstuffs, so that they are in that respect at one with the rest of society. It also affects their livelihood since it is the loss of some of their stock in trade.

Two specific types of sacrifice required plant products that are now lost to the locusts. The first offering (1:13; 2:14) is either the grain offering, described in detail in Leviticus 2, or a general term for all grain and animals offerings (e.g., Gen. 4:3–5; Mal. 1:8–10).[30] Because of the context, the former is preferable, since the following context mentions only vegetable products. This offering required olive oil and flour, part of which was burnt on the altar. Since both oil (Joel 1:10)[31] and grain (1:11) are gone, so is the potential for offering. This loss directly impacts the priestly larder, since it comprises some of their food supply (Lev. 2:10), especially so since this offering in particular is a perpetual or regular offering (e.g., Lev. 6:13; Num. 4:16).

The second plant-based offering is the less fully detailed drink offering (1:13; 2:14). This, also called a libation offering (NJPS, JB), is inappropriately named a "drink offering," since, while it can be wine (Ex. 29:40; Lev. 23:13; Num. 15:5) or even water (cf. 2 Sam. 23:15–17), can also be oil (Gen. 35:14), which is not a beverage. "Liquid" or "poured" offering is a more appropriate translation, since this is the means by which it is offered. Just as wine is cut off from the mouths of those who would drink it (Joel 1:5), so these sacrifices are cut off from the temple, "the house of the LORD" (1:14; 3:18; cf. 1 Kings 8:11), the place where they are to be offered.

The priests mourn this loss like one mourns the death of a loved one (e.g., Gen. 37:35; 50:10). They are ministers (Joel 1:13[2x], of the altar and God; 2:17, of Yahweh), a term always accompanying "priest" in Joel. This word can indicate an assistant to a leader (e.g., Joshua for Moses; Ex. 24:13; Josh. 1:1; also 1 Kings 1:15; 2 Kings 4:43) or even a personal valet (2 Sam. 13:17–18). In the

---

29. NLT, GNB; Wolff, *Joel*, 30. The LXX reads "the husband of her maidenhood," i.e., the one who took her virginity, namely, her first husband.

30. The term is also used in secular contexts for a gift, present, or tribute; *HALOT*, 601.

31. A different word (*yiṣhār*) is used in this verse. It will be discussed below.

prophets it indicates those serving in a religious context (e.g., Isa. 61:6; Jer. 33:21, 22; Ezek. 44:11; see also 1 Sam. 2:11). Their very role is in jeopardy. There are serious theological and sociological ramifications if the sacrificial system, the regular means of approaching God, is not able to function as it was established to do. The people must be reminded from whom these sacrifices actually derive, Yahweh himself (Joel 2:14).

In verse 10, the grounds for the deprivation and mourning are established: Three staples of life—grain, wine, and oil—fail from earth and field. The assault on life is accentuated at many levels through literary means that are lost in translation: through staccato pounding of five, two-word clauses,[32] each having an identical beat number for both words;[33] through pervasive alliteration and assonance;[34] and through piling on verbs of destruction. Devastation comes to the cultivated field (vv. 11, 12, 19, 20; Gen. 37:7; Mic. 3:12) as it does to its grain (Joel 1:17; 2:19), the source of flour for daily bread (2 Kings 18:32).

The verb *šdd* ("ruin") is a strong one, used of military destruction (Isa. 21:2; Jer. 49:28) and even death (Judg. 5:27; Jer. 6:6), continuing the stark picture begun in Joel 1:7. The very ground (*ʾᵃdāmâ*), the source of humanity itself (*ʾādām*; Gen. 2:7), is affected. The author plays on two uses of the second verb (*ʾbl*). Playing off of Joel 1:9, the anthropomorphized ground joins the priests in mourning (Hos. 4:3).[35] The verb also means "dry up," the sense also of the verbs in the fourth (*ybš*; cf. Joel 1:11, 12, 20) and fifth (*mll*; cf. 1:12) clauses, which is equally contextually appropriate. The writer could be engaging in a wordplay looking both back to the previous verse and forward to the concluding verbs here.

Along with grain, the new wine and oil are lost. These three terms regularly occur together in the Old Testament (e.g., 2:19; Num. 18:12; Deut. 7:13; 11:14; 12:17). The firstfruits of all three are for personal use by the priests (Num. 18:12, 27), in addition to their cultic function in sacrifices. These divine gifts (Deut. 7:13; 11:14; Jer. 31:12) are now absent.

The crop loss also devastates the agriculturalists responsible for production (v. 11). These include the farm laborer ("farmers"), those using ox and plow to prepare annual grain crops (Jer. 51:23), and the tenders ("growers")

---

32. The third clause has a linking, supraclausal particle *kî* ("because").

33. 2–2 / 3–3 / 2–2 / 2–2 / 2–2.

34. The litany of destruction shows literary craftsmanship through the Hebrew sounds. Those that would have struck the ear are underlined in the transcription that follows, where each strophe is separated: *šuddad śādeh* / *ʾābᵉlâ ʾᵃdāmâ* / *kî šuddad dāgān* / *hôbîš tîrôš* / *ʾumlal yiṣhār*. The recurring initial vowel /u/ also links clause 1–3–5.

35. Crenshaw, *Joel*, 99; see the NIV note with "dried up."

of grape vines, a perennial plant requiring different cultivation practices (2 Kings 25:12//Jer. 52:16).[36] The terms often occur together exemplifying the range of crop production (Isa. 61:5; 2 Chron. 26:10; cf. Amos 5:16–17), and probably indicate the poorest of the land (Jer. 52:16), those who tend land not their own (2 Chron. 26:10).

The two verbs used here were encountered previously (*ybš, yll;* 1:10 and 1:5 respectively), though the first has a different nuance here. Wine itself dries up (1:10), but that is not an appropriate verb for the farmers. A homonym of the same root carries a meaning of shame (e.g., Jer. 2:6; 8:9), an appropriate response for those unable to fulfill their vital societal role.[37] Some suggest that this meaning is appropriate for most or all occurrences of the verb in Joel,[38] but there seems rather to be a conscious play on the ambiguity of meaning, just as there is play on sound in these verses. The two verbs are morphologically ambiguous, equally able to be masculine plural imperatives (so most translations) or third common plural perfect forms (cf. LXX; Vulgate; Berkeley; Moffat; NJPS). The existence of so many imperatives in this section (Joel 1:8, 13[5x], 14[4x]) and chapter (1:2[2x], 3, 5[3x]) supports the majority reading.

More specific than verse 10, this verse concentrates on field crops, namely "wheat," which is ground for choice flour for breads (Ex. 29:2) or parched and eaten dry (Lev. 23:14), and "barley," a quicker-growing crop that is also eaten parched (2 Sam. 17:28) or raw (2 Kings 4:42) or ground into flour (Num. 5:15) for baked goods (Judg. 7:13; 2 Kings 4:42; Ezek. 4:12).[39] The former seems to be held in higher regard since, while barley is also used in offerings (Num. 5:15; Ezek. 45:13), wheat plays a more regular role there, often in a form designated "fine [i.e., not course] flour" (Ex. 29:2; Lev. 2:1–7; 5:11; 2 Kings 7:16; 1 Chron. 9:29; Ezek. 16:13). Barley also is relegated to use as horse feed (1 Kings 5:8). It is "because" these are lost that mourning happens; the harvest (Deut. 24:19) has been utterly "destroyed" (4:26; Ps. 102:27).

Other, perennial crops are listed in verse 12, with numerous links to previous verses.[40] Vine and fig join other fruits: pomegranate (Num. 13:23; Deut. 8:8), date palm (only here noted for its fruit bearing; cf. Song 7:7), and apple

---

36. *kōrmîm,* "vine-dressers," an artificial participial form from *kerem,* "vineyard."

37. *DCH,* 4:77; *HALOT.* This verb is a biform of the much more common root *bôš,* which carries the same meaning (2:26, 27). This verb is used of farm laborers in Jer. 14:4.

38. Marti, *Dodekapropheton,* 121; *DCH,* 4:77 for 1:10, 11, 12, 17.

39. The harvesting seasons for barley (cf. Ruth 2:23) and wheat (cf. Gen. 30:14; Judg. 15:1) were listed sequentially in the Gezer Calendar (*COS,* 2, 222). The relative harvesting dates are also evident in Ex. 9:31–32.

40. "Vine," 1:7; 2:22; "fig tree," 1:7; 2:22; cf. also "field," 1:10, 19; "dry up," twice in two Hebrew stems, Hiphil in 1:10, 11 and Qal, 1:20; "wither," translated "fails" in 1:10.

(Song 2:3, 5; 7:9; 8:5; Borowski suggests it is instead the apricot).[41] These are summarized as "all the trees of the field," even though this is not literally true, since other tree crops are also significant in the economy of Israel.[42] They do serve as representative of this important element of the diet of the people.

A concluding analogy is made with the emotional state of the people. All humanity, those previously identified and more, suffer the desiccation of joy, the normal emotional response to a good harvest (Isa. 9:3; 16:9–10). There is another clever play on sounds and words between this and the immediately preceding clause.[43] Food and drink, which make the heart glad (Ps. 104:15), by their absence now remove that gladness.[44]

In verse 13, the focus returns to the priesthood, those initially identified as serving Yahweh (1:9; 2:17), but now as ministers of his altar. This is the place where for practical purposes the people most intimately encounter the deity ("my God") himself. "My" indicates that, at least in this verse, Joel the narrator rather than Yahweh himself is speaking (see 1:6 and comments).[45] The priests are repeatedly commanded in a string of five imperatives.

They are first to gird themselves like the bereft virgin (1:8), though the object of the girding, the sackcloth, is left implicit, being clear from the previous verse and made explicit later in this verse. This time the sackcloth is to be worn overnight.[46] Mourning (Gen. 23:2; 1 Sam. 25:1) and wailing (Joel

---

41. For the fruits mentioned here, see Oded Borowski, *Agriculture in Iron Age Israel* (Winona Lake, Ind.: Eisenbrauns, 1987), 116–17, 126–30; cf. John Goldingay, *After Eating the Apricot* (Carlisle: Solway, 1996).

42. E.g., the olive and sycamore (see 1 Chron. 27:28; Ps. 78:47; Amos 7:14), a different species than that found in North America, which also produces an edible fig (see Borowski, *Agriculture*, 117–26, 128–29, respectively).

43. The last five words of the preceding clause and the first three of this are: kol-ʿᵃṣê haśśādeh yābēšû / kî hôbîš śāśôn. There is much repetition of actual letters or phonetically similar elements (sibilants, vowel classes) within these few words. There is also a chiasm, pivoting on two stems of the same verbal root.

44. The NIV took the initial conjunction of the last clause (kî) as emphatic ("surely"), though many of the other uses of this conjunction have been interpreted as causal ("because"). C. Frankfort, "Le kî de Joel I 12," *VT* 10 (1960): 445–48, suggests that a causal sense carries through here as well; the farm laborers lost the joy of their work because of the loss of their other crops, so they let their fruit trees go to ruin.

45. The LXX reads simply "God," but all other occurrences of "God" in Joel have a pronominal suffix—3mp (2:17), 1cp (1:16) or, more regularly, 2mp (1:13, 14; 2:13, 14, 23, 26, 27; 3:17). The occurrence of the same noun with "my" and "your" in the same verse is irregular. Wolff's proposal of "your house of God" (*Joel*, 19) would solve this difficulty.

46. In addition to the biblical passages exemplifying this ritual of sackcloth, see also the practice within the later Jewish community in fifth-century B.C. Israel (A. Cowley, *Jewish Documents of the Time of Ezra* (New York: MacMillan, 1919), 73, lines 15, 20.

1:5, 11) are not things quickly accomplished. Like the mourning for a departed loved one, which takes a season to go through, the loss of sacrificial material does not right itself immediately; at least a new harvest season must pass.

The priests are then to "come," though the destination is not specified. This is usually clear from the context (e.g., 1 Kings 20:33; Ezek. 33:30), but that is not the case here. Since the altar is mentioned and the priests' regular service is in the Jerusalem temple, that is probably where they must come (cf. Ps. 95:6; 100:2). While it may be reading too much into the verb, there could be in it an indication that the priests are not actually where they are supposed to be and have to be recalled to their God in whose house they should already be serving (cf. 2 Chron. 29, where Hezekiah has to start his reform by recalling the negligent priesthood).

Finally, they are again reminded of the reason for mourning. As conception is withheld from a barren womb with resultant grief (Gen. 30:1–2), so grief ensues from life-giving sacrifices that are withheld.

In verse 14, further steps are demanded in order to restore what is lost. This is done through four more imperative verbs, apparently also directed toward the priests. "Sanctifying a fast" (2:15; cf. 1:12) uses a common Hebrew root for purification and setting things apart for sacred service (*qdš*). This is applied to preparation for "holy war" (3:9; Jer. 6:4; 51:27), for feast (Ezra 3:5), or for fast. Fasting (1 Sam. 28:20) is done either privately (2 Sam. 12:16) or publicly (e.g., the one national fast on the Day of Atonement, Lev. 16:29, 31; Num. 29:7; fasts increased in number after the Exile, e.g., Zech. 8:19), as a sign of mourning (2 Sam. 1:22; 1 Kings 21:27) and/or as an accompaniment to petitionary prayer (Ezra 8:21; Dan. 9:3), both being closely related actions.

The speaker calls (1:19; 2:15, 32; 3:9) not only for a cessation from food, but also from work (from the root "restrain, hold something back," Gen. 16:2; Jer. 36:5; cf. Deut. 16:8 regarding work). In English this is often rendered as a "(sacred) assembly," not only directed toward Yahweh but also called for pagan gods (e.g., Baal in 2 Kings 10:20). The priests are not to be alone in these endeavors, however, since elders (1:2; 2:16, 28)—and indeed all the land's inhabitants (1:2; 2:1)—are to gather (2:10; 3:15) at the temple ("the house of the LORD your God"; cf. 1:8, 13, 16; 3:18). When the nation assembles, they are to implore Yahweh's name and "cry out" to him for help (cf. Judg. 12:22; Mic. 3:4; Hab. 1:2). He is the key for this verse, his ministers being called to cry to him because of the deprivation of his house.[47] He is also the One to whom the people are driven by the disaster that befalls them.

---

47. Prinsloo, *Theology of Joel*, 24.

Lament (1:15–20)

A NEW SECTION is discernable here because of the change of address to the first person; the speaker himself comes more to the fore (see 1:6). The previously dominant litany of imperatives also stops. This is a cry of distress (cf. Judg.11:35). It introduces for the first time in this book the concept of "the day of the LORD," an important event developed in previous and subsequent prophecies (see "Theology" in the introduction). It provides the speaker's own perspective on the calamity that has happened to him and his people.

The cry begins with an interjection of concern and woe, "alas!" (*ʾᵃhâ;* 2 Kings 3:10).[48] The subject follows: (lit.) "the day," that is, the day of Yahweh (see also Ezek. 30:2–3). A definite article normally refers back to something previously mentioned or to something well known in the shared universe of speaker and audience.[49] This is probably an example of the latter, and the specific day is identified in the next clause. The conjunction "for" either indicates the cause of the cry (so NIV) or is emphatic, indicating that the following is "indeed" true (e.g., Amos 3:7). Either fits the present context, though the majority of the thirty examples of this word with the former connotation in this prophecy suggest the former interpretation.

The cry concerns the proximity of "the day of the LORD" (cf. 2:1, 14), a statement familiar from other prophecies (e.g., Isa. 13:6; Ezek. 30:3; Obad. 15; Zeph. 1:7, 14[2x]). Some anticipate the Day as positive (Amos 5:18a; Zech. 14:1), a welcome perspective for those whose very subsistence is in jeopardy because of the locusts. They anticipate a day of relief in that finally God will come to help in catastrophe. Joel quickly corrects their misconception. What they have experienced so far is but a glimmer of what is yet to come; they have seen trouble, but the Day will be worse (2:1, 11; 2:31; 4:14), and it is coming (Zech. 14:1; Mal. 3:23).

The manner of this day's coming is compared to "destruction [*šōd;* cf. the verb of the same root twice in 1:10] from the Almighty [*šadday*]," an old name for God (e.g., Gen. 17:1; 28:3; Ex. 6:3), probably chosen to provide yet another alliteration (see notes on 1:10, 12). This juxtaposition of sounds attracts the ear of the hearers, also shocking them when they hear the meaning lying behind the sounds; Yahweh uses his awesome might for destruction instead of salvation!

---

48. This interjection is usually followed immediately by the person addressed (Judg. 11:35; 2 Kings 6:5, 15), most commonly "my Lord Yahweh" (e.g., Josh. 7:7; Judg. 6:22). For a survey of passages in which it occurs, see Siegfried Bergler, *Joel als Schriftinterpret* (BEATAJ 16; Frankfurt: Peter Lang, 1988), 78–84.

49. Williams, *Hebrew Syntax*, §83, 85 respectively. This could also be an example of what Williams calls the "distinctive," i.e., "the God" (§88).

The prophet seems to be combining quotations from earlier prophecies, such as Ezekiel 30:2b–3 ("Alas [*hâ* instead of *ʾahâ*] for that day! For the day is near, the day of the LORD is near") and Isaiah 13:6 ("for the day of the LORD is near; it will come like destruction from the Almighty"; cf. also Zeph. 1:7b). Previously these verses threatened other nations with God's approaching judgment; here his own people realize that judgment curses face them, right before their very own eyes (cf. Deut. 28:31; Isa. 13:16). Previously the threat had been theoretical—it would happen someday; here it is actualized. Joel shows this by rhetorically inviting his audience to join in the message by answering the rhetorical question (see 1:2). "Can't we all see the truth of the claims I am making? Hasn't the Day really already arrived?"

The evidence of the Day's arrival involves two elements, both governed by the verb *krt* (1:16; "cut off," cf. 1:5, 9),[50] which bridges two clauses, doing double duty and having both elements as direct objects. Both "food" and "joy and gladness" are denied to the temple, just as wine and the grain and drink offerings are denied to drinkers and the temple (1:5, 9). "Food" fits the context in its literal meaning (Gen. 41:35, 48; Prov. 13:23). Also, since main elements of Israelite food are the grain, wine, and oil, which, being cut off, result in the impossibility of sacrifice (Joel 1:9–10), so the term here may refer back to those sacrificial verses.

But another possibility fits within this verse as well. The term also includes liquids, including wine,[51] so this may be synonymous with what follows, leading to the second direct object. "Joy and gladness" can be understood literally,[52] but they instead may be a poetic expression for wine, as they only occur together elsewhere in this exact form in the context of the joy of winemaking and consumption (e.g., Isa. 16:10; Jer. 48:33; cf. Hos. 9:1–2; Joel 2:21–24). Whatever interpretation is followed, the people face deprivation of provisions that lighten the heart (Ps. 104:15). The writer continues his sound play in this verse by repeating the 1cp pronominal suffix ("our")—the only times it is used in the book.[53]

Unlike most verses in Joel, 1:17–18 are mainly words not repeated elsewhere in the book.[54] Their interpretation is at best uncertain, as shown by the different translations (cf. the NIV note on v. 17).[55] In the first clause, only

---

50. The morphological form of *krt* is ambiguous—either 3ms Niphal perfect in pause or a Niphal ms participle. In either case, however, the Day would have already arrived.

51. See among the Dead Sea Scrolls, 11QT 47:6, 13; 4Q370.

52. Cf. also 1:12, where the same theme had been expressed with different words.

53. *ʿênênû* ("our eyes") / *ʾĕlôhênû* ("our God").

54. Of the 25 words and particles, 14 are not repeated anywhere else in Joel. Four are used only here in the Old Testament.

55. Simkins, *Yahweh's Activity*, 146–47, suggests leaving the first clause untranslated.

one word occurs more than once, and it could mean either "under" or "instead of," so provides little help. The remaining three verbs in verse 17 concern destruction (*šmm*, "be in ruins," Ezek. 6:4; 36:36; Zeph. 3:6; cf. Joel 1:7; 2:3, 20; 3:7, 19[x2]; *hrs*, "be broken down," Jer. 50:15; Ezek. 36:35; *ybš*, "dry up," Joel 1:10, 12), so one assumes that the unique first verb (*ʿbš*) does so as well. Some take it to mean "shrivel," based on an Arabic cognate,[56] presumably from dryness and heat (see 1:19–20), while others translate "rot, grow moldy," based on Aramaic and Modern Hebrew uses.[57] Since the latter state comes from excess moisture, the opposite of the problem in this context, the former suggestion is preferable.

The subject noun is generally taken as "seeds," fitting with "grain" in the last clause of this verse. The constituent root (*prd*) means "separate, divide, set apart" (Gen. 2:10; 25:23), so it may refer to the individual grains rather than the collective mass of grain, though others propose different interpretations based on this root.[58] That under which the seeds come to ruin is most frequently taken as "clods,"[59] though others suggest "shovels."[60]

The second two clauses concern destroyed installations. The first is a common term for "storehouse," which can, depending on what is stored, be a treasury (Josh. 6:19, 24; 1 Kings 14:26), an armory (Jer. 15:25), or, as fits in this context, a larder (2 Chron. 11:11; Neh. 13:12, 13). The second is another unique term, but the context, and that of a closely related form (Hag. 2:19), suggest another place for food storage. Thus, these two clauses are in synonymous parallelism, with the cause of the devastation explained in the final clause of the verse.

With an exclamation of wonder, the writer notes in 1:18 that the domesticated animals, important for Israelite household and cultic economy,[61] also feel the negative effects. Those affected are first cited with the more general designation "cattle" (1:20; 2:22; Gen. 8:1; Ex. 20:9; Deut. 14:4),[62] then with two specific subcategories—herds of cattle and flocks of sheep. They are pictured anthropomorphically in terms used elsewhere of human suffering, moaning or sighing in anguish (Isa. 24:7; Ezek. 9:4), perplexed without any means of escape (Ex. 14:3), or even suffering punishment from humanity's

---

56. See BDB; HALOT; NASB; NIV; NJPS; NRSV.

57. See KJV; ASV. See Wolff, Joel, 19, for a comparison of the versions.

58. HALOT, 963, prefers "that which was put aside," referring to the seed grain for the next year's planting.

59. See KJV; ASV; NASB; NJPS; NIV; NRSV; cf. GNB, NLT (dry/parched ground).

60. See BDB; HALOT, 546 (based on Syriac and Arabic).

61. See O. Borowski, *Every Living Thing: Daily Use of Animals in Ancient Israel* (Walnut Creek, Calif.: AltaMira, 1998).

62. Better translated "livestock," since the term is broader than simply bovines.

guilt (Zech. 11:5).[63] The reason for their disturbance is lack of pasturage (Gen. 47:4). The ripple effect spreads: Humans and animals suffer, as does the cult, which cannot receive vegetable sacrifices, and now also suffers through the loss of the animals necessary for blood sacrifice (Ex. 20:24; 1 Kings 8:63). There is no dichotomy in Israel between humanity and nature; all life suffers together.

Finally (1:19–20), after a detailed description of the problem and lament over it using the third person, the writer turns, using second person verbal and suffix forms, to the only "you" who can help, Yahweh himself, to whom he now calls (1:14; 2:15, 32; 3:9). He speaks in his own voice, using first person singular forms, rather than as a member of the people, using the first person plural forms found in the previous section (1:16). Again the following particle (cf. v. 15) is ambiguous, either indicating the reason for the call ("for," NIV) or emphasizing its contents, "indeed." The emphatic meaning fits better literarily, since the clause at the beginning of the cry concerning the burning fire (v. 19b) also concludes it (v. 20c), resulting in an inclusio.

The destruction now takes a different slant, comparing voracious locusts with all-consuming fire (cf. 2:3, 5; 2:30) and flame (2:3). The former metaphorically "eats" (ʾkl; Deut. 32:22; Ezek. 19:14), just as do the locusts (1:4). Here it is (lit.) "pastures of the wilderness" (cf. 2:3, 22; 3:19) that are consumed. Rather than land far from human occupation, as "wilderness" can imply (Job 24:5), it probably denotes here the open, communal grazing region just outside of the inhabited village areas, where shepherds can graze their flocks. They are the same as "the fields" (1:10, 11, 12, 20), whose trees (1:12; 2:22) also are burnt. This may be yet another metaphor for the all-consuming locust swarms, or an indication that all of nature works together at one time against these poor folks, hitting them either simultaneously or sequentially with locust, drought, and fire. The latter is a natural consequence of the death and desiccation caused by the former, leaving tinder-dry remains, vulnerable to the first spark.

The animals of 1:18 join the writer in panting longingly (Ps. 42:2) for water streams (Joel 3:18), which dried up because of the heat of flame and drought. These are most likely not natural streams, for which Hebrew has several other words, but artificial irrigation channels.[64] The repetition of the

---

63. The last verb, *neʾšāmû*, has also been understood as *nāšammû*, "be made desolate" (from the root *šmm*, 1:7, 17, etc.; LXX, BHS, HALOT; DCH, 1:415; 2:127). This reading might be preferred since this verb does occur in the context (though the MT root does not have this type of metaphorical extension to animals elsewhere), and it makes better theological sense, especially since no human wrongdoing had been adduced as precipitating the devastation so far in the prophecy.

64. Frankfort, "Le *kî* de Joel I 12," 447.

same clause at the ends of verses 19 and 20 shows formally that their theme of fiery destruction is central to these verses.

PROPHETIC IDENTIFICATION. Prophets in the Old Testament are regularly identified at least by name, though usually extra information is given about them or about the book associated with them. This information includes such things as: the father's name (e.g., Isa. 1:1; Jer. 1:1), additional ancestors (e.g., Zeph. 1:1; Zech. 1:1), the hometown or ancestral home and/or profession (e.g., Jer. 1:1; Amos 1:1), the genre of the book (e.g., Isa. 1:1; Jer. 1:1), the book's divine source (e.g., Jer. 1:2; Hos. 1:1–2), and the book's date (e.g., Jer. 1:2; Hos. 1:1).

One of the purposes of identification could have been for verification or "quality control." We have little information on the actual process of the collection and recording of individual prophetic utterances, whether by the instigation of the prophet himself (cf. Jer. 36) or by a group of disciples (cf. Isa. 8:16). Those reading the prophetic "transcripts" may have consulted their prophetic originator or at least recognized him as an accepted authority whose name and credentials are known (cf. Jer. 26:18, referring to the prophecy of Micah). Of greater import, at least regarding the nature of the document as a true prophecy, is the identity of the true Author, the deity who is its divine source. In this case, it is Yahweh, Israel's covenant God.

What's in a name? In the West today, names for one's children are most commonly chosen in order to honor family members who preceded them, to sound good in conjunction with the family name, or else just to follow what the fashionable *nom du jour* might be. Most people have no understanding of any meaning underlying the names they choose. The meaning of most Western names has become opaque; that is, it is not readily clear even to native language speakers what the historical background or meaning of a name might be.

In a number of languages this is not the case. In them, personal names are transparent, carrying a readily identifiable meaning. This is the case for the Semitic language family, of which Hebrew is a member. They build their names from regular words in the language. For example, David means "beloved," a meaning that comes through for the form of the word appearing in Song of Songs 1:1; Nabal means "fool," as his wife readily acknowledges (1 Sam. 25:25); and Mahlon and Kilion, the sons of Elimelech and Naomi (Ruth 1:2), derive from roots that mean "sicky" and "on his last legs," appropriate names for the context of their story.

Since Hebrew names have meanings, they are often chosen because of the relevance of the meaning to the parents, either reflecting a prayer for divine aid (e.g., Nathaniel, "God has given [a son]") or to indicate their state of mind at the time. For example, Benjamin, originally named by his mother, who was dying in childbirth, was named Ben-Oni, "son of my sorrow." Again, Leah, Jacob's first wife, thought that by bearing a son for her husband she would garner her husband's love, so she named him Reuben, which means "Look! A son."

Joel's name, meaning "Yah[weh] is God," is therefore an affirmation of Yahwistic monotheism. *ʾEl* is the general Semitic noun for deity, usually translated with the upper case ("God") if referring to the proper name of a deity and with the lower case ("god") if referring in general to a foreign deity. It is also the name of the deity at the head of the Canaanite pantheon, El. For a major portion of her existence, Israel was particularly attracted to the Canaanite religious practices, and Israelite prophets and priests had to be ever vigilant lest syncretistic practices be incorporated into Israel (cf. 1 Kings 18; Hos. 2). Joel's name reflects his parents' religious sentiments. For them it is not El who is god, but Yahweh is the true El.

Literary craftsmanship. There is a difference between setting words on paper and crafting them into art. Both deliver information, but care in craftsmanship can deliver it with greater power and impact. Numerous biblical writers, including Joel, use word choice and structure with skill. Joel uses sounds to tie together some of his work, though since the sound of words are specific to the original language, they do not readily translate into English.[65] Structural elements are more transportable when translated, so non-Hebrew speakers are fortunate that biblical writers used a number of these structural features in their work.

The structural form Joel uses in 1:5–14 is a chiasm or envelope construction (see also comment on 2:6). It can be diagrammed something like an arrow point, with the first and last elements of the piece repeating the same ideas or even the same vocabulary, likewise for the second and next-to-last elements, and so on. Frequently the middle element, the actual point of the arrow, is the highlighted key point of the passage. An excellent example is the book of Amos, which appears to be entirely structured as a chiasm around the central turning point of 5:8b. While the sentence looks like it interrupts a doxology and may have been placed where it is by mistake, the chiasm form shows that the theologically pivotal element of the entire book is "Yahweh is his name."[66]

---

65. E.g., 1:10, 12, 16 and notes there.

66. See J. de Waard and W. A. Smalley, *A Translator's Handbook on the Book of Amos* (Stuttgart: United Bible Societies, 1979), 192.

Using this principle, the highlighted element of Joel's lament is the loss of opportunity to offer to God the sacrifices due him. While the loss of food is significant for any nation (1:16), loss of sacrifice is even more severe. Not only is physical life endangered, but so is a continuing covenant relationship between Israel and her God.

Wine and alcohol. Wine was a common staple in the Israelite diet[67] and thus an important part of the agricultural life of the community. In a two-month period during the summer (August–September; Num. 13:20),[68] juicy wine-grapes and other summer fruit (Jer. 40:10–12) are gathered with rejoicing in the bounty of the harvest (Isa. 16:10; Jer. 48:33). They are then taken to the winepress (Isa. 16:10; 65:8).[69] Such a press is formed from natural stone or is stone purpose-formed for the process (Isa. 5:2). The grapes are laid in its upper basin and trodden underfoot, squeezing out the juice (Job 24:11; Neh. 13:15; Isa. 63:3; Jer. 25:30; 48:33; Joel 3:13; Amos 9:13; Mic. 6:15). The juice in turn runs down a channel into a lower, holding basin, where the natural fermentation process immediately commences.

Early stage juice is ʿasîs ("must"; Song 8:2; Isa. 49:26; Joel 1:5; 3:18; Amos 9:13). When most of the active fermentation is complete, the result is transferred to jars or wineskins to allow the process to continue. This is the stage identified as tîrôš ("new wine"). After approximately forty days it becomes wine (yāyin) and is now suitable for drinking (see Mic. 6:15 for the two stages of wine-making, the juice of newly trodden grapes and the wine itself). Some of this is allowed to mature with its lees, so it needs straining (Isa. 2:6). Usually after the forty days, it is decanted into a new vessel or skin in order to separate the liquid from the lees. Otherwise, the resultant wine becomes too sweet and thick and is more prone to spoil (Jer. 48:11–12).[70]

Alcohol use was part of daily life in the ancient Near East. In Israel wine was a daily staple, a blessing from God (e.g., Gen. 27:5; Deut. 7:13; 11:14; Judg. 19:19; Ruth 2:14). It was cause for celebration and

---

67. See Carey Ellen Walsh, *The Fruit of the Vine: Viticulture in Ancient Israel* (HSM 60; Winona Lake, Ind.: Eisenbrauns, 2000), 209–47, concerning the consumption of wine.

68. See the Gezer Calendar, which had "two months for grape harvesting" (*COS*, 2, 222). This seems to be the time of "ingathering" (Ex. 23:16), which is placed at the end of the Israelite agricultural calendar.

69. See Walsh, *The Fruit of the Vine*, 142–65. For a thorough discussion of the harvesting process, see 167–86.

70. See D. J. Clark, "Wine on the Lees (Zeph. 1.12 and Jer. 48.11)," *BT* 32/2 (1981): 241; P. J. King and L. E. Stager, *Life in Biblical Israel* (Louisville: Westminster John Knox, 2001), 99–101; *DDD*, 871–72.

gladness (e.g., Judg. 9:13; Ps. 104:15; Song 5:1; Zech. 10:7; John 2:1–11) and accompanied formal occasions (e.g., Gen. 14:18), even forming part of the people's tithes to Yahweh himself (e.g., Deut. 12:17; 14:23, 26; Tobit 1:7).

Wine apparently contains alcohol even in its earliest stages, though this increases during the fermentation process. The must (ᶜasîs) causes inebriation (Isa. 49:26), which is also implied for new wine (tîrôš; Judg. 9:13; Hos. 4:11). Wine (yāyin) is regularly associated with other fermented drink, most probably beer (e.g., Lev. 10:9; Num. 6:3; Mic. 2:11), and is intoxicating (e.g., Gen. 9:21; Isa. 29:9). In spite of its possible misuse leading to intoxication, wine drinking is never generally prohibited. Priests are forbidden intoxicants when they are actively involved in Israel's rituals in order that their powers of discernment will not be clouded (Lev. 10:9–10).

While drunkenness is discouraged, there does not seem to be an understanding of its being evil per se, though it can produce evil results. Even Noah, the first recorded inebriate (Gen. 9:18), was not condemned for his drunken state. While wisdom literature and the prophets note its debilitating effects, neither do they condemn its use outright. It is just its use in excess that is warned against (e.g., Tobit 4:15; Eph. 5:18).

Wine use continues in the New Testament. Some, such as John the Baptist, carried on the practice of abstinence from alcohol established for the Nazirites (Num. 6:3; Luke 1:15; 7:33). Jesus, in contrast, did partake of wine (Luke 7:33), even providing it for a wedding party in his first miracle at Cana as evidence of his power and glory (John 2:1–11).

Ritual disruption. Some Israelite rituals were annual events (e.g, the festivals described in Lev. 23:4–44; Num. 28:16–29:39). Others occurred more frequently, on weekly or monthly cycles (Lev. 23:3; Num. 28:9–10 and Num. 28:11–15, respectively), or even on a twice daily basis (Num. 28:3–8). They formed the organizing structure for Israelite religious life, providing opportunity for celebration and repentance. The loss of cereal crops and grapes and the subsequent impossibility of presenting cereal and drink offerings affected these twice daily rituals, which included both burnt and cereal offerings, along with accompanying drink offerings (Ex. 29:38–41; Num. 28:5–7). Their loss also affected the occasional sacrifices, such as those to purify people cleansed from a skin disease (Lev. 14:10, 20, 21, 31), those part of the jealousy ritual (Num. 5:15, 18, 25, 26), and most of the annual festivals (Num. 29). Religious life in Israel is being seriously disrupted during the time of Joel.

Among Israel's neighbors, especially those in Mesopotamia, the inability to bring a sacrifice caused an even severer difficulty, since sacrifice by humans provided food for the gods.[71] With disruption of sacrifice also came the disruption of the mealtimes of the gods, with serious consequences. This is shown in the Epic of Gilgamesh, the Babylonian Flood story. There the sacrifices stopped because of the ill–planned actions of one of the gods, whose flood, which was brought to destroy humanity, frightened even the gods themselves. When sacrifices finally resumed after the flood had subsided, the starving "gods crowded around the sacrificer like flies."[72] They became dependent on humans and were starving without them.

The continued dependence is shown in Assyrian royal inscriptions, in which Mesopotamian kings listed some of their more important accomplishments. Often included are building temples for various named gods, where they received worship, including offerings. Several inscriptions also mention building beer vats and storage areas, places to prepare and keep the necessities of life for their survival;[73] several also mention bringing regular offerings.[74]

It was important to look after the gods, because they in turn looked after the city, blessing its inhabitants with provisions. Therefore, if the gods should for some reason depart from a city, that was a serious concern indeed. The capture of one city by another is described in royal annals by saying that the gods of city X (the defeated) left to go to city Y (the conqueror), or that they were taken away by force.[75]

This necessary care for the gods, in order for them to care for the people, was used on a political level by Cyrus, the Persian king who brought the Babylonian empire to an end (see 2 Chron. 36:22–23; Ezra 1:1–2:1). He claimed that his ability to take over from the Babylonian rulers was because they neglected their own gods, who turned to Cyrus himself for aid.[76] While Israel has a completely different view of the relationship between their God and the sacrifices brought to him than do the

---

71. This is stated as the reason for creating humanity in the Epic of Atraḥasis as well as in the Babylonian creation account Enuma Elish, see *COS*, 1, 402, 450.

72. *COS*, 1, 459–60.

73. See, e.g., A. K. Grayson, *Assyrian Royal Inscriptions I: From the Beginning to Ashur–resha–ishi I* (Wiesbaden: Otto Harrassowitz, 1972), 7, 9, 88.

74. Ibid., 80, 102; A. K. Grayson, *Assyrian Royal Inscriptions II: From Tiglath–Pileser I to Ashur–nasir–apli* (Wiesbaden: Otto Harrassowitz, 1976), 18.

75. E.g., A. K. Grayson, *Assyrian and Babylonian Chronicles* (TCS 5; Locust Valley, N.Y.: J. J. Augustin, 1975), 79, 86, 88, 91.

76. "Irreverently, he put an end to the regular offerings.... Marduk [the chief god] ... surveyed and looked throughout all the lands, searching for a righteous king whom he could support. He called out his name: Cyrus" (*COS*, 2, 315).

Assyrians and Babylonians, the inability to bring offerings and sacrifices he expected was still a serious concern.

Agriculture and religion. Prinsloo rightly observes that, for Israel, "farming and religion are intimately linked."[77] A physical link has been suggested for Canaanite Baal worshipers through the fertility cult and ritual prostitution (cf. Jer. 2:23; Hos. 2:13 are suggested).[78] In contrast, orthodox Israelite tradition is monolithic in its ascription of agricultural bounty to God for theological rather than physical reasons. He initially established vegetation (Gen. 1:11–12) and provided it for the sustenance of his creatures (1:29–30). His provision for humanity was special (2:8–9, 16), though its misuse had eternal ramifications (Gen. 3). Thus, good or ill could blossom from the same branch.

For a people living in a marginal agricultural zone such as the land of Canaan/Israel, agricultural produce was especially seen as divine blessing (e.g., Deut 8:8), the very mainstays of life.[79] If one maintained a correct relationship with God, this blessing would flow (Deut. 28:1–12); but if one became estranged, it would be withheld as punishment (28:15–18, 23–24). The loss of agricultural provision was thus not understood as a "natural" calamity, happening apart from God and his working. It was in fact a clarion call to return to him, following his covenant, so that blessing could then flow. He was still the covenant God, Yahweh, who was committed to his people, which is the focus of Habakkuk's message. He declares:

> Though the fig tree does not bud
>   and there are no grapes on the vines,
> though the olive crop fails
>   and the fields produce no food,
> though there are no sheep in the pen
>   and no cattle in the stalls,
> yet I will rejoice in the LORD,
>   I will be joyful in God my Savior. (Hab. 3:17–18)

Habakkuk is directing the people's attention to the Giver rather than to the gift. They must remember that it is the relationship with their Great King that needs to be carefully preserved. If that is in good order, all the rest falls into line.

---

77. Prinsloo, *Theology of Joel*, 27.

78. This understanding of Canaanite religion has recently been questioned (see, e.g., W. Hermann, *DDD*, 138).

79. See Borowski, *Agriculture*, 88; Ferdinand Deist, *The Material Culture of the Bible: An Introduction* (Biblical Seminar 70; Sheffield: Sheffield Academic Press, 2000), 185; cf. David W. Baker, "Agriculture," *DOTP*, 21–26.

SELF-IDENTIFICATION. In today's world, what is the mark of a Christian? In Joel's day, one's religious commitments could at times be determined by the name you bore. Some parents still choose names today because of their religious associations (e.g., David, Paul, even Jesus in many Spanish-speaking countries), but because of rampant biblical illiteracy, at least in the First World, most people do not make the biblical tie-in when they hear the name. This is no different from using the English names of the days of the week, all of which are etymologically related to either astral bodies or pagan deities. Anyone who doesn't know their historical grammar doesn't make the connection.

Some today wear religious jewelry—crucifixes among the more traditional, and WWJD ("What Would Jesus Do?") items among evangelicals. These may at times carry a message to the initiated, those on the inside who know what they symbolize, but most do not know this or even notice them as anything more than jewelry. We don't know for sure what Jesus would do, but most probably he would not present his religious awareness in this manner. He knew the history of his people, who were taught that "man looks at the outward appearance, but the LORD looks at the heart" (1 Sam. 16:7). His disciples understood that it is not outward finery that indicates who one is, but rather one's inner character (e.g., 1 Tim. 2:9; James 2:2; 1 Peter 3:3).

This is not a discussion about acceptable clothing practices, however, but about one's self-identification with God. While some of the means mentioned might be an indication to the initiated, that is not to be the approach of the Christian. We are not to be isolated from anyone unlike us, but to be a light on the hill for those who have not received their own new identity in Christ. We need a public self-identification, which is one of the functions of baptism. While that step is important, it is not readily discernable, something that a colleague or classmate sees. In this context, there is truth in the words sung by the last generation: "They will know we are Christians by our love," not by our name or our jewelry.[80]

Alcohol and the Christian. Many North American churches have developed a view of the appropriateness of alcohol use at variance with that found in the Bible, where it is clearly used without condemnation.[81] Some prohibitionists argue that the Hebrew and Greek terminology also allows for grape juice, which is unfermented. This may be so in some cases, but the

---

80. "The Spirit Song," words written by Peter Scholtes (Los Angeles: F.E.L., 1966).

81. For a helpful discussion of the topic from an "open" perspective, see A. S. Bustanoby, *The Wrath of Grapes: Drinking and the Church Divided* (Grand Rapids: Baker, 1987).

terms also clearly apply to fermented drinks, since drinking them at times resulted in drunkenness (e.g., Gen. 9:21; Acts 2:13–14; Eph. 5:18). What Scripture condemns is intoxication, the loss of one's facilities to distinguish appropriate from inappropriate actions as a result of excess consumption of alcohol (Lev. 10:9).[82]

To protect people from intoxication is laudable, but it is inappropriate to deprive people of Christian freedom based on their potential abuse. What the church should seek is Christian maturity, discipling its members into moderation, not only in alcohol consumption (see Sir. 31:27–28), but in all things. While alcoholism is a real problem, even the daily news reports point out that obesity is much more pervasive and potentially devastating. Consistency in Christian concern for the welfare of others must not stop, therefore, with sobriety but must also include gluttony. In the end, while the church can educate in these areas of excess, it is individual Christians who must monitor their own behavior.

Teachable moments. Formal education is planned with an established curriculum that is previously designed with some goal in mind. This holds for schools whether in the traditional educational system or on Sunday morning. Informal education (e.g., in a family) is most regularly serendipitous and unrehearsed, but it is no less formative. The latter is particularly driven by teachable moments, events encountered during the course of life that provide a natural segue into something that can be learned.

An example of the difference between formal and informal education could involve teaching children the facts of life. Educational systems have sex education curricula in place, and these have often proven lightning rods for controversy for various reasons. One of the reasons for the debate derives from the artificial nature of the process; when is it appropriate to provide certain levels of information? This type of question seems to have arisen in the main since so many people have lost contact with life on the farm or since pets are regularly neutered. While this is not advocating either rural life or the merits of spaying, the actual encounter with child (or puppy) birth does provide a natural teachable moment on the subject of reproduction.

The locust plague in the time of Joel supplies a teachable moment for God, especially since he has a rapt audience because of the vital nature of the topic. The inability of the people to bring their vegetable sacrifices was a time of national importance of which everyone was aware. God uses it to teach

---

82. See D. W. Baker, "Leviticus," *Cornerstone Biblical Commentary* (Wheaton: Tyndale, forthcoming).

concerning his power and his grace, the present and the future, and his own relationship with nature. Much of the power of the teaching derives from its real-life relevance to the questions being asked at that particular moment.

Part of the role of the church is to be on the lookout for teachable moments. My own preferred preaching style is expository, following through a text from beginning to end over a period of time. This allows the entire message of the passage to come to the fore, not just those bits I prefer or am more comfortable with. Part of this process, however, is to be constantly exegeting the congregation as well as the text. While one may have only been partway through a ten-week series on an epistle, the message preached in North America on September 16, 2001, demanded its focus be on the events that had taken place in New York, Washington, and a Pennsylvania field several days previously. Sometimes we don't need to search for teachable moments; they come crashing into our lives.

There must be advance preparation for these moments, however, since often their force and immediacy make it difficult to render a reasoned response directly after the event. This preparation includes the ability to process and address things theologically and with our minds as well as emotionally. Jesus is an example of this on many occasions, but certainly on the cross. One of his colleagues in crucifixion called on Jesus to use his claimed power to spare himself and them from the real pain and death they faced (Luke 23:39). The natural, visceral response was to do just that, since it was certainly within his power to do so. His theology did not allow his bodily pain to determine his response, however. The reason for his incarnation was to provide atonement for sin and to show the victory of the Christ over the power of sin and death. Neither of these could happen if he had left the cross. His theology won out over personal expediency.

This is a problem for much of the contemporary church, at least in the West. Our encounters with God are too often based only on personal experience rather than on theological reflection. When we find ourselves facing an experience of pain or grief, our theology is only a veneer, a surface without substance that does not allow us to address the deep questions of the heart. When a child dies, a business fails, or a horror is perpetrated, previous encounters with God with the mind and soul as well as in the heart are needed to provide what is necessary for the teachable moment. It is these prior reflections that help us to be ready to explain the hope that is within us (1 Peter 3:15).

Destruction. Since most Westerners are not agriculturalists, our comprehension of the magnitude of crop devastation through swarming locusts is meager. For many, the only reality of insect swarms has been a mess on the car windshield. This has not always been the case, however, since even in

North America farmers still experience the helpless horror of such events. A powerful reminder of the psychological, physical, and economic impact is found in Laura Ingalls Wilder's *On the Banks of Plum Creek*.[83] For others of us, a starker comparison is the total destruction caused by explosions at the Federal Building in Oklahoma City or the World Trade center in New York. In the latter, there is physical loss, which has subsequent psychological and economic ramifications leading to consequences far beyond the physical zone of destruction. Like locusts that cut a swath through an entire territory, depriving many families of not only livelihood but also sustenance, so the entire U.S. economy has felt the impact.

It is events such as these, whether deriving from natural or human causes, that force us to realize that we are not ultimately in control of our own destiny. We can send people to walk on the moon, but a loose piece of shielding can also bring our rocket tumbling to the ground. We can protect the life of a severely premature baby who can't even breathe on its own, but we can't stop its parents from using the drugs to cause the premature delivery in the first place, and which also render the baby addicted before it is even born. We can prepare for our family's well-being through IRAs, insurance, and a financial plan, but we have no control over the cancer cells starting to form in our own body.

In each of these instances, we have no control, and we can but scream into the night, "Why?" Our scream does not go into the void, for the Bible, through such books as Joel, shows us that there is a listening ear for these heart cries. We may not get the answer that we sought, as in the instance of Job 38–42, or even any answer at all, as in Jesus' own cry of dereliction (Matt. 27:46; Mark 15:34; cf. Ps. 22:1). We do know through Scripture and through our own prior encounters with the God revealed in Scripture that he exists, that he creates and thus is sovereign, and that he knows and cares about our lives. When we, individually or as a community, face the "dark night of the soul" spoken of by John of the Cross and experienced by each one of us, we do not stand alone or in darkness.

Our experience needs to be informed by our theology, that the God of life and light suffered through his Son as we do (Rom. 8:17; 2 Cor. 1:5; Phil. 3:10; 1 Peter 4:13; 5:1). He is not just the God of light, however. After delivering the Ten Commandments to the people, Moses went back up the mountain and "approached the thick darkness where God was" (Ex. 20:21). In going into the darkness, neither Moses nor we are leaving the presence of God, since he is the God who is there as well. While we might not know the

---

83. Revised edition (New York: Harper Collins, 1953), chapters on "The Glittering Cloud" (192–205) and "Grasshoppers Walking" (259–67).

"why" in our despair, we can stand on the foundation of the "Who" that is with us in it.

Warning. There seem to be two extremes in popular preaching and writing, with vacillation between the two at different times and locations. One is the "hellfire-and-brimstone; turn-or-burn" type of message, which seeks to scare people into the kingdom by describing God the Judge (cf. the classic "Sinners in the Hand of an Angry God," preached by Jonathan Edwards on July 8, 1741).[84] The other is the "gentle Jesus, meek and mild; God our Father, Christ our brother" type of message, which seeks to woo people into the kingdom by describing God the Lover of our soul and the One who meets our daily needs (e.g., much "seeker-sensitive" preaching or more liberal, social-gospel types of sermons).[85]

Both types of message are appropriate on different occasions, and part of the pastoral/prophetic task is to determine which occasion it is. While it does no good to provide pious platitudes of hope to those heading for destruction unless they alter their path, it is also unhelpful to present unmitigated woe to those defeated and beaten down. Great prophets like Joel, Jonah, and Jesus read the times and spoke elements of God's truth relevant to those times. For Joel, the message needed to be "hear, listen up, you are in danger." Does our message today need to look beyond self-actualization and the abundant life, which are indeed provided by God, to the message that our lifestyle as Christians in many areas puts our relationship with God in question? When do we mix warning with weal?

Provider of peace and plenty. The grape and the fig symbolize peace, plenty, and prosperity for Israel (Deut. 8:8; 1 Kings 4:25; Zech. 3:3).[86] Their destruction, by contrast, symbolizes deprivation and want, not only for Israel (Jer. 5:17) but also for others, even her enemies (e.g., Egypt, Ps. 105:33). Israel was aware that Yahweh's hand was involved in both of these aspects, positive and negative.

Human nature, however, seems to look mainly to oneself in both of these circumstances. When things go well, when we enjoy provision and plenty, we see them as arising from our own efforts; they are our due. The unparalleled advances in the financial markets during the 1990s arose from the United States having the most productive economy in history because of our

---

84. See http://www.ccel.org/e/edwards/sermons/sinners.html for a copy of the sermon.

85. E.g., Dorothy Day's article "Our Country Passes from Undeclared to Declared War; We Continue our Christian Pacifist Stand," from early in the Second World War (*The Catholic Worker* [January 1942] 1, 4 [http://www.catholicworker.org/dorothyday/daytext.cfm?TextID=868]).

86. See Prinsloo, *Theology of Joel*, 17.

hard work and good business practices. We produced our own grapes and figs. There was little consideration that sending jobs to places where wages, anti-exploitation, and safety laws are much less rigorous helped fuel these economic gains considerably.

Are we draining needed water from the vines and groves of others, or are we appropriating their few weak shoots to strengthen our many hardy ones? Perhaps God is providing more than we could ask or think to give us an opportunity to support those at home and abroad who are not so blessed, those who need a brother to be their keeper. Do we notice that our neighbors are short of bread and water, much less sweet wine and succulent fruit?

On the other hand, when the U.S. financial markets tumbled down at the turn of the millennium, we claimed it was due to terrorist attacks or unfair steel trade practices. Somebody was vandalizing our trees and vines! There was little consideration that exorbitant executive salaries or illegal accounting practices might be detrimental to the whole superstructure, since they were undermining its foundation of integrity and trust. The royal bureaucracy was taking the majority of the produce of grove and vineyard for its own private enjoyment, stripping the vines and trees without care for the irreparable damage being done to them.

Perhaps God is providing an opportunity for us to reexamine the source of both prosperity and responsibility as he did for Israel. Is it time to turn to the Source of the sun and the rain, the ultimate Provider of both seed and growth, in both apology and adoration? After all, the vineyards and trees are his, not ours.

Joel 2:1–11

¹ Blow the trumpet in Zion;
>   sound the alarm on my holy hill.
Let all who live in the land tremble,
>   for the day of the LORD is coming.
It is close at hand—
²   a day of darkness and gloom,
>   a day of clouds and blackness.
Like dawn spreading across the mountains
>   a large and mighty army comes,
such as never was of old
>   nor ever would be in ages to come.

³ Before them fire devours,
>   behind them a flame blazes.
Before them the land is like the garden of Eden,
>   behind them, a desert waste—
nothing escapes them.
⁴ They have the appearance of horses;
>   they gallop along like cavalry.
⁵ With a noise like that of chariots
>   they leap over the mountaintops,
like a crackling fire consuming stubble,
>   like a mighty army drawn up for battle.

⁶ At the sight of them, nations are in anguish;
>   every face turns pale.
⁷ They charge like warriors;
>   they scale walls like soldiers.
They all march in line,
>   not swerving from their course.
⁸ They do not jostle each other;
>   each marches straight ahead.
They plunge through defenses
>   without breaking ranks.
⁹ They rush upon the city;
>   they run along the wall.
They climb into the houses;
>   like thieves they enter through the windows.

¹⁰Before them the earth shakes,
   the sky trembles,
the sun and moon are darkened,
   and the stars no longer shine.
¹¹The LORD thunders
   at the head of his army;
his forces are beyond number,
   and mighty are those who obey his command.
The day of the LORD is great;
   it is dreadful.
Who can endure it?

DISASTER PILES UPON disaster, with the prophet turning from a description of agricultural catastrophe to the description of an invading army. While this is most likely a metaphorical description of the invading locusts, it drives home the destructive capability of the invaders. This further elucidates the Day of the Lord, a day so momentous that the entire nation needs to be warned of its approach. The description of the Day builds up throughout this passage, starting with the warning (v. 1), a description of the darkness of the Day (v. 2a), which is compared to the approaching army (v. 2b). The metaphor changes to overwhelming fire (v. 3) and then to an inexorable army (vv. 4–9). Its coming results in an apocalyptic cataclysm affecting the entire universe (v. 10). Possibly even more devastating than its physical presence is the identity of the army's commander, God himself (v. 11).

A Warning concerning the Day (2:1–2a).

A NEW SECTION commences with the speaker turning from addressing Yahweh (1:19–20) to Yahweh addressing the people (2:1). He still uses the second person, but now a plural ("all") rather than the singular forms. He rejoins the theme of the Day of the Lord (1:15), expanding on events comprising it. This theme of "the Day" both opens and closes 2:1–11.

The section begins with an urgent series of commands, the first two imperatives and the third a jussive ("let us"). The signaling "trumpet" (*šôpār*) made from a ram's horn is to be blown, as it is in war, heralding an attack (e.g., Judg. 7:8; Job 39:25), or on other occasions announcing news of great import (1 Sam. 13:3; 1 Kings 1:34). The second verb is more general, indicating that a loud noise is to be raised, whether by horn or voice (*rw^c*; Josh.

6:5; 1 Sam. 10:24). The inhabitants of the land shake, either in anger (Ezek. 16:43) or, more likely, in terror (Deut. 2:25) at the news they hear.

The place where the alarm is raised is called "Zion" (cf. 2:15, 23, 32; 3:16, 17, 21) and "my holy hill." In 3:17, the latter modifies the former in apposition. As the site of the temple, the dwelling of God himself (Ps. 76:2), it is the natural source for his warnings. It is also where the people gather to meet the onslaught. During war, they man the battlements from whence comes the call (Ezek. 33:2–4), but this type of attack rendered by nature demands a different type of response, a cultic one, which is also an occasion for trumpet and cry (Lev. 25:9).

The reason for this alarm is again "the day of the LORD" (cf. 1:15). It is not always clear whether the Day is recollected or anticipated, but in either case, it is a matter of consternation.[1] The Day's nearness indicates its imminence, as is usually the case with this predicate adjective "at hand" (*qārôb*; e.g., Deut. 32:35; Obad. 15).

The nature of the Day is described in terms used verbatim in Zephaniah 1:14–15. These are used elsewhere of a theophany, a visible manifestation of God in his awesome power (Joel 2:31; see Bridging Context section). There is particularly a strong tie-in with the Exodus event, where "darkness" was one of God's plagues on Egypt (Ex. 10:21–22; cf. also 10:14–15, where the plague of locusts also brought darkness), in the description of which the synonym translated here as "gloom" also occurs (10:22; cf. also Isa. 8:22; 58:10). What God delimited at creation (Gen. 1:2–5) now returns, an appropriate parallel to this empty, lifeless landscape, denuded of the vegetation that he also created (1:11–12). The second clause also has Exodus ties, but these are later in that story, when God guides Israel using a "cloud" (Ex. 13:21–22; Deut. 1:33) and actually appears to them and Moses in a theophany.

Note how Amos uses "darkness" and "gloom" to correct Israel's optimistic conception of the Day of the Lord (Amos 5:18, 20). Israel thought the Day to be one of blessing, light, and brightness, but Amos corrects them of that perception. Zephaniah picks up these terms to develop his concept of the Day more fully, as a warning to his own period. Joel then uses these terms to indicate that Zephaniah's predictions are coming about; these calamitous events befalling his people are part of the Day. Joel joins himself to the "official," cautionary view of the Day rather than the popular, optimistic one countered by Amos.

---

1. The morphological form of the verb used here is ambiguous, either a perfect ("past tense") or a participle (present continuous) form. This ambiguity may have been playing in the writer's mind, since the locust swarm had already come (perfect), but it and its effects were by no means over (participle) (cf. 2:31; 3:14; see Prinsloo, *Theology of Joel*, 41, n. 5).

Expansion on the Nature of the Day (2:2b–11)[2]

JOEL NOW EXPANDS on the nature of this Day. It is like a "mighty army," already introduced in 1:6–7 and developing themes encountered there and elsewhere in the book. A possible linking feature leading to this comparison is the encroachment of a people (*'am*; cf. 1:6, where the related term *gôy* is used) like either "the dawn" or "darkness"[3] as it spreads out like a net (cf. Isa. 19:8; Hos. 5:1) over the hills of Jerusalem (Joel 2:32; 3:17–18) in its slow, inevitable approach. From the following verses with their military aspect, this army must still represent the nation of locusts. Number and strength have swapped places from 1:6, here with the more frequent "large, great" (*rab*; Ex. 12:38). The army is without comparison from time immemorial (Ps. 119:52; Isa. 27:8; cf. the future orientation of the term in Joel 2:26, 27; 3:20, where the present negative connotation is to be reversed), and also nothing will be its duplicate afterward, in the future (lit., "years of many generations," Deut. 32:7; cf. Joel 1:3; 3:20).

Joel now discusses this invasion spatially, with a play on what happens "before" it (i.e., the encroacher, v. 3a, c) and "behind" it (v. 3b, d). The first two clauses have parallel actions of fire and flame already encountered in 1:19–20. The encroacher pursues a "scorched-earth policy." The previous and resultant states of the countryside are starkly contrasted in the last half of the verse. Previously there was land "like the garden of Eden," a place of beauty, fruitful and luxuriant with trees and water (Gen. 2:9–10; Ezek. 28:13).[4] After the marauders' passing, it is only destruction (cf. 1:7, 17), as lifeless as a true desert (cf. 1:20; 3:19).

This second half-verse takes two other prophecies of hope and turns them on their head. Both Isaiah 51:3 and Ezekiel 36:35 declare that Yahweh

---

2. Leslie C. Allen, *The Books of Joel, Obadiah, Jonah, and Micah* (NICOT; Grand Rapids: Eerdmans, 1976), 64, n. 3, suggests that the end of v. 1 should have been here.

3. *Šaḥar* has been read here in two, seemingly opposite, ways: as "dawn, daybreak" (LXX, ASV, KJV, NASB, NIV, NKJV, NLT) or "darkness" (ESV, NRSV, GNB, NJPS [soot]; based on a revocalization like that suggested by *BHS* as *kiš'ḥōr*, "soot" [Lam. 4:8]). The MT vocalization shows that the Masoretes prefer the former option, though the context of this verse leans toward the latter, providing a tie to the first part of the verse.

4. At least two derivations for Eden have been suggested. The word in some contexts connotes joy and delight (Ps. 36:8; Jer. 51:34; cf. the Akkadian cognate suggested by A. R. Millard, "The Etymology of Eden," *VT* 34 [1984], 105), leading to the concept of Eden as a paradise (see LXX of Gen. 2:15). Others have suggested a derivation from Sumerian EDIN ("steppe, plain") through Akkadian *edinu* (*CAD*, 4:33) to Hebrew (BDB). Both derivations serve equally well in the context of our verse, since either special delicacies or the abundant grass needed for livestock will be greatly missed if destroyed.

restores his errant people, including making their ruins and deserts like the Garden of Eden.[5] Apparently Joel knows this traditional message of hope and also the rhetorical power it will have when reversed. People's expectations, raised in hearing the familiar words, are shattered as they listen to the new meaning.[6] While from a conventional war one might expect refugees (NIV "escapees"; 2:32, "survivors"; Gen. 32:8; Obad. 14), in this case "even" these (using an emphatic adverb) do not survive this attacker. From the context, these survivors are not human but plants that will not be able to escape the locust horde (see Ex. 10:4).

Verses 4—5 provide five different comparisons of the invader with an army. Thus, this is not a literal army but rather a metaphorical one—the locust horde (cf. 1:4, 6). The first three liken the locusts to cavalry forces: the fierce look of charging horses, the swiftness of war horses (NIV "cavalry"), and the sound of the careening chariots. The description of the latter indicates the figurative nature of these analogies, since chariots cannot operate in mountain heights but need level terrain (Josh. 17:16).[7] The verb is appropriate, since "skipping, skittering around" (*rqd*) applies to both animals (and insects) and chariots (Ps. 29:6; Isa. 13:21; Nah. 3:2).[8] This poetic heightening of the actual illustrates the dread this unprecedented force brings on those who encounter it. Habakkuk 3:8 also uses this image of Yahweh as a divine charioteer with horses.

All three of these analogies are new to Joel. Not so the two that follow, however, since a "flame of fire" (1:19, 20; 2:3) and the "mighty army/nation" (*'am*; see comment on 2:2) occurred previously in this section. The flame makes a noise (cf. 2:11; 3:16) as it consumes the chaff or stubble, the dry waste remaining after all the useful grain is gone (Isa. 40:23; Jer. 13:24). The army/nation is not only powerful but is set out in full military array (Judg. 20:20; Jer. 6:23), ready for battle (cf. Joel 2:7; 3:9). The litany of military metaphors drives home the awareness that this force is awesome indeed.

Looking back on all that has just been described, in light of the dread evoked by this advancing marauder, the people respond like a woman in labor, writhing in anguished pain (Isa. 13:8; Jer. 4:31). A common metaphor

---

5. Neither passage is an exact parallel. It seems that Joel conflates them. Underlining indicates exact verbal parallels with Joel, and italics indicate equivalent variants in these literal renditions: Isa. 51:3: "he will establish *her garden like Eden*"; Ezek. 36:35: "this *ruined* <u>land</u> was like the garden of Eden."

6. See the introduction for a discussion of borrowing and relative dates.

7. Mary A. Littauer and J. H. Crouwel, "Chariots," *ABD*, 1:890; Barry J. Beitzel, "Travel and Communication (OT World)," *ABD*, 6:645.

8. In Ps. 114:4, 6, the mountains themselves skip around.

for physical and psychological torment, it was real and immediate to the audience. Without hospitals, babies were born at home with the help of midwives (Ex. 1:15–21), so the process and the attendant pain, unameliorated by anesthetics, were part of everyone's experience. It is not just Israel who has this response, but "nations" (cf. Ex. 15:14–16, where four named nations writhe). Such natural pestilences as drought, famine, or locust swarms knew no natural boundaries, so entire regions felt their effects.[9]

The second clause in verse 6 apparently indicates a physiological response to the stress of the situation. It involves the peoples' faces (a play on the first word in the verse, [lit.] "because of," which in Hebrew derives from the word for "face"). Literally they are said to "gather a glow/glory."[10] The verb is straightforward, used for collecting such things as people, crops, or water (2:16; 3:2, 11; cf. Isa. 22:9; 62:9). Most translations understand this as the color caused by blood flow being removed, resulting in a pallor, which is indeed a result of fear. What appears more likely, based on word meaning as well as context, is that this refers to the glow or pinkness from the collected blood in the face, resulting in flushing, which is the opposite physiological phenomenon to pallor.[11] The verb usually indicates a gathering toward, not away from a place. Also, flushing is more in keeping with labor contractions and strain than is pallor, which more often follows delivery. An almost verbatim parallel to this clause occurs in Nahum 2:11, also in the context of enemy attack, but with no mention of labor pains. This is yet another place where Joel uses material from another source. He also structures his material to provide a multileveled chiasm.[12]

After this parenthetical interlude looking at those under attack, attention returns to the attackers, with two further explicit military comparisons (v. 7a). They are like "warriors" and "soldiers" (lit., "mighty [men]"

---

9. Cf. the regional famine that drove Jacob's family to Egypt finally also struck Egypt (Gen. 41:54–55).

10. *HALOT*, 908 (*p'r* II) as "show glory." Cf. 909 for a discussion of possible etymologies for this word.

11. See KJV, JB: "gather blackness"; cf. NWT: "collect a glow."

12. The verse shows a partial chiasm of sound as well as syntax, which diagrammatically looks like this, with sound parallels underlined:

mippānāyw
    yāḥîlû (verb)
        ʿammîm (subject noun)
           kol-pannîm (subject noun)
      qibbᵉṣû (verb)
pāʾrûr

[Josh. 10:7; 1 Sam. 2:4] and "men of war" [Ex. 15:3; Isa. 3:2]), two synonymous terms. They attack at a run, scaling the protective city walls (Deut. 28:52), without which a city is in disgrace (cf. Neh. 1:3). Just like at Jericho (Josh. 6:5, 20), this horde advances as if the walls are not even there.

Verses 7b–9 detail what each of the members of these two groups does, these mighty warriors.[13] The first four clauses describe the unswerving commitment that each has to his own course. Like runners in their lanes, each soldier moves straight ahead, "through" rather than around obstacles. The meaning of the first verb in verse 8 is uncertain, occurring only in Judges 2:18, where it describes oppressors.

The next six clauses may form another chiasm, beginning and ending with sentences with almost the same structure, with the middle four also sharing similar structures. The four middle clauses in particular are short and staccato, rushing along like the attackers themselves. "Defenses" (here the handheld weaponry for attack or defense [Neh. 4:17, 23]) and "windows" (put in walls to provide light and air but able to be closed [Gen. 8:6; 2 Kings 13:7]) are both expected to keep people out, but now serve rather as the means of the enemy's entry.

The last clause of verse 8 is variously interpreted. The verb usually means "cut off, i.e., kill" (Job 6:9; 27:8), which some translations see here as wounding (KJV, NJPS; cf. "cut off, complete," LXX; "halted," NRSV). Others perceive it as paralleling the negative clauses in verse 8, maintaining military ranks (ASV, NASB, NIV). Due to Joel's penchant for reusing literary motifs, the latter is preferred.

Verse 9 describes the actual progression of events for the marauding forces: ranging around the city (Isa. 33:4; Nah. 2:5), attacking the walls, and climbing up to and into the house windows. The final comparison to a thief likely does not refer to their means of entry, by stealth at night (Jer. 49:9; Obad. 5), but to their purpose, taking what is not rightfully theirs (Gen. 31:19, 20, 26, 27; Ex. 22:6–7). This, then, is the awe-inspiring picture of an unswerving foe.

In verses 10–11, the description concludes with a depiction of the reaction from another perspective. The NIV and NRSV see universal turmoil coming "before them" (i.e., the mighty army of the previous

---

13. The first two clauses of the verse use plural forms of the nouns, indicating ordinary countable plurality. Then the two nouns are given in their singular forms, which is a means of indicating distribution, that is, "each, every" (*DCH*, 1:221–22; 3:313). They are presented in these two verses in reverse order, mighty one–men–each/every man–each/every mighty (one), another modified chiasm.

verses). The Hebrew makes it even more ominous, however, anticipating new information revealed in verse 11. There the turmoil is "before *him*," the same force referred to twice by the identical form in 2:3. The elements of the universe are in turmoil, just as the nations being attacked are in verse 6. The earth shakes like the land's inhabitants are called to do in verse 1, and the very heavens (2:30; 3:16) also tremble like the earth moving in an earthquake (Judg. 5:4; Isa. 13:13; 24:18).[14]

Even the heavenly bodies—the sun, moon, and stars—lose their light (see the same two clauses in 3:15; cf. 2:31). The first two blacken like the night (Mic. 3:6), a verb also used in texts of grief and mourning (Ps. 36:14; Jer. 8:21). The stars literally "remove their light," as God removes his favor from his wayward people (Jer. 16:5; cf. Ps. 104:29).

The mounting litany reaches its climax in verse 11. The focus moves from humans (attacker and attacked) to the earth and heavens, and now specifically to the Creator of all, Yahweh (1:1), Israel's own covenant God. He now reveals what is going on from his perspective, and it is not a comforting message to his people. The first audience knew that something dire was afoot, since Yahweh's thundering (lit., "gave/lifted his voice") is usually an awe-inspiring event that does not bring good news (2 Sam. 22:14; Jer. 25:30; Amos 1:2). The location of his thundering is what is troubling here: "at the head of *his* army." The locust swarm is not just some freak of nature, a random storm that, though devastating, is entirely natural. It is rather a force brought and controlled by God himself.

This revelation of the actual source of the calamity makes the first audience go back over what they had just heard and experienced, reviewing it from the perspective of this new understanding. The author does the review literarily, reusing terms describing the numerous, mighty force that he used previously (cf. 1:6; 2:2, 5). The force itself is given a new description: "forces," a term not found elsewhere in this book. Elsewhere it is the structured encampment of the Israelites in the desert wanderings (e.g., Num. 2:17), but also an organized army (1 Sam. 17:46). This ordered troop of nature is at the same time the troop of Yahweh himself, obeying his commands.

The "day of the LORD" is also revisited (cf. 1:15; 2:1). Its previously noted nearness is replaced by its magnitude and awesomeness (cf. 2:31; repeated with the same terminology in Mal. 4:5). The latter indicates the

---

14. The two Hebrew verbs are used interchangeably with heavens and earth.

result of being in the presence of God (Gen. 28:17). It is not just approaching; it is already here, and it is overwhelmingly unbearable (Jer. 10:10; Amos 7:10).

THEOPHANY—THE APPEARANCE OF GOD. The God of the Old Testament is not a deistic being, someone who starts his creation going and then leaves the scene, nor is he that of the animist, seeing deity as being resident in natural objects. While the Old Testament does not articulate a specific understanding of an omnipresent God, God does appear in physically discernable ways numerous times in the biblical text. Such an appearance is technically known as a *theophany*.

Divine appearances are at times accompanied by physical manifestations similar to those that accompany the Day of the Lord in this passage. Many of these are associated with the most important theophany in the life of the nation, Mount Sinai, where the Israelites received their foundational covenant document, making them a special people under God. A trumpet blast accompanies his appearance there (Ex. 19:16, 19; 20:18; Ps. 47:5; Zeph. 1:16; Zech. 9:14). Joel 2:2 reflects other elements of the Exodus tradition, with the divine manifestation in cloud (Ex. 16:10; 19:9) and blackness (Ex. 20:21; cf. Deut. 4:11, where darkness, blackness, and cloud unite; Ps. 97:2; also Amos 5:20; Zeph. 1:15 relating these elements to the Day).

Fire is also a manifestation of the presence of God at Mount Sinai (Ex. 19:18; 24:17; Deut. 5:23) as well as elsewhere (e.g., Gen. 15:17; Ex. 3:2; 13:21; Deut. 1:33; Ps. 97:3; Isa. 29:6; 66:15). It here accompanies the terrible Day (Joel 2:3). God's appearance is associated with his "arm," a symbol or metaphor of his strength and military might (Ex. 15:16; Deut. 4:34; 5:15; 1 Kings 8:42; Isa. 51:9). Joel 2 pictures the locust swarm also as being the army of God.

Earthquake is also associated with the appearance of God, as its sound, caused by military/locust advance (v. 10), here accompanies the Day of the Lord. At Mount Sinai, an earthquake accompanies smoke, fire, and trumpet, when Yahweh made a covenant with his people (Ex. 19:16–19; cf. Judg. 5:4), as it does when he comes to their aid in judgment on their enemies (e.g., Ps. 18:7–15; Isa. 13:13; Ezek. 38:19–20). The quaking accompanies his voice here (Joel 1:11) as it does elsewhere (e.g., Ps. 29:6–9). All of these elements unite this passage around the concept of the dreadful appearance of the mighty God, a general at the head of his natural, inhuman army.

THE DARK IS RISING.[15] Darkness, thunder, and destructive power are often not seen in the first instance as manifestations of God's power, but often as just the opposite. The growing presence and power of evil, at times accompanied by these same natural phenomena, is not only a biblical theme, but one that is common in literature. It has made itself especially apparent in children's literature of late, being a core motif of the continuingly popular Chronicles of Narnia by C. S. Lewis,[16] and also in the Lord of the Rings movie trilogy, based on the novels of Lewis's friend J. R. R. Tolkien.[17] The interest is not restricted to those with a Christian perspective, however, as evidenced by the currently burgeoning Harry Potter phenomenon.[18] The motif is not restricted to this genre, however, finding a home from the story of Beowulf to modern romance novels and westerns.

In most iterations of this story, good ultimately wins out, leaving one with a spirit of optimism. Some of its darker examples, however, do not end this way, leaving the future bleak indeed.[19] The latter better reflects the point of view of one suffering the onslaught of the darkness, evil, and suffering in whatever form. In the midst of the anguish, the darkness seems complete, with any light of hope vanished. What is not needed in this situation is some subjective attempt to pull oneself up by one's bootstraps, or even worse, a claim that one should be able to do so on one's own. Rather, there needs to be an external source of light and hope, a voice from outside indicating that the darkness is not universal and permanent.

It is this seemingly overwhelming blackness, both literal and metaphorical, that overwhelms Joel's contemporaries in the shape of a devastating invasion of locusts. While this passage describes a bleak and chilling picture, it is bracketed by rays of hope—acknowledgment that God hears (1:19–21)

---

15. Taken from the title of a book by Susan Cooper, *The Dark Is Rising* (New York: Macmillan, 1973).

16. With the stage set for the series by the strong picture of it in the first book of the series, *The Lion, the Witch, and the Wardrobe* (London: Geoffrey Bles, 1950, and subsequent reprints).

17. J. R. R. Tolkien, *The Fellowship of the Ring* (London: George Allen & Unwin, 1954); *The Two Towers* (London: George Allen & Unwin, 1954); *Return of the King* (London: George Allen & Unwin, 1955).

18. Starting with J. K. Rowling, *Harry Potter and the Philosopher's Stone* (London; Bloomsbury, 1997; published in the U.S. as *Harry Potter and the Sorcerer's Stone* [New York: Scholastic Press/Levine Books, 1999]), with subsequent novels and the movies being made from them.

19. E.g., *The Planet of the Apes, Dr. Strangelove,* and the Gilgamesh Epic.

and that he can turn back to them in grace if they respond to him in an appropriate way (2:12–14). The message to those of Joel's day, and to ours, is not a claim that the darkness does not exist—that is, that we should deny that any pain or anguish exists. Rather, the message is that, though the darkness is rising, it will be overcome by the light. In reality, that light has already dawned (e.g., Isa. 9:2; Matt. 4:16).

It is also important to be aware that darkness does not have an independent existence apart from God. He has been in control of it from the very beginning of creation (e.g., Gen. 1:1–5). He is now present and at work in it even when human eyes cannot see or experience him. Christian mystics have called this phenomenon "the dark night of the soul."[20] It is during these times of what appears to be abandonment when one can become closest to the One in whom we live and move and have our being. While God does appear in blessing, too often the blessing becomes the center of attraction; when he comes in darkness and pain, one is driven to concentrate on God rather than the darkness in order to survive it.

Where is God? What would be the response, even within the church, if God appeared today in smoke and fire, or even in darkness? Have we in reality become so blind to his presence, so used to his absence to our physical eyes, that we don't see him when he is present? Eli, the priest of God, did not recognize God when he revealed himself to Samuel (1 Sam. 3). Visions were not widespread in that day (3:1), just as they are rare today, but one wonders whether that is because God is not speaking or because his people are not listening.

I remember a news story a number of years ago of a man landing at the Toronto airport after an international flight but without a passport. His claim was that God had revealed to him that he should come to Canada to tell the Canadians about God's love for them, even though they are among the most unchurched English-speaking nations. He was turned back by the immigration authorities. His claim seems laughable; surely he was delusional, since God doesn't work this way in our tidy, rational lives. That is why God at times turns to mighty locust swarms to reveal himself, and at other times to an evening breeze (Gen. 3:8) or a newborn baby (Matt. 1:18–25).

---

20. See John of the Cross, *Dark Night of the Soul* (trans E. Allison Peers; Garden City, N.J.: Image, 1959). See also E. Underhill, *Evelyn Underhill: Selected Writings*, ed. E. Griffin (Maryknoll, N.Y.: Orbis, 2003); G. May, *The Dark Night of the Soul: A Psychiatrist Explores the Connection between Darkness and Spiritual Growth* (New York: HarperSanFrancisco, 2004).

Each of these events can be rationalized, since each has a natural explanation. The question does not seem to be whether or not something can be explained naturally, but who is behind the natural? God the Creator, who does things decently and in order, putting his creation in order in Genesis 1, is the One who defines natural, the One who sets it in order. Perhaps a better biblical approach would be not to deny the possibility of God acting here or there because each incident has a rational explanation, but rather to look for his providential hand of care, or discipline, even in the mundane, the natural things of life. Why take a negative, exclusionary view of God's presence when he wants us to take a positive, inclusionary view, hearing his praises, like the psalmist, even in mute creation (see Ps. 19).

Joel 2:12–17

¹²"Even now," declares the LORD,
>"return to me with all your heart,
>>with fasting and weeping and mourning."

¹³Rend your heart
>and not your garments.
Return to the LORD your God,
>for he is gracious and compassionate,
slow to anger and abounding in love,
>and he relents from sending calamity.
¹⁴Who knows? He may turn and have pity
>and leave behind a blessing—
grain offerings and drink offerings
>for the LORD your God.

¹⁵Blow the trumpet in Zion,
>declare a holy fast,
>call a sacred assembly.
¹⁶Gather the people,
>consecrate the assembly;
bring together the elders,
>gather the children,
>those nursing at the breast.
Let the bridegroom leave his room
>and the bride her chamber.
¹⁷Let the priests, who minister before the LORD,
>weep between the temple porch and the altar.
Let them say, "Spare your people, O LORD.
>Do not make your inheritance an object of scorn,
a byword among the nations.
Why should they say among the peoples,
>'Where is their God?'"

Original Meaning

WHEN YAHWEH NEXT speaks, it is not in warnings of judgment but in tones of grace. Destruction is not inevitable if the people show repentance. God himself and his character (vv. 12–14) are now the center of attention, not the people and their wrongs, which are not mentioned. Only then are specific ritual instructions given to the people (vv. 15–17); after it is established to whom the people are to return and that Yahweh might be willing to receive their repentance (the "who" and the "why"), the people are given the "how."

This last section returns to the chapter beginning, reiterating the warning cry of alarm (vv. 1, 15). But this time there is more offered than helpless trembling (v. 1). All of the people, described in detail in verse 16, in contrast to the general description of verse 1, can act by assembling for sanctification. The people, through their representatives the priests, can pray, not directly for their own salvation but rather for the honor of God himself (v. 17).

The appropriate response to the devastation brought by God is repentance (v. 12). Triple transition indicators mark it. "Even" (cf. 2:3, 29) and "now" (Gen. 50:21; Ps. 2:10) indicate a new, sequential element to what precedes. It allows a brief window of opportunity to respond in the face of the rapidly approaching Day of Yahweh. The direct discourse indicator ("declares the LORD") identifies the exhortation to repent as originating from Yahweh himself (e.g., Gen. 22:16; Hos. 2:15; Obad. 8).[1] Yahweh does not wait for the people to turn to him; he initiates the discussion.

The new word directed to the audience is an imperative, "return/repent" (*šûb*; cf. Jer. 5:3; Hos. 3:5), which forms a small inclusio with repetition of *šûb* in Joel 2:13b. Joel follows this up with the manner of repentance: It must be total (Deut. 4:29; 6:5; Jer. 29:13), accompanied not only by the traditional outward signs of grief ("fasting," Joel 1:14; 2:15; "weeping," Gen. 45:2; 2 Kings 13:36; "mourning, wailing," Gen. 50:10; Amos 5:16–17), but also with a true, inner reflection of sorrow ("with all your heart").

Verse 13 indicates the latter by contrasting what is customary but unwanted, tearing one's clothes (Gen. 37:29; 2 Sam. 3:31), with a desired response, the metaphorical tearing of the heart. The clause only occurs here, but its meaning is clear from the context. The verb "return" is applied also in the case of the second, desired action (cf. Joel 1:2). The target toward which one is to turn is indicated first as Yahweh as speaker ("to me," 2:12) and then in the third person as "the LORD your God" (2:13). This shows that while the people have committed wrong, Yahweh still allows them to use his covenant, personal name; he still maintains a personal relationship with them. The prophet is taking up the call to repentance initiated by God in verse 12.[2]

The reason for the command to repent follows in a litany of descriptors of God. Repentance is to be based on who God is, not on anything of the

---

1. For a discussion of the clause and its use, see Meier, *Speaking of Speaking*, 298–314.
2. Prinsloo, *Theology of Joel*, 59.

one who repents. These descriptors consist of four adjectives ("gracious, compassionate, slow to anger, abounding in love") and a participle ("relents"), which has an adjectival function. The whole section expresses characteristics of God, not simply actions that he performs sporadically. The adjectives seem to form a fixed unit, since they often occur together, with some variation (Ex. 34:6; Ps. 86:15; 103:8; 145:8; Neh. 9:17). The entire unit is repeated verbatim in Jonah 4:2, with an ironic reversal. Here it is given as a reason for hope, but there it is the reason why Jonah does not want to offer repentance to Nineveh.

Joel most likely is borrowing from Jonah, since the next three verbs in verse 14 also occur in the same context in Jonah (Jon. 3:9).[3] From the multiple uses of this saying, it appears to be a common understanding that God is not only a judge but also someone who wishes to temper his judgment, if the correct response is forthcoming. It is theologically vital to note the hesitancy, however, "Who knows?" (cf. Jer. 17:9; Eccl. 2:19; 6:12). While God has shown his graciousness in the past and one expects him to be consistent in his actions and show graciousness again, one must not become either complacent or presumptuous. God is by no means obligated to show compassion and forgiveness. Each time it must be seen from the perspective of human sinners as an unexpected grace, one that is by no means deserved (cf. Lam. 3:29; Amos 5:15; Jon. 1:6; Zeph. 2:3).

God's pity is here expounded by describing an actual blessing, a gift of grace (Gen. 33:11; Mal. 3:10), that God "may turn and have pity."[4] This translation hides the fact that the first verb is in fact "return" (*šûb*), the verb already encountered twice in the two preceding verses. If Judah returns to God, he returns to them. "Leave behind" is probably a reference to what the locusts left behind (though the verb itself is not used in that context): devastation and destruction. They had deprived people and priest of the means to bring grain and drink offerings (1:9, 13), but these God restores. These in turn are to be directed back to him in worship.

After establishing that there is reason to hope for God's gracious restoration, the prophet instructs the people to respond further, using another string of seven imperatives and three imperative-like verbal forms (2:16–17). The imperatives in these two verses all occur in earlier passages in Joel (see 1:14

---

3. The only difference between the two passages is in the final verb "have pity," which are phonetically identical in both but morphologically distinct (in Jonah a 3ms perfect form and in Joel a ms participle). The noun "disaster, evil, calamity" (Joel 2:13) also occurs in Jonah in reference to this same episode in his life (Jon. 3:10).

4. Deist, *Material Culture*, 167, n. 2, suggests that the word regularly translated "blessing" (*b'rākâ*) could in this and several other contexts (Lev. 25:21; Ezek. 44:30; Mal. 3:10) have been seen as "(reciprocal) gift," an equal response to an action of another.

for verbs 2–5, 7; 2:1 for verb 1; 2:6 ["turns pale"] for verb 6 ["bring together"]), as do all the nouns save three.[5]

The people are called by a trumpet blast (see 2:1), though for a different reason. Earlier it was a call of alarm, signaling fear and dread. Here it is a call to assemble for more hopeful reasons.[6] The "assembly" indicates a gathering of people for cultic, that is, "sacred" purposes (2 Chron. 30:13; Neh. 8:17). The people gathered here include even the very young (nursing infants; cf. Ps. 8:3; Lam. 2:11; 4:4),[7] who are the polar opposite of the "elders," the only ones called in the first several summons in the book (Joel 1:2, 5, 11, 13; 2 Chron. 20:3–4, 13).

Also included are the bridegroom and bride, thematically related to the couple mentioned in 1:8, though the vocabulary is different. They are newly wed, since they are called out of the privacy of their nuptial chambers (Song 1:4; Ps. 19:5). Ministering priests, who wept in frustrated ineffectiveness (Joel 1:9), now weep in fervent prayer in the area where they perform their cultic service, between the altar (1:13) and the "temple porch" (the vestibule of temple or palace: 1 Kings 6:3; 7:6).

The priestly prayer in verse 17 is the second in the book (see 1:15–20). It also includes an imperative and a jussive verb directed toward Yahweh. He is requested to "spare, show pity" (*ḥûs*; 1 Sam. 24:10; Ps. 72:13) on his unfortunate people (Joel 2:16), also called his "inheritance" or "property" (Deut. 9:26, 29; Isa. 47:6).[8] Both people and property are God's by virtue of the covenant.[9]

The priests request that God's own be spared from "scorn" and ridicule (1 Sam. 11:2; Ps. 69:9–10), from becoming an international "byword" or word of contempt.[10] In the case of Israel, their claim to be God's people and

---

5. Joel 1:14 has nouns 2, 3, 6 (cf. 1:2, 14); 2:1 has noun 1; 2:2 has noun 4. Two of the previously encountered noun–verb combinations are not repeated here.

6. Prinsloo, *Theology of Joel*, 52.

7. There does not appear to be any distinction between the two words Joel uses. "Children" is etymologically related to suckling infants and animals (*HALOT*, 797), while the latter word clearly has that connotation.

8. "Your people" and "your inheritance" are the only words in Joel with the 2ms pronominal suffix, compared to 37 uses of the 2mp pronominal suffix. "Your inheritance" with its suffix occurs a total of nine times in the Old Testament, referring either to a people (Israel: Ps. 74:2; 106:5; Isa. 63:17; Mic. 7:14; others: Ps. 2:8) or a place (Ex. 15:17; Ps. 68:10). The juxtaposition of these two terms occurs also in Ps. 28:9, another prayer for help and salvation. In the first prayer the speaker is self-identified as "us" (Joel 1:16).

9. Prinsloo, *Theology of Joel*, 56.

10. Unfortunately, even today most groups use terms referring to those different from them in a derogatory fashion, the subject of humor, and the means of insult. This is evident in the saying quoted in Titus 1:12 about the nature of Cretans; Jesus countered such stereotyping through the parable of the good Samaritan (Luke 10:25–37; cf. 17:16).

inheritance would become a lie if they were destroyed. People would ridicule not only their claims but also the very existence or power of their God. "Where is he, if he can't even help you?" (cf. 2 Kings 18:34//Isa. 36:19; Ps. 42:3; Mic. 7:10; Luke 23:35). The last sentence in Joel 2:17 is found almost verbatim in Psalm 79:10; 115:2. This theme of concern for the reputation of God and his people seems to have been common.

Rather than thinking that the disaster that befell them is only a fluke of nature, the people realize that it is from God. While God is instigator, he also desires to restore the relationship and actually commands his people to approach him for restoration. All society has suffered; now all must turn to the Lord for aid. Their attention is now directed away from the calamities of the past and toward the possibility of restoration through God's response in the future to their previous laments.

REPENT/CHANGE THE MIND. The expression of God's willingness to "relent from sending calamity" (v. 13) needs cautious handling. The verb (*nḥm*) occurs 108 times in the Old Testament, with various meanings. It is used of people facing a situation of loss or suffering, causing them to need "comforting."[11] As an extension of this meaning, it is used of sinful humans to indicate their repentance, which is understood as realizing the error of, and turning away in sorrow from, a wrong action (Job 42:6; Jer. 8:6). This may be entertained as the meaning here in Joel, since the noun "calamity" often denotes "evil" in the ethical sense (Gen. 44:4; 1 Sam. 12:17).

The larger theological context of Scripture does not allow this interpretation, however, since Yahweh does no evil, so he has no need to repent of it. The noun translated "calamity" can also mean "evil, suffering, disaster" in the physical, nonethical sense (Ezek. 7:5; Eccl. 12:1), "on account of which" (Gen. 20:3; Ex. 17:7) Yahweh acts (see Ex. 32:14, where the same verb–preposition–noun combination occurs with this meaning). The sense of the verb *nḥm* that best fits Yahweh as subject is to feel grief or sorrow and subsequently to relent from a course of action.[12] It is this characteristic that is hoped for in Joel 2:14, where the two identical verb forms are hidden by the NIV translations of "relent" and "have pity."

---

11. In several different Hebrew verb stems (P= *piel*; N= *nifal*; T= *hitpael*), for example Gen. 24:67[N]; 37:35[N,T]; 2 Sam. 13:39[P]; cf. Ps. 77:2[N]; Isa. 40:1[P, P]; 49:13[P]; Jer. 31:13[P]; Ezek. 14:22[P], 23[P].

12. Gen. 6:6–7; Ex. 32:12–14; 1 Sam. 15:35.

There is a heated debate over this topic in contemporary theology, precipitated by what is called "openness theology."[13] It is a variation of Arminianism, which diverges from Reformed theology in four areas: God and time, God and change, the sovereignty of God, and God's foreknowledge.[14] Relevant to the issue at hand in Joel, classical Reformed theology has seen God as immutable or changeless.[15] This causes problems to any of the proposed interpretations of the verb: God as holy cannot sin, so does not repent of sin; God as immutable does not change his mind; God as immutable and "without . . . passions" cannot feel sorrow. To address this concern, this verb, and other verbs of "passion," can be taken as being metaphorical, an anthropomorphism attributing to God emotions that he does not have.[16] The topic is vast and important, but beyond the scope of what can be adequately addressed in this commentary.

Outward versus inward. The prophet draws a sharp contrast between internal and external realities when he distinguishes between torn clothing and a torn heart. The former is a formal, visible indication in Israelite society of an inner reality of grief, mourning, or other upset (cf. Gen. 44:13; Num. 14:6; Judg. 11:35; 2 Kings 2:12; 5:7; 11:14; 18:37–19:1; 22:11, 19; 2 Chron. 34:19; Ezra 9:3, with pulling hair and sitting; Job 1:20, accompanied by shaving and prostration; Jer. 41:5, accompanied by self-mutilation and shaving the beard). It could be accompanied by other symbolic gestures, such as wearing garments of coarse cloth (Gen. 37:34; 2 Sam. 3:31; 1 Kings 21:7, accompanied by fasting; 2 Kings 6:30; Esth. 4:1), falling on one's face (Josh. 7:6), or putting dust or ashes on one's head (Josh. 7:6; 1 Sam. 4:12; 2 Sam. 1:2; 13:19; 15:32; Esth. 4:1; Job 2:12). These mourning practices, perfectly acceptable for the people, were forbidden for the priests (e.g., Lev. 10:6; 21:10).

---

13. See in particular the works of Clark Pinnock (e.g., *Most Moved Mover: A Theology of God's Openness* [Grand Rapids: Baker, 2001]); John Sanders (e.g., *The God Who Risks: A Theology of Providence* [Downers Grove, Ill.: InterVarsity Press, 1998]; with C. A. Hall, *Does God Have a Future? A Debate on Divine Providence* [Grand Rapids: Baker, 2003]); and Gregory Boyd (e.g., *God of the Possible: A Biblical Introduction to the Open View of God* [Grand Rapids: Baker, 2000]; idem, *Is God to Blame? Moving Beyond Pat Answers to the Problem of Evil* [Downers Grove, Ill.: InterVarsity Press, 2003]).

14. For a useful introduction to the topic, identifying various players and options, see B. B. Colijn, "Open Theism: Framing the Discussion," *ATJ* 34 (2002): 55–65.

15. The Westminster Confession states: "There is but one only living and true God, who is infinite in being and perfection, a most pure spirit, invisible, without body, parts, or passions, immutable" (Chapter II).

16. Cf. N. L. Geisler and H. W. House, *The Battle for God: Responding to the Challenge of Neotheism* (Grand Rapids: Kregel, 2001), 71, 272–74. Regarding anthropomorphic/ anthropopathic or analogical language, see, e.g., K. Vanhoozer, ed., *Nothing Greater, Nothing Better: Theological Essays on the Love of God* (Grand Rapids: Eerdmans, 2001).

Joel does not condemn the practice per se here. Rather, he denounces an outward show that does not correspond to an inner reality; a public show of mourning when there in fact is none is hypocrisy. If there is to be a choice between the two, inner posture should be chosen over outer posturing.

Surface appearance is more readily apprehended, but since it can mislead, one's true character is key, as God informs Samuel at the anointing of David (1 Sam. 16:7; cf. Gal. 2:6; James 2:1–4). Amos condemned the sham of hypocritical religious cult among a people who did not in reality hold to a covenant commitment (Amos 5:21–24), and Jeremiah warned that one of the external trappings of religion, even if it is the temple itself, has no value if the practices of the people fail to meet their obligations (Jer. 7:1–11). In the Sermon on the Mount, Jesus took the inward/outward distinction a step further. While some understood the law as something that could only be broken in practice (the outward), Jesus stated that attitude and thought (the inward) could also contravene it (Matt. 5:28; cf. 15:8). One's essential character is inward and will produce external fruit commensurate with its nature (13:33–35; 15:18–19). God's ultimate goal is that the inward and the outward coalesce in the image of his Son (cf. 1 Cor. 14:24–25).

A GOD OF PASSION. God's immutability (i.e., whether he ever changes or even if he knows real emotions) is not only a theological question but also a personal issue, one that touches the heart. One pastoral point will be raised here. In some discussion about this issue, it is proposed that, for the comfort of the believer, the immutability of God is the most important theological concept. I find this theologically and pastorally troubling. In an experience of personal crisis, there seems to be much more practical assurance of hope in knowing that I am in the hands of a God who loves me and cares for every aspect of my life than in knowing that I have to do with a God who is emotionless and dispassionate. A child growing up with a parent who only shows emotional detachment and distancing, one who cannot or will not exhibit love or intimacy, experiences personal dysfunction. How much more so if this is the attitude of a heavenly Parent!

Related to this discussion is the divine "perhaps" of verse 14 ("he may turn"). However one understands God's foreknowledge and immutability, this is not an attribute he shares with human beings. Whether his actions are always predetermined or at times might be contingent either on human request or response, they are not something that can be known to his creatures in advance, apart from divine revelation. One might hope for a gracious response based on such occurrences in the past, but it must not become expected; each time grace comes, its recipients should be surprised.

As Prinsloo states, "there is no direct causal connection between the people's penitence and Yahweh's response."[17]

Who knows? The prophet presents a healthy view of God. He calls for the people to respond in penitence, with its appropriate rites (vv. 12–13). This is in their power to do; it is a choice they can make. On the other side, God can also choose to respond to this repentance as he wills. Based on his prior reactions to Israel's return to him, Joel and his contemporaries hope that he will accept them back. This is within his power to do; it is a choice he can make.

Some in the church today, however, see both choices lying within the hands of God's human creatures. Human actions compel God to act in a certain way, usually to bless the actor. This is in reality a magical, esoteric view of human power found most commonly in neopaganism. In this view, such things as the pronunciation of the true name of God or possession of the Holy Grail endow one with powers beyond the natural.[18] The increasing numbers involved in these beliefs and practices is apparent by the spate of published titles on such things as witchcraft and spells, the many internet sites devoted to neopagan practices, ranging through druidism, wicca, and satanism, and the acceptance by the U.S. military of neopaganism as a valid religion.

Some forms of Christian theology approach this type of coercive manipulation, claiming its power when directed against God. The "name-it-and-claim-it" prosperity gospel movement says that statements of God's promised blessings in relation to one's self guarantee their reception.[19] There is no discussion of the theological context, of such matters as obedience and faithfulness on the part of the believer. Nor is there a discussion of the sovereignty of God. Rather, there has developed an arrogant expectation that a creature can force the hand of the Creator. The prophet's "perhaps" becomes rather "God owes me." Even prayer itself can be perverted, a coercion of God, "but coercion by prayer is yet coercion."[20]

A proper understanding of the relationship between human and divine is better expressed by a certain Christian leader shortly before he passed away. When asked how he grappled with the theological question of how he could be dying despite the prayers of many faithful Christians, he said: "When I am

---

17. Prinsloo, *Theology of Joel*, 58.

18. A powerful picture of the outworking of this kind of perspective and its place within a Christian understanding of the world can be seen in the fictional writings of Charles Williams, a friend and writing companion of C. S. Lewis, most particularly in *All Hallow's Eve* (London: Faber & Faber, 1945; Grand Rapids: Eerdmans, 1981).

19. See Bridging Contexts section of Mal. 3:6–12.

20. M. M. Shideler, *The Theology of Romantic Love: A Study of the Writings of Charles Williams* (Grand Rapids: Eerdmans, 1962), 137.

in the presence of God, it seems uniquely unbecoming to demand anything."[21] This shows the correct attitude toward God; he is the Father Almighty, Creator of heaven and earth, as stated in the Apostle's Creed. Any view that espouses divine coercion envisions only a diminished God, placing him a little lower than his creatures, who are in control. This is neither the God of orthodox Christianity, nor is it the God of Joel.

Theological community. Theodore Geisel, writing as Dr. Seuss, shows in several of his works that the community is made up of individuals, and that individual actions can have direct bearing on the life of the community. This is most clearly illustrated in *Horton Hears a Who*.[22] In this story, an entire community is endangered because one of its members does not take part in an action that requires the involvement of everyone. When that one joins in, he sways the balance, even though he is the smallest member of the community; as a result, the community is saved. The Bible also records incidents when the actions of a single person affect their entire community for either good (e.g., Esther's willingness to risk all for their people, Esth. 4) or ill (e.g., Achan's withholding for his own use things dedicated to God, Josh. 7).

Western Christianity too often suffers from this individualistic tendency. While many give lip service to a body theology as articulated by Paul (e.g., 1 Cor. 12:12–31), they act on the theology articulated by Frank Sinatra, "I did it my way." This is exhibited through disconnecting from both the past and the present. While the Roman Catholic Church may have laid too great an emphasis on tradition, evangelicalism has denigrated tradition. We share testimony on how God has worked in "my life," which is of some encouragement, but we sell short, or are completely ignorant of, how God has also worked mightily in the lives of our fathers and mothers.

It is the community memory of God's actions in the life of Israel that prompts hope in generations of the nation of Israel (e.g., in Deuteronomy, which itself is in the literary form of an aging leader's reminiscences to his followers before he bids them farewell; cf. also Josh. 24:2–13; Ps. 44:1–3), as well as in the hearts of individuals (e.g., Ps. 22:4–5, 9–10). While not all of our tradition is helpful, it all molds our beliefs and our being in some way. What we must strive for is not an abandonment of tradition, which is impossible; rather, Christians need to develop a theological lens through which to critique and evaluate tradition. This will allow us to appreciate that which draws us closer to God and to discard that which shadows him from us.

The present is also hindered by typical Western individualism, since the body does not grow when individual members feel autonomous and

---

21. Reported in L. Crabb, *Inside Out* (Colorado Springs: NavPress, 1988), 150.
22. Dr. Seuss, *Horton Hears a Who* (New York: Random House, 1954).

self-sufficient. This can manifest itself in many ways, but an egregious example brought to my attention is of an itinerant preacher who said that he never uses commentaries or study aids for sermon preparation; rather, he relies solely on the guidance of the Holy Spirit. I am not trying to downplay the role of the Spirit in sermon preparation (though he seems to be ignored often in such pursuits, judging by many of the sermons I hear preached!), but this is laying something to the charge of the Spirit that is never mentioned by Scripture. It also flies in the face of an expectation that we use our own gifts and intellect in the service of God (cf. 2 Tim. 2:15), including showing enough intellect that we do not think that everyone must reinvent the wheel. If believers through the ages have diligently and correctly interpreted Scripture, why be a fool by not taking their advice and instruction (Prov. 12:15)?

Self-absorbed individualism can also deny the community of much-needed ministry. In the parable of the good Samaritan (Luke 10:30–35), the priest and the Levite do nothing wrong, from their viewpoint of self-interest. Both obey the law that warns any who minister in the sanctuary not to touch a corpse (Lev. 22:4). They follow a negative ethic of avoidance, but they are not ministering to the present and pressing need of a member of the community. They do not follow an ethic of engagement, putting a community need above their own individual need. Using contemporary evangelical jargon, they are more worried about their own salvation than they are about that of the other.

Individualism often manifests itself in the most mundane areas of life, such as greeting those we encounter. When we see someone on a Sunday morning, we say, "Hi. How are you?" The acceptable response is, "Fine. And you?" When someone instead says that their spouse has just been diagnosed with cancer or that their business has just declared bankruptcy, we are brought up short and often find ourselves irritated. Don't these folks realize that our greeting is just rhetorical, that I just want you to notice that I have noticed you? You see, it's not really about the other person at all, it is about me. My outward façade of caring hides an inner reality that is quite different.

Even in this simple area of greetings, community plays an important role. Paul exhorts his readers in Galatia to "carry each other's burdens" (Gal. 6:2) if we are to truly live in God's kingdom community. In order to do this, we must know what these burdens are, and in order to know, we must care about them and really ask as if we do care. This can be dangerous to our self-centered lives, since it can cost in terms of time, emotions, and commitment. But after all, these three things seem to be what turns a simple collection of people into a community.

A strong concern for community, and that in its entirety, is the concern of Joel in this passage (v. 16). The prayer of the priests is for the entire nation, not just for themselves. This is the call to the church as well (e.g., Gal. 6:2).

Joel 2:18–32 [2:18–3:5]

¹⁸ Then the LORD will be jealous for his land
    and take pity on his people.

¹⁹ The LORD will reply to them:

"I am sending you grain, new wine and oil,
    enough to satisfy you fully;
never again will I make you
    an object of scorn to the nations.

²⁰ "I will drive the northern army far from you,
    pushing it into a parched and barren land,
with its front columns going into the eastern sea
    and those in the rear into the western sea.
And its stench will go up;
    its smell will rise."

Surely he has done great things.
²¹   Be not afraid, O land;
    be glad and rejoice.
Surely the LORD has done great things.
²²   Be not afraid, O wild animals,
    for the open pastures are becoming green.
The trees are bearing their fruit;
    the fig tree and the vine yield their riches.
²³ Be glad, O people of Zion,
    rejoice in the LORD your God,
for he has given you
    the autumn rains in righteousness.
He sends you abundant showers,
    both autumn and spring rains, as before.
²⁴ The threshing floors will be filled with grain;
    the vats will overflow with new wine and oil.

²⁵ "I will repay you for the years the locusts have eaten—
    the great locust and the young locust,
    the other locusts and the locust swarm—
my great army that I sent among you.

²⁶You will have plenty to eat, until you are full,
>and you will praise the name of the LORD your God,
>who has worked wonders for you;
>never again will my people be shamed.

²⁷Then you will know that I am in Israel,
>that I am the LORD your God,
>and that there is no other;
>never again will my people be shamed.

²⁸ [3:1]"And afterward,
>I will pour out my Spirit on all people.
>Your sons and daughters will prophesy,
>your old men will dream dreams,
>your young men will see visions.

²⁹ [3:2]Even on my servants, both men and women,
>I will pour out my Spirit in those days

³⁰ [3:3]I will show wonders in the heavens
>and on the earth,
>blood and fire and billows of smoke.

³¹ [3:4]The sun will be turned to darkness
>and the moon to blood
>before the coming of the great and dreadful day
>of the LORD.

³² [3:5]And everyone who calls
>on the name of the LORD will be saved;
>for on Mount Zion and in Jerusalem
>there will be deliverance,
>as the LORD has said,
>among the survivors
>whom the LORD calls.

Original Meaning

GOD IS RESPONSIVE to the prayers of his people. When they cry to him, he answers them in a threefold reply (2:18–20, 25–27, 28–32), separated by a request for them to continue calling on him (2:21–24).¹ Attention turns at this point from an understandable concern with the fearful depredations of the recent past, the subject of the

---

1. The same plea–response form is found Ps. 22 on the personal level, and in Ps. 60:1–5, 6–8; 65:1–7, 8–13; 2 Chron. 30:6–13, 14–17, on the national level; cf. Wolff, *Joel*, 58.

prophecy up to this point, to the bountiful promises of God for the future, anticipating the final Day of the Lord, the concern of the rest of the book. This will be a time of true blessing for those who call on God.

Yahweh's First Response (2:18–20)

THIS NEW SECTION is separated from the preceding context by a new speaker, Yahweh himself, and by different grammatical constructions, indicative rather than imperative verbal forms. It is not a completely separate unit from what precedes, as some have claimed,[2] since the Hebrew verbal construction with which it begins ties it to the preceding context. Yahweh appropriately responds (cf. "reply," v. 19) to the mourning of "his land" (v. 18; cf. 1:6, 10) and to anguished cries of "his people" (2:18), who have suffered under "his army" (2:11).[3] The strong association with Yahweh indicated by the pronominal suffixes ("his") explains his jealousy for them (Zech. 1:14; 8:2), his desire for an exclusive relationship with them.[4] Yahweh's jealousy is spelled out in the Ten Commandments and as such is a foundational principle for Israel's life (Ex. 20:5; Deut. 5:9), one they too often neglect (see Bridging Contexts section).

The next verb ("takes pity") looks inward toward the people rather than outward toward other interests. Yahweh directs his compassion and pity on his suffering people, just as Pharaoh's daughter did on the crying baby Moses (Ex. 2:6; cf. 2 Sam. 21:7). Joel 2:13 anticipates this pity from the compassionate God. He responds through promised restoration of what was previously destroyed: "grain, new wine and oil" (2:19; cf. 1:10). God is not a debtor but rather makes good even beyond that which is lost, going beyond "enough" to "satisfaction, satiety" (2:19; cf. Deut. 6:11; Isa. 1:11; cf. Job 42:10–17). All this replaces the "scorn" Yahweh allowed neighboring nations to lay on them (Joel 2:19; cf. 2:17).

Verse 18 is a literary pivot in the book.[5] Up to now, the problem has been presented and the response of the people has been called for. Now God's response unfolds. It is not introduced here *de novo*, however, since

---

2. E.g., B. Duhm, "Anmerkungen zu den Zwölf Propheten," *ZAW* 31 (1911): 184–88.

3. See the same order of land, then people, who are restored in 2 Chron. 7:13–14; Braaten, "God Sows," 126, notes that in this section of Joel it is land (v. 21), animals (v. 22), people (v. 23).

4. The verbal form used here is unusual, following a form that most regularly occurs in narratives. Note the NIV's alternate translation in the textual note on v. 19. The use of the perfect here may be a "persistent perfect," describing a permanent characteristic of God (his jealousy) that is past, present, and future.

5. Cf. Ahlström, *Joel and the Temple Cult,* 132; Keller, Joël," 102; Wolff, *Joel,* 67; Prinsloo, *Theology of Joel,* 63.

the possibility ("who knows?") of restoration was laid out in 2:14. Now that possibility is reality ("the LORD will"). The same structure is found in the Flood story, which built up to the climax of God's remembering Noah (Gen. 8:1).[6] This verse is also the physical center of Joel according to a word-unit count.[7]

God's promises expand in 2:19, eradicating the problem and not simply making up for the loss of agricultural produce (1:10). The uncertainty of God's "perhaps" of 2:14 now becomes the certainty of his "yes, I will." In Hosea, God promises to respond to Israelite faithfulness by having the earth provide grain, wine, and oil (Hos. 2:21–22). This happens "in that day," the Day of the Lord. God here responds (using the same verb, ʿnh) through the same three agricultural products. For Joel, these events following the Judean response to God fulfill Hosea's prophecy.

God's reply is one of two mentions of God "saying" (ʾmr) anything in the book (cf. also 2:32), a marked contrast to the frequent prophetic usage elsewhere of the verb ʾmr for speeches of Yahweh (e.g., Isa. 3:16; 7:3, and *passim*). The book does contain his direct speech, but this specific verb, common elsewhere, is intriguingly missing in Joel. The scorn that the priests pray to avoid (Joel 2:17) will be removed, showing God's attentiveness to his people's requests. He "sent" them blessing, in contrast to the plagues brought on Pharaoh, who neglected to "send" Israel out in order to be able to worship (Ex. 10:4).

The locust army (1:4; 2:2–11), now identified by its place of geographical origin ("the northern army," 2:20), will be driven away (Deut. 30:1; 2 Chron. 13:9) from the land, reversing the proximity of the coming at the Day of the Lord (Joel 1:15; cf. 3:14). As Yahweh previously drove the plague of locusts away (Ex. 10:17, 19), so he now does with the encroaching army. Since their arrival results in a dry and destroyed land (Joel 1:7, 10, 12; 2:3; cf. 3:19[2x]), it is only appropriate that this be the locust's final destination, a "tit-for-tat" type of conclusion.[8]

The huge expanse of the swarming army is indicated by its finally reaching between two seas (lit., those "in front" and "behind"). From the perspective of those already settled within the land, these are "eastern" (Dead Sea)

---

6. See G. J. Wenham, "The Coherence of the Flood Narrative," *VT* 28 (1978): 336–48[338].

7. E. R. Wendland, "Recursion in the Prophecy of Joel: Its Form, Function, and Significance for the Translator," United Bible Society Triennial Workshop manuscript, Stuttgart (1984) 24; cited in Bliese, "Metrical Sequences," 74.

8. Dryness here uses a different root (ṣyh) than that used previously, but the concept is the same. Cf. D. W. Baker, "Aspects of Grace in the Pentateuch," *ATJ* 29 (1997): 7–22, concerning the concept of appropriateness in this type of situation.

and "western" (Mediterranean Sea) respectively (Job 18:20; Ezek. 10:19; Zech. 14:8). Their removal results in the death of the ousted locusts, killed by water (cf. Ex. 10:19) and lack of food in the desert. A rising "stench" often results from decaying organic material (cf. Isa. 34:3; Amos 4:10—both passages in the context of death in battle, continuing the military metaphor for the locusts; cf. Ex. 7:18, 21).

The last clause of verse 20 is one of the most grammatically and literarily obscure in the book. Literally it reads "for/indeed he magnified to do" (cf. v. 21d; Ps. 126:2–3). Most see the combination of finite verb + infinitive, or even the finite form on its own, as meaning "to do great things" (BDB; KJV; NASB; NIV; NJPS; NRSV; LXX: "he made his work great"), even though there is no explicit direct object for the verb. Even if accepted, the subject is not at all clear. Many take it as Yahweh, an anticipation of the same clause with him as subject at the end of verse 21 (NCV; NJPS; NIV, as indicated by punctuation and spacing; NLT). Others see it as concluding the previous section, contributing to the locusts' destruction, with the locust swarm ("it") as the subject (MT; ASV; ESV; KJV; RSV; NASB; NJB; NKJV, "Because he has done monstrous things"; NRSV).[9]

If the latter is the correct interpretation, there is a contrast between the powerful deeds and the poor end; magnification precedes destruction. As pride in power affects human nations and their armies (e.g., Assyria, Isa. 10: 5–19; Moab, 16:6; Judah, Jer. 13:9; Israel, Hos. 5:5), so it metaphorically does to locust hordes. This interpretation is preferred, for the clause then provides a segue, a catch phrase that leads to the following section.

People, Rejoice! (2:21–24)

THE VERBAL FORMS in verses 21–22 revert to imperative-like forms in a call to praise, not directed only to people who suffered but also to inanimate creation and dumb beasts, who are also directly affected ("land," v. 21, cf. 1:10; "wild animals," v. 22; cf. 1:18, 20). Rather than terror (2:11), God's people reexperience the gladness and joy they lost (1:16; cf. 2:23). Why? Because of the mighty acts of Yahweh (see comment on 2:20), exemplified in verse 22 by the restoration of pasture (the "greening" of what has been consumed in 1:19–20), fruit trees (the resumed bearing by what has been dried out and scorched in 1:12, 19), and most specifically the fig tree and grape vine (1:7, 12). The latter two "yield their riches" (*ḥêl*; Gen. 34:29; Num. 31:9), a play on this same word elsewhere used of the "forces" or "army" of the locusts

---

9. See Allen, *Joel*, 89; Crenshaw, *Joel*, 152.

(2:11, 25); the one is overturned and replaced by the other, both physically and semantically.

Subsequently the people, those previously summoned to fear, weep, and pray in Zion (2:1, 15), now join the rest of creation in celebration (2:21). The basis of their rejoicing is God himself, and secondarily his actions on their behalf. These include his acts in nature, now not in removing the locusts but in relieving from drought (2:23; cf. 1:10).

Instead of making (*ntn*) them an object of scorn (v. 19), Yahweh provides (*ntn*; NIV "has given" in v. 23) rain by causing it to come down ("sends"). For many of us, rain is only a bother, but for agriculturalists in a semiarid climate, it is the difference between plentiful crops and starvation. Since rain is vital for their society, Israel has several terms for different types and periods of rain (see Bridging Contexts section). The more general term is more specifically identified as "autumn rains" and "spring rains." These two types of rain form a merism (a literary form using two polar extremes to include everything in between them; cf. Deut. 11:14; Jer. 5:24), which indicates the resumption of all rains. That resumption is indeed cause for celebration.

Two different adverbs describe God's sending rain in verse 23. The first is literally "for righteousness."[10] In the three other occurrences of this exact form (Ps. 106:31; Isa. 5:7; Hos. 10:12), righteousness is the goal sought, so that is probably what is meant here, though whose righteousness is unclear. The second adverb ("as before"; lit., "in the first") is only used outside Joel in the context of dating events, referring to the "first (month)" (e.g., Gen. 8:13; 9:5). While no month is specified here, context suggests that it refers to the situation at the beginning of the time of destruction just past, before all the locusts, drought, and flame had come.

There may be a similar thematic link between these two concepts as well as the gracious gift of rain in Deuteronomy 11:8–12, which can help us understand this passage. There the Israelites were promised that, if they live in covenant faithfulness with Yahweh, he will provide abundant moisture for the land over which he keeps his eye all the year, from beginning to end. In Joel, the previous time of plenty, as promised in Deuteronomy, will be the result of Yahweh's righteousness in remembering his promises, but it will also serve as a reminder to Israel that they must show righteous obedience as well. Thus there could be in the Joel passage an implicit reference to covenant.[11]

Ahlström notes a purposeful progression in these verses, calling for rejoicing starting with the land, progressing to the animals, and ending with the

---

10. *Môreh* ("autumn rain") is also used of a "teacher" (Isa. 30:20). A combination of the two terms could be taken as "teacher for righteousness" (Joel 2:23, Young's; NIV mg.).

11. Cf. Allen, *Joel*, 93 and n. 29.

people of Zion—that is, moving from the periphery to those who actively worship God.[12] The Hebrew emphasizes "O people of Zion," placing them at the start of the sentence with an emphatic or affirmative conjunction.[13]

The final stage of restoration follows (2:24). After the locusts are expelled (v. 20) and the trees start to bear (v. 22) because the rains have returned (v. 23), other crops are prepared for consumption and storing away. Two places of production are mentioned for the first time in the prophecy, since previously they lay unused as a result of the lack of raw material. The "threshing floor" (Ruth 3:2; Job 39:12) is where the wheat and barley (cf. 1:10–11) are processed, removing the edible kernel (the "grain," cf. Amos 5:11; 8:5) from the waste chaff through the process of winnowing. The previously unused site will now be filled, probably by the farmers who previously were without any work (1:11), though the subject is unspecified.

The presses (NIV, "vats"; cf. 3:13; Job 24:11; Isa. 5:2) for processing raw material for their liquid content, such as grapes, resulting in wine (1:10; 2:19), and olives, resulting in oil (1:10; 2:19), will now overflow like a river that overflows after God's rain (Ps. 65:9; Joel 3:13). The locusts previously destroyed all of these, but God makes them good in abundance.

Yahweh's Second Response (2:25–27)

YAHWEH AGAIN SPEAKS directly to his people, promising his covenant faithfulness. He continues to be "your God" (v. 26), just as they are still "my people" (v. 26; cf. Ex. 6:7; Lev. 26:12; Jer. 7:23; 30:22). Referring back to the devastating locust horde, Yahweh repeats each destructive locust type found in Joel 1:4. He also acknowledges that they are his own great "army" ("forces" in 2:11), sent by him just as are the grain, new wine, and oil (2:19). This acknowledgment has not yet been specifically mentioned. Now he "will repay," restoring the situation to its state prior to the devastation (cf. 3:4; see the interpretation of 2:24; also Job 8:6). He brings both woe and weal.

New information is given regarding the length of time the people have suffered. Taking this verse at face value, the devastation does not last just for a season, but rather for "years" (v. 25). This is expected even in the event of a regular crop failure, since it takes at least two years under those circumstances before the people can use the next crop. The vivid descriptions of the horror in this case indicate that this episode is distinctly worse, so recovery will, in the normal course of events, take even longer. However, Yahweh promises that this long delay will not happen; the time of lack is now over.

---

12. Ahlström, *Joel and the Temple Cult*, 6–7; see also Prinsloo, *Theology of Joel*, 69.
13. Williams, §438; Prinsloo, *Theology of Joel*, 69.

Instead of locusts eating, the people will now eat—and not just for subsistence, but to satiety (2:26–27; cf. 2:19). As a result of his deliverance, people "will praise" Yahweh's name and reputation (cf. Gen. 12:2; Neh. 9:10; Ezek. 16:14), lifting it high, in contrast to those demeaning it, bringing it to scorn (Joel 2:17, 19). This contrast is also brought out in the verb translated "work wonders" (*plʾ*), which is in the causative stem in Hebrew, indicating an outward focus. It is not just that Yahweh does mighty acts, but that those wonders inspire others with awe and reverence (cf. Ex. 15:11; Isa. 25:1), not the scorn and derision they intended. Shame and humiliation are reversed forever (cf. Joel 3:20), reminding the hearers that the power of Yahweh is in reality stronger and more enduring than any seemingly unparalleled and permanent threat. The assurance of no further shame is sufficiently important that it is repeated in both verses 26 and 27.

This repeated clause forms an *inclusio* around what is arguably the theological center of the prophecy. Israel has been psychologically defeated by the natural attacks it suffered, with even its neighbors convinced that God abandoned them, because he is apparently nowhere to be found. Now Yahweh proclaims that Israel ("you"), and secondarily her neighbors, knows three things for a surety. This is a bold affirmation, unlike the uncertainty of knowing whether God would forgive noted previously (2:14). Yahweh has forgiven, God will restore, and they can know the following (2:27):

1. He has not abandoned Israel, his people whom he for the first time calls by their name, "Israel." He is still in her midst in power, as he was when the nation was first being born (cf. Num. 14:14).
2. His relationship with them has not changed from the time he entered into a covenant relationship with them (see Bridging Contexts section).
3. In stark contrast to the apparently absent God for whom Israel's neighbors sought to ridicule her, Yahweh is the only God there is; none other exists.

These three are sufficient reasons for Israel to forget any of her shame, not only now but forever. The ultimate ground for her confidence and hope does not ultimately lie within her and her identity, but in Yahweh, her eternally present God.

Statements 2 and 3 call to mind the strong proclamation of monotheism in Isaiah 45–46, where variations of it occur no less than seven times.[14] Each

---

14. While there were strong similarities between these, internal variations indicate that they were not simply copies from some source, whether one of these passages or some other.

of these, plus Joel 3:17, where a variation recurs, is here laid out for comparison with our passage:

Joel 2:27   *waᵓᵃnî   yhwh ᵓᵉlōhêkem wᵒên   ᶜôd*
                      For I (am) Yahweh your God, and there is none other.

Joel 3:17   *kî   ᵓᵃnî   yhwh ᵓᵉlōhêkem*
                      That I (am)   Yahweh your God

Isa. 45:5   *ᵓᵃnî   yhwh   wᵒên ᶜôd zûlātî ᵓ ên ᵓᵉlōhîm*
                    I (am) Yahweh,   and there is none other. Except
                                            for me there is no *god.*

Isa. 45: 6   *ᵓᵃnî   yhwh   wᵒên ᶜôd*
                    I (am) Yahweh,   and there is none other.

Isa. 45:14   *ᵓak bāk   ᵓēl   wᵒên ᶜôd*
                Only in you (is there) a   God, and there is none other

Isa. 45:18   *ᵓᵃnî   yhwh   wᵒên ᶜôd*
                    I (am) Yahweh,   and there is none other.

Isa. 45:21   *hᵃlōᵓ   ᵓᵃnî   yhwh   wᵒên - ᶜôd ᵓᵉlōhîm mibbalᶜāday*
               Am not I Yahweh,   and there is no other <u>god</u> apart
                                                from me.

Isa. 45:22   *kî   ᵓᵃnî-   ᵓēl   wᵒên ᶜôd*
                For   I (am)   God and there is none other.

Isa. 46:9   *kî   ᵓᵃnōkî   ᵓēl   wᵒên ᶜôd*
                For   I (am)   God and there is none other.

While Joel could know Isaiah, or vice versa, there is authorial intent in the modifications made between the two books. In the case of Joel, it is clear from the context that the emphasis is on the jealousy of God (2:18). He and he alone is Israel's God, and a relationship has already been pronounced four previous times in the prophecy (1:13, 14, 23, 26). This, then, is a theological pivot point of the book, the truth that provides the nation with the psychological boost they need to overcome their extreme distress: Yahweh exists, Yahweh is present with them, and Yahweh, and no natural phenomenon of force, has divine power over them.

Yahweh's Third Response (2:28–32 [3:1–5])

IN THE PRECEDING sections, the prophet has presented God as restoring to fullness what he punished for some unidentified wrongdoing. Now he moves beyond restoration to promising a new thing, advancing beyond anything his people, or any people, experienced before.

Yahweh continues his direct speech here. The section begins with a variant of an introductory formula to a new section (e.g., Jer. 21:7; 49:6). The formula also ties in that which precedes to that which follows. These things happen ("and it will take place," at the beginning of Joel 2:28, omitted in NIV; also in 2:32; 3:18)[15] in a period temporally subsequent to ("afterward") God's restoration of Israel's livelihood. This is not a return to a previous state, but the beginning of a new one. As the locust plague is without parallel (1:2), so is this event.

Following the time-setting element, the first aspect of God's new activity is marked by an inclusio in verses 28b and 29, with Yahweh promising, "I will pour out my Spirit" (cf. Ezek. 39:29). The literal use of the verb *špk* involves pouring either liquid or dry material from a container (e.g., Ex. 4:9; Lev. 14:41). The audience was all too familiar with the metaphorical use of outpouring God's anger on people (e.g., Ezek. 7:8; Hos. 5:10), and of the ritual blood being poured out in the sacrificial system for the sin offering (Lev. 4:7, 12, 18, 25, 30; cf. Ex. 29:12) or of other things for the drink offering (Isa. 57:6)—aspects that are appropriate to the context of Joel (Joel 1:9, 13; 2:14). This time it is God's Spirit that is poured out like a liquid (cf. Isa. 44:3).[16]

From the preceding context of blessing, first-time readers would suppose that this spiritual outpouring is a positive event rather than a punishment. This is confirmed in what follows. The recipients of the outpouring are clear from the text: "all people" (lit., "flesh"), but the phrase is probably misheard by readers to be nationally restricted, since in the subsequent development, all those affected are Israelites, as indicated by the pronominal suffixes "your." "Flesh" is not limited to Israel, however, but can refer to humanity generally as contrasted to God (e.g., Gen. 6:3; Deut. 5:23), to animals as distinct from humans (e.g., Gen. 6:19; 8:17–including birds and reptiles), and to all creatures generally (e.g., Gen. 6:13; 9:11; Isa. 40:5).

While it is most suitable to see the following promises as restricted to humanity, limiting them to Israel alone is a misreading of this text. While the Spirit in the Old Testament is many-faceted (see Bridging Contexts section), here she (the noun is grammatically feminine in Hebrew) is associated with receiving revelation from God. This comes in three forms: prophecy, dreams, and visions, terms that often overlap in meaning. The new thing is not in the revelation per se, but in its recipients.

---

15. Note the NASB here: "It will come about after this."

16. There is here a play on the various meanings of "spirit" in Hebrew, which can also mean "wind, breath." As God's Spirit here will bring blessing on all, so at the time of the Exodus, it was a "wind" brought by God that removed the earlier locust plague (Ex. 10:13, 19; M. Sweeney, "The Place and Function of Joel in the Book of the Twelve," in Redditt, *Thematic Threads*, 145).

Two more merisms (see comment on 2:23) exemplifying what is meant by "all flesh" follow. The first indicates that this gift is available to both genders: "sons" and "daughters." While the terms foundationally designate male and female biological descendants of a single generation (Gen. 4:25; 30:21), they also are used without the single generation connotation for males and females (Gen. 30:13; Lev. 6:18; Judg. 12:9).[17] No one is excluded by gender.

The second merism seems more related to age (Prov. 20:29; Jer. 31:13; Lam. 5:14), since "elders" in this context is best understood as those toward the end of life (see comments on Joel 1:2), while "young men" contrast with the elderly and infants and also with young women (Deut. 32:25; Lam. 2:21; 5:14), being old enough to marry and fight at war (2 Chron. 25:5; Isa. 62:5). Since both genders have already been included, and will be again, one should not take these two groups as being exclusive but representative of the entire people. Moses' prayer that all might be prophets (Num. 11:29) is fulfilled at this time.

This spiritual endowment is most certainly not exclusive, as shown by verse 29, since it is given, using exactly the same sentence structure, to both male and female slaves or servants. This category receives heightened semantic focus because of the use of the connector (lit.) "and even."[18] The "men" servants can refer to males owned by another (e.g., Gen. 39:17), but it can also be gender neutral (e.g., Deut. 5:15). It may also indicate those who serve but are not necessarily the chattel of another ("servant" or "subject"; e.g., Gen. 18:3, where the word is a way of address showing honor when spoken to a superior, e.g., "I am your humble servant"). Here, however, it is probably denotes male slaves since the other term is restricted to female slaves (e.g., Gen. 12:16) or servants/subjects (showing the same semantic range as the previous term; 2 Kings 14:2).[19]

In the socioeconomic scale, these servants or slaves are close to the bottom. Israelites were not the permanent property of a master, but they could be forced into servitude because of economic difficulty.[20] Foreign prisoners of war, however, could be owned outright and sold or bartered.[21] Being at this

---

17. At times the former term lost any gender connotation (e.g., Gen. 3:16; Ex. 1:9).

18. Heb. *wᵉgam*, identified as a "focus inducing connecter" (C. H. J. van der Merwe, *The Old Hebrew Particle Gam: A Syntactic-semantic Description of Gam in Gn–2Kg* (ATSAT 34; St. Ottilien: EOS Verlag, 1990).

19. Ruth 2:13 seems to capture the two different nuances of the term. Naomi acknowledges that she is of a more lowly state than Boaz, so is his "servant" (*šipḥâ*) even if she is not one of his chattel-slaves (also *šipḥâ*).

20. See G. C. Chirichigno, *Debt-Slavery in Israel and the Ancient Near East* (JSOTSup 141; Sheffield: Sheffield Academic Press, 1993).

21. See G. Haas, *DOTP*, 778–83.

rung in the socioeconomic ladder makes receiving a blessing such as this poured-out Spirit an astounding thing. It indicates to the audience that the promise is indeed to "all flesh."

This all happens "in those days" (cf. 2:29b; 3:1). This exact form, which occurs only eight times in the Old Testament,[22] refers back to past events when used in historical narrative (Neh. 13:15). In prophetic texts, since the natural referent of the demonstrative pronoun is to the most recent time indicator, which itself refers to future events, the events so described occur simultaneously to these. In this case, the latest time reference ("and afterward," 2:28) indicates the time of the outpoured Spirit, with which the events of the following passage occur. Sometimes this phrase describes events both predicted from the viewpoint of the writer but then fulfilled within the period of the Old Testament, such as the Lord's preserving a remnant from the Babylonian army that, at the time of the message, was yet to invade Judah (Jer. 5:18), or a return from Mesopotamian exile (3:18; 50:4).

Sometimes, however, there are elements that are not ever fulfilled in this way, such as the predicted restoration of both Judah and Israel (Jer. 3:18; 50:4) and a turning by all nations to Israel and Jerusalem as the only source for help and guidance from God (Jer. 3:16–17; Zech. 8:14), neither of which have happened up to this day. There can be, therefore, an eschatological implication with this phrase, pointing beyond the original context and situation. This fits the present passage, which Christian interpreters understand as referring to a much later Pentecost (Acts 2:1–21) and beyond (Rev. 8:7).

Displays in the astral ("the heavens") and terrestrial ("the earth") spheres accompany the Spirit's outpouring (vv. 30–31), just as they did with the locust army (2:10). They are "wonders" ("portents," LXX; NRSV; "warnings," GNB), tokens or signs of power used to convince observers of the truth of a statement or of God's power (Ex. 7:9; Deut. 7:19; 28:46; 1 Kings 13:3, 5). The plagues in Egypt served both of these functions (e.g., Ex. 7:3; Ps. 78:43; 105:27; 135:9). Blood (Joel 3:19, 21), fire (1:19, 20; 2:3, 5), and smoke billows are also aspects of the same Exodus–Sinai episode (blood: Ex. 4:9, 25–26; 7:17–21; 12:7, 13, 22–23; fire: 3:2; 9:23–24 [translated as "lightning"]; 12:8–10; 13:21–22; 14:24; 19:18; smoke: Ex. 19:18; 20:18).[23]

Other theophanies have fire and smoke, though blood is much rarer (e.g., Gen. 15:8–17, where fire and smoke are mentioned and blood is implied

---

22. Neh. 13:15; Jer. 3:16, 18; 5:18; 50:4; Joel 2:29; 3:1; Zech. 8:23. Cf. the equivalent phrase *bayyāmîm hāhēm*, which occurs an additional 28 times with equivalent usages.

23. This particular word for "billows" only occurs again in relation to the smoke arising from burning incense (Song 3:6).

from the context; cf. 2 Sam. 22:9//Ps. 18:8). Blood, fire, and smoke appear together frequently, however, in another context of divine-human contact, the sacrificial ritual in the tabernacle or temple (e.g., Lev. 1–7).[24] These ambiguous symbols of life and death raise ambivalent feelings in those who observe them, not knowing what they portend. Will they issue in good or ill? Or it can be both, as in the Exodus–Sinai event, depending on whether one is Egyptian or Israelite!

This verse does not specify the manner in which these phenomena show themselves. This could be the function of verse 31, at least as regards "the heavens." The sun and moon were both affected on a natural level in similar ways by the locust swarm (2:10; 3:15). Now it is precipitated by the approaching "day of the LORD." These two astral bodies are part of the pantheon among Israel's neighbors—the Egyptians,[25] Assyro–Babylonians,[26] and most immediately, the Canaanites.[27] It is against this background that this verse is heard. Rather than picturing the sun and moon as autonomous powers in their own right, they are under Yahweh's control, he who can go as far as altering and negating their very character.[28]

This is the sole occurrence of the sun or moon as subject of the verb *hpk*, but the resultant blood is governed by the same verb when Moses, through Yahweh's power, turns the Egyptian water supply to blood during the plague episode (Ex. 7:17, 20).[29] Light to darkness is found elsewhere in the Old Testament (e.g., 2 Sam. 22:12), but its occurrence as another one of the Egyptian plagues (Ex. 10:21–22; cf. 14:20; Deut. 4:11; 5:23; Ps. 105:28) provides yet another thematic and lexical link with that story.[30] God as Creator of both light and darkness is in control of both (Isa. 45:7; Amos 5:8).

---

24. The burnt sacrifices produced much smoke, which wafted up to the nostrils of Yahweh as a "pleasing odor" (e.g., 1:5–9). Nowhere in this passage or in any sacrificial context is the specific term for smoke used, however, so any possible tie-in to sacrifice in the Joel 2:30–31 context is conceptual rather than lexical. See Sweeney, "Place and Function," 145.

25. Re was the sun god: J. Assman, *Egyptian Solar Religion in the New Kingdom: Re, Amun and the Crisis of Polytheism* (New York: Kegan Paul, 1995); *DDD*, 689–92; I. Shaw and P. Nicholson, *British Museum Dictionary of Ancient Egypt* (London: British Museum Press, 1995) 239; Khons was the moon god (ibid., 151–52).

26. UTU/Shamash was the sun god: J. Black and A. Green, *Gods, Demons, and Symbols of Ancient Mesopotamia: An Illustrated Dictionary* (London: British Museum Press, 1992), 182–84; Nanna-Suen (Sîn) was the moon god (ibid., 135); see also *DDD*, 586–93.

27. Shemesh was the sun god: *DDD*, 764–68; Yarikh was the moon god: *DDD*, 587–93.

28. Cf. G. Hasel, "The Polemic Nature of the Genesis Cosmology," *EQ* 46 (1974): 81–102 (esp. 88–89).

29. Cf. the same motif in Rev. 6:12.

30. Blood and darkening sun and moon also were part of God's judgment and punishment (e.g.. Ezek. 32:6–7).

All of these phenomena are harbingers of the "day of the LORD," which this time is not described by its proximity (1:15; 2:1; 3:14) but by its character; it is "great" ("important," 2 Sam. 3:38; 2 Chron. 2:4) and "dreadful" (2:11), a description found verbatim in Malachi 4:5. Both of these terms apply to Yahweh himself (e.g., Neh. 1:5; 4:8; Ps. 99:3). This Day is associated with darkness by other prophets too (Amos 5:18, 20; Zeph. 1:15), each time with a threatening, negative overtone.

The NIV translation seems, however, to bring too negative a connotation to the term here since "dreadful" in common usage has moved from an archaic usage based on its etymology of "inspiring awe, dread" (the connotation here) to something that is disagreeable or bad, which is not the implicit connotation of the Hebrew term here. The verb can mean "to fear," but it does not hold the feeling of shaking terror such as one feels before an immediate threat to life;[31] rather, it denotes the awe and reverence felt in the presence of a greater power who, while potentially threatening, is also potentially beneficent.

In conjunction with ("and," NIV; Heb., "and then it will be") these physically powerful events are those equally powerful on a psychological and personal level: Salvation is offered to all. The NIV translation is not the best since in Christian jargon "salvation" usually carries the theological meaning of deliverance from the consequences and power of sin, which is not in view here. The Hebrew noun used in the second clause of the verse is well-rendered by the NIV as "deliverance" (*p⁺lêṭâ*), used of escaping with one's life from physical captivity, danger, or judgment (e.g., Gen. 32:9; Jer. 50:29). In this context, the verb used in the first clause has this same physical nuance, "fleeing or escaping with one's life," as Lot and his family did from Sodom (*mlṭ*; Gen. 19:17–22; 1 Sam. 19:10–12), rather than a theological meaning.

This deliverance was in Jerusalem, also known as Mount Zion (e.g., Isa. 2:3//Mic. 4:2; Amos 1:2), the dwelling place of God that suffered severely from the natural disasters (Zion: see Joel 2:1; cf. 15, 23; 3:16, 17, 21; Jerusalem: see 3:1). For people convinced that life is finished, since their food supply was irremediably destroyed, Yahweh is offering deliverance, a reprieve from death.

Relief is not automatic, however, but must be requested. "Calling on God's name" means invoking him, praying for his help, and even expressing allegiance and belonging to him (Gen. 12:8; 2 Kings 5:11; Isa. 44:5). Those who do this realize that they are in themselves powerless against natural disaster; only the Lord of nature has the necessary power to deliver. The promise

---

31. See Deut. 7:21, where the two types of fear seem to be contrasted; also Neh. 1:5, where God has this characteristic along with love.

is confirming one Obadiah delivered previously. Deliverance in Mount Zion is repeated almost verbatim in Obadiah 17a,[32] and Joel acknowledges that Yahweh spoke on that earlier occasion.

Unfortunately, there are casualties, since those making the request of God are "among the survivors," a synonym of those delivered earlier in the verse. This implies that there are also some who have perished (Num. 21:35; Isa. 1:9).[33] Calling is mutual, since these are also ones whom Yahweh calls over a period of time as he did young Samuel (1 Sam. 3:8). The intended nuance of the clause is difficult to perceive, which may explain some seeing it as a later addition.[34] This is in fact begging the question, however, since the present text is a unit, so someone, whether the original author or subsequent editor(s) or redactor(s), must have made sense of the present text.

JEALOUS GOD. Yahweh demands an exclusive relationship with his people. To my knowledge, this is unique to Israel from among her immediate neighbors. In a polytheistic society such as theirs, a deity would be hard pressed to expect undivided allegiance, since there were many other gods in the society also laying claim on its members. A monotheism such as Israel had leads more logically toward a deity who could be jealous for the sole position in the hearts and minds of his people. The problem arose when Israel, called to be monotheistic (e.g., Deut. 6:4–5), became polytheistic, inviting other, pagan deities into her religious system.

From the time of creation, Israel's God has wanted humanity to rely on him and his directions rather than on either their own incomplete understanding of reality (cf. Gen. 3, where the result of abandoning this by listening to the blandishments of another is powerfully presented) or the deities of her neighbors—gods who are in fact not gods. The very first words of the preface to Israel's national constitution echoes this exclusivity, "I [and no other] am the LORD your God" (Ex. 20:2). The concept is reiterated and made formal in the first of the Ten Commandments: "You shall have no other gods before/beside me" (v. 3). God is a jealous God (cf. v. 5; 34:14; Deut. 4:24; 5:9;

---

32. The two passages differ in only two Hebrew words. They read: "for on Mount Zion and Jerusalem there will be deliverance" (Joel 2:32; Jerusalem also parallels Zion in 3:16); "but on Mount Zion there will be deliverance" (Obad. 17; cf. also Obad. 14, where "deliverance" and "survivors" occur together as they do in this verse.

33. The same term occurs in Obad. 18 and could have been chosen here because of this association with the portion previously cited from that prophecy.

34. See Wolff, *Joel*, 68; Wilhelm Rudolph, *Joel, Amos, Obadja, Jona* (KAT 13/2; Gütersloh: G. Mohr, 1971), 70, n. 5.

32:16; 1 Kings 14:23; Ps. 78:58), who views his "marriage" with Israel as inviolable. Association with any other deity comprises spiritual adultery.

This marriage/adultery metaphor is brought out most emphatically by Hosea. He was called to literally marry an unfaithful wife (Hos. 1:2), symbolizing the unfaithfulness the Israelites display by their liaison with Baal. This act undoubtedly brought Hosea's neighbors to him sharing their repugnance, to which he could then reply, "Aren't you doing exactly the same thing with Baal, and doesn't Yahweh feel the same repugnance?" Part of Israel's adultery involved crediting Baal, the Canaanite storm god, with their agricultural bounty of grain, wine, and olive oil (2:8), things in fact provided by Yahweh himself. To bring the actual source of all provisions to Israel's attention, he was going to withhold them (v. 9; cf. also the contest between Baal and Yahweh in 1 Kings 17).

In Joel, Yahweh's jealousy is reversed, using vocabulary reminiscent of the Baal conflicts. His jealousy is not just to punish, but it is ultimately for their restoration (cf. Isa. 9:6; 37:32; Zech. 1:14; 8:2), since Israel is his dearly beloved wife. His desire for their good will restore the same elements—grain, wine, and oil (Joel 2:19)—that he removed in Hosea.

Army from the north. Though describing the locust swarm in Joel, the northern army may well have a wider referent. Locusts most regularly swarmed into Israel from the east and south (cf. Ex. 10:13, 19), so swarms from the north were unusual. Human armies regularly came from either the north (e.g., the Syrians [Aram, Judg. 3:8; 1 Kings 20; 22:31], Assyrians [2 Kings 15:19–20, 29; 17:3–6], and Babylonians [2 Kings 24:1–2, 10–12; 25; Ezek. 26:7]) or the south (the Egyptians [1 Kings 9:16; 14:25–26; 19:9; 23:29]), since the east and west are effectively blocked by the Arabian Desert and the Mediterranean Sea, respectively.

Two biblical prophets also envision an eschatological army from the north that threatens Israel (Jer. 1:13–15; 4:6; 6:1, 22; 10:22; 25:9; Ezek. 1:4; 38:6, 15; 39:2).[35] Pagan deities, and most particularly the Canaanite Baal, are also associated with the north, most specifically a mountain there (Zaphon; cf. Isa. 14:13).[36] This is a motif countered by the Yahweh-worshiping writer of the Psalms, who has Zion replacing it in importance (Ps. 48:2), and also in Job, where Yahweh himself is portrayed as coming from the north (Job 37:22).

God's Spirit in the Old Testament. The "Spirit [of God/the LORD]" (*rûaḥ* [*ʾĕlōhîm/ yhwh*]) plays an important, though often behind-the-scenes, role in

---

35. See E. M. Yamauchi, *Foes from the Northern Frontier: Invading Hordes from the Russian Steppes* (Grand Rapids: Baker, 1982).

36. See *DDD*, 132–39, 152–54, 927–29.

the Old Testament. Mention of the Spirit spans the opening verses of the Jewish canon (Gen. 1:2), where she[37] broods over the primordial deep, to its last book (2 Chron. 24:20), where she provides prophetic revelation.[38] There is no systematic presentation in the Old Testament of a theology of the Spirit (or of anything else, for that matter), but the Spirit is encountered periodically in its story.

The Spirit's presence is usually seen to be beneficial and empowering (e.g., Ex. 31:3; 35:31; Judg. 14:6, 19; 15:14; 1 Sam. 10:10; 11:6; 19:20, 23; 1 Kings 18:12; 2 Chron. 15:1; 24:20; Isa. 63:14; Ezek. 11:24; Mic. 2:7), even by pagans (e.g., Gen. 41:38), to whom she also provides revelation (Num. 24:2–3).[39] The Spirit comes on several people to empower them in a special way for a leadership role, such as judge (Judg. 3:10; 6:34; 11:29), prophet (1 Sam 10:6; 19:20–24; 2 Chron. 20:14; Ezek. 11:5; Mic. 3:8; cf. Num. 11:16–20), king (1 Sam. 16:13–14; cf. 2 Sam. 23:2, where David's words of song are ascribed to the Spirit), or Messiah (e.g., Isa. 11:2; 59:21; 61:1 [Luke 4:18]).

There is also evidence of a wider function of the Spirit beyond to individual people. In Isaiah, Yahweh's Spirit and his words remain not only with the prophet himself, but also with his children and their descendants forever (Isa. 59:21). The office of prophet is not hereditary, but their role seems here to be viewed as spreading beyond the formal office to many others.

God also promises to place his Spirit in the midst of his people, who will be restored after their punishing exile, enabling them to adhere to his covenant commands (Ezek. 36:27; cf. 39:29). The context indicates that the Spirit is not some force working on the people from the outside but rather an element of their inner being, since 36:26 states: "I will give you a new heart and put a new spirit in you." The Spirit provides the nation life (37:14), renewing their freshness and vitality like water in the desert (Isa. 44:3; contrast 40:7).

The same verb as used in this Joel passage is associated with the Spirit in Zech. 12:10 ("And I will pour out on the house of David and the

---

37. The noun is most commonly feminine in Hebrew, esp. so when identified as that of God (feminine: Gen. 1:2; Num. 24:2; Judg. 3:10; 6:34; 11:29; 14:6, 19; 15:14; 1 Sam. 10:6, 10; 11:6; 16:15, 16, 23; 18:10; 19:9, 20, 23; 2 Chron. 15:1; 20:14; 24:20; Isa. 11:2; 40:7; 59:19; 63:14; Ezek. 11:24; masculine: 2 Sam 23:2; 1 Kings 18:12; 22:24//2 Chron. 18:23; 2 Kings 2:16), so this pronoun is consciously chosen here. A masculine pronoun would go counter to the regular Hebrew grammar, and a neuter pronoun ("it") is theologically problematic, for the Spirit is a personal being rather than an inanimate force.

38. In the order of the Old Testament books in the Christian canon, the Spirit arguably appears for the last time in Zech. 12:10, but definitely so in 7:12.

39. At times, however, the Spirit has a more negative role; cf. 1 Sam 16:15–16, 23; 18:10; 19:9, where an evil spirit came from God. The Spirit also blows on grass and flowers to desiccate them (Isa.40:7).

---

inhabitants of Jerusalem a spirit of grace and supplication"). It is not specifically identified as the Spirit of God (cf. NIV text note), though that could be what is in mind.

The widespread dispersion of the Spirit is thus not a novelty for Joel's prophecy. What it does, however, is to draw out the fuller meaning of this dispersion. It is to be poured out on Israel, David's house, but not just a bestowal on its religious or political leadership. People from all walks of life, all social strata, and even from all nations ("all flesh," 2:28), will be blessed, empowered, and vivified through the gift of the Spirit of God.

Peter picks up this theme in his Pentecostal sermon in Jerusalem (Acts 2:17–21). He recognizes the event of the filling of the Spirit for those gathered on that occasion as an element of fulfillment of Joel's promise. It is not completed on that occasion, however, for Peter also explains that the promised Spirit comes "for you and your children and for all who are far off" (2:39; cf. Isa. 59:21). To the surprise of the Jewish members of the early church, this goes even beyond their number to include the despised Samaritans (Acts 8:14–17; cf. John 4:10–14, 23–24) and Gentiles (Acts 10:44–48).

Peter made the indwelling conditional in a way also related to what is previously mentioned in the Old Testament. It follows repentance and baptism (Acts 2:38) and involves commitments to following God and being members of his covenant community. It is the ability to do so that Ezekiel previously envisioned (Ezek. 36:27). God's people in the Old Testament are to be known by their renunciation of self–determination by submitting to God's directives in the covenant and by the outward sign of circumcision, while his New Testament people are to be known also by repentance from sinful self-determination and by the outward sign of baptism. The Spirit is available to all who "call on the name of the Lord" (Acts 2:32).

This theme is picked up by Paul (Rom. 10:13). He does not limit the application to the Israelites, as the Joel passage could be read, but uses it as a universalizing statement, since he says in verse 12, "there is no difference between Jew and Gentile—the same Lord is Lord of all and richly blesses all who call on him." This argues for the universal availability of the Spirit.

Divine revelation in the Old Testament. God is not silent, in spite of the claims of some who consider him dead.[40] This concept would have been

---

40. Originated by Friedrich Nietzsche (*Joyful Wisdom* [New York: F. Ungar, 1960], sec. 125). See, e.g. T. J. J. Altizer, *The Gospel of Christian Atheism* (Philadelphia: Westminster, 1966); T. J. J. Altizer and W. Hamilton, *Radical Theology and the Death of God* (Indianapolis: Bobbs–Merrill, 1966); idem, *Godhead and the Nothing* (Albany: State Univ. of New York Press, 2003); S. R. Haynes and J. K. Roth, ed., *The Death of God Movement and the Holocaust* (Westport: Greenwood, 1999).

especially foreign to people from the biblical period, within Israel itself and also among her neighbors. For them, divine revelation is, if not a daily experience, at least something that is not completely foreign (as a counterexample, see the mention of the rarity of God's revelation in 1 Sam. 3:1). According to the biblical text, the medium of revelation for Israel varied. On the canonically earliest occasions, the text mentions direct communication between God and humanity, whether laity or leaders, with God speaking directly (e.g., Gen. 1:29; 3:9–19; 4:6–7, 9, 15; 6:13; 7:1; 8:15; 9:8; 12:4; 17:9, 15, 19, etc.). Upon seeing the powerful theophany at Mount Sinai, the people request an intermediary between themselves and God (Ex. 20:18–21), and record of direct human-divine contact diminishes.

At other times, a specific revelatory medium is mentioned. These are often dreams[41] or visions.[42] These two seem to have become standard means of revelation to prophets.[43] They could be misused, however, as could other, less acceptable means of hearing from God or the gods (e.g., 1 Sam 28; Jer. 23:16; 27:9; 29:8–9; Ezek. 13:6–7, 16). These two means were also used among Israel's neighbors, Egypt and Mesopotamia.[44] They were not reserved solely for prophets, however, in either Israel or the ancient Near East, as previous references indicate.[45]

The innovation in this Joel passage is, therefore, not in the means of revelation but in its recipients. The beneficiaries of the Spirit-gift and its accompanying revelation will not only be a special class, the prophets, or even a few folk, whose prophetic gift is rare enough to be a matter of note. Rather, this bestowal will be universal, blessing young and old, male and female, free or slave; it will affect all of humanity. God desires his Word to be widely known (cf. Prov. 1:23).

---

41. The first of these recorded is not even to an Israelite, but to the pagan Philistine king Abimelech (Gen. 20:3, 6; cf. also Laban, 31:24; cf. the Egyptian pharaoh, whose dreams need interpretation by the Yahweh worshiper, Joseph, in Gen. 41; 42:9; Egyptian functionaries, 40:5–17; Nebuchadnezzar, a Babylonian king, Dan. 2, 4; Mesopotamian astrologers, Matt. 2:20; Pilate's wife, Matt. 27:19). Abraham's descendants also had revelatory dreams; e.g., Jacob, Gen. 28:11; Joseph, Gen. 37; Solomon, 1 Kings 3:5; Joseph, Matt. 1:20; 2:13, 19, 22.

42. Gen. 15:1; 46:2; Num. 24:4 (of Balaam); Isa. 1:1; Dan. 8; Hos. 12:10; Obad. 1; Nah. 1:1; Hab. 2:2–3.

43. See, e.g., Gen. 12:6; Num. 12:6; Deut. 13:1; Jer. 23:28; Ezek. 7:26; Dan. 1:17.

44. Beside the biblical references noted above, see A. L. Oppenheim, *The Interpretation of Dreams in the Ancient Near East* (Philadelphia: American Philosophical Society, 1956); S. A. L. Butler, *Mesopotamian Conceptions of Dreams and Dream Rituals* (AOAT 258; Münster: Ugarit–Verlag, 1998); J.-M. Husser, *Dreams and Dream Narratives in the Biblical World* (Biblical Seminar 63: Sheffield: Sheffield Academic Press, 1999).

45. From Mari, a city on the Euphrates, come several letters from the eighteenth century B.C. reporting revelatory dreams received by laypeople, *ANET*, 623–24.

This kind of universalistic promise is not unknown in Israel (cf. Gen. 9:8–11; 12:3; Isa. 2:2–4; 56:3–8). Israel kept forgetting this truth, however, seeking to limit God's power and provision of the Spirit (cf. Isa. 44:3; 54:13; Ezek. 39:29) to themselves alone, so God had to remind them of the wideness of his mercy (e.g., Isa. 40:3–5; 49:6; Amos 9:7; cf. Luke 3:6). He revealed himself in these ways again and in a special way in the events surrounding the birth of Jesus (e.g., Matt. 1:20; 2:12, 13, 19, 22; Luke 1:22; cf. v. 67; 2:36–38).

Rain in an agricultural society. Water is one of life's necessities, and its long-term lack makes an area uninhabitable.[46] Some regions in the ancient Near East relied on river water supplemented by irrigation. In Mesopotamia the rivers flowed regularly (cf. Isa. 8:7) while in Egypt there was an annual flooding (Ex. 7:19; Isa. 19:5–8). Other areas depended on rainfall for agriculture and daily use. This distinction is noted in Scripture (Deut. 11:10–11).[47] Israel did have several rivers, and there is evidence of limited irrigation,[48] but she depended much more on rainfall (1 Kings 8:35–36; Isa. 30:23) and water storage, such as cisterns and wells (Gen. 21:25; Deut. 6:11; Isa. 22:9, 11; Jer. 2:13).

The entire agricultural calendar was dependent on "rain in its season" for the crop cycle to produce the most bounty (Lev. 26:4–5; Deut. 11:13–17; this word for "rain," *gešem*, is a common, general term for natural watering that can be beneficial or devastating, causing floods [Gen. 7:12; 8:2; Ps. 68:9]; cf. also with the same meaning for *meṭar*, Deut. 11:11, 14). The dry season ran generally from April to September, the rainy season from October to April. The ground could only be plowed and planted after the softening of the early rains, which came in September to October. These are called the *yôreh*, having the same root as the term occurring twice in Joel 2:23, *môreh*

---

46. For a more detailed discussion of the human endeavors to meet this need, see J. P. Oleson, "Water Works," *ABD*, 6:885–93. See also J. L. Kelso and F. N. Hepper, "Agriculture," *NBD*, 19–20.

47. Compare the Amorites, whose territory in northern Mesopotamia spread over several regions, each requiring different types of water provision; see G. E. Mendenhall, "Amorites," *ABD*, 1:199–200.

48. Several terms could indicate irrigation canals, such as *yûbal* (Jer. 17:8; cf. the proper noun in Gen. 4:21) and *peleg* (Ps. 1:3; 65:9; cf. the proper noun in Gen. 10:25//1 Chron. 1:19, whose name could indicate the beginning of irrigation [cf. S. R. Driver, *The Book of Genesis*, 15th ed. (London: Methuen, 1948), 130]). Of the Siloam channel, see Y. Shiloh, "Underground Water Systems in Eretz-Israel in the Iron Age," in *Archaeology and Biblical Interpretation: Essay in Memory of D. Glenn Rose*, ed. L. G. Perdue et al. (Atlanta: John Knox, 1987), 203–44 (esp. 220). Irrigation may have been in use in the area of Jericho from as early as the Neolithic period (late 9th century B.C.; R. Miller, "Water Use in Syria and Palestine from the Neolithic to the Bronze Age," *World Archaeology* 11 [1980]: 331–32).

(cf. Ps. 84:7). Special rains close out the season—the latter or spring rains, called the *malqôš* (Prov. 16:15; Jer. 3:3), with which *yôreh* always appears, serving as a merism (see comment on Joel 2:23). A delay of the first rains leaves a season too short to allow the crops to fully ripen, while if they come too soon, there may not be enough moisture during the rest of the season to be able to adequately provide for the crop's maturation.[49]

Numerous other words also describe aspects of rain, such as its abundance (*ᵃrubbâ*, a gushing flood as if through open floodgates, Gen. 7:11; 8:2; Isa. 24:18; *zerem*, heavy downpour, Isa. 30:30; 32:2; *nepeṣ*, cloudburst, Isa. 30:30; *sagrîr*, persistent downpour, Prov. 27:15; *sᵉpîḥâ*, downpour, Job 14:19).[50] Rain in all of its forms shows God's continued covenant loyalty to his people (Deut. 28:12).

Covenant language. Pronouns are easy to ignore while reading, since they appear less concrete and have less impact than the attendant nouns. They do carry considerable baggage, however, especially if one is careful to determine which nouns they are referring to and the relationships to which they point. Jesus' cry of dereliction on the cross, "My God, my God, why have you forsaken me" (Matt. 27:46; Mark 15:34; citing Ps. 22:1) derives its poignancy and power from the fact that it indicates a prior relationship, one established before this abandonment. God is not just "a" God, or even "the" God, but he is "my" God, a relationship that engenders expectations. Others who identified God in this way experienced his salvation (e.g., Ex. 15:2; 2 Sam. 22:3) or desired to do so (e.g., Mic. 7:7; Zech. 14:4); based on this, they promised obedience, even if it was at a cost (Deut. 26:14; Josh. 14:8; 2 Sam. 24:24). Jesus is not, at least in the near term, able to experience this salvation from suffering, in spite of the relationship with "my God," but was rather obedient to death.

These verses in Joel pick up a covenantal relationship between God and his people, one often expressed through pronouns: "your God" and "my people" (2:26–27). These pronouns of relationship, which we can so easily glide over, are of special impact for Israel because they have been instrumental in their very birth as a nation. At that time God promised this mutual relationship (Ex. 6:7). The relationship's import is evident since its two-sided nature is reiterated by both Jeremiah (Jer. 7:23; 11:4; 30:22) and Ezekiel (Ezek. 36:28), prophets who had to provide God's people with messages of hope since they faced destruction and exile. The relationships are also stated

---

49. Borowski, *Agriculture*, 47–48; F. S. Frick, "Rain," *ABD*, 5:612.

50. For this and other words, see P. Reymond, *L'eau: sa vie et sa signification dans l'Ancien Testament* (VTSup 6; Leiden: Brill, 1958); D. W. Baker, "The Wind and the Waves: Biblical Theology in Protology and Eschatology," *ATJ* 34 (2002): 13–37.

by using just one half of the pair, "my people," occurring over two hundred times in the Old Testament, most often in the mouth of God,[51] and "your God," occurring over five hundred times, mostly referring to Yahweh.[52]

THE SOURCE OF **good things.** When prosperity or success comes to a nation or a church today, we do not credit it to God's gift of rain, because most Westerners have lost a tie to the earth. In reality we rarely acknowledge God at all, usually crediting it to our own strength or ingenuity. If we can but show more of this strength and ingenuity, more success will naturally and inevitably result. Another way this is manifest is through following the latest model and application of someone's ingenuity or insight that is sure to lead to results: seven habits for effectiveness,[53] ten steps to growth,[54] twelve steps to sobriety,[55] seventeen or twenty–one laws or qualities for leaders and teams.[56]

There is, of course, nothing wrong with disciplined action, and planning is noble and productive, so many of these models benefit numerous people. It is not the model that is effective, however, but rather a knowledge that things are not completely as they should be, a desire for improvement, and a heightened awareness of the goal. For the believer, these are all accompanied by the empowerment of the Holy Spirit, accompanied by the awareness that all good gifts, all progress in sanctification, and every blessing come from God himself and not from our planning and perseverance, as good as that is (cf. 1 Cor. 3:6–7). This is because it is not ultimately for our benefit but for his glory that these things come (cf. Ps. 115:1).

This attitude not only provides a needed corrective against arrogance, but it also brings an antidote for discouragement. In situations such as Joel's, where

---

51. A. Even–Shoshan, *A New Concordance of the Bible* (Grand Rapids: Baker, 1985), 886–87.

52. Ibid., 73–74.

53. E.g., S. R. Covey, *Seven Habits of Highly Effective People: Restoring the Character Ethic* (New York: Simon & Schuster, 1989); *The Seven Habits of Highly Effective Families: Building a Beautiful Family Culture in a Turbulent World* (New York: Franklin Covey, 1997).

54. E.g., D. A. McGavran and W. C. Arn, *Ten Steps for Church Growth* (San Francisco: Harper & Row, 1977).

55. Bill W, *Twelve Steps and Twelve Traditions* (New York: Alcoholics Anonymous Publishing, [1953]); B. Pittman and Dick D, *Courage to Change: The Christian Roots of the Twelve-Step Movement* (Center City, Minn.: Hazelden, 1994).

56. J. C. Maxwell, *The 17 Indisputable Laws of Teamwork: Embrace Them and Empower Your Team* (Nashville: Nelson, 2001); idem, *The 17 Essential Qualities of a Team Player: Becoming the Kind of Person Every Team Wants* (Nashville: Nelson, 2002); idem, *The 21 Indispensable Qualities of a Leader: Becoming the Person That People Will Want to Follow* (Nashville: Nelson, 1999).

locusts and drought could not be directly averted by the people of Israel, no matter their great physical efforts, they could but turn to the one with ultimate control over these "natural" elements. This is like Job, who is vexed after butting heads with his dialog partners to no avail. He finally hears God himself (Job 38–41), and though he does not get any more answers to his questions from God than he did from his human interlocutors, he is satisfied because he knows that he has been heard. He ends up in the same posture as he begins, acknowledging God's blessedness and wonderfulness, even though he does not comprehend him (1:21; 42:1–6). For our own lives, a lack of ability or no results from our efforts lead to discouragement, but the results are not ultimately in our hands. Ours is to strive, God's to bring to fruition.

Here our understanding of God's jealousy also comes into play. We understand this emotion on a human level as wanting to keep something completely and solely for ourselves and not sharing it with anyone else. Our resources, whether financial or relational, are finite, and we feel as if they are only sufficient for our own needs. God's jealousy must not be understood in this same way. This is not the picture of jealousy painted by Joel. God's jealousy is to shower his people with all good blessings, wanting to raise them to the heights rather than keeping them low and impoverished. He desires all of their allegiance and love to be directed toward him, since it is finite and should not be squandered on another deity (see 2 Cor. 11:1–4, esp. v. 2). His infinite blessing, however, is completely available to those who so worship him.

Gifts of nature. In common vernacular we talk about "gifts of nature," the enjoyable things that come from the natural realm: budding flowers and shrubs in the spring, ripening fruit from the garden, colorful leaves in the fall, and a clear, crisp day in which one can speed down the ski slope. We also speak of nature being harsh or cruel, with hurricanes and tornados destroying swathes of houses, and earthquakes, tsunamis, or forest fires leaving destruction and loss. Joel indicates that this type of description of these events is theologically problematic.

A literal understanding of this concept could honor nature with not only personality but also with power. Paganism or pantheism, in which elements of the divine inhabit all things, animate and inanimate alike, is closer to this understanding than is classical Judeo-Christian theology. God reminds the people of Joel's time that nature is neither inherently malevolent, working for their ill through the calamity of locust and drought, nor is it autonomous and self-determining. Rather, it is under Yahweh's ultimate control, since he is its Creator and Organizer (Gen. 1–2).

This has pastoral implication for people today. From a biblical perspective, events are neither simply random nor inevitable. While we may not be directly masters of our own fate, we have been created by one who is master and who desires to be known by his creatures not as fate but as Father. His control extends not only over human armies but also armies of locusts, and he provides not only human support and encouragement but also provisions through nature, which is a secondary provider under his primary impulse and direction.

I will repay. Our family first encountered the phenomenon while teaching in South Africa, but found that it spread there from the United States. People came to our small church having been severely wounded by a large church in the area. Their self-esteem was in tatters and their security in God's love nonexistent, for they were taught that a correct relationship with God results in only blessing; any suffering or loss can result only from sin or falling short of God's desires for us. Christians will not face battles and opposition, only victory. When sincere Christians attending that church met disaster through illness, unemployment, or death of a loved one, there was no succor for them; they were considered less than worthy and ostracized. Many who did not abandon the church altogether found their way to us for ministry and healing.

While we might wish that the Christian life is indeed as it was preached by that pastor, and many others, the uniform experience of saints throughout the ages gives the lie to this understanding. While some pain is God-given discipline to punish those who have turned away from him, the final goal of it is restoration, not ostracism (cf. Gal. 6:1). All suffering is not like this, however, lest Paul or even Jesus be branded as sinners, since they both suffered greatly (e.g., Paul, 2 Cor. 12:7–10; Jesus in his Passion). Paul states a reason for such suffering, namely, to be able to experience God's grace and strength through a period of his own weakness.

God does not promise those in covenant relation with him a detour around life's battles, whether the Christian of today facing life's challenges or Joel and his contemporaries battling their locust armies. What he does promise is a companion as one goes through the battles (Deut. 31:6; Josh. 1:5; 1 Kings 8:56; Matt. 28:20). God also promises restoration after them, not only to Joel but also to many others in numerous promises of renewed blessing (e.g., Isa. 2:1–5; 44:24–28; Ezek. 36–37; Hos. 14; Amos 9:11–15; Obad. 17–21).

Prophetic responsibility. Christians are rightly pleased that Peter and Paul both apply Joel's promise of the Spirit to others besides the Israelites. After all, if the promise is to Jews alone, the Gentile church is not its beneficiary. With the benefit of the Spirit comes obligation, however. While revelation from God through dreams, visions, and prophecies is a gift to be desired, it is not directed ultimately toward its recipient but toward others.

Prophets in the Old Testament were God's intermediaries to the people and their rulers. Paul states the same thing in his teaching to the Corinthians (1 Cor. 14:1–25). The contrast he made between self-edification through tongues and the lack of it through prophecy may indicate that the latter may not be of great personal advantage. Jeremiah, and numerous other prophets, have found that the "gift" is in fact exercised at great personal cost.[57]

One could then ask, "Why should I want this, or any of the gifts of the Spirit?" This reflects an attitude that is unfortunately all too prevalent among many in the church. The secular attitude of "What's in it for me?" is unfortunately not restricted to the secular. In some ways, this is what Jesus taught his disciples in the Upper Room. While they hoped for personal position and prestige (Matt. 20:21; Mark 10:37), Jesus showed them the way of service (John 13:1–17). Jesus exhibited the same attitude with his entire life, and especially with his death, which brought him no personal gain (in fact, it brought the opposite), but did bring inexpressible gain to others.

The correct Christian question should not be, "What is in it for me?" This is one of the dangers of an evangelical understanding of salvation as being strictly personal. While that is necessary, it is not a sufficient view of what salvation is (see the Contemporary Significance section of 2:10–17). A truly Christlike question is, rather, "What can I do for you? How can I aid in bringing you into a correct relationship with our covenant God?" A useful definition of spiritual formation describes "a process of being conformed to the image of Christ for the sake of others."[58] Too often contemporary Western Christianity engages in theological narcissism by omitting the last phrase.

---

57. E.g., Jer. 20:1–2, 7–10; 26:7–11; 36:1–38:13; cf. 1 Kings 19:10, 14 [Rom. 11:3]; Matt. 5:12; Luke 6:23; 1 Thess. 2:15.
58. M. Robert Mulholland, *Invitation to a Journey: A Roadmap for Spiritual Formation* (Downers Grove, Ill.: InterVarsity Press, 1993), 15.

Joel 3[4]:1–12

"In those days and at that time,
  when I restore the fortunes of Judah and Jerusalem,
²I will gather all nations
  and bring them down to the Valley of Jehoshaphat.
There I will enter into judgment against them
  concerning my inheritance, my people Israel,
for they scattered my people among the nations
  and divided up my land.
³They cast lots for my people
  and traded boys for prostitutes;
they sold girls for wine
  that they might drink.

⁴"Now what have you against me, O Tyre and Sidon and all
you regions of Philistia? Are you repaying me for something I
have done? If you are paying me back, I will swiftly and speed-
ily return on your own heads what you have done. ⁵For you
took my silver and my gold and carried off my finest treasures
to your temples. ⁶You sold the people of Judah and Jerusalem
to the Greeks, that you might send them far from their
homeland.

⁷"See, I am going to rouse them out of the places to which
you sold them, and I will return on your own heads what you
have done. ⁸I will sell your sons and daughters to the people
of Judah, and they will sell them to the Sabaeans, a nation far
away." The LORD has spoken.

⁹Proclaim this among the nations:
  Prepare for war!
Rouse the warriors!
  Let all the fighting men draw near and attack.
¹⁰Beat your plowshares into swords
  and your pruning hooks into spears.
Let the weakling say,
  "I am strong!"
¹¹Come quickly, all you nations from every side,
  and assemble there.

Bring down your warriors, O LORD!

¹²"Let the nations be roused;
    let them advance into the Valley of Jehoshaphat,
  for there I will sit
    to judge all the nations on every side.

STILL LOOKING TO the future, God directs his attention away from his own people, as he has been doing, to speak judgment and restoration on the nations. His people become secondary in chapter 3 (cf. 3:1, 16–18). Different sections are marked by shifts of grammatical person and division indicators. The first section (vv. 1–3) speaks about the nations, using the third person ("them"). The rest speaks directly to the hearers in the second person ("you"). The second section (vv. 4–6) details the wrongs committed, while the third (vv. 7–8) describes the results of God's judgment. The fourth section (vv. 9–12) exhorts these nations in a series of imperatives.

The entire passage is bracketed as a unit by mention of judgment in the Valley of Jehoshaphat. God's people have been subject to great loss through natural phenomena as well as at the hand of her neighbors. Now those nations in general will suffer at the hand of God.

Wrongs Committed (3[4]:1–3)

BOTH SYNTAX AND semantics indicate this as a new section. There is a shift of interest to foreign nations that is also tied to God's promised deliverance of his people.[1] Verse 1 sets the stage for what follows.[2] There is a new time indicator with several elements. First is an emphatic demonstrative indicator of proximity to the previously mentioned events:[3] *"those* days" and *"that* time." The most immediate referent of these is the period described in 2:28–32, that these new things happen right in conjunction with sending the Spirit (3:2). Jeremiah uses a similar time indication to describe God's future restoration

---

1. Prinsloo, *Theology of Joel,* 92.

2. On circumstantial clauses, especially those in this episode-initial position, see Andersen, *Sentence,* 77–91 [79–80]. See also 86–87 for the use of such clauses as time marginal references.

3. This is done by using the combination of the conjunction *kî* ("for") plus *hinnēh* ("now, behold"). See, e.g., T. O. Lambdin, *Introduction to Biblical Hebrew* (New York: Scribners, 1971/ London: Darton, Longman & Todd, 1973), 168–69; Muraoka, *Emphatic,* 140. *Hinnēh* functions to indicate immediacy in relationship to the speaker or the event, something happening immediately preceding ("just," e.g., Gen. 48:2) or following ("about to; just then," e.g., Gen. 6:17; 37:7–9).

of the fortunes of his repentant and forgiven people (Jer. 33:15; 50:4, 20). This same repentance of the people is seen in Joel 2:32.

The time is described further in a relative clause concerning the restoration of Judah and its capital, Jerusalem (cf. Jer. 33:15).[4] What is restored (*šûb*)[5] is a matter of debate. The cognate noun (lit., "returning," *šᵉbût*; NIV "fortunes"; elsewhere also *šᵉbît*) can mean "captivity" (LXX, KJV, ASV, NKJV), referring to the restoration from exile (Jer. 29:14; 30:3; 31:23; 32:44; Amos 9:14 [so NIV]; cf. Ezek. 29:14 of Egypt). Return from Judah's captivity in this case most likely indicates the end of the Babylonian exile in 535 B.C., necessitating a late date for Joel.

There are a number of contexts, however, where *šᵉbût* indicates hardship and loss, not specifically captivity and exile. It is used of other nations (e.g., Jer. 48:47 [Moab]; 49:6 [Ammonites], 39 [Elam]; Ezek. 16:53 [Sodom]) and individuals (Job 42:10) who suffer but are not exiled. In light of this, the more general "restoration of fortunes," which may include return from exilic captivity but does not demand it, has been adopted by many translations (e.g., ESV, NASB, NIV, NRSV, NLT; cf. Rudolph, Allen, Barton, Crenshaw). This would not necessitate a late, postexilic date for the prophecy (cf. Zeph. 3:20, a pre-exilic prophecy, where the same clause is used), though it allows it. It also fits well into the context of real loss suffered in the first chapters of the book, losses already stated as having been put right (Joel 2:25).

Many interpreters see here in 3:1–2 an eschatological formula, anticipating some as yet future restoration.[6] While this may be part of what is envisioned, the more immediate return from exile also makes sense of the historical context and itself can anticipate a fuller restoration of fortunes. Even with eschatological overtones, the text need not be postexilic, since the terminology is also used in earlier centuries as well.[7]

"All nations" now becomes the subject of Joel's prophecy (3:2), just as all resident Israelites were previously (cf. 1:2). These nations are those who previously taunted a devastated people (2:17, 19). They are now gathered together as God's people were gathered in Jerusalem for prayer in the face of devastation (2:15–16; 3:11).

When "I will gather" occurs elsewhere, Israel is usually the object, and it refers to a return from exile (Jer. 29:14; Ezek. 11:17; 20:34, 41; 36:24; 37:21;

---

4. The relative pronoun is omitted by some ancient manuscripts (*BHS*, 1013, n). Most English translations render it as a temporal adverb ("when"; *DCH*, 1:426)

5. The MT *kᵉtîb* reads the verb as a Hiphil (*ʾāšîb*), while the *qᵉrîʾ* took it as a Qal (*ʾāšûb*). The former is more common with this direct object, though the latter also occurs five times (Jer. 32:44; 33:7; 49:6; Lam. 2:14 [Q]; Ezek. 39:25)

6. See Prinsloo, *Theology of Joel*, 104–5 and sources cited there.

7. Ibid., 108–9.

39:27). Others gather in the context of judgment (Ezek. 16:37), which is the context here, while the nations in particular gather either for battle (Zech. 14:2) or to see the glory of God (Isa. 66:18).[8] The verbal form in "I will enter into judgment" implies taking up a legal case against someone, usually with Yahweh as the plaintiff subject of the verb.[9] The nations have done something wrong to Israel, for which they are charged. Rather than being the northern kingdom, the term "Israel" here most likely refers to the entire nation, identified in Joel 3:1 as "Judah." She is described as belonging to Yahweh as "my people" (cf. also 2:26, 27; 3:3), explaining his special concern for them as his special "inheritance, possession" (2:17).

The nations are to congregate at "the Valley of Jehoshaphat" (3:2, 12). There is a play on words here, since "Jehoshaphat" ("Yahweh has judged") is related to the verb "judge" (*špt*). Jehoshaphat was the fourth Judean king (c. 873–849 B.C.). In his war with the neighboring ruler, Mesha of Moab (and his ally Ammon), Judah, Israel, and their ally Edom stood by and watched as Yahweh provided the victory (2 Kings 3:4–27//2 Chron. 20:1–30). The victory proved short-lived, however. This event took place in a valley south of Bethlehem, which, in the battle accounts themselves, receives the name of "the Valley of Blessing [Beracah]" (2 Chron. 20:26). This could be what is intended here, in which case it was a site with a history of God's intervention known to the Judean audience, who would be encouraged by its association. Bad news for their bothersome neighbors is good news for them. God will "bring down" these nations there, in contrast to the other, locust "nation," which went up against Israel (cf. Joel 1:6; 2:7, 9).

The nature of the evil of these nations is scattering God's people "among the nations." This may refer to the Babylonian exile of the early sixth century B.C. or to the earlier Assyrian exile of Israel in 722 B.C. The nations are accused of "dividing up my land." This verb-noun combination describes the allocation of the land under Joshua (Josh. 13:7; 18:10; 19:51; cf. Ezek. 47:21), but here it is parceled out by Yahweh's enemies (Mic. 2:4, where the object is "fields"). This expression is not used elsewhere in the context of the Exile.

The list of wrongs continues in verse 3 (note that verse divisions are not original to the text, since the first clause fits better with v. 2). To "cast lots" is a random means of ascertaining something. The "lot" was a small item such as a stone or piece of bone thrown in some way to help determine

---

8. This may be an allusion to Deut. 30:2, where "gathering" and "restoration of fortune" are also juxtaposed—there with a positive benefit for those gathered, the reverse of the situation in Joel.

9. *špt*, Niphal + preposition *ʿim*; cf. Prov. 29:9; Jer. 2:35; 20:35, 36, all with the semantically equivalent preposition *ʾet*; Prinsloo, *Theology of Joel*, 94.

God's will. Even though prophecy was the primary means of revelation, casting the lot was an acceptable practice in Israel to find out, for example, which goat was to be used on the Day of Atonement (Lev. 16:8–10) or who had done wrong (Josh. 7:14). The lot seems to have worked on the principle of binary opposition, indicating one of two things (e.g., "yes" or "no"). Its human randomness allows impartiality in such things as determining who gets spoil or land (Num. 26:55; Josh. 14:2; John 19:24). In the context of land division (Joel 3:2), this may be what is meant here. The nations care so little for God's land and people that they gamble for them (cf. also Obad. 11; Nah. 3:10).

This disregard for the value of fellow human beings is clear from the next two clauses. They misuse both male and female children (lit., "the boy and the girl," the definite article indicating an entire class) as the means of barter, treating them like foreign chattel slaves by selling them. They give or sell them (cf. 3:6, 8[2x]) in exchange for the means of debauchery, prostitutes, or wine.[10] While wine is a blessing from God (1:5; Deut. 14:26), the Bible warns against its misuse (Gen. 19:32–35; 1 Sam. 1:14), though never condemning it outright.

Prostitution in the Old Testament was of two types. Cultic prostitution was part of pagan fertility practices and is condemned outright (Deut. 23:18). Regular, secular prostitution also appeared in Israelite society, and this is what is spoken of here (Gen. 34:31). The two types of prostitution are distinguished (cf., e.g., Gen. 38:15, 21; Hos. 4:14). Prostitution does not seem to be condemned per se, though the money earned by it is unsuitable for payment of a religious vow (Deut. 23:19), and the condemnation of adultery is one of the foundational principles of Israelite life (Ex. 20:14; Deut. 5:18). What seems condemned by Joel is the disregard for the value of human beings, especially that of the young; something as necessary for the continuation of society as her next generation is squandered on something so fleeting.

What Are You to Me? (3:4–6)

JOEL NOW SPEAKS directly to some of Israel's neighbors to the north (Tyre and Sidon) and southwest (Philistia), addressing them through questions. He opens with the same sequential transition marker as used in 2:12 (see comments), made up of the coordinating conjunction "and" (showing continuity with what precedes) and the adverb "moreover, in addition," which accentuates the same thing (NIV simply uses "now").

---

10. If it were not for the parallelism in the verse, the first of these two could have been read just as well syntactically with the preposition *b*ᵉ with the function of identity (Williams, §240), "they gave boys as prostitutes."

The first rhetorical question is grammatically straightforward, but it raises several different interpretations, all of them sobering. "What [are] you to me?" is a verbless clause,[11] with the various interpretational options arising from the verb that needs to be supplied in English, and also from how the preposition is understood. A number of interpreters take the question literally as translated above (e.g., LXX, ASV, ESV, NASB, NRSV). They understand the preposition as expressing interest or benefit: "Of what interest/advantage are you to me?" While on a surface level this seeks information, a rhetorical question such as this most regularly expects a negative response, so the deep-level meaning is, "You are of no interest to me." This results from their disregard for human compassion through the plundering and kidnapping mentioned.

Others see the clause as meaning, "What have you to do with me?" (KJV), an opposite perspective to the previous one. Here it is God who is of no interest to the nations; they want to have no dealings with him, as evidenced by their lack of care for his people. Still others suggest a form of the verb "to do" has been elided, this being an abbreviated form of "What have you done to me?"[12] Wolff suggests that this is the opening of an actual legal dispute between Yahweh and the nations, a literary form found in other passages where they are summoned before him (Isa. 43:9; Mic. 1:2; Zeph. 3:8). While this may be a lawsuit, the fuller form suggested by Wolff is not used, and there is no compelling evidence for an elided verb.[13] The NIV and others see the preposition as indicating opposition ("against me," cf. NCV, NLT). The following context, then, appropriately continues this thought, explaining in which ways they do so.

Only three names are singled out for specific mention from among "all nations" (3:2). But Joel likely sees these three as representative of all the enemy nations of God's people. Note, for example, how in Obadiah, one nation, Edom, is representative of "all nations" (see the commentary).

Note too that Joel has used several merisms (extreme parts representing the whole, e.g., 2:23, 32), so he may well be doing the same thing here. This suggestion is strengthened by the geographical location of the nations. Tyre and Sidon are a frequently recurring word pair (e.g., Isa. 23; Jer. 25:22; 27:3; Ezek. 27:3, 8; Zech. 9:2). They are located about twenty-five miles apart on the Phoenician seacoast north of Israel in what is now Lebanon (see the introduction). Bracketing Israel to the south is the Philistine region, whose

---

11. See F. I. Andersen, *The Hebrew Verbless Clause in the Pentateuch* (Nashville: Abingdon, 1970); C. L. Miller, ed., *The Verbless Clause in Biblical Hebrew: Linguistic Approaches* (Winona Lake, Ind.: Eisenbrauns, 1999).

12. This assumes a perfect ternse; see Wolff, *Joel,* 77; cf. NJPS, "What are you doing," which apparently assumes a participle; cf. Allen, *Joel, in loc.;* GNB).

13. See on this, Rudolph, *Joel,* 77.

inhabitants lived in tension with Israel since they both arrived in the land about the same time. Among other things, the Philistines were slave traders (Amos 1:6). These northern and southern neighbors, both sharing the same wrongdoing, geographically bracket Israel in Amos 1:6–10 as they do in Joel, only there it is in a south-north order. This bracketing strengthens the suggestion that they are a merism for all of Israel's neighbors, similar to that of Dan and Beersheba as northern and southern extremities serving as a merism for the entire land of Israel (Judg. 20:1; 1 Sam. 3:20).

The next question in verse 4 asks literally, "Is it a recompense that you are paying back concerning/against me?" That is, have I done anything wrong, that you should make it up to me as I made up the destroyed years for Israel (2:25)? The noun "recompense" and the root from which it derives (*gml*) is neutral, used either in a positive sense as a reward (2 Sam. 22:21//Ps. 18:21; Prov. 19:17) or, more commonly, in a negative sense as a punishment (Deut. 32:6; Ps. 7:5). The context here falls most definitely in the latter category, since the precipitating actions themselves are negative. The response is not delayed but comes quickly, as does the Day of the Lord (Zeph. 1:14). The fact that the deeds of the nations return on their own heads is a direct quote from Obadiah 15, with the sole difference being the number of the pronoun "your" (cf. also v. 7 below). Here it is plural, referring to the three representative nations, while in Obadiah it is singular, referring to Edom, which is also representative of "all the nations."

Verses 5–6 detail some of the wrongs for which the nations are to be repaid. The first is plundering the treasure of God and taking it to their own temples. The silver, gold, and "finest treasures" are God's, as are the land and its people (cf. 1:6; 2:26, 27; 3:2, 3), grape vines and fig trees (1:7), Zion (2:1), and even the locust army (2:25). Everything belongs to God, including these valuables. "My finest treasures" (lit., "my good desirable things") is not specific but can include gold, silver, and family members (1 Kings 20:6–7; Ezek. 24:16–18, 25; Hos. 9:6, 16) as well as Jerusalem, the temple, and its implements (Isa. 64:10–11; Ezek. 24:21; Lam. 1:10; 2 Chron. 36:19), and even necessities like food (Lam. 1:11), all being liable to plunder. This may refer to such things as the goods that the Assyrian king Tiglath-Pileser received from Menahem (2 Kings 15:20), (Jeho)ahaz (2 Kings 16:8; 2 Chron. 28:21), or Hoshea (2 Kings 17:3), or that Sennacherib claimed as tribute from Hezekiah (2 Kings 18:14),[14] or

---

14. On the tribute received from these kings, see *COS*, 2:285, 287, 288, 289, 291, 293, 303. According to Sennacherib's inscription, the tribute included gold, silver, precious stones, and ivory, as well as family members and numerous other items. Many of these were included among the "finest treasures" in Scripture.

perhaps even the pillaging of the temple by the Babylonians (2 Kings 25:8–21; 2 Chron. 36:17–20).

In none of these episodes elsewhere in the Old Testament is any of the three nations named in Joel mentioned as perpetrating such acts, though not all such events are likely to have been recorded (cf. Obad. 10–14, where Edom is implicated of complicity in the sack of Jerusalem, an involvement not mentioned elsewhere). There are many times in Israel's history when these three nations, and other neighboring nations they represent, did prey on Israel (e.g., 2 Chron. 16:2). This does not, therefore, have to be a historically inaccurate substitution of some people for others, nor does it necessitate a date for the prophecy from at least the exilic period, though that is not precluded either.

An even more egregious wrong is the slave-trading these peoples engaged in, possibly the same actions as referred to in Amos 1:6–10 (a passage already shown to have formal similarities to this one; see comments on Joel 3:2–3). Judeans, more specifically Jerusalemites (3:1), are sold, referring either to the events of 3:3 or to more general practices for prisoners of war (Deut. 20:10–15; Neh. 5:8).[15] Kidnapping an Israelite for slavery is a capital offense (Ex. 21:16; Deut. 24:7), so this strong reaction may well be an extension of this prohibition. The purchasers of these slaves are the Greeks (*y⁽ʷānîm*; i.e., "Ionians"), in whose culture slavery was ubiquitous.[16] This slavery distances the Israelites from their own land (Joel 2:20), a horrible fate for a people so tied to their land (cf. Jer. 27:10; Ezek. 11:16).[17] Those sold are literally "sons" (cf. 2:28; NIV "people"), here being gender inclusive to include all the inhabitants of the land regardless of age or gender.

No biblical text mentions Greek involvement in this practice with Israel, though there is frequent mention of the return from exile of Israelites from the "coastlands" (e.g., Isa. 10:11; Jer. 25:17–26),[18] a locale associated in at least some cases with Greece (cf., e.g., Gen. 10:4–5). In Jeremiah 31:10–11, the

---

15. For the more common and culturally accepted form of slavery that is entered into because of debts, see see I. Mendelsohn, *Slavery in the Ancient Near East* (New York: Oxford Univ. Press, 1949); M. A. Dandamaev, *Slavery in Babylonia: From Nabopolassar to Alexander the Great (626–331 B.C.)*, rev. ed. (DeKalb: Northern Illinois Univ. Press, 1984); idem, "Slavery," *ABD*, 6:58–65.

16. One writer states: "There was no action or belief or institution in Graeco-Roman antiquity that was not one way or other affected by the possibility that someone involved *might be* a slave" (M. I. Finley, *Ancient Slavery and Modern Ideology* [New York: Viking, 1980] 65).

17. Many read the preposition *l⁽ma⁽an* (NIV "that [you might]") as a purpose clause (Williams, §277; LXX, ASV, ESV, KJV, NASB, NCV), but this makes no sense. It is better read as a result, "so that you removed them" (Joüon §169g; NLT, NRSV).

18. In Isa. 59:18–19 these coastlands, associated with the west, would be recompensed for what they had done to Israel, using the same terminology as Joel 3:4, a text to which this may be alluding.

Israelites are brought back from these coastlands by "ransom" and "redemption," both words associated with release from slavery ("ransom": Deut. 7:8; 13:6; Mic. 6:4; "redemption": Ex. 6:6; Lev. 25:48, 49). While Joel 3:6 may refer to those dispersed during the Babylonian exile, this exile was by no means the only case of Israelite dispersion, and the Greeks were active in the area of the eastern Mediterranean from the late third millennium B.C., with much trade in later periods.[19] Mention of trade with Greece, therefore, does not support or preclude any dates proposed for Joel. This trade could include trafficking in humans.

Role Reversal (3[4]:7−8)

A NEW SUBSECTION opens with the same interjection with which Yahweh earlier spoke words of encouragement and restoration to his people (2:19; *hin*'*nî*, both untrans. in NIV). This time they are words to an opposite effect. Previously God promised restoration of what his people had lost; now he promises a recompense for the loss inflicted on his people. There is even a parallel in verbal structure between the two passages, since both express the action in the form of a participle. Here God says that he will "rouse them" (ʿ*wr*), that is, "the people of Judah and Jerusalem" in 3:6. Like those sleeping, he awakens them (cf. Isa. 50:4). Israel has become habituated to the slavery into which they were sold (Joel 3:3, 6), but God will rouse them out of their despondency and repay their captors, as he previously promised (v. 4).[20]

The slave traders receive the same treatment they inflicted on Judah (v. 8): They too will be sold. God himself is the seller, through the agency of the Judeans. Those sold include "sons and daughters," with the former term now being gender specific, in contrast to its use in relation to Judah (see comment on v. 6). God metaphorically sells them, placing them into the control of Judah, who literally sells them in turn.

The buyers this time are "the Sabaeans." These peoples are identified in the Table of Nations as "Sheba" (Gen. 10:7), probably located on the southwest corner of the Arabian peninsula in what is now Yemen.[21] It was a nation rich from its own products and from trade (e.g., 1 Kings 10:1−13//2 Chron. 9:1−12; Job 6:19; Isa. 60:6; Ezek. 27:22, 23; 38:13), which also probably included trade in slaves. It was also known for its distance from

---

19. Cf. John MacRay, "Greece," *ABD*, 2:1093.

20. The verbal form here is *waw* conversive + perfect, while in v. 4 it is a prefix. Both share the same meaning, and the remainder of the clause is identical.

21. E.g., Y. Aharoni and M. Avi-Yonah, *The Macmillan Bible Atlas* (New York: Macmillan, 1968), 15.

Israel (Jer. 6:20), so just as Judean slaves were distanced from their native land as slaves (v. 6), so too these slaves would be sent to a land far away.

The section closes with a somber boundary indicator: It is Yahweh himself who is speaking. This form almost always occurs at the beginning of an episode (Isa. 1:2; Jer. 13:15; cf. Ps. 50:1) or at its end (1 Kings 14:11; Isa. 22:15; 25:8; Obad. 18), as it does here.[22] This marker of direct discourse is especially concentrated in Isaiah, which, along with its occurrence in Micah 4:4, becomes particularly relevant in the discussion of verse 10, below.

You Nations! (3[4]:9-12)

A CALL TO battle is made up of a new set of imperatival forms, many repeated from previous sections.[23] This separates it from its preceding context, where such forms are not used. Yahweh continues to speak (cf. v. 8), calling unnamed hearers to proclaim (*qr*ʾ) the following message to all of the gathered "nations" (cf. 3:2). The previous two times this imperative is used in Joel, it is directed to Israel (her priests, 1:14; 2:15), so they may again be the subject here. The demonstrative pronoun "this" refers to the message that follows.

While suffering Judah was to sanctify a fast (1:14; 2:15) and themselves (2:16), the nations are to (lit.) "sanctify a war" (NIV "prepare for war"). Since the deities of nations actively involved themselves in the warfare and religious dedicatory practices were often part of the preparation (see Bridging Contexts section), this juxtaposition of theology and warfare was familiar to Joel's hearers. Calls for preparation for war are part of other prophetic messages (Jer. 49:14; Obad. 1).The terminology here strongly reflects that language describing the encroaching locust swarm. The swarm is metaphorically at war against Judah (Joel 2:5, 7), its "warriors" (cf. 2:7; 3:10, 11) also called "fighting men" who "attack" ("scale," 2:7). It is clear that the one fighting force is deliberately described in reference to the other. Yahweh now calls for the mustering of the troops, as he promised (3:7).

There is a juxtaposition of the sedentary, agricultural life, with its implements such as plowshares and pruning hooks, with the life of war, with its swords and spears. The first of these (ʾittîm) is a cutting implement made out of iron, a metallurgical technology unavailable to Israel early in her nationhood, necessitating going to the Philistines, who developed iron technology. In 1 Samuel 13:20–21, this word joins several similar other implements, including axes and plowshares, so the ʾittîm seem to be something other than

---

22. The Masoretic setumah division marker (ס) that follows v. 8 confirms this.

23. *BHS* suggests reading the fourth and fifth verbs as imperatives instead of the jussive forms, which were in MT. There is little appreciable change in meaning.

plowshares. A related Akkadian term is part of a plow,[24] and this is how the English translations generally take the word, though it may be better to see it as a more general term for a sharp cutting implement. It is clearly made of metal in Joel, since it is shaped by beating. Deist suggests that it is the implement used to clear and open new land, which could later be kept productive through the use of a plow.[25]

The verb "beat" applies to the second noun (*mizmērôt*, "pruning hooks") as well. Another context in which this implement is used is to cut thin shoots from a grape vine (Isa. 18:5).[26] In other words, what the farmers are giving up here is the ability to open new land and to adequately harvest what they produce.[27]

The resulting implements are clearly implements of war. The "sword" is a hand weapon, at times with two edges, used for cutting (Judg. 3:16; 1 Sam. 17:51), and the "spear" is one that is thrown or thrust (Num. 25:7), often used with a shield (Judg. 5:8; 1 Chron. 12:8).[28] The nations are warned that they will face the same situation as regards their agricultural life as the Israelites whom they have oppressed. Israel loses her agricultural livelihood to natural disaster; the nations lose theirs to war.

Joel here provides an interesting reversal of a saying known from previous prophetic utterances. Both Isaiah (Isa. 2:4) and Micah (Mic. 4:4) use almost a mirror opposite to the Joel saying: "They will beat their swords into plowshares and their spears into pruning hooks." This saying appears familiar to Joel and his audience, and he reverses it for rhetorical impact.[29] The reversal of the expected is a powerful means of attracting attention. Where in the original context the peaceful aspects of Yahweh's reign in Jerusalem, the "city of peace," are the subject, this reversal indicates that it will not be so peaceful for those who oppose him or his people. Yahweh warns them to get ready for a fight! It is not only the warriors who are going to be involved in conflict; even the "weakling," one who is close to death (cf. Job 14:10) or already defeated (cf. Ex. 17:13; Isa. 14:12),[30] now has to claim fighting vigor.

---

24. *Ittû*; CAD, 7:312.

25. Deist, *Material Culture*, 191.

26. See the related *mᵉzammeret*, one of the temple implements used in the Holy Place, most likely a knife used to trim the wicks of the golden candlestick (1 Kings 7:50; Jer. 52:18).

27. Deist, *Material Culture*, 191.

28. See stone reliefs of swordsmen, spearmen, and shield-bearers in, e.g., *ANEP*, 332, 364, 366, 372.

29. It appears likely that Isaiah is the original source, with Micah citing it, using the direct discourse indicator, "for the LORD Almighty has spoken," which is characteristic of Isaiah. See Meier, *Speaking of Speaking*, 156–58.

30. Whether these were homonyms or one root is debated among the dictionaries (cf. BDB, *HALOT*), though the meanings seem close enough not to require two separate roots.

He too is one of the warriors (Joel 3:9; 2:7; 3:11). Even those unable or unexpected to fight will be called upon to do so.

All the surrounding "nations" (v. 11; cf. v. 9) are summoned to "come" in response to these events. The exact nature of their coming is unclear, since the verb (ʿwš) only occurs here in the Bible. Translations such as "hurry" or "help" have been proposed. Either fits the context, and neither is compelling. They must also gather (2:16), just as the nations were already told to gather (3:2). In this verse the place of assembly is not identified apart from their being called "to there." The nearest location is in the next verse, the Valley of Jehoshaphat, the same gathering place as at the beginning of this chapter (3:2).

The final imperative in verse 11 has a different subject. The prophet himself steps back into the frame, directly addressing Yahweh. As the enemy's warriors were previously called to action (vv. 9, 10), Joel now calls Yahweh to bring his own warriors down (nḥt) just as he had at other times brought his hand down in punishment (Ps. 38:2). The repetition of "warrior" in each of these three verses ties them together (cf. Obad. 9). The verb nḥt signifies military attack (cf. Jer. 21:1 and context).[31] Reading the clause in this way shows an impatient prophet who is almost saying, "Enough talk, God. Get moving!" (cf. Hab. 2:1).

Yahweh's directions resume in verse 12. He repeats his call for the arousal (cf. vv. 7, 9) and ascent (cf. v. 9) of the surrounding nations to the same valley to which he promised they would be gathered in 3:2. This shows that the summons, while worded as a call to war, is in fact for a different end: God will bring them to judgment (cf. 3:2).

Literarily, the episode in 3:11–12 is coming back to its inauguration in 3:2, signaled by the use of many elements repeated from that verse: "gather," "all of the nations," judgment, "there," and a Niphal verbal form. Over this entire procedure, Yahweh sits, not in patience as he did for Gideon (Judg. 6:18), but rather as a mighty, enthroned king (1 Sam. 4:4; Ps. 61:8; 99:1; 132:14) or judge (Ex. 18:13).

ISRAEL AND THE LAND. Land was central to Israel's self-identity. From its prenational period under Abram, land was part of Israel's promise (Gen. 12:1). At first unspecified, it was soon identified as "this land" (15:7, 18) and "the land of Canaan" (17:8; cf. Ex. 6:4), where Abram dwelt (Gen. 13:12; 16:3), followed by his descendants (28:4; 31:18;

---

31. Cf. T. Gaster, "The Battle of the Rain and the Sea: An Ancient Semitic Nature Myth," *Iraq* 4 (1937): 28, n. 13, who proposes "launch into the fray," based on an Ugaritic cognate.

37:1). When separated from the land, return to it was a strong desire and greatly anticipated (31:3, 13; 48:21; cf. 49:29; Ex. 3:8, 17; 13:5, 11; Lev. 14:34; 20:24; 25:38).

One of the problems of Israel's settling into the land relates to one of its previously mentioned designations: land of Canaan. It was already inhabited by the Canaanites, who were comprised of several subgroups (e.g., Ex. 13:5), people who also felt an affinity with the land, which is theirs by possession, having been out of direct control of Abraham's descendants for centuries. Even though the land was often identified with their name, Israel was not to identify with them, since Yahweh clearly distinguished between its current residents and those who moved in by right of ancestral inheritance. One of the distinctions made was moral, that Israel must have nothing to do with the Canaanite practices (Lev. 18:3). Israel used Yahweh's land promise as an apologetic for their right to it when they returned. This was based on God's ultimate right to the land since he created it in the first place (Gen. 1:1).[32]

On the verge of entering the land, God reiterated his promise to the Israelites (Num. 13:2), but they lost their focus on the land as one of promise and also lost faith in the One who promised; thus, they were instead terrorized by its inhabitants (13:32).[33] As a result, that entire generation was unable to enter into the land (14:21–22). The promise was not abrogated, however, since God did allow the next generation to complete the journey, arriving in the land and settling it (Joshua–Judges).

Before even settling the land, however, God announced that failure to keep her covenant regulations would result in Israel's exile from it (Deut. 28:64), but he also promised that a return to the covenant would precipitate a return to the land and the life it held (30:5, 16). It is this promise and warning that the prophets repeatedly held up in front of Israel and its leaders: As their relationship with the covenant was, so would be their association with the land.[34]

This emphasis on land as home rather than as property is something foreign to many in the West. Especially in North America, geographical ties are held lightly since we are a mobile society. This is not the case for many, who have a much closer tie to the land, which is often described as the "mother

---

32. Joel seems to have chosen the words for what is created here with thought, since the word translated "earth" (ʾereṣ) is also the word translated in the passage referred to as "land."

33. It is ironic that the people still recognized the land as "this land" (Num. 14:3), but, having lost faith in God, this same land of promise became this land of terror.

34. This is reflected in positive (e.g., Isa. 9:2; 11:9; 25:8; Hos. 1:11; Mic. 5:3–6; Zech. 3:9) as well as negative (e.g., Isa. 6:12; 7:22, 24; 9:19; Zeph. 1:18; 5:3; 7:14) terms—restoration or exile, depending on belief or apostasy.

land," emblematic of the love felt for it. An example of this attachment is the Nobel Prize-winning author Alexandr Solzhenitsyn. He was exiled from Russia in February 1974, but in spite of his great suffering there, he returned in 1994 at the end of the Cold War, because in spite of the comforts of his American residence during exile, that is still home.

Selling people. Israel's neighbors are strongly condemned for human trafficking (3:3, 6, 8). People in Israel and in the wider ancient Near East became enslaved for numerous reasons. Sometimes economic deprivation led to selling one's family or even one's self into slavery (e.g., 2 Kings 4:1). In Israelite practice, Israelites who found themselves in this position were to be released after six years of service (Ex. 21:2; Deut. 15:12; Jer. 34:14), in effect serving their master as an indentured servant (Lev. 25:39–41). Foreigners often became slaves through being prisoners of war (Deut. 20:11–14), though usually this involved only the women and children, since the men were killed as enemy combatants (Num. 31:9, 35). They became the permanent property of their owners. Slaves could also be acquired from neighboring nations (Lev. 25:44–46). These presumably were non-Israelites, who would have been treated differently.

The slavery denounced by Joel could well be of people obtained by a different means, one strongly condemned by Israelite law: kidnapping. This was a capital offence under Israel's covenant obligations (Ex. 21:16; Deut. 24:7). Regardless of how the people trafficked in Joel's day were obtained, they seem to be treated as nothing but chattels, objects to be bartered for fleeting personal gratification. Whether the issue is the concept of slavery itself (and that of Israelites in particular by their enemies) or the deprivation of basic human dignity, God is upset at Israel's neighbors for their actions.

Holy war. This theme of holy war appears also in other Old Testament passages. The verb used in Joel 3:9 (lit., "to sanctify") is used twice with war as the direct object (Jer. 6:4; Mic. 3:5). In another case (Jer 22:7), it is warriors who serve this grammatical function, and in yet another passage the context indicates that the verb itself, without a specific direct object, is used with the meaning of "prepare for war" (Jer. 51:27–28; cf. ESV, NCV, NIV, NLT, NRSV, GNB).

In Israel, war was initiated by divine oracle (e.g., Josh. 6:2–5; Judg. 1:2; 20:1, 18, 23, 27–28), and preparation for war included rituals (e.g. Judg. 20:26; 1 Sam. 7:4, 9). Yahweh (or at least his cultic symbols or personnel) was involved in the battle (Josh. 6:8–16; Judg. 4:15; 1 Sam. 14:1–18, 23; 23:6–12; 30:7–8),[35] and the results of war included dedication of plunder to God

---

35. See, e.g., M. Lind, *Yahweh Is a Warrior: The Theology of Warfare in Ancient Israel* (Scottdale: Herald, 1980); T. Longman III and D. G. Reid, *God Is a Warrior* (Grand Rapids: Zondervan, 1995); cf. P. C. Craigie, *The Problem of War in the Old Testament* (Grand Rapids: Eerdmans, 1978).

(Josh. 6:17−7:1; 1 Chron. 26:27). War for Israel was more than simply a sociopolitical act; it was also theological, and in this could be understood as "holy."

Deities were also credited as taking part in warfare in the ancient Near Eastern world. The eighth-century B.C. inscription of Zakir, a Syrian king, credits his military victory to the intervention of his god, Ilu-Wer (Hadad).[36] The Hittites had a ritual they performed before entering into battle,[37] in which they not only appealed to all their own gods but also to those of their enemy to come over to join them. They also anointed their warriors and accoutrements before battle.[38] In Mesopotamia, magic rituals were thought to help in times of war.[39]

The Israelite ethos was different from that presented among her neighbors. While prayer was a real part of Israelite life and prayers against one's enemies are recorded (e.g., Ps. 3:7; 7:6; 30:1; 59:1; 60:11), most of these were not in a battle context. In a military situation, the call often went in the other direction. God called his people to battle, with him at their leader. Theirs was holy war in that it was divinely instigated. This is a completely different thing from what is called "holy war" today. Today wars of national or partisan interest, such as that in Iraq or of Islamic extremists against their opponents, are designated so as to baptize something that is humanly instigated and definitely not "holy" with some kind of theological veneer.

Journeying to Jerusalem: a reversal. Coming up to Jerusalem is an important motif in the Old Testament. Especially after the establishment of the temple and its rituals, Jerusalem was the center for service, worship, and pilgrimage (e.g., 2 Chron. 11:14; 30:3, 11; 32:23; Ps. 24:3; 122:4; Jer. 31:6; cf. Ezra 1:3; 3:8). Since it was also the nation's capital, people came to it for sociopolitical reasons as well (e.g., Jer. 35:11; Obad. 21). Other nations also are said to come up to the holy city, not only for worship (e.g., Isa.2:3//Mic. 4:2; Jer 3:17; Zech. 8:20−23; cf. Zech. 14:18, 19), but also for war (Jer 6:4−5; cf. animals, Isa. 35:9).

In 3:10, Joel plays off these two reasons for coming up to Jerusalem in his reversal of Isaiah 2:3 and Micah 4:2. In the two earlier prophecies, people are urged to come up to Jerusalem to learn about, and worship,

---

36. *ANET*, 655.

37. *ANET*, 354−55.

38. E. Laroche, *Catalogue des texts hittites* (Paris: Klincksieck, 1971), 162, 8−14.

39. M. Elat, "Mesopotamische Kriegsrituale," *Bibliotheca Orientalis* 39 (1982): 5−25; W. H. P. Römer, "Rituale und Beschwörungen in sumerischer Sprache," in *Religiöse Texte*, ed. W. C. Delsman, et al. (*TUAT* 2/2; Gütersloh: Gerd Mohn, 1987), 169−71.

---

the God who lives there. A stated attraction for this teaching is that it is one of peace, one leading to the conversion of war materiel to agricultural purposes. Joel also calls people to come up to Jerusalem (Joel 3:9), but not for peacemaking; these are makers of war, those who reconstitute the decommissioned weapons so that even the least warlike becomes aggressive (v. 10).

SLAVERY. Slavery is outside of the experience of most Western Christians. Some of them have ancestors who were enslaved, while others have within their family tree those who owned slaves, and yet others have both. While this is all part of our heritage, it is not an active element of our daily experience. This is not so for Joel's Israel, nor of many in the world today. Slavery was only banned in Yemen and Saudi Arabia in 1962, and in Mauritius only as recently as 1980.[40] Recently a Yemeni girl from Birmingham, England, wrote an account of her father who sold her and her sister as brides back in Yemen.[41]

This is not just an issue affecting others, however. In 1999, the CIA estimated that between 45,000 and 50,000 women and children are trafficked into the United States each year.[42] This does not include internal traffic within the United States itself. Most of these women and children are used within the sex industry, for prostitution and/or pornography. Christians also make use of both of these, especially through internet viewing or pornography.[43] There are members of our churches, both those in the pew and those behind the pulpit, who are supporting this slave trade through their participation.

---

40. Bernard Lewis, *Race and Slavery in the Middle East: A Historical Enquiry* (New York: Oxford Univ. Press, 1990), 79.

41. Zana Muhsen with Andrew Crofts, *Sold: A Story of Modern Day Slavery* (London: Warner, 1994); cf. Eileen MacDonald, *Brides for Sale? Human Trade in North Yemen* (Edinburgh: Mainstream, 1988); Mende Nazer, *Slave* (New York: Public Affairs, 2003).

42. Amy O'Neil Richard, "International Trafficking in Women into the United States: A Contemporary Manifestation of Slavery and Organized Crime," available at http://www.odci.gov/csi/monograph/women/trafficking.pdf.

43. A 1991 study of a questionnaire sent to 500 pastors indicates that 45 percent of the respondents have used pornography (J. O. Balswick and J. W. Thoburn, "Demographic Data on Extra-marital Sexual Behavior in the Ministry," *Pastoral Psychology* 46/6 ([1998]: 453); see also D. Hughes, "The Internet and Sex Industries: Partners in Global Sexual Exploitation," *Christian Social Action* 14/4 (2001): 17–19.

This must be addressed in at least two ways, both involving education. (1) The church needs to be made aware that this is not just the "world's" problem, or if so, it is one of many ways in which the world has infiltrated the church. It is also not something that is just done "in the privacy of one's own home," but has national and global implications. (2) There also needs to be assurance that, though the matter is serious indeed, it is not the "unforgivable sin"; there is hope, and a way out of sexual addiction.[44] The church, recognizing that all human beings are in God's image and are valuable enough to God that he sacrificed his Son for them, needs to strive mightily to free people from slavery in the twenty-first century, just as they did in England and the United States in the nineteenth century.

Holy/just war. War and peace are still vexing topics for the church and the wider society in the twenty-first century. Some in the United States justify a de facto unilateral invasion of Afghanistan and Iraq through a just war theory.[45] Moreover, some Muslims call on the concept of *jihad* to justify attacking civilian as well as military targets around the world. This is another case where theology is a life-and-death issue. This becomes clearer when one understands that *jihad* is a spiritual as well as physical war against "infidels." Christians get justifiably upset when this is directed against them, but this exemplifies the relativity of terminology. Since an "infidel" is one who does not hold to a particular belief system, Christians are infidels in the sight of Islam, and Muslims are definitionally the same in relation to Christians. This is clear from the Crusades, when this very term was applied to Muslims.

At its root, a more foundational question is how one views one's fellow human beings. If an enemy has become someone "other" than us and

44. Several resources available, among many, are: H. W. Schaumburg, *False Intimacy: Understanding the Struggle of Sexual Addiction* (Colorado Springs: NavPress, 1997); J. K. Balswick and J. O. Balswick, *Authentic Human Sexuality: An Integrated Christian Approach* (Downers Grove, Ill.: InterVarsity Press, 1999); S. Arterburn and F. Stoeker, *Every Man's Battle: Winning the War on Sexual Temptation One Victory at a Time* (Colorado Springs: WaterBrook, 2000), with other related volumes on the topic by the first author; J. Harris, *Not Even a Hint: Guarding your Heart Against Lust* (Portland: Multnomah, 2003).

45. Just war theory has a long history, going back to Thomas Aquinas's *Summa Theologica*, part II, question 40. Hermeneutical approaches to the topic are delineated in, e.g., W. M. Swartley, *Slavery, Sabbath, War, and Women: Case Issues in Biblical Interpretation* (Scottdale: Herald, 1983). See also, among others, S. Hauerwas, *The Peaceable Kingdom* (South Bend, Ind.: Univ. of Notre Dame Press, 1983); R. G. Clouse, ed., *War: Four Christian Views*, 2nd ed. (Downers Grove, Ill.: InterVarsity Press, 1991); J. Daryl Charles, *Between Pacificism and Jihad: Just War and Christian Tradition* (Downers Grove, Ill.: InterVarsity Press, 2005).

therefore does not merit human dignity, we forget that we all are created in God's image and the object of his self-sacrificing love. While the human default setting since the Fall seems to be violence, are not Christians called to represent Christ's kingdom, with a different ruler and different rules? While this brief note cannot persuade in any of the myriad positions proposed by people of good faith, the thinking Christian needs to at least be aware that there are options held by sincere Christians of good will. Each of us needs to come to our own position on this and many other vital ethical issues, since theology cannot stay just in our heads but must also live through our hearts in our hands.[46]

46. A position less familiar to many among Reformed and Arminian Christians is pacifism, represented particularly among the Anabaptists. For an entrée, see works in the previous note, and see also H. J. M. Nouwen, *The Road to Peace: Writings on Peace and Justice* (Maryknoll, N.Y.: Orbis, 1998), and E. M. Sider and L. Keefer Jr., *A Peace Reader* (Nappanee, Ind.: Evangel, 2002).

Joel 3[4]:13–21

¹³ Swing the sickle,
    for the harvest is ripe.
  Come, trample the grapes,
    for the winepress is full
    and the vats overflow—
  so great is their wickedness!"

¹⁴ Multitudes, multitudes
    in the valley of decision!
  For the day of the LORD is near
    in the valley of decision.
¹⁵ The sun and moon will be darkened,
    and the stars no longer shine.
¹⁶ The LORD will roar from Zion
    and thunder from Jerusalem;
    the earth and the sky will tremble.
  But the LORD will be a refuge for his people,
    a stronghold for the people of Israel.

¹⁷ "Then you will know that I, the LORD your God,
    dwell in Zion, my holy hill.
  Jerusalem will be holy;
    never again will foreigners invade her.

¹⁸ "In that day the mountains will drip new wine,
    and the hills will flow with milk;
    all the ravines of Judah will run with water.
  A fountain will flow out of the LORD's house
    and will water the valley of acacias.
¹⁹ But Egypt will be desolate,
    Edom a desert waste,
  because of violence done to the people of Judah,
    in whose land they shed innocent blood.
²⁰ Judah will be inhabited forever
    and Jerusalem through all generations.
²¹ Their bloodguilt, which I have not pardoned,
    I will pardon."

    The LORD dwells in Zion!

A RENEWED BATTLE cry opens the last section with loose ties with the previous section through mention of agricultural implements, and with the beginning of the prophecy through mention of agricultural products (here in abundance, there in scarcity). The double allusion to a valley recalls the double mention bracketing the beginning of this chapter (3:2, 12), and the Day of the Lord makes its appearance yet again (cf. 1:15; 2:1, 11; 2:31), uniting the entire book.

The prophet then anticipates an ideal future for Judah (3:18–21). Those oppressing and opposing her will be done away with, and she will receive not only blessing but unexpected forgiveness. In the immediate context of desiccation and depredation, blessing is presented in terms of much needed water. Something beyond just the physical and ordinary is meant, however, since the water flows not from a spring but from the very presence of God, his house. This will all happen "in that day."

The Valley of Decision (3[4]:13–17

GOD COMMANDS AN unidentified group to set its hands to attack, using a harvest metaphor, something denied the Judeans by the locust swarm army (1:7).[1] The sickle (Jer. 50:16) is used for grain crops, whose plentiful harvest has ripened (cf. Gen. 40:10; Sir. 51:15). After gathering, the crop is so plentiful that the processing facilities are full. The crop is unidentified, possibly being grain since the processing places are associated with threshing floors (Judg. 6:11; Num. 18:27, 30). The verb associated with the "vats" is only used of liquids, however, though its occurrences are few (šûq; 2:24; Ps. 65:9), so the common understanding of this crop to be grapes has merit, though olives, and their oil, is possible as well. God promised this type of agricultural abundance for his people (Joel 2:24), and now this literal profusion is applied metaphorically to the wickedness of the nations. For this cause they are cut down like grain.

Since the nations are the ones doing wickedness, they cannot be the subject of this call to punish them. Though the nations are roused to prepare for battle (3:12), it must be God's own forces (v. 11) here called to the offensive.

The confluence of punishers and punished results in a large gathering (vv. 14–15). This is associated with the crowd of an army (Judg. 4:7; 1 Kings 20:13, 28), but also often with the accompanying tumultuous commotion and uproar (1 Sam. 4:14; Isa. 13:4). This turmoil is emphasized by

---

1. See Prinsloo, *Theology of Joel*, 102, concerning some suggestions as to the identity of the recipients of the imperatives.

its repetition.[2] The lack of a verb in Hebrew also draws attention to the repeated nouns.

The valley, previously fully identified as that of Jehoshaphat (3:2, 12), is now identified twice as that of "decision" (*ḥārûṣ*, "take decisive action"; cf. "judgment," LXX, GNB). This relates it to the judgment associated with the previous mentions of the valley, both in its name and the related verbs. There are numerous cognates for the word "decision," however, another one of which also fits the literary context.[3] That is, *ḥārûṣ* can also be an agricultural tool, a threshing sledge used to process grain (Job 41:22; Isa. 28:27; 41:15). Damascus used such sledges made of iron as inhumane instruments of war (Amos 1:3). Joel just referred to the conversion of metal agricultural implements into weapons of war (3:10), and this motif may be continued here, where the nations receive what they, in another context, inflicted on others.[4] This suggestion receives greater weight by Joel's knowledge of Amos's prophecy, evidenced by the quote in Joel 3:16.

Once again the approaching "day of the LORD" is mentioned (3:14; cf. 1:15; 2:1), this time as it affects the nations rather than God's people. In fact, the focus of the Day turns in a completely different direction.[5] It is not only near, but it is "awesome" (NIV "dreadful," 2:11; 2:31; see comments), though that descriptive term is not used here. Nations experience the same upset of earth and heavens as Judah suffered, with the exact clauses of 2:10 repeated.

The exact words of Amos 1:2 (cf. Jer. 25:30) occur in the first half of Joel 3:16, where they also concern the herald of the power of God's response in judgment and punishment against the nations, there including also Israel and Judah. Zion, as the residence of Yahweh in his temple, is the place from which Yahweh's call goes out (cf. Joel 2:1, 15).[6] This quotation uses a word different from Joel's other terminology for divine utterance. This is not a feeble cry but a mighty roar, as of a lion or thunder (2:11; Judg. 14:5; Job 37:4; Ps. 22:13; Isa. 5:29). The heavens and earth tremble as they did at the advance of the locust army (Joel 2:11), giving a modification of the first part of the same verse, the latter part of which is cited in 3:15.

In marked contrast to the turmoil facing the nations, Yahweh stands firm on behalf of his people (2:16, 17[2x], 18, 19, 26, 27; 3:2, 3), in contrast to the "people" of the locusts (2:2, 5) and the neighboring peoples (2:6). He is

---

2. Waltke-O'Connor, § 119.

3. *DCH*, 3:315–16 lists three adjectival uses as well as one proper name (2 Kings 21:19). It also lists "gold" and "channel, moat."

4. See Bliesse, "Metrical Sequences," 71.

5. Prinsloo, *Theology of Joel*, 103.

6. This strong tie between the ending of Joel and the beginning of Amos is not determinative for establishing which quoted the other.

the place where one can take "refuge" (cf. Jer. 17:17) as from the rain (Isa. 4:6). The natural elements do none of the harm they did earlier in the book. It is not just a place of hiding, however, but a "stronghold," a place of strength. There is a contrast here between security in Yahweh and the insecurity of those against whom he moves.

The section concludes (3:17) by an address to a "you" for whom Yahweh is God, a favorite self-description of the first part of the prophecy (1:13, 14; 2:14, 23, 26, 27). Now, after seeing the recompense brought on those who oppress them and after being restored from the depredations of nature, the people can see the identity of God and his relationship to them that is stated in similar terms in 2:27 (see Bridging Context section).

Instead of simply being in their midst, Yahweh "dwells" on Zion, his temple mount. The participle, with its durative function (see 2:32), along with the verb itself (*škn*), shows that Yahweh is not a temporary resident, an alien, but one who is sinking down roots with his people (2 Sam. 7:10; Ps. 102:29). Because of God's presence there, Zion can be called his "holy hill." While for Israel Zion is a place of action as she prepares to face her attackers (cf. 2:1), it can also be a prayerful place where destruction and tumult are distant (Isa. 11:9; 55:7; 65:25). Since holiness denotes separation from that which is unclean (Lev. 7:19–21; 12:4), Jerusalem, like Zion within it, is sanctified by separation from "foreigners," those called in Isaiah 52:1 "the uncircumcised and defiled" (cf. Ps. 74:7; Ezek. 7:22; Dan. 11:31).

Unlike Zion, described by an adjective (*qādôš*; 2:1), Jerusalem's state is described by a predicate nominative: (lit.) "Jerusalem will become a holy place/a sanctuary" (*qōdeš*). The tabernacle and temple are called holy places (e.g., Num. 4:15; 2 Chron. 29:7), and this sanctity, deriving from the presence of God within them, extends to the entire city when what is unclean is removed (cf. Zech. 14:20, 21). The foreigners are to be kept away permanently, for they will "never again . . . invade her."

In That Day (3[4]:18–21)

THIS LAST SECTION begins with a new time reference (cf. 3:1), continuing the theme of restoration from the beginning of the chapter. The audience needs encouragement on one more level: Their human oppressors have been eradicated through the power of Israel's mighty God (3:1–17), but their physical world is still in disarray because of the severe losses arising from the locusts and the drought (chs. 1–2). God now promises that this worry also will be no more, with produce aplenty.

The mountains, where previously there was the call to prayer for aid before the advancing army (2:1, 2, 5), now "will drip new wine," like water poured from the rain clouds (Judg. 5:4; Ps. 68:9). The new wine, previously cut off from drinkers' lips (Joel 1:5), is now restored in abundance. The other half of the common word pair with "mountains," "the hills" (cf. Hos. 10:8; Hab. 3:6)[7] "will flow" with milk, a verb (*hlk*, "go, walk") previously only used of the encroaching locust army (Joel 2:4, 7). Milk forms part of the people's staple diet (Gen. 18:8; Deut. 32:13–14; Isa. 7:15, 22) and is a gift of God. Note that one of the signs of the richness of the land promised to Israel is that it would be "flowing with milk and honey" (e.g., Num. 13:27; Deut. 6:3). These are not new delicacies added to Israel's diet here; rather, the emphasis is on their plentitude and the ease of obtaining them. This promise seems to allude to a prophecy with similar wording in Amos 9:13, another promise of God's abundant restoration after a time of hardship.[8]

Not only milk, but also an even more valuable commodity, water, will flow. Israel was a semiarid agricultural country, especially in the southern region of Judah. It was dependent on a water supply that was not only somewhat regular but was sufficient to meet not only their need for drinking but also for irrigation. That the once-dry ravines or channels (1:20) "will flow" is welcome news indeed to Judah. Not only will there be sufficient water for her needs, but its "fountain" (better "spring"; cf. 1 Kings 18:5; 2 Kings 3:19) is a source of fresh water for others (cf. Ezek. 47:1–12).

The exact location of this spring is not certain. "The valley of the acacias" ("valley of Shittim," NIV text note) uses a different word for "valley" than that used in Joel 3:2, 12, 14[2x], so a different location is in mind. This word, also translated "wadi" (e.g., Num. 34:5), designates an occasional streambed that carries water when rains fall but is dry for much of the year. Many of them exist, so the designation does not help pin down its location.[9] The identification with acacias (*šiṭṭîm*) provides little help, since acacias, which do not require much water, are common throughout the area. Israel's final encampment before entering the land was at Shittim in the Jordan rift valley (Num. 25:1). But Shittim itself cannot be meant here since it is in Transjordan, across the Jordan River from this source of water. That Jordan valley is also not appropriate since that river is not a wadi. Wherever it is, the once dry and devastated land will now be a source of blessing for others.

---

7. See S. Gevirtz, *Patterns in the Early Poetry of Israel* (SAOC 32; Chicago: Univ. of Chicago Press, 1963), 56; Y. Avishur, *Stylistic Studies of Word-Pairs in Biblical and Ancient Semitic Languages* (AOAT 210; Kevelaer: Verlag Butzon & Bercker, 1984), 698.

8. Joel 3:18 literally reads, "they will drip (imperfect) the mountains new wine and the hills they will go milk," while Amos 9:13 reads, "and they will drip (*waw* conversive + perfect) the mountains new wine and all of the hills will flow with it." There is sufficient alteration between the two to indicate that authors were not slaves to their source.

9. E.g., R. Cleave, *The Holy Land: A Unique Perspective* (Oxford: Lion, 1992), 271, lists eleven sites with this as part of their name.

The nations, in contrast, receive no blessing, but rather the devastation that once was Judah's (v. 19). Egypt, Judah's mighty neighbor to the southwest, and Edom to its southeast will become the same desert wasteland (2:3, cf. 1:7, 17, 19, 20; 2:22), a place that is uninhabited. Neither nation has been mentioned previously, but they are included among "all the nations" condemned earlier in this chapter (3:2). This does certify that those nations mentioned earlier—Tyre, Sidon, and Philistia (3:4)—are just representative of many others who now join them in their judgment.

Egypt was a major power throughout Israel's history in the land and a regular source of attack.[10] Their association with Israel's enslavement (e.g., Ex. 1:11; 13:3; 20:2) could make them an appropriate choice of target here (cf. 3:6). Edom, the descendents of Jacob's brother, Esau (Gen. 36), also had a long history of animosity with their neighbors,[11] including atrocities in Amos 1:11–12 (which may have influenced the two books being side by side in the canon).

Both Egypt and Edom treated Judah violently, including the shedding of blood, a frequent enough event that using it for dating to any specific incident is impossible. The blood is shed (lit.) "in their land," referring either to the land of Judah or to the lands of Egypt and Edom. The former is the understanding of the NIV (also NASB, NLT, NRSV, GNB), in which case it refers to one of their campaigns against Israel. Other interpreters leave it ambiguous, which is truer to the original text. The blood is "innocent," not guilty of some particular offence (e.g., Deut. 19:19; 21:8–9; 1 Sam. 19:5) rather than being absolutely free from sin.

The contrast with Egypt and Edom's demise through the lack of inhabitants is in the permanent existence of Judah and Jerusalem (v. 20). They will "be inhabited" (cf. Isa. 13:20; 45:18; Zech. 7:7; the verb serves both separate locations; cf. Joel 1:2) "forever," the same period for which Judah will be unashamed (2:26–27), and "through all generations" (lit., "to generation and generation"; cf. 1:3; 2:2). The prophet uses both concepts to refer back to the destruction that is without equal in previous times, in contrast to this great time of blessing for his restored people, which continues through future time.

The first two clauses of verse 21 have been variously interpreted. Literally they read, "I will declare clean/innocent their blood I have not declared clean/innocent" (see Num. 14:18; Nah. 1:3).[12] The interpretational variety

---

10. See, e.g., W. A. Ward, "Egyptian Relations with Canaan," *ABD*, 2:401–8.

11. See, e.g., J. R. Bartlett, "Edom," *ABD*, 2:287–95.

12. What Waltke-O'Connor calls the "psychological/linguistic" factitive, through means of a speech act estimating or declaring that something is the case (402–3); Williams, §145, calls it "delocutive."

arises depending partly on the various understandings of who the pronoun "their" refers to. Some refer it to the Egyptians and Edomites of Joel 3:19 (NCV), but that seems too distant a referent for the pronoun. Moreover, proclaiming the innocence of the oppressive neighbors of Judah would be unique in Scripture, so that interpretation is unlikely.

More likely, therefore, "their" refers to Judah and Jerusalem (v. 20; NLT). Their blood, unjustly shed by Egypt and Edom, is to be avenged by God himself. The verbal root of "declare innocent" (*nqb*) is the same as that of the adjective "innocent" in verse 19. Their "blood," using a literary figure called metonymy, where a part stands for the whole, refers to God's people suffering shed blood and the resultant death.[13] Those previously lacking innocence are now made or declared right, released from any obligation or guilt brought about by wrongdoing (cf. Gen. 24:8, 41; Ex. 21:19; Jer. 2:35).

God's own people were previously called to repentance (2:12–16), and this is the promise that forgiveness is granted.[14] As Joel is wont to do, he picks up a motif from earlier in his prophecy in order to note its coming to pass. In this case, the entire prophecy comes to a close with these two positive statements to God's people: "I will forgive you, and I am with you." This last statement picks up the statement of 3:17, a surety he wants them to know in that verse and one he repeats here so as to be branded in their awareness as his concluding promise. Though locusts, droughts, enemies, and devastation come, from natural causes or from their own guilt, Yahweh is there.

KNOWING GOD. Among Israel's polytheistic neighbors, it is important to know one's personal deity from whom help might be expected. Uncertainty seems a troubling part of life. This is shown by a seventh-century B.C. "Prayer to Every God" found in the library of Ashurbanipal and written in interlinear Akkadian and Sumerian. Part of it reads:

> O Lord, my transgressions are many; great are my sins.
> O my god, (my) transgressions are many; great are (my) sins.
> O my goddess, (my) transgressions are many; great are (my) sins.
> O god whom I know or do not know, (my) transgressions are many;
> great are (my) sins.

---

13. K. F. de Blois, "Metaphor in Common Language Translations of Joel," *BT* 36 (1985): 214.

14. Van Leeuwen, "Scribal Wisdom," takes this as an allusion to Ex. 34:6–7, which he finds as being a key verse regarding the Day of the Lord, showing both positive and negative aspects of his works in God's self-revelation.

> O goddess whom I know or do not know, (my) transgressions are
>   many; great are (my) sins.
> The transgressions which I have committed, indeed I do not know;
> The sin which I have done, indeed I do not know.
>
> ....
>
> Man is dumb; he knows nothing;
> Mankind, everyone that exists—what does he know?[15]

At this level, knowledge is simply the intellectual awareness of a fact.
The one praying does not even know to whom he is praying or for what he
might be praying. This foundational level of awareness seems to be what
Yahweh intends to address when he provides the grumbling Israelites meat
and bread in the desert for this specific purpose: "Then you will know that
I am the LORD your God" (Ex. 16:12). This is Yahweh, the one who is speaking to them, who is their deity, not any of the numerous gods whom they left
behind in Egypt or whom Abram may have known in Mesopotamia.

A lack of this basic recognition caused serious difficulties for the pharaoh
of the Exodus (Ex. 5:2), and living in such a situation of unknown gods was
to be the punishment of a rebellious Israel (Deut. 28:36; cf. Jer. 15:14; 17:4).
Ironically, Israel, in turning to unknown gods (Deut. 29:26), was punished by
having to live among them. It might be expected that non–Israelites would
not know God in this way (cf. John 15:21; 17:25; 1 Cor. 1:21; Gal. 4:8;
1 Thess. 4:5); but Israel was expected to know him (e.g., Ex. 10:2; Ezek. 6:7;
7:4, 9 and numerous other instances in Ezekiel). Though having a close
covenant relationship with the Creator of the universe, she knew less than
a dumb animal: "The ox knows his master, the donkey his owner's manger,
but Israel does not know, my people do not understand" (Isa. 1:3).

A deeper level of understanding, beyond the simple knowing of a fact (cf.
German *wissen*), is knowing a person or other animate being, becoming
acquainted with them (cf. German *kennen*). God acts not only to let Israel and
others know the fact that he exists, but also that they might experience and
appreciate his character and very being. God declares that the special
covenant relationship between him and his people produces this deeper intimacy (Ex. 6:7), using the same clause as that in Joel 3:17 ("Then you will know
that I [am] the LORD your God"). This will not be simply an intellectual
awareness but a personal encounter, since he said that he is the One "who
brought you out from under the yoke of the Egyptian" (Ex. 6:7). Part of this
knowledge of God is to be able to distinguish him and his being from other
gods competing for Israel's attention and worship (e.g., 1 Kings 20:28).

---

15. *ANET*, 391–92; ll. 21—27, 51–52.

Part of the magnitude of Israel's sin is turning away from the God whom they know in this intimate way:

I brought you into a fertile land
    to eat its fruit and rich produce.
But you came and defiled my land
    and made my inheritance detestable.
The priests did not ask,
    "Where is the LORD?"
Those who deal with the law did not know me;
    the leaders rebelled against me.
The prophets prophesied by Baal,
    following worthless idols. (Jer. 2:7–8; cf. 4:22)

A deeper experience of God and his grace, as well as of his expectations, brings with it a fuller responsibility (e.g., Prov. 10:17; Hos. 4:5–9; Amos 2:4–16, where Judah and Israel are more culpable since they know God's revealed will through the law; Luke 12:48; Acts 17:30; 1 Peter 1:14–15). Jesus on several occasions also brings out the distinction between knowledge of God cognitively and experientially. In John 4:22 he said: "You Samaritans worship what you do not know; we worship what we do know, for salvation is from the Jews." He anticipates the day when all will worship "in spirit and in truth" (v. 23), with a fuller awareness and deeper knowledge of God (see also 7:28–29; 8:19, 55; 1 John 4:7–8).

HEAD AND HEART. Evangelism Explosion has refined the use of the evangelistic question "If God were to ask you, 'Why should I let you into My Heaven?' what would you say?" The question is effective in causing the person on the street to think about life and the future. Responses come back such as: "I go to church regularly" [read: "at Christmas and Easter"]; "I pray to God" [read: "when I am really in trouble"]; "I am a good person" [read: "at least I don't get caught very often"]. Unfortunately, if the same question is asked in many churches, the same range of answers returns. One is then forced to ask the question, "What difference does church make?" The answer too often must be, "Not much difference at all."

A contributing factor to this problem is a wrong perception, that "church" makes a difference when it is in fact God who makes the difference. "Church" is not an end in itself; rather, it is a means to a greater end, developing an intimate relationship with God. The megachurch phenomenon brings many new folk through the doors, which is laudable indeed, but that is not the end, but rather only the beginning. It is not numbers through the door that are determinative of success, but rather the number of maturing disciples; it is not even a convert score that is important, but rather people who are developing in Christlikeness. The aim of the church should not be to get people to know about God, but rather to get to know God. In a way similar to relationships on a human level, true intimacy is not attained quickly but in a sustained encounter in which the details of one's very being are shared and appreciated.

This deepening encounter involves what Eugene Peterson calls "a long obedience in the same direction."[16] Time spent with an acquaintance can develop into a friendship, and time spent with a friend can transform that person into one's beloved. This is the way to move a human relationship from one of the head to one of the heart, and it also is the way to develop intimacy with God, getting to know him. Joel equates this intimacy of knowing God with holiness (3:17), with sharing relationship leading to a changed being. Peterson's subtitle (*Discipleship in an Instant Society*) indicates one way in which this kind of shared time is achieved: through discipline. While "discipline" can have a negative connotation to our ears, sounding of punishment, it is not the attitude with which one should face spiritual discipline. This is rather a way to be purposeful about spending time with the Beloved.[17] After all, it is in both word etymology and in actual practice that *discipleship* relates to *discipline*.

Unfortunately, human relationships today are disintegrating at an alarming rate, inside the church as well as outside of it. Approximately 43 percent of first marriages end in separation or divorce within the first fifteen years, based on a 1995 study.[18] The church does not fare much better, with its divorce rate (23 percent) almost matching that of the general population (26 percent) according to a 2000 study by the Barna

---

16. E. H. Peterson, *A Long Obedience in the Same Direction: Discipleship in an Instant Society* (Downers Grove, Ill.: InterVarsity Press, 1980).

17. The topic has produced many publications. Some of the best are by Richard Foster (e.g., *Celebration of Discipline: The Path to Spiritual Growth* [San Francisco: Harper & Row, 1978]; *Prayer: Finding the Heart's True Home* [San Francisco: HarperSanFrancisco, 1992]; *Streams of Living Water: Celebrating the Great Traditions of Christian Faith* [San Francisco: HarperSanFrancisco, 1998]); see also Eugene Peterson (*Answering God: The Psalms as Tools of Prayer* [San Francisco: Harper & Row, 1989]; *The Contemplative Pastor: Returning to the Art of Spiritual Direction* [Waco, Tex.: Word, 1989]; *Leap over a Wall: Earthy Spirituality for Everyday Christians* [New York: HarperCollins, 1997]).

18. M. D. Bramlett and W. D. Mosher, "First Marriage Dissolution, Divorce and Remarriage: United States," *Advance Data from Vital and Health Statistics* 323 (Hyattsville, Md.: National Center for Health Statistics, 2001): 5.

organization.[19] Lack of communication is a major contributing factor to relationship breakups such as this. This is exemplified by one estimate that married couples spend approximately fourteen minutes per week in elective conversation.[20] The foundation on which a relationship is initially born and fostered, getting to really know a person, has been eroded and diminished to such an extent that the edifice of the relationship cannot be expected to stand. In order to counteract this erosion, a couple needs to do what John urges on the lukewarm Ephesians: "Do the things you did at first" (Rev. 2:5), spend time together, and become reacquainted.

How can the human-divine relationship be expected to flourish without an equal amount of care and attention? While God is one party in the relationship, and he knows and loves those who are in relationship with him, the necessary precautions are not needed for him but for us humans. We must spend time, not only in our talking to him in prayer, but also in our listening to him, in reading Scripture, and in being in his presence. The church needs to return to a realization that we very much need to know God.[21]

---

19. http://www.barna.org/FlexPage.aspx?Page=Topic&TopicID=11. Non-denominational church members had the highest rate (34 percent), with Baptists following in second place (29 percent) according to a report (http://www.adherents.com/ largecom/ baptist_divorce.html).

20. Oral presentation by John Shultz, Ashland Theological Seminary, May 4, 2004.

21. See, e.g., A. W. Tozer, *The Knowledge of the Holy* (New York: Harper & Row, 1961); J. I. Packer, *Knowing God* (Downers Grove, Ill.: InterVarsity Press, 1973).

Introduction to Obadiah

AN ELEMENT NECESSARY for well-being, whether of an individual or a nation, is a feeling of safety and security. Even a developing newborn must learn trust before he or she can thrive. On the political level, a nation that fears for its national security, especially if that was compromised in the past, is in serious jeopardy. Its very existence feels threatened.

This is the situation facing Judah in the short prophecy of Obadiah. Her next door neighbor, Edom, whose inhabitants are related to the Judeans by blood, not only stood by when the Babylonian world power moved against Judah, she actively collaborated in that aggression. Edom, situated in a geographically superior position to Judah, and the vastly superior armies of Babylon were, to the eyes of Judah, invincible. In her ignorance, Judah's doom was sealed.

What Judah needs to be reminded of, however, is that neither geographical nor military advantage is the sole deciding factor of international relations, especially when these involve the very people of God. The nation previously faced similar situations of strategic disadvantage. For example, the superior forces of Aram besieged them in the days of Elisha (2 Kings 6:8–25). Judah, through Obadiah, needs to hear the words that encouraged Israel at that time: "Those who are with us are more than those who are with them" (6:16b). For Elisha the help was in the form of the heavenly host (6:17), and Judah finds itself under the protection of the very "LORD of hosts," the "Sovereign LORD" (Obad. 1).

Obadiah's message is only secondarily a promise of hope to Judah, since it primarily presents itself as a threat to Edom and to all others who mistreat God's people. When you see your enemies brought low, you expect that your own fortunes will rise, and God shows that this scenario lies in store for Judah. Pride in position or power is humbled by the God who is over all in both position and strength.

This small book is not just relevant to two small nations in a remote corner of the globe long ago, however. It is a reminder for larger nations much closer to us in time that they also can display arrogance and intimidate others, however unwittingly. Even today "national interest" can be too easily used as a politically correct euphemism for national greed. The best interest of neighbors cannot enter into consideration if we, at our neighbor's expense, fatten either our own pocketbook or stomach. Who today stands beside the weak nations who are unable to withstand the encroachments of today's superpowers? May it not be the same "Sovereign LORD"!

Obadiah the Person

UNLIKE SOME OLD TESTAMENT prophets who are well identified with lengthy genealogies (e.g., Zeph. 1:1; Zech. 1:1) or of whom we can determine much from detailed accounts of life events (e.g., Isaiah, Jeremiah), Obadiah is a shadowy figure. The only thing we can be certain of is that the person called Obadiah is a visionary on at least one occasion (v. 1). A special revelation of God has come to Obadiah as it had to others before (Isa. 1:1; Nah. 1:1; Hab. 2:2), an indication that he is included among the prophets.

Apart from that fact, we cannot be certain of much else concerning Obadiah, including his name. In Hebrew, the name means "servant or worshiper of Yahweh." While all Israelites should have been able to carry this title, it is one often used of the prophets ("my servants the prophets," e.g., 2 Kings 9:7, and sixteen further times in the Old Testament; also of individual prophets, e.g., Moses [Deut. 34:5; Jos. 1:1], Ahijah [1 Kings 14:18], Elijah [2 Kings 9:36], Jonah [2 Kings 14:25]). The name "Obadiah" could simply be a title, indicating the writer's subservient position to his Lord. It is also used as the proper name of about a dozen people in the Old Testament,[1] and this could also be the case for the writer of this book. We do not have sufficient information to argue convincingly either possibility.

Chronological Context

THE BOOK OF OBADIAH is also shy of information concerning its date. Neither links to kings (e.g., Isa. 1:1; Jer. 1:2–3; Hos. 1:1; Amos 1:1; Mic. 1:1; Zeph. 1:1; Hag. 1:1; Zech. 1:1; cf. Ezek. 1:1–2) nor natural phenomena (Amos 1:1) provide an easy handle by which to tie Obadiah's prophecies to a particular period. Any dating suggestions thus come mainly from internal evidence within the book itself.

Suggesting the earliest (*terminus a/ante quo*, "the end from/after which") and latest (*terminus ad quem*, "the end to which") possible dates of a work is based on equal parts detective work and speculation, with the latter often gaining the upper hand. These can be suggested from seeing what is included and what is omitted. An event can only be referred to after its occurrence, so the earliest recorded event in a document serves as its *terminus a quo*. On the other side, a major incident that happens but is not mentioned in a text even though

---

1. J. M. Kennedy, "Obadiah (Person)," *ABD*, 5:1–2.

this event appears important enough to the interest of the book to be included suggests that a book was completed before that event happened. This provides a *terminus ad quem*. This dating method is particularly valuable in narrative texts. In prophetic texts such as Obadiah, however, historical allusions are at times of less relevance and are thus relatively infrequent. There is also the complicating factor of a predictive prophecy, raising the question as to whether an event is described has already happened or is predicted to happen.

Two series of events lead toward at least a broad indication of date for Obadiah. The first is the complicity of Edom/Esau in the destruction of Judah (vv. 10–14), an event pictured as already in the past (v. 15b). The clearest referent to a period of invasion, plundering, destruction, and betrayal of Jerusalem and Judah is their capture by the Babylonians under the rule of Nebuchadnezzar in 586 B.C.[2] Judah and her neighbors, including Edom, were called by God to demonstrate their trust in his deliverance by submitting to Babylon (Jer. 27:3–11), but instead Edom turns against neighboring Judah (Ps. 137:7; Ezek. 35:5; 1 Esdras 4:45). Ironically, some of the Judeans dispossessed in this incident end up living in neighboring Edom (Jer. 40:11). Babylon captures the whole region at this time, including the Negev (40:20). Now, the entire nation of Israel is under foreign domination, including the northern nation of Israel who, under the Assyrians and their kings Shalmaneser and Sargon,[3] had lost its territory, including Ephraim, Samaria, and Gilead (v. 19), in 722 B.C.

Others date the historical event of verse 15 earlier. Early Jewish tradition suggests that this Obadiah is the same one who supported Elijah against Ahab in the early ninth century B.C. (1 Kings 18:1–15).[4] In the next century, Edom, conquered and placed under Israelite control by David (2 Sam. 8:12, 14; 1 Kings 11:15–16; 1 Chr. 18:11–13), rebelled against Jehoram (c. 845 B.C.; 2 Kings 8:20–22; 2 Chron. 21:8–10). Among reasons why neither of these seems to fit with the Obadiah context, however, are that there is no mention of Edomites entering Judah, as Obadiah 12–14 describes, and there is an implication that Israel has already been exiled (vv. 19–20).[5] The vivid detail with which the events are portrayed suggests that the author is an eyewitness to them and that they are not too far past in his experience.

---

2. R. H. Sack, "Nebuchadnezzar (Person)," *ABD*, 4:1058–59.

3. A. K. Grayson, "Shalmaneser (Person)," *ABD*, 5:1155.

4. See P. R. Raabe, *Obadiah: A New Translation with Introduction and Commentary* (AB 24D; New York: Doubleday, 1996), 49, for sources and other suggested links with this period.

5. For a discussion of other suggested dates, see ibid., 49–51; C. Armerding, "Obadiah," *Expositor's Bible Commentary*, ed. Frank E. Gaebelein (Grand Rapids: Zondervan, 1985), 350–51.

Obadiah pictures the destruction prophesied for Edom/Esau to lie in the future (vv. 6–10, 18, 19, 21), which happened under the Babylonian king Nabonidus in 553 B.C.[6] While the name "Edom" continues even into the New Testament period (where it becomes the Greek "Idumea," Mark 3:8; cf. 1 Macc. 4:29), this came to refer to an area southwest of the Dead Sea, in the Negev region, where the Edomites were displaced by the Arabs.[7] These events fit Obadiah most comfortably into the thirty-year period 586–553 B.C., more probably toward the beginning of that period.

Geopolitical Context

OBADIAH'S PROPHECY CONCERNS a great number of peoples and places within its brief span. These include Edom (vv. 1, 8), Sela ("the rocks," v. 3), Esau (vv. 6, 8, 9, 18[2x], 19, 21), Teman (v. 9), Jacob (vv. 10, 17, 18), Jerusalem (vv. 11, 20), Judah (v. 12), Mount Zion (vv. 17, 21), Joseph (v. 18), Negev (vv. 19, 20), Shephelah ("the foothills," v. 19), Philistines (v. 19), Ephraim (v. 19), Samaria (v. 19), Benjamin (v. 19), Gilead (v. 19), Israel (v. 20), Canaan (v. 20), Zarephath (v. 20), and Sepharad (v. 20). This is a total of a possible twenty people or place names in a short twenty-one verses. Since these names are unfamiliar to most of us, we will discuss them here, placing them into two categories, depending on their relation to Obadiah and his fellow Israelites: those with whom he would have felt connected ("Us") and the others from which he would have felt distinct ("Them").

Us

IN OBADIAH, the broadest ethnic and geographic term for God's people is "Israel," denoting the descendants of the twelve sons of Jacob/Israel (cf. Gen. 32:28; 34:7 and elsewhere). It is not only the most common self-designation for God's people, it is also used of them outside the Bible by foreigners, such as the kings of Egypt, Assyria, and Moab.[8] Later the name Israel is also used just for the northern kingdom in contrast to the southern kingdom of Judah, so we must be careful to determine exactly who is referred to. In Obadiah 20, the entire nation is meant. Jacob in Obadiah also had this broad meaning, at least in verses 17–18 (though the reference in v. 10 could also be to the southern kingdom of Judah, which is mentioned in v. 12).

---

6. P. A. Beaulieu, *The Reign of Nabonidus, King of Babylon, 556–539 B.C.* (YNER 10; New Haven, Conn.: Yale University Press, 1989), 166; cf. Raabe, *Obadiah*, 54.

7. U. Hübner, "Idumea (Place)," *ABD*, 3:382–83.

8. *COS*, 2:41, 263, 138 respectively.

Obadiah's audience most naturally would understand the designation Jacob/Israel as referring to the southern kingdom alone, since by his time the northern tribes of Israel had already been exiled by Assyria (722 B.C.). To indicate that the prophet indeed had in mind the people of both kingdoms, in verse 18 "the house of Jacob" is paralleled to "the house of Joseph." Joseph is the father of Manasseh and Ephraim (Gen. 41:51–52). Tribes descending from both sons settled in what becomes the northern kingdom (Jos. 16–17), and Ephraim rose to such a position of prestige that at times its name is used to refer to the entire northern kingdom (e.g., Isa. 7), as it does in Obadiah 19. Samaria, the city built by Omri as the northern capital (1 Kings 16:24), is also mentioned in Obadiah 19.

One further northern reference is to Gilead (v. 19). This is the area of Transjordan occupied by the tribes of Reuben, Gad, and half of Manasseh lying north and east of the Dead Sea (Num. 32:1–3; 2 Kings 10:33).[9] It later became an Assyrian province (2 Kings 15:29).

In addition to Judah, the south is represented by several peoples and places as well. While lying on the geographical border between Judah and Ephraim, Benjamin becomes most closely associated with the south (e.g., 1 Kings 12:21; 2 Chron. 11). Two other geographical areas of Judah were not identified by tribal names. The Negev (Obad. 19) refers to the arid land in the south (Josh. 15:21–32), and the "foothills" (Shephelah; so NASB, NRSV) lay between the coastal plain and the more mountainous central highlands.[10] Jerusalem, the city established as the national capital by David (2 Sam. 5:6–10; 1 Chron. 11:4–7), was later the capital of Judah, while Israel's capital is Samaria. It is also at times called by one of its topographical features, Zion (2 Sam. 5:7).

In sum, by the time of Obadiah, the northern tribes had been exiled by Assyria, and only the southern tribes remain in the land. The prophecy, however, concerns locations indicating that both parts of the original had a future role to play in the plans of their God.

Them

THE MAJOR POWER of the period was Babylonia, but it is not explicitly mentioned in Obadiah. Judah's major antagonist here is Edom, the geographical area of Transjordan stretching from the Wadi Zered at the southern extreme of the Dead Sea to the Gulf of Aqabah, part of what is present-day Jordan. The area had several names throughout history, even in the short prophecy of Obadiah itself. The most common alternative, Esau (vv. 6, 8, 9, 18, 19, 21),

---

9. M. Ottosson, "Gilead (Place)," *ABD*, 2:1020–22.
10. H. Brodsky, "Shephelah (Place)," *ABD*, 5:1204.

reflects the history of the area and its people. Esau, the elder twin of Jacob (Gen. 25:24–26), is nicknamed Edom ("red"), purportedly after the red stew of which he was fond (v. 30), but also a logical choice because of the color of his hair (v. 25).

There was conflict between the two brothers from even before their birth (vv. 22–23), and this continued as they grew (vv. 27–34; 27:1–28:9), finally forcing the younger brother to flee. Though they were reconciled later in life (Gen. 33), Esau eventually was dispossessed to the east to accommodate their growing livestock holdings (36:6) and ended up in the area of Seir (36:8), a synonym for Edom (not used in Obadiah; see Num. 24:18; Ezek. 25:8; 35:2, 3, 7, 15).[11]

The Israel–Edom/Esau national relationship is fraught with as much tension as occurred between the brothers from whom they were descended. Though biologically "family," blood did not preclude bickering. When Israel attempted to pass through their territory in Transjordan on the way from Egypt to Canaan, the Edomites refused passage (Num. 20:14–21). David conquered Edom (2 Sam. 8:12, 14; 1 Kings 11:15–16; 1 Chron. 18:11, 13), but only after Saul's inability to do so (1 Sam. 14:47). Solomon controlled Ezion Geber long enough to build ships in that Edomite seaport (1 Kings 9:26; 2 Chron. 8:17), but Hadad, a member of its royal house, rebelled against him (1 Kings 11:14–22).

Judah seems to have regained control by the time of King Jehoshaphat (871–848 B.C.), who also built trading ships associated with Ezion Geber (1 Kings 22:47). He had apparently set up a puppet ruler in place of the Edomite king ("deputy"; v. 48).[12] Soon thereafter, Jehoshaphat sallied forth in battle against Moab and his allies, including King Jehoram of Israel and "the king of Edom" (2 Kings 3:9). This is probably still the Judean puppet rather than a newly enthroned ethnic Edomite, since Edom did not enjoy such self-rule until the reign of Jehoram/Joram, the son of Jehoshaphat (848–841 B.C.; 2 Kings 8:20–22; 2 Chron. 21:8–10).

King Amaziah of Judah (800–783 B.C.) regained control of Edom with the slaughter of ten thousand of its inhabitants and the capture of its capital, Sela (2 Kings 14:7; 2 Chron. 25:11–12, 19–20). This city, mentioned in Obadiah 3, was renamed Joktheel as a sign of total control over it (2 Kings 14:7). This longstanding, antagonistic relationship between sibling groups makes it easy to understand why Edom is grouped among Israel's, and God's, perpetual enemies in poetry (Ps. 60:8, 9; 83:3; 108:9, 10) and prophecy

---

11. A. E. Knauf, "Seir (Place)," *ABD*, 5:1072–73.

12. T. J. Finley, "Obadiah," in *Joel, Amos, Obadiah* (WEC; Chicago: Moody Press, 1990), 346; Iain Provan, *1 and 2 Kings* (NIBC 7; Peabody, Mass.: Hendrickson, 1995), 169–70.

(e.g., Isa. 11:14; 63:1–6; Jer. 25:21; 49:7–22; Ezek. 25:12–14; Joel 3:19; Amos 1:6, 9, 11; Mal. 1:4).

A synonym to Edom is Teman (Obad. 9), the name of one of the tribes comprising Edom (cf. Gen. 36:11, 15).[13] Teman is also used as a geographical term, but it is unclear whether it stood for a specific place or an area within Edom.[14] It is used as a variant of the other national designations, Edom and Esau. This is a similar usage to that of the name Sela, translated "rocks" in the NIV (Obad. 3; cf. text note). The name is also that of the capital of Edom captured by Amaziah (2 Kings 14:7; see also Judg. 1:36; Isa. 16:1; 42:11; Jer. 49:16), an appropriate name since Sela is identified by the LXX with the Nabataean city of Petra, which was literally carved from the rock. Petra is best known to people today from its depiction in the movie *Indiana Jones and the Last Crusade*. While this identification of Petra as the location mentioned in Obadiah 3 is romantic, it is probably not correct, since no remains have been discovered in Petra that predate the fourth century B.C.[15]

Other geographical terms refer to places having a history of opposition against Israel. The Philistines (v. 19) were part of the Sea People who originated in the Aegean. They invaded the eastern Mediterranean coast from Egypt to Syria in the late second millennium B.C., and so were vying for the same territory as Israel during this period, with the Philistines settling in five cities in the coastal and lowland areas of Palestine: Gaza, Ashkelon, Ashdod, Gath, and Ekron.[16] The two nations had several military encounters (see Judges; 1 Sam. 4, 13, 31), with David defeating them, breaking their strength but not wiping them out (1 Sam. 17; 18:6–9, 25–27, 30; 19:8).

Canaan (Obad. 20) is the name of the Promised Land prior to Israelite occupation (Gen. 50:11), from part of Syria in the north through what is now Lebanon as well as Israel east of the Mediterranean and west of the Jordan River. Remnants of this population in the land after Israelite occupation caused theological problems, since Israel was constantly tempted by the Canaanite religious practices.[17]

Zarephath (Obad. 20) is one of the northern Canaanite cities, located equidistantly between Tyre and Sidon. Even though a pagan city, it is the place to which Elijah escaped from both famine and the Israelite king Ahab

---

13. E. A. Knauf, "Teman (Person)," *ABD*, 6:347–48.

14. Raabe, *Obadiah*, 166.

15. A. Negev, *NEAEHL*, 1181.

16. H. J. Katzenstein, "Philistines, History," and T. Dothan, "Philistines, Archaeology," *ABD*, 5:326–28 and 328–33, respectively.

17. P. C. Schmitz, "Canaan (Place)," and J. Day, "Canaan, Religion of," *ABD*, 1:828–31 and 831–37, respectively.

(1 Kings 17:8–24; Luke 4:26). The irony of this incident is that this is the area from which Ahab's Phoenician wife Jezebel had come (1 Kings 16:31).

The last named location, Sepharad (Obad. 20), has been difficult to identify, since its name is unique here. Suggestions in Spain (*Tg. Jon.*; contemporary Jewish identification of Spanish-speaking Jews as "Sephardic" comes from this identification), Asia Minor (Sardis, capital of the Lydians c. 685–547 B.C.), and Media (based on an Assyrian text; cf. 2 Kings 17:6; 18:11) have been made.[18]

Literary Context

OBADIAH, WITH ONLY twenty-one verses, is the shortest Old Testament book. It occurs fourth among the Minor Prophets, but any reason for its placement there is uncertain, since the Twelve are not arranged either by size or by date. A word tie with Edom in Amos 9:12 could explain why Obadiah immediately follows that book.[19]

Literary Form

THOUGH BRIEF, Obadiah consists of several different literary genres. The two main types are prose and poetry. The main body of the book (vv. 1a–18) is poetry, as shown by the Hebrew poetic devices of parallelism of ideas and syllable or stress patterns.[20] This is "sandwiched" between two prose passages, the brief superscript or title and messenger formula (1a-b), and a brief statement at the end of verse 18.

The superscript identifies the entire book as a vision report (Heb. *ḥªzôn*). While the Hebrew term *ḥzh* at times relates to natural, physical sight (e.g., Ps. 58:8; Prov. 24:32; Isa. 33:20), it could be used of seeing God (e.g., Job 19:26–27; Ps. 17:15), and it most commonly describes the content of the message received upon seeing God in the context of prophecy.[21] This divine source is reiterated in the second prose note in verse 18b.

The poetic section starts with a divine summons to battle (Obad. 1c), followed by a direct divine speech of judgment directed to a single nation (Edom, vv. 2–14, 15b), which is interrupted by a declaration of divine speech (v. 8b). Then follows a reported judgment speech directed to all the nations

---

18. J. D. Wineland, "Sepharad (Place)," *ABD*, 5:1089–90; Raabe, *Obadiah*, 266–68.
19. Leslie C. Allen, "Obadiah," in *The Books of Joel, Obadiah, Jonah, and Micah* (NICOT; Grand Rapids: Eerdmans, 1976), 129.
20. Raabe, *Obadiah*, 6–14.
21. Ibid., 94–96; see also J. A. Naudé, "חזה," *NIDOTTE*, 2:56–61.

(vv. 15a, 16–18a-f), which concludes with a divine speech marker (v. 18g). The entire prophecy concludes with a promise of salvation (vv. 19–21).

Composition

FOR SUCH A small book, Obadiah is brimming with questions regarding the process of its composition. The mixtures of prose and poetry, Edom and the nations, judgment and hope, and second and third person sections contribute to the discussion. Raabe describes no less than nine different views as to the history of the composition of the book, ranging from it being completely from the hand of a single author, whether on one occasion or several, to coming from eight originally separate fragments.[22]

Whatever the prehistory of the work, there are clear uniting elements across its present form. The pervading presence of geographical terms has already been discussed, and Yahweh ("the LORD") both opens (v. 1[2x]) and closes (v. 21) the book (see also vv. 4, 8, 15, 18). It is significant that God is only identified in it by this personal name, not by the more general description "God" (*ʾĕlōhîm*; see "Theology," below). Two other words used throughout the book are "the nations" (vv. 1, 2, 15, 16) and "day" (vv. 8, 11[2x], 12[4x], 13[3x], 14, 15). While these unifying points could be the work of an editor, to my mind there is no compelling reason to deny it to the hand of one author, especially since with this kind of literary artistry, the distinction between author and editor becomes problematic. A mixture of prose and poetry is not at all a rare phenomenon in Hebrew prophecy (cf. Isa. 36–37:22a, 36–38:9, 21–39:8; Amos 7:12–17 as only several examples of many prose passages sandwiched within poetic material).

Obadiah and the Old Testament

SINCE OBADIAH IS part of a national literature, one expects themes and concepts to be shared with other literary pieces from the culture. There are some parallels, however, that point to more than simply a common culture. The closest of these are between Obadiah and Jeremiah. Note Obadiah 1–4 and Jeremiah 49:14–16 below, with exact Hebrew verbal parallels in bold face and differences within these in italics, so that the parallels can be more readily seen:

---

22. Raabe, *Obadiah*, 16–17; see also Allen, "Obadiah," 133–35; Finley, "Obadiah," 348–49.

Obadiah	Jeremiah 49
¹ ***We*** have heard a message from the LORD: An envoy was sent to the nations to say, "Rise, and let us go **against her for battle**"—	¹⁴ ***I*** have heard a message from the LORD: An envoy was sent to the nations to say, "Assemble yourselves to attack it! **Rise up [against her] for battle!**"
² "See, **I will make you small among the nations**; you will be utterly **despised**.	¹⁵ "Now **I will make you small among the nations**, despised among men.
³ The **pride of your heart has deceived you, you who live in the clefts of the rocks** and make your home on the **heights**, you who say to yourself, 'Who can bring me down to the ground?'	¹⁶ The terror you inspire and **the pride of your heart have deceived you, you who live in the clefts of the rocks,** who occupy the **heights** of the hill.
⁴ Though **you soar like the eagle** and make **your nest** among the stars, **from there I will bring you down**," declares the LORD.	Though **you build your nest** as high as the eagle's, from **there I will bring you down**," declares the LORD.

Jeremiah provides further parallels, such as Jeremiah 49:9–10c with Obadiah 5–6.

Obadiah	Jeremiah 49
⁵ "**If thieves** came to you, if robbers in the **night**—Oh, what a disaster awaits you—would they not steal **only as much as they wanted?**	⁹ᶜ**If thieves** came during the **night**, would they not steal **only as much as they wanted?**
If grape pickers came to you, would they not leave a few grapes? ⁶ But how **Esau** will be ransacked, his hidden treasures pillaged!	⁹ᵃ **If grape pickers came to you, would they not leave a few grapes?** ¹⁰ But I will strip **Esau** bare; I will uncover his hiding places,

Parallels between Obadiah 7–8 and Jeremiah 49:7 are subtler and less sustained, as well as being hidden in English translation, as shown below.

Obadiah	Jeremiah 49
[7] but you will **not** detect it. [8] "In that day," declares the LORD, "**will I not destroy the wise men of** Edom, men of understanding in the mountains of Esau?	[7] **Is there no** longer **wisdom in** Teman? Has counsel **perished from** the prudent? Has their **wisdom** decayed?

Obadiah 7 contains a sentence found almost verbatim in Jeremiah 38:22, with only three consonants differing between the two.

Obadiah	Jeremiah 38
[7] your friends will deceive and overpower you;	[22] They misled you and overcame you—those trusted friends of yours.

The cumulative evidence indicates that there is some dependence between Obadiah and Jeremiah. There are three possible relationships here: (1) Jeremiah borrows from Obadiah, (2) Obadiah borrows from Jeremiah, or (3) both Jeremiah and Obadiah borrow from a third source. There is no compelling evidence leading to any of these three alternatives, though Jeremiah's activities, if not the penning of his prophecies, were in the late seventh to early sixth centuries B.C., prior to the date for Obadiah adopted here (though the dating of the material in Jeremiah is not without its own complications).[23] This argues against option 1. Option 3 cannot be ruled out, even though there is no known copy of the possible third source. The fact that the two writers differ from each other in such significant ways in spite of the numerous parallels could indicate that both freely adapt a third source. Alternatively, if one borrows from the other, they did not do so slavishly, but show their own literary creativity in their adaptations.[24]

---

23. E.g., B. D. Sommer, "New Light on the Composition of Jeremiah," *CBQ* 61 (1999): 646–66; W. McKane, *A Critical and Exegetical Commentary on Jeremiah*, 2 vols. (ICC; Edinburgh: T. & T. Clark, 1986, 1996), 1:xv–xcvii; 2:cxxxiii–clxxiv.

24. See Allen, "Obadiah," 132–33; Finley, "Obadiah," 342–45, and Raabe, *Obadiah*, 22–31 for further discussion of Jeremiah's relation to Obadiah.

Theology

Yahweh

JUDAH AS A NATION is vulnerable, since those to whom they might turn for support based on fraternal ties repeatedly turn against her. The prophet shows her that she is not without trustworthy support, however, since she is cared for by Yahweh, who is the Creator of heaven and earth (Gen. 2:4). Rather than using the more distant title "God" (*ʾĕlōhîm*), Israel's deity speaks to them using his personal, covenant name ("the LORD" [*yhwh*, Yahweh]).

While intimate, Yahweh is also powerful, the king of nations (v. 21) who engages in battle (v. 2) against both warrior and sage (vv. 9, 8), allowing neither human brilliance nor might to thwart his aims. This stark contrast to the powerless state in which Judah finds herself convincingly points her, and her enemies, to the necessity to turn beyond natural national resources for real aid. Yahweh is also the God of the ages. He takes his people, whom he established at Mount Sinai (Ex. 19–24), in their present difficulties with their lifelong fraternal rivals, and he offers them hope. He will restore his kingdom on Zion, the site captured by David (2 Sam. 5:7; 1 Chron. 11:5). There he had chosen to erect his temple (1 Kings 8:1; 2 Chron. 5:2), but allowed it to be destroyed because of Israel's sin (Mic. 3:12).

Responsibility and Justice

ACTIONS DO AND must have consequences. Choices, whether for good or ill, have results, and part of the maturation process is learning this, whether as a child or as a nation. Neither can attain independence if protected from understanding this. The lack of a punishment for a willfully wrong action cheapens one's humanity.[25] This being so, the punishment meted out on Edom is an indication of their responsibility for their choice to harass rather than assist their brothers in their national plight.

"Will not the Judge of all the earth do right?"(Gen. 18:25), Abraham reminded the Judge himself. Obadiah is not simply a nationalistic diatribe by Judah against her enemies and thus something below a true theology of compassion and forgiveness, as some claim.[26]

---

25. See C. S. Lewis, "The Humanitarian View of Punishment," reprinted in *God in the Dock: Essays on Theology and Ethics* (Grand Rapids: Eerdmans, 1970), 288.

26. E.g., G. A. Smith, *The Book of the Twelve Prophets* (London: Hodder & Stoughton, 1928), 2:179.

Grace

MEANING DERIVES FROM context, and the historical context of this prophecy is vital in order to understand the grace of Yahweh in it. Judah was destroyed and taken into captivity in 586 B.C. because they had broken covenant loyalty. Her sister, Israel, had suffered the same fate for the same reasons in 722 B.C. The Babylonians and Assyrians do not take to vassals defying their authority by ignoring the obligations laid on them, which include fealty to the overlord accompanied by material donations of tribute to keep the overlord's coffers full. Breach of covenant leads to swift and severe retaliation, including destruction, deportation, and barbaric cruelty.[27] This is what Judah and Israel have received from their secular overlords (2 Kings 15:19–20, 29; 17:1–18:12; 18:13–19:37; 24:10–17, 20b–25:22; 1 Chron. 5:6, 26; 2 Chron. 32:1–23; 33:11; 36:10, 15–21; Ezra 4:2; Isa. 36–37; Jer. 52:3b–30).

This is also the just response to turning their back on obligations to the "Great King," Yahweh, with whom Israel also entered into a covenant. The curses brought for breaking this relationship involved exile and suffering, though not the barbarity imposed by humans (e.g., Lev. 26:14–39; Deut. 29:28; 1 Kings 8:33–46; 14:16). The destruction of Jerusalem and the end of the Davidic monarchy, at least its enthronement in Zion, should not, therefore, be surprising. What is surprising, and unique among ancient Near Eastern covenants, is that forgiveness, the possibility of a second chance, is incorporated into the covenant document itself (e.g., Deut. 30, esp. 1–5). The very fact of the continued existence of the recipients of the prophecy, even after they earn annihilation, is itself an aspect of God's grace. The punishment, which is wholly justified, serves its disciplinary purpose of driving the people back to a relationship with their God. Even pain can be a grace.[28]

God's grace to his people extends beyond their basic survival in Obadiah. Judah receives blessing in that their tormenters will be punished. But it does not even stop there. While a mortally wounded soldier might feel some reward in seeing that his enemy is also doomed, it is much more beneficial to know that he himself will survive. In Judah's case, they are assured not only of survival, but they will even flourish, being not only delivered but restored.

27. B. Oded, *Mass Deportations and Deportees in the Neo–Assyrian Empire* (Wiesbaden: Ludwig Reichert Verlag, 1979).

28. See, e.g., D. W. Baker, "Aspects of Grace in the Pentateuch," *ATJ* 29 (1997): 7–22.

Outline of Obadiah

1. Modified from A. Pope, *Essay on Man*, Epistle 1, line 123.

Annotated Bibliography on Obadiah

Baker, D. W. "Obadiah." Pages 12–44 in *Obadiah, Jonah and Micah*. Ed. D. W. Baker, T. D. Alexander, B. K. Waltke. TOTC 23a. Downers Grove, Ill.: InterVarsity Press, 1988. A brief, popular level exposition.

Barton, John. *Joel and Obadiah*. OTL. Louisville: Westminster John Knox, 2001. A useful mainline look at historical and linguistic backgrounds.

Ben Zvi, E. *A Historical-Critical Study of the Book of Obadiah*. BZAW 242. Berlin/New York: Walter de Gruyter, 1996. Not a commentary, but an in-depth study using untransliterated, untranslated Hebrew.

Clark, D. J., and N. Mundhenk. *A Translator's Handbook on the Books of Obadiah and Micah*. Helps for Translators. London/New York: United Bible Society, 1982. Useful analysis of individual words and phrases for translation. Not a regular commentary.

Finley, T. J. "Obadiah." Pages 339–80 in *Joel, Amos, Obadiah*. WEC. Chicago: Moody Press, 1990. Useful in-depth analysis of Hebrew text. Mostly accessible to those without Hebrew. Reprint: Finley Reprint. Dallas, Tex.: j1 Biblical Studies Press, 2003.

Limburg, J. "The Book of Obadiah." Pages 127–36 in *Hosea–Micah*. Interpretation. Atlanta: John Knox, 1988. A brief commentary seeking to find application for the church.

Niehaus, J. "Obadiah." Pages 495–541 in *The Minor Prophets: An Exegetical and Expository Commentary*, vol. 2. Ed. T. E. McComiskey. Grand Rapids: Baker, 1993. Short but useful look at textual, historical, and theological issues from a conservative perspective.

Raabe, P. R. *Obadiah: A New Translation with Introduction and Commentary*. AB 24D. New York: Doubleday, 1996. An excellent, detailed study of the book as a unified work.

Stuart, D. "Obadiah." Pages 402–22. *Hosea–Jonah*. WBC 31. Waco, Tex.: Word, 1987. A useful commentary, especially for bibliography and the Hebrew text.

Wolff, H. W. "The Prophet Obadiah." Pages 15–71 in *Obadiah and Jonah: A Commentary*. Minneapolis: Augsburg, 1986. A technical commentary with extensive bibliography, viewing the prophecy as a composite.

Obadiah 1–4

THE VISION OF Obadiah.

This is what the Sovereign LORD says about Edom—

We have heard a message from the LORD:
    An envoy is sent to the nations to say,
    "Rise, and let us go against her for battle"—

² "See, I will make you small among the nations;
    you will be utterly despised.
³ The pride of your heart has deceived you,
    you who live in the clefts of the rocks
    and make your home on the heights,
you who say to yourself,
    'Who can bring me down to the ground?'
⁴ Though you soar like the eagle
    and make your nest among the stars,
    from there I will bring you down,"

declares the LORD.

OBADIAH 1 GIVES the title of the book, its author, and an indication of its nature. It is a summons, not to peace and tranquility, as in some prophetic messages, but to the violence and destruction of war. The summons is also not to God's people, a call for them to respond and return, but rather to outsiders, unusual recipients of God's message. It includes a word to those who will be attacked, showing why they will be brought low.

In the sparsest title in the prophets the writer indicates the literary genre of the work and its originator. He identifies his work as a "vision" (*ḥᵃzôn*), which is used as a title for only two other Old Testament prophets (Isaiah, Isa. 1:1; cf. 2 Chron. 32:32; and Nahum, in the slightly longer form "the book of the vision," Nah. 1:1). Verbs from the same root (*ḥzh*) have as their subject other prophets (e.g., Moses, Ex. 18:21; Balaam, Num. 24:4, 16; Isaiah, Isa. 1:1; 2:1; 13:1; Amos, Amos 1:1; Habakkuk, Hab. 1:1).

Where the noun *ḥᵃzôn* relates to a named person, it is as a subjective genitive, with the person named performing the visionary action. Though the verb can be used of physical sight (e.g., Ps. 58:8), the noun only refers to prophetic perception, indicating the content of what is seen rather than the act of perceiving (cf. Ps. 89:19). For example, in Balaam's fourth oracle, it parallels the words and knowledge that derive from God (Num. 24:16–17). It is a neutral term as regards content, needing modification to indicate whether it is good (e.g., Ps. 17:2; Isa. 30:10) or ill (e.g., Isa. 30:10; Lam. 2:14; Ezek 13:6, 8, 9).

The original hearers of the prophecies would expect "vision" in such a title to mean a message from God through his named prophet. This expectation is confirmed here when Yahweh affirms four times that he is the One speaking (vv. 1, 4, 8, 18). The expectation of a divine source is of first importance, so the lack of some of the material commonly found in other prophetic books regarding specific dates (cf. Amos 1:1) or family background of the prophet (cf. Isa. 1:1) is not a concern.

The next sentence is a "messenger formula" (v. 1b), since the speaker is acting on behalf of another—a common practice in Israel (e.g., Gen 32:5; Ex. 5:10). It derives from its Near Eastern context where literacy was rare, and messages, even if transmitted in writing, needed to be read aloud by the messenger.[1] Readers/hearers were aware that this formula indicates that the messenger did not speak on his own authority but on the authority of the one whose name follows.

The framer of the message is identified by the modified proper noun "Sovereign LORD," or more literally "my lord [ᵃdōnay; title], Yahweh [proper name]." This combination has become fossilized, so that the personal designation has become lost. Note the various instances of God using the title of himself (e.g., 2 Kings 19:23; Ezek. 29:16), so it comes to be read as "the Lord Yahweh." Most English translations hide the personal name of God, "Yahweh," behind a substitute "LORD," thus resulting in a translational difficulty in this case, where consistency demands a rendering "my Lord LORD." This complication is avoided among the major English translations only by JB, where "Yahweh" more accurately reflects the Hebrew.

The divine title indicates the subservient position of the speaker in relation to the addressee, acknowledging the authority of the latter. This could be metaphorical, since it is used in polite address as we do with the English "sir" (e.g., Ruth 2:13), but at times the social distance is literal. The usage is therefore appropriate when speaking of the Creator of the universe.

The message regards Edom, Israel's eastern neighbor. In every other case where the present construction is used in the exact order of "messenger formula + preposition *lᵉ* + indirect object" (e.g., Gen. 32:4 [Esau]; 2 Chron. 20:15 [king of Jerusalem and its inhabitants]; Isa. 45:1 [messiah Cyrus]), the

---

1. See the study by S. A. Meier, *The Messenger in the Ancient Semitic World* (HSM 45; Atlanta: Scholars, 1988); Raabe, *Obadiah*, 99–105.

preposition indicates the one "*to whom*" the vision is to be delivered, and NIV uniformly translates accordingly. Obadiah 1 is the only instance where NIV translates this construction as "about," though it does translate *lᵉ* elsewhere as "concerning, about" (e.g., Num. 9:8; Jer. 46:2; 48:1; 49:1, 7, 23, 28), though never where the other two elements of the construction used in Obadiah 1 are present.[2] In general, "concerning, about" translates the preposition *ᶜal* (e.g., Gen. 24:9; 47:26; Amos 1–2; Micah 3:5).[3] In other words, based on customary usage, the message in Obadiah is directed *to* Edom rather than just being *about* Edom.

Most regard the prophetic messages found in Scripture to address the Israelites, even if other nations are named in their headings (e.g., Jer. 1:4–10, which designates Jeremiah as a prophet to the nations; cf. 46:1). While only one prophet, Jonah, actually addresses a foreign nation directly (3:3–5), it is possible that prophets were, at least indirectly, addressing those outside the land. Prophecies were not given in secret, and word likely reaches the intended hearers without undue difficulty. Evidence for domestic and international delivery of news comes from several sources. In Amos 7:10 a message is relayed from a priest to the king. In Number 23–24 Balaam delivers his oracles, which are couched in terms of the promises to Abra(ha)m from Genesis 12:1–3; 17. Balaam would have had no firsthand knowledge of these promises since he is not an Israelite. He had, therefore, become aware of these promises by some other means of news delivery, whether by human or divine messenger.

Verse 1c introduces Yahweh as the originator of another message, this time a report (cf. Isa. 28:19; 53:1; Ezek. 21:7) concerning a call to battle (see Jer. 6:22–24 for another reported battle). Obadiah and others "have heard" the report, with "we" identifying Obadiah either with his contemporaries in Judah or with the tradition of prophets of which he is a part (cf. Jer. 49:14, where the [earlier?] prophecy had a singular, "I heard").[4] The extent of the report is most likely the rest of this verse.[5]

A messenger, an official representative from Yahweh (cf. Isa. 57:9; Prov. 25:13), is sent to call the nations to war against the land of Edom ("her"; cf. Jer. 49:17). They were not simple witnesses of Yahweh's case against wrongdoers (e.g., Isa. 43:9; Ezek. 16:37) or recipients of his punishment

---

2. See *DCH*, 4:482; *HALOT*, sub ל, 6.

3. *HALOT*, sub ל, II, 3.

4. For the former position, see Allen, "Obadiah," 145; for the latter position, see Raabe, *Obadiah*, 113.

5. So Raabe, *Obadiah*, 113; Allen ("Obadiah," 144) suggests that the actual report is not included in the book.

(e.g., Joel 3:1; Zeph. 3:8), but participators in it. It is not just the nations who fight, however, but Yahweh himself joins in with them ("let us").

National pride is a characteristic of nations, in the biblical period and even today. What starts as justifiable pride in national achievements can become chauvinistic when others are either ignored in their need or put down as below one's self-inflated position of superiority. The Edomites had this attitude, and their neighbors in Judah were feeling the brunt of it. They are now, and for the remainder of the book, addressed through the use of masculine ("you") forms, referring to the people in contrast to the grammatically feminine land.[6]

"See, look, something of immediate importance is coming next" (*hinnēh*) all are possible renderings of the Hebrew particle that opens God's message to Edom in verse 2. This particle and the Hebrew word order emphasize that the Hebrew word "small, insignificant" does not regard number but rather size or significance. Size was usually not an issue, since most of the other regional states in the area, such as Moab, Ammon, Israel, Judah, and the Philistines, were not geographically large (cf. Eccl. 9:14). Significance, honor, or status was a different matter, however, especially for those like Edom who had a vaunted self-image. To be small in significance was to be "despised," as the second half of verse 2 indicates. In an area vying for national prominence, diminution of esteem was degrading as well as dangerous, because it was viewed as a sign of weakness and an opportunity to attack.

According to verse 3, Edom vaunts herself because of the strategic advantage she enjoys over her neighbors as a result of her geographical setting. A topographical map indicates that the land of Canaan steadily rises going eastward from the Mediterranean Sea. Jerusalem is situated in the central highlands in Judah, but after the steep descent toward the Dead Sea and the Arabah to its south, the land rises precipitously to the even higher plateau (up to 5,500 feet), on which Edom is situated. Land passage through this territory is often through narrow passages between towering rocks, a way that is easily blocked by a few well-placed soldiers.

Geographically, therefore, Edom is impregnable to outside military forces. This is in contrast to neighboring Judah to the west. She has the disadvantage of lying athwart a coastal plain along major trade routes. This opened her up not only to the wealth of passing merchant caravans, but also to the pillaging of army movements, which happened all too frequently in her history.

Edom's military advantage puffs up her national pride to a point of arrogance. She is convinced of her inviolability enough to brag of it. This

---

6. H. W. Wolff, "The Prophet Obadiah," in *Obadiah and Jonah: A Commentary* (Minneapolis: Augsburg, 1986), 33.

is not a justified self-esteem deriving from some actual preeminence, but rather a deceptive self-vaunting. As the first woman was deceived by the serpent in the Garden into rising above her level of adequacy (Gen. 3:13), so Edom leads herself astray. Her pride raises her even above her earthbound heights. She likens herself to an eagle who can soar and nest above the high terrain (Obad. 4; cf. Job 39:27; Prov. 23:5), or even above the earth itself, to the very stars, the outer reaches of their existence (Job 22:12).

Unfortunately for Edom, her survey to every horizon of the military might to which she considers herself superior does not include a glance heavenward, where the greatest threat to arrogance lies. It is not a human army who brings Edom down, but the warrior God (Amos 9:2). He leaves the nation a diminished and "despised" people. She does not consider Israel's God, who created those same stars (Gen. 1:16) and who is also referred to as an eagle (Deut. 32:11; Jer. 49:22). It is this God, Yahweh, who speaks these words of judgment, as indicated by the phrase "declares the LORD," which occurs numerous times in the prophets.

Bridging Contexts

MESSENGERS AND MESSAGES. Literacy was rare in the ancient Near Eastern world because of the complex writing systems of the major societies such as Egypt and Mesopotamia. Messages, if written, were recorded by scribes and delivered orally to the recipient, who also likely was illiterate. It is, therefore, of vital importance to indicate clearly both the source and the recipient. The former is necessary since it is under the sender's authority, rather than that of the messenger, that the message is to be understood. The words were not those of the messenger but of his sponsor. This is clear also in the context of Old Testament prophecy, where the authority of the message does not lie in the prophetic messenger but in the divine sender, Yahweh himself.

This position of the messenger as intermediary is how God pictures the roles of Moses and Aaron when confronting Pharaoh (Ex. 7:1–2) and is indicated frequently in the prophetic books when they state that the words are those of Yahweh (e.g., "This is what the LORD says," over 300 times in the prophets; "declares the LORD," over 350 times). In the same way that neither Moses nor any kings claimed authorship of the law, so the prophets do not claim to be originators of their messages to the people. In fact, prophecies of human origination were specifically declared as false (Jer. 23:30–31, 36). It is due to Obadiah's position as a messenger of God that his warning to Edom needs to be heeded.

God as warrior. Israel as a nation entered into the Promised Land through battle (Joshua), and through battle lost it again (2 Kings 17:3–6; 18:9–11; 25:1–7; Jer. 39:1–7; 52:4–11). Throughout its history Israel faced armed conflict, so the metaphor of the Lord as a warrior God is most appropriate (Ex. 15:3; Ps. 24:8).[7] Starting life as a slave race with no army, Israel needed instruction in warfare from God, even in as elementary matters as determining potential able-bodied fighters (Num. 1:2–3). Yahweh himself takes their side numerous times in battle, leading them with "an outstretched arm" (e.g. Deut. 4:34; 7:19; cf. Exod. 17:16; 1 Sam. 17:47; 1 Chron. 5:22; 2 Chron. 20:15, 17). Deities depicted as warriors were common among Israel's Near Eastern neighbors.[8] Yahweh defends his people through warfare, but his end goal is peace, not only for Israel but for all humanity. This is a role carried on by Jesus in his defeat of natural calamities, the demonic, disease, and even death (e.g., Mark 4:35–5:43).

Nationalism. Nationalistic pride is not the domain of Edom alone but characterizes the human race, both in terms of ethnic as well as ecclesiological associations. Humanity is pictured as reaching toward heaven from their habitation in Babylon early in human history (Gen. 11:1–11, esp. v. 4; cf. Job 20:6; Prov. 21:24) just as Babylon did much later (Isa. 14:12–14; Jer. 51:55; cf. Isa. 13:19; Hab. 2:2–5). While one might expect such self-confidence on the part of the world powers (cf. Assyria, 2 Kings 19:22; Isa. 10:12; Zech. 10:11; Egypt, Ezek. 32:12), it is also evident among smaller states (Moab, Isa. 16:6; 25:10–11; Jer. 48:29; Tyre, Isa. 23:9; Ezek. 28:2; Philistines, Zech. 9:6). Even Israel and Judah are not immune (Israel, Isa. 9:9; 28:1–3; Hos. 5:5; Amos 9:2; Judah, Jer. 13:9, 17; Zeph. 3:11). Pride in might, whether through armed forces, chariotry, or horses, is misplaced, however, since it is Yahweh who brings these into being (Isa. 43:16–17), and he brings them down (Jer. 51:20–21; Zech. 9:10). The battle is ultimately in God's hands (Prov. 21:31), not in that of any nation.

---

7. See M. C. Lind, *Yahweh Is a Warrior: The Theology of Warfare in Ancient Israel* (Scottdale, Pa.: Herald, 1980); D. Bergant, "Yahweh: A Warrior God?" in *The Church's Peace Witness*, ed. M. E. Miller and B. N. Gingerich (Grand Rapids: Eerdmans, 1994), 89–103; T. Longman III and D. Reid, *God Is a Warrior* (Grand Rapids: Zondervan, 1995); E. Gerstenberger, *Yahweh the Patriarch: Ancient Images of God and Feminist Theology* (Minneapolis: Fortress, 1996), 38–54; G. A. Boyd, *God at War: The Bible and Spiritual Conflict* (Downers Grove, Ill.: InterVarsity Press, 1997); M. Klingbeil, *Yahweh Fighting from Heaven: God as Warrior and as God of Heaven in the Hebrew Psalter and Ancient Near Eastern Iconography* (Göttingen: Vandenhoeck & Ruprecht, 1999).

8. M. Weinfeld, "Divine Intervention in War in Ancient Israel and in the Ancient Near East," in *History, Historiography and Interpretation: Studies in Biblical and Cuneiform Literatures* (Jerusalem: Magnes, 1983), 121–47; S-M. Kang, *Divine War in the Old Testament and in the Ancient Near East* (BZAW 175; Berlin: Walter de Gruyter, 1989), 11–110, concerning Mesopotamia, Egypt, Syro-Palestine, and Anatolia.

Contemporary Significance

"IN THE NAME of the LORD." Like the false prophets of old who spoke their own words for their own gain, society and the church today hear siren calls to follow.

- "Invest in technology, because its growth is assured!"
- "Commit suicide so we might be able to become one with the God of the comet!"
- "Send money to my ministry and God will increase it a hundred times!"

Israel listens for a word from Yahweh, which they will recognize if it comes to pass (Deut. 18:22, ruling out the first statement above), if it points toward God and not another (Deut. 13:2; 18:20, ruling out the second statement), and if it is not self-appointed and self-serving (Jer. 14:14; Ezek. 13:19; cf. 2 Cor. 2:16, ruling out the third statement). God spoke to his people through his messengers the prophets, and he continues to do so, through his Word of Scripture and through his servants today. What is needed is careful discernment, openness to God's revelation, and also continuing acknowledgment that the evaluative criteria for that Word have not changed. If attention is directed to the messenger instead of the One who sent her, those who hear must be very cautious.

Personal pride. There is a fine line between self-confidence, self-reliance, and pride. God calls and equips people to various tasks from the garden (Gen. 1:28) through the Exodus (Ex. 3:7–12a; 6:30–7:2), from the time of the settlement of the land (Judg. 2:16) to its resettlement after the Exile (Neh. 1), from the commissioning of the church (Matt. 28:16–20) to its culmination (Rev. 22:9). In each instance the primary focus is to be on the task and the preparation for it, not on the obstacles challenging it or on the person to whom it is delegated.

A diversion in either direction can easily derail the mission. When Israel was directed to take the land, she sent in spies to survey it. When they concentrated on the obstacles, they were overwhelmed and refused to fulfill their calling (Num. 13:26–29, 31–33). Only those who understood the capability that accompanied the commissioning were confident in themselves because they were confident in God (v. 30). He was the warrior on their behalf; they did not need to take the land themselves. The church today needs to take this to heart as well: God does not leave us to defeat sin and the enemy on our own.

At other times attention to one's self and one's own capabilities or calling get in the way. Saul was commissioned to defeat and annihilate the Amalekites (1 Sam. 15:1–3). Formerly unable to believe that he had anything to offer

God or his people (9:21; 10:22), now he felt that he did not even need God's instruction; he was able to make his own decisions even if they ran counter to God's specific instructions (15:9, 15, 20–21). He had become so self-confident he did not even understand what he had done wrong.

Pride, defined in the dictionary as "a high or inordinate opinion of one's own dignity, importance, merit, or superiority," characterizes our age, at least in Western culture. "I did it my way," says a popular song of not too long ago, and unfortunately the same attitude invades the church. One of the problems of self-reliance and pride is that one is not open to correction; after all, if I am right, why should I listen to what anyone else thinks? One of the advantages of the community of faith is not only to find support when one is hurting, but also to find guidance when one is lost. Edom is sure of its safety and impregnability. Some individuals and churches think they too have it all together; they know what God is saying since they believe that he is speaking directly to them. The church is still hurting from leaders with these ideas—Jim Jones and David Koresh, Jimmy Swaggart and Jimmy Bakker.

Americans pride themselves in freedom, autonomy, and self-reliance, but where is there also accountability? Denominations and structures are not God's ultimate answer to the unity of his body, because they too often degenerate into ecclesiological nationalism. However, if we are out of fellowship with a wider body of believers, whether within a church or as a church in a wider circle of influence, where is our accountability? What will temper our pride and keep us from doing what is right in our own eyes?

⁵"If thieves came to you,
   if robbers in the night—
Oh, what a disaster awaits you—
   would they not steal only as much as they wanted?
If grape pickers came to you,
   would they not leave a few grapes?
⁶But how Esau will be ransacked,
   his hidden treasures pillaged!
⁷All your allies will force you to the border;
   your friends will deceive and overpower you;
those who eat your bread will set a trap for you,
   but you will not detect it.

Original Meaning

EDOM FINDS THAT far from being impregnable, after her arrogance is brought low, she is open to attack, even from her allies. She is a prime candidate for such incursions, since she has gained a measure of wealth through overland trade that passed through her via the King's Highway (Num. 20:17),[1] as well as through maritime trade (1 Kings 9:26–28). There are also copper mines in the region.[2] A country that has resources but is unable to defend them is ready prey. The Hebrew perfect or affix verb forms used in this section most often indicates completed action, though we can discern no specific episode in Edom's past to which this might refer.

The prophet begins this section by asking a rhetorical question, thus capturing the people's attention. He draws on national experiences of looting and plunder, which, though bad enough, are far less than what Edom could expect. The loss is due to habitual sneak-thieves (Gen. 31:39; cf. Ex. 20:15) or more violent, devastating plunderers (Jer. 12:12). Their crimes are accentuated since they happen at night, a time when unsuspecting citizens are not vigilant.

The author highlights the heinous nature of the crime by inserting an almost involuntary exclamation, whose introductory interjection "Oh" can

---

1. S. C. Carroll, "King's Highway (Place)," *ABD*, 4:48–49.
2. B. Rothenberg, "Timnah," *NEAEHL*, 4:1475–86.

indicate horror (Jer. 51:41) or lament (Isa. 1:21; Jer. 48:17). The exact content of the interjection is unclear, since the Hebrew verb involved (*dmh*) can mean either "to be similar" (e.g., Ezek. 32:2) or "to be destroyed" (NIV "disaster"; e.g., Isa. 6:5). Either use fits the context, and the author perhaps uses this ambiguous verb on purpose. It is a thing of horror, whether Edom is destroyed or whether they are themselves acting like the plundering thieves (vv. 11–14). This multi-meaning word was possibly selected on purpose since it supplies a wordplay with the sound "Edom" (*ʾdm*).[3]

These plunderers limit their haul, taking only enough to satisfy their needs (cf. Ex. 36:7) and not completely stripping their victims. At least these brigands have boundaries, and these are understood by the hearers, who are expected to answer the rhetorical question in Obadiah 5a-b in the affirmative. The same holds for the question in verse 5c, which is similar in structure. Here it is common agricultural practice, not criminal activity, that is called upon for support.

One staple of Edom's crops is the grape (cf. Num. 20:17). According to Israelite regulations, the poor are to be provided for through leaving gleanings, or unharvested portions, for their use (Lev. 19:9–10; Deut. 24:19–22; cf. Ruth 2). Even though these Israelite laws did not hold in Edom, agricultural practices were similar, and nonmechanized harvesting results in incomplete harvests even if leaving some produce was not mandated. Both of these pictures, whether of violence or of agriculture, show at least a small portion remaining.

By contrast, Edom in its punishment is completely denuded (v. 6). Even the stores hidden away in her rocky nooks and crannies (v. 3) will be ferreted out, purposefully sought for (cf. Gen. 31:34–35), and, by implication, plundered.[4] The nation is identified by a different name here, that of Esau, its founder (Gen. 36), a name common in the rest of the book (Obad. 8, 9, 18[2x], 19, 21). It is referred to in this verse as both singular ("his treasures") and plural ("they will be ransacked"). This could indicate that it is being used as a collective noun that at times refers to a unit and at other times to a collection of individuals within that unit (cf. 1 Kings 18:39, where one noun governs both singular and plural verbs).

Rather than criminals or ancient enemies plaguing Edom, it is her former friends and allies who turn against her. They are identified in Hebrew literally as covenant partners ("allies"; lit., "those of your covenant"), "friends" (lit., "those of your peace"; Jer. 38:22; cf. Ps. 41:9; Jer. 20:10), and "your

---

3. Raabe, *Obadiah*, 142.

4. In spite of the NIV's making the pillage and ransacking explicit, the two verbs used involve only a careful search for hidden things, not their removal.

bread." The latter term appears odd in the context. Poetically parallel to the two previously mentioned phrases, it must indicate a positive relationship with Edom, in contrast to some of the early versions that revocalized the text to read "those who do battle with you."[5] In Psalm 49:9, "those of your peace" were synonymously parallel with "those who eat your bread," so this could be a scribal error where the verb "eat" dropped out accidentally, or else "those of," using the first two phrases, could be understood to apply here as well.[6] In the Old Testament, meals (or sharing bread) often indicate an amicable, even covenantal relationship (e.g., Abram and Melchizedek, Gen. 14:18; Abimelech and Isaac, 26:28–31; Jacob and Laban, Gen. 31:51–54; Yahweh and the Israelite elders, Ex. 24:11; Israel and Gibeon, Josh. 9:14–15; David and Abner, 2 Sam. 3:20–21; cf. 1 Cor. 11:23–25).[7]

Rather than receiving the support expected from friends, Edom finds them to be enemies. The Edomites are forcefully expelled (cf. Gen. 3:23; Jer. 15:1) from their dwellings and driven to the periphery of their land. Like their own deceitful heart (Obad. 3), former friends deceitfully overpower Edom— an example of a hendiadys in which two nouns, "deceive" and "overpower," make up one concept (e.g., "kith and kin") rather than two separate actions. Often used in terms of conflict (e.g., Judg. 16:5; 1 Sam 17:9), the erstwhile friends overpower Edom, driving her out of her holdings.

The third response, to "set a trap," is unclear because of the difficulty with the Hebrew, which in the three other occurrences of this word (Jer. 30:13; Hos. 5:13[2x]) means "sore," which is difficult in this context. The NIV, admitting its uncertainty, follows some of the ancient versions.[8] An alternative proposal that does not require textual emendation derives the word from a Hebrew verb "be strange, foreign," resulting in a noun "place of foreigners."[9] The next term "under you" (NIV "for you") could equally mean "in place of you,"[10] indicating that foreigners replace Edomites in

---

5. *BHS*, note a. The same verbal root can mean "to eat," so a revocalization and scribal deletion has been suggested from an original *lōḥmê laḥmᵉkā* ("those who eat your bread"; see G. I. Davies, "A New Solution to a Crux in Obadiah 7," *VT* 27 [1977]: 484–87).

6. Armerding, "Obadiah," 345–46.

7. See J. D. Nogalski, "Obadiah 7: Textual Corruption or Politically Charged Metaphor?" *ZAW* 110 (1998): 67–71, who sees "your bread" as a political metaphor synonymous to "your covenant" and "your peace" and thus understands this verse as condemning Edom for her political alliances.

8. The LXX, Vulgate, Targum, Syriac, Theodotian, and Aquila apparently read either *māṣôr* ("siege"; e.g., Mic. 4:14) or *māṣôd* ("snare, net"; Job 19:6; Eccl. 7:26) instead of the MT *māzôr*.

9. P. K. McCarter, Jr., "Obadiah 7 and the Fall of Edom," *BASOR* 221 (1976): 87–91; Raabe, *Obadiah*, 155.

10. *HALOT*, תַּחַת, 3.

their abandoned territory, a practice of exile and resettlement common for ancient Near Eastern conquerors (cf. 2 Kings 17:6, 24–26).

The NIV and NRSV view the final clause in verse 7 as referring to the trap that is undetectable. The suggested reading above makes this unworkable, and the grammar of the Hebrew also tells against this. A better rendering is "there does not exist any understanding *in* it/him" (so, e.g., Vulgate, KJV, NASB; cf. Deut. 32:28), referring either to "in Esau" (Obad. 6) or "in the place of foreigners." In either case, the self-vaunted wisdom of Edom, picked up in the next section of the prophecy, is unknown to the new inhabitants of their land. This is similar to Jeremiah's reference to Shiloh (Jer. 7:12), which in the past had been a place of significance but has subsequently been forgotten.

COVENANTS. In the ancient Near East, nations related themselves to each other through covenants. At times, major regional powers allied themselves with each other as equals for mutual protection and support. Documentation of this kind of relationship exists between, for example, the Egyptians and the Hittites, who lived in what is now Turkey. During the thirteenth century B.C. these two countries allied themselves by treaty so they could look after other concerns, such as the encroaching "Sea Peoples" (including the Philistines), rather than having to worry about each other.[11] In the Old Testament, there seem to be hints of this kind of treaty between Israel and the Midianites (Ex. 18),[12] as well as the relationship inferred here between Edom and her unnamed allies.

Other treaties were imposed by conquerors, when a mightier nation subdued a smaller neighbor. Israel entered into this kind of relationship with the Gibeonites (Josh. 9–10), as did David with surrounding nations when he established his empire. He conquered some and intimidated others into becoming vassal tributaries (2 Sam. 8:1–14; cf. 3:3; 5:11). The relationship between Israel and her God is also pictured in covenant terms: He is their Great King and they are his vassal servants (e.g., 1 Sam. 12:12; Ps. 68:24; 95:3; cf. Matt. 5:35).

This covenant concept continues into the New Testament, but in a modified form. There the divine Great King is incarnated in Jesus of Nazareth (Matt. 21:5; 27:11, 29), and his rule is over all humanity, not just Israel

---

11. See *ANET*, 199–201, also 201–3, and other treaties between equals, e.g., 203–6; cf. *COS*, 2:93–106.

12. See *NBD*, "Covenant, Alliance," sec. 2.2.

(Rev. 15:3–4; cf. Ps. 47:7). He rules through service and suffering (e.g., Matt. 26:28; 1 Cor. 11:25) rather than through the use of physical power.

Common to covenant relationships is mutual fidelity; covenant partners are to show commitment to each other, whether the relationship is coerced or voluntary. Breach of such a relationship is an egregious wrong and runs counter to the practice of covenant-making. It is not unheard of, however, since most covenant documents contain punishments for such breaches (e.g., Deut. 28:15–68). It is in this context that Edom is called to task for her behavior toward Judah. As she is biologically kin to Israel and also geographically close, their relationship should be one of covenant loyalty, but instead it is one of betrayal (cf. Obad. 10–15). Her punishment is to suffer such covenant betrayal herself. Even her friends and partners will turn against her in ways threatening her very existence.

HITTING YOU WHERE **it hurts**. Judah and her neighbors were mainly agricultural societies, depending for livelihood and sustenance on what crops and animals their people could raise for their own use and for the market. This is why theft of produce was such a serious thing, threatening family and nation (cf. Judg. 6:11). A sign of covenant blessing was an abundance of produce and crops (Deut. 28:11), but a result for breach of covenant was their loss (vv. 18, 29–30, 33).

Today, most people depend on things other than agriculture for their livelihood, so the examples from this sphere have less impact than they did to Obadiah's original audience. The equivalent today is the pink slip (notice that one's job is coming to an end), an all-too-common occurrence with the changing economic climate and multinational shifts of manufacturing sites. The compounded threat of loss of retirement and medical benefits because of either corrupt financial practices or the threatened collapse of the Social Security system creates the same anxiety today as did loss of crop and treasure. The corporate or governmental "friend" that is expected to be available might prove illusory or even be an enemy.

Biblical answers to this are difficult, especially since even the church has become dependent on the state. Some clergy in the United States are able to opt out of the Social Security system, providing for retirement and disability needs through other means. This is an option worth exploring if one is convinced that responsibility in this area should lie elsewhere than with the government. Much of this type of care is provided by the community, whether the people of Israel in the Old Testament, who dispersed God's covenant bounty equitably through such things as leaving part of the crops for the poor (e.g., Lev. 19:9–10; Deut. 24:19–21), or the church in the New Testament, through distribution of wealth (e.g., Acts 2:44–45). Some evangelicals in the past decades have been challenging the church to examine its role not only in economic assistance but also in decrying economic exploitation.[13] In terms drawn from Obadiah, they are asking whether the church is fulfilling the role of covenant partner by sharing God's provisions with others, or covenant breaker by denying these provisions to others.

---

13. Cf., e.g., R. J. Sider, *Cry Justice! The Bible on Hunger and Poverty* (New York: Paulist/Downers Grove, Ill.: InterVarsity Press, 1980); R. J. Foster, *The Challenge of the Disciplined Life: Christian Reflections on Money, Sex and Power* (San Francisco: Harper & Row, 1985); H. Schlossberg, et al. eds., *Christianity and Economics in the Post-Cold War Era: The Oxford Declaration and Beyond* (Grand Rapids: Eerdmans, 1994); Max L. Stackhouse, ed. *On Moral Business: Classical and Contemporary Resources for Ethics in Economic Life* (Grand Rapids: Eerdmans, 1995); S. W. Carlson-Thies and J. W. Skillen, eds., *Welfare in America: Christian Perspectives on a Policy in Crisis* (Grand Rapids: Eerdmans, 1996); R. J. Sider, *Rich Christians in an Age of Hunger: Moving from Affluence to Generosity*, 20th anniversary ed. (Dallas: Word, 1997); idem, *Just Generosity: A New Vision for Overcoming Poverty in America* (Grand Rapids: Baker, 1999).

Obadiah 8–9

⁸"In that day," declares the LORD,
   "will I not destroy the wise men of Edom,
   men of understanding in the mountains of Esau?
⁹Your warriors, O Teman, will be terrified,
   and everyone in Esau's mountains
   will be cut down in the slaughter.

IN A NEW section marked again by a speech of Yahweh (cf. v. 4), the demeaning defeat of Edom is carried even further. This section ties to the previous passage through content as well as through the use of rhetorical questions, with which verse 8 begins in the Hebrew (cf. v. 5). Another uniting feature is reference to "in that day," in which the events previously discussed are simultaneous to what follows. The form also serves as an anticipation of a fuller discussion of "the day of the LORD" in verse 15. This day of judgment for Edom in verses 8–9 is precursor of that day of universal judgment.

Yahweh promises that he will not only deprive Edom of tactical geographical advantage (vv. 2–4) and strength derived from either wealth or allies (vv. 5–7), but he will also deny them two other means of national support, the wise and the strong. The "wise men" are important figures in the court and society (Jer. 18:18; cf. Deut. 1:13–15; Prov. 24:3–7; Isa. 29:14), providing sage intellectual insight or good sense (e.g., 2 Sam. 13:3; 1 Kings 5:7) as well as practical skill (e.g., Isa. 3:3; 40:20).

Edom had a particularly strong tie to wisdom. The wise man Job comes from Uz, which, while unidentified, is associated with Edom (Lam. 4:21), and one of his "friends," Eliphaz, also has links with Edom (Teman; see Obad. 9; cf. Job 1:11). Edomite wisdom is also noted in other passages (Jer. 49:7; Bar. 3:22–23, Teman; cf. Job 15:17–19). All of this—the people and their practical skills—is removed. Edom is here paralleled with "the mountains of Esau"—or better, Mount Esau (cf. Obad. 9, 21), since the noun is singular. This seems to be a wordplay designed by the author, playing off Mount Zion (vv. 17, 21) and Mount Seir, a common designation of Edom/Esau (Gen 36:8, 9; Deut. 2:5; see the note on Obad. 6), and is a reminder of Edom's mountainous strongholds in verse 3.

Trained soldiers are called upon to act with valor (e.g., Judg. 11:1; 1 Chron. 5:24), but those of Edom are terrified (Obad. 9), psychologically demoralized by the catastrophe befalling them (Isa. 31:9; cf. Jer. 8:9, where the verb applies to "the wise"). The result of this loss of military resolve is a defenseless citizenry who face massacre (cf. "cut down" in Ex. 12:15, of wrongdoers in Israel; Ruth 4:10, of a family line; Prov. 2:22, of the wicked; Joel 1:16, of food). They are not simply driven away but killed (Job 13:15; 24:14; Ps. 139:19). The ones who do this to them are most likely members of the nations mustered against them (Obad. 1).

NATIONAL LEADERSHIP. Even though leadership in Israel for a good part of its history appears to reside in the hands of the king, there was a well-established, decentralized system of leadership prior to the monarchy that served as a means of "checks and balances." In addition to the tribal hierarchy moving up through father, clan chief, and tribal ruler (such as the "judges" or war chiefs of the book of Judges), the prophet was chosen by God to bring king and country back into a correct relationship with him, and the priest was to lead and teach. The "wise" also provided insight from their own resources and from previous tradition (2 Sam. 14:1–7; 20:14–20; cf. Jer. 18:18, where these last three occur together).

Good leadership requires all of these elements, and at times several functioned within a single individual (e.g., Solomon, who was a wise king). Military might was also necessary for national development. Loss of any of these elements, or even worse, of several of them simultaneously, posed a threat to a nation's continued existence.

Edom shares types of leadership with their Israelite neighbors, especially in their kings (Gen. 36:31–39) and their wise ones. The threatened loss of wisdom and might from Edom means that they do not know how to live, nor do they have that means to attain any goals they might have. This threat of a lack of vision and lack of means is common among the prophets (e.g., Isa. 29:14; Jer. 51:57), and the confusion and defeat are among the curses following breaking covenant relationships (Deut. 28:20, 25). These, coupled with the previously mentioned loss of livelihood, leave a nation such as Edom destitute indeed.

LEADERSHIP INTEGRITY AND STRENGTH. Israel and her neighbors would be shocked at today's threatened loss of leadership insight and strength. We do not seem to expect either one from leaders. The 2000 presidential election in the United States left a leader without great power because he was without a clear mandate from the majority of the people. The need for consensus and the fear of political pitfalls and of alienating even a tiny portion of the small majority often mean that decisions are made based on expediency and special interest rather than on justice and righteousness. Things seem to aim more toward the safe common denominator, which is of much lower value than are criteria based on what is best and right. In this, the church shares a belief with both Israel and its neighbors: There are actions expected of rulers that are either right or wrong. While society at large might question this, Christians cannot do so.

Part of the cause of loss of moral strength is an accompanying loss of integrity. This is a problem not only in the political arena but also in the church. Political leaders are joined by religious leaders in not only engaging in immorality, but also in lying and covering up for what are euphemistically called "indiscretions." Our moral horizon, even within the church, has become lowered, and we need to ask the question raised in another context, "Whatever became of sin?"[1] While the threatened loss of guidance and power would have concerned the ancients, the fact that neither today's society nor the church seems to be bothered about the loss of both moral vision and the ability to accomplish good in leading society is even more of a concern. We could well be looking back on the realization of an event like Obadiah's prophecy. Where are today's leaders who will base decisions on integrity rather than on either pragmatism or politics?

---

1. Taken from the title of a book by K. Menninger (New York: Hawthorn, 1973).

Obadiah 10–15

¹⁰Because of the violence against your brother Jacob,
  you will be covered with shame;
  you will be destroyed forever.
¹¹On the day you stood aloof
  while strangers carried off his wealth
 and foreigners entered his gates
  and cast lots for Jerusalem,
  you were like one of them.
¹²You should not look down on your brother
  in the day of his misfortune,
 nor rejoice over the people of Judah
  in the day of their destruction,
 nor boast so much
  in the day of their trouble.
¹³You should not march through the gates of my people
  in the day of their disaster,
 nor look down on them in their calamity
  in the day of their disaster,
 nor seize their wealth
  in the day of their disaster.
¹⁴You should not wait at the crossroads
  to cut down their fugitives,
 nor hand over their survivors
  in the day of their trouble.
¹⁵"The day of the LORD is near
  for all nations.
 As you have done, it will be done to you;
  your deeds will return upon your own head.

Original Meaning

THE EXTERNAL REASONS for the fall of Edom are now identified. The surprising reversal of verse 7 (friends turning to enemies) is not that surprising after all! Instead, Edom will receive back on her own head what she had done to her own "family." What goes around comes around!

The first two verses of this section break the normal Hebrew word order by beginning with prepositional phrases. They emphasize causes of judgment: violence and noninvolvement. Verses 12–14 continue with a litany of eight sentences, each beginning with the adverb "(and) not." By emphatic ordering and the emphasis of repetition, the prophet is hammering away at the heinous nature of that in which Edom is involved. The inseparable preposition "(deriving) from violence," which opens this section in verse 10, is the same preposition that closed the previous section ("[deriving] from slaughter" in v. 9). This provides a noticeable syntactic tie between cause and effect.

Edom's Violence (v. 10)

EACH OF THE three Hebrew terms in the first clause of verse 10 has a strong rhetorical impact on the hearers. The causal element ("violence") was the precipitating factor for the destruction of humanity by flood during the time of Noah (Gen. 6:11, 13). This word can indicate both personal physical abuse (e.g., Gen. 49:5–6; Jer. 13:22) and practices destructive of institutions and society (e.g., Ex. 23:1; Zeph. 3:4). In this case, both physical and psychological destruction are introduced by this term. Specific instances are explored in the following verses.

This violence is (lit.) "of your brother Jacob." This is an objective genitive, indicating that the brother is the recipient of the action done by someone else, who in this case is Edom.[1] A political treaty can be described as being between neighbors who call themselves brothers (e.g., 1 Kings 9:13; 20:30–34),[2] but here the actual biological fraternal relationship is highlighted. This not only reminds hearers of the biological ties between the Israelites and Edomites, but also emphasizes the monstrous nature of the wrongdoing. This is not just an outrage against an enemy, or even a neighbor; this is against one's own blood!

This close relationship is accentuated by identifying the brother as "Jacob," the physical brother of Esau (Gen 25:25–26), here indicating the nation of Judah, Jacob's descendants (cf. Joel 3:19). Readers are reminded of previously strained relationships between the two "brothers" (e.g., Num. 20:14), a strain that had by now become a serious rupture. The prophet, by using

---

1. In Hebrew, as in English, such a genitive construction can be ambiguous, and it is vital to determine the exact function in any particular case. For example, it is of some importance in a construction such as "my killing" whether it is a subjective genitive ("I am the one killing another") or an objective genitive ("another is killing me"). Sometimes the context clarifies the function (e.g., in 1 Kings 10:9, "the love of God" is stated to be "for Israel," so it is clearly a subjective genitive), but other examples are not as clear (e.g., 1 John 2:5).

2. Cf. *CAD*, 1/1:200–201

these three terms in this relationship, starts his punishment justification phase with a powerful thunderclap.

Violent Edom, instead of being cloaked by its pride (v. 3), is now "covered with shame," just as the flood covered Noah's violent neighbors (Gen. 7:19–20) or as one might be wrapped in a garment (e.g., Ex. 28:42; Deut. 22:12). The ironic twist is that garments are used most commonly to cover one's shame (e.g., Gen. 9:23; Hos. 2:9; cf. Gen. 3:7, 21), but here it is shame that covers the nation. Shame is in contrast with honor, an external consideration of worth—an important concept in the Near East, including contemporary Arabic culture. Honor is unlike pride, which is an internal, subjective consideration of worth. Edom is deprived of the former as she already had been deprived of the latter (Obad. 2–3).

Shame is not the only result, however, since shame, while psychologically damaging, is not of itself fatal. Edom will be "destroyed" (the same verb as "cut down" in v. 9, providing yet another verbal tie between this section and the last). The nature of this total destruction (cf. Gen. 9:11; Jer. 11:19) is accentuated here, since it is eternal ("forever"). There is no hope for future restoration since there will be nothing to restore.

The Specific Nature of Edom's "Violence" (vv. 11–14)

THE MAIN CLAUSE of verse 11 is followed by four subordinate clauses that explain the background events of which Edom is guilty. They seem to contrast Edom, the "you" of the first and last clauses, with the unidentified enemies and foreigners who despoil "his" (i.e., Jacob's/Judah's) wealth. The verb "carried off" indicates that military action is involved, with the conqueror removing either people (whether soldiers or citizenry; e.g., 1 Kings 8:46–48) or property ("wealth"; cf. 2 Chron. 21:17). In a society where gates and walls protect cities, open access for nonnative "foreigners" (Deut. 17:15) is not only a disgrace, but it is also dangerous. Jacob's/Judah's gates are open, those of Jerusalem as well as those of her other towns.

These strangers, rather than respecting the authority of Judah's capital or the sanctity of the site of the temple, treat it as a commodity won by the lucky gambler. The instrument determining the winner is the "lot," most likely a pebble with inscriptions on its surfaces. These indicate various possible outcomes that are determined randomly by throwing, much like dice.[3] While used to determine who might receive clothing or property (e.g., Num. 26:55; Ps. 22:18), it is also used in a grammatical form similar to that found here to indicate the division of prisoners of war for exploitation as slaves (Joel 4:3;

---

3. Cf. W. W. Hallo, "The First Purim," *BA* 46 (1983): 19–29; Raabe, *Obadiah*, 175–76.

Nah. 3:10). While no such practice is associated with any specific date in Judean history, the reference of this whole section is probably to the Babylonian exile of Jerusalem and Judah in either 597 or 586 B.C.

The last clause of verse 11 comes as a shock, since Edom, at whom the finger is dramatically pointed through the pronoun "you," acts the part of enemy and foreigner rather than that of neighbor and brother. She stands aloof, separate but within visual distance of the events taking place. She sees what is happening, so she cannot plead ignorance. She does not take part here, either as participant or as rescuer. But as the next verses show, Edom's involvement becomes steadily greater, moving from silent complicity to active participant.

The eight sentences in verses 12–14 each begin with a negative command "don't" (NIV "you should not"). The context of verses 10–11 places the perspective after the actions have already taken place, and numerous translations put this form into the past, even though that is incorrect since, from a grammatical standpoint, it is directed toward the present or the future as a universal prohibition (so translated by ASV, NIV, NASB, NEB). The author may use this form to express the immediacy of the horror to him, placing himself back directly into the time of the action and calling out "STOP!"

The three sentences in verse 12 indicate increasing levels of psychological intimidation that Edom shows. They "look down on" their brother (the regular verb for looking intently at something [*r'h*] can also connote gloating [e.g., Ps. 22:18; 37:34]), they "rejoice maliciously" (e.g., Isa. 14:8; Mic. 7:8), and they "open wide the mouth" (which the NIV takes as "boast"). This last phrase more likely indicates scornful laughter rather than boasting (boasting would indicate Edom had something to do with the situation, which is not the case).[4]

The situation is first called (lit.) "the day of your brother" (the NIV omits "the day of"), picking up terms from verses 10 ("brother Jacob") and 11 ("day" when they were defeated). It is further defined as "the day of his misfortune," a term that only occurs here and in Job 31:3, where its use with "misfortune" indicates that this is probably a synonym. This is clarified in the next sentence as the time of their destruction, when the people of Judah were carried off into exile and destroyed as a people (e.g., Jer. 48:46; Amos 1:8); in a true time of great trouble or distress—a common phrase in the prophets (Obad. 14; Nah. 1:7).

Edom moves from mental to physical assault in four of the next five sentences in verses 13–14. They join the foreign enemy of verse 11 by entering

---

4. See Raabe, *Obadiah*, 179; cf. similar phrases in Ps. 35:19–21, where "rejoicing" also occurs with "opening wide the mouth"; Isa. 57:4.

Judah's gate—either that of their capital or a collective noun for the gates of all her towns. Here Judah is called "my people," a covenant term showing the strong relationship between Yahweh and his people (Lev. 26:11). This should serve as a severe warning to Edom: She is not just attacking little Judah, but also Judah's covenant partner, the Creator of the universe.

Obadiah uses a synonym for "misfortune" three times in verse 13. "Their disaster" (ʾêdām) refers to that of Judah, but the term also supplies a clear wordplay on the name Edom. Edom looks around from close quarters (cf. v. 12) at Judah's calamity after they enter her gate.[5] But Edom does not stop with observing. She joins in the looting and pillage of their wealth. The verb "stretch out [the hand]" (NIV "seize") has a peculiar grammatical form,[6] but is often used of taking things (with the implied direct object "your hand"; see also 2 Sam. 6:6; cf. Gen. 3:22; Ex. 22:7, 10). The identification of Edom with the enemy of previous verses again accentuates the surprising statement closing Obadiah 11.

The most despicable acts are those in verse 14, where Edom physically lays hands on defeated and fleeing neighbors. She stands waiting (or actively fighting against; cf. Judg. 6:31; 2 Chron. 20:23) refugees. The location where this takes place is unclear (NIV "crossroads"),[7] but the heinous nature of the act is not. Literally, they "cut off/down" those who flee, a verb regularly used of putting someone to death (e.g., Jer. 9:20; 44:7), though death is not the only means of elimination and does not work well in this context, since survivors remain in the next sentence. Separation is meant here, not by death but by exile, just as an unclean person is separated from the Israelite camp (cf. Ex. 12:15; cf. the related word for divorce, Deut. 24:1, 3). Edom aids the exile of a defeated people by turning over the defeated survivors (Num. 21:35; Josh. 8:22). Those to whom she commits them are not mentioned, lest they also share the blame, which is here left wholly on Edom.

The Reason for the Warning (v. 15)

THE REASON FOR the warning against this cumulative litany of escalating evil is now given. Edom will receive as she has given. As she exploited Judah's days of calamity (vv. 11–14), so a day will cause her distress. This is "the day of

---

5. The NIV omits two emphasizing words, "even you," from this sentence.

6. The Hebrew has it as a 2/3fp imperfect Qal, but there is no clear subject for this form. The best interpretation is to see it as a 2ms form, which fits contextually in this address to Edom, with an energic ending (Raabe, *Obadiah*, 183–84; Ehud Ben Zvi, *A Historical-Critical Study of the Book of Obadiah* [Berlin: Walter de Gruyter, 1996], 156–57).

7. See Raabe, *Obadiah*, 184, and Ben Zvi, *Historical-Critical Study*, 160–62, for a discussion of options.

the LORD," a time that affects not only Edom but all nations, of which she is a representative. One way this representation might be seen is linguistic, since "Edom" and "humanity" are comprised of the same consonants (*ʾdm*) in Hebrew.[8] The next section of the prophecy expounds the nature and effect of this day, but this verse serves as a hinge, drawing one section to a close while it opens the next.[9] Along with the numerous key words sprinkled throughout, this adds to the cumulative evidence for the textual unity of the book.

"The day of the LORD" is not a concept originating with Obadiah, but rather one that started with the earliest of the writing prophets (see Amos 5:18[2x], 20; cf. Isa. 13:6, 9; Ezek. 13:5; 45:35; Joel 1:15; 2:1, 11, 31; 3:14; Zeph. 1:7, 14[2x]; Mal. 4:5). The origins of the concept are debated, but its contents are clear from what is probably the first of the biblical uses of the phrase—Amos 5:18. It concerns a time of divine intervention in history, bringing good and blessing on those who please God and gloom and destruction on his foes.[10] The day is not only an eschatological concept at the end of the age, but a time that is near (Joel 1:15; 3:14; Zeph. 1:7) and approaching quickly (Zeph. 1:14). Its nearness is one of the compelling reasons for the current predicament in which Edom finds itself and why the people are called to reform while there is still a chance to do so.

Yet another surprise awaits the readers in verse 15. The nations called to participate in the campaign against Edom in verse 1 may well have felt themselves on the side of good since they had been given this task. The situation is shown to be otherwise, however, since they, along with Edom, are recipients of judgment (cf. esp. v. 16). Their fate will follow later, since the author returns attention to Edom, who again is addressed in the second person in a comparative sentence. The past, Edom's prior actions, have a result in the future; they will be done to her.

This response is based on one of the foundations of Israelite law, an appropriate response to a wrong that had been done. Called talion law, or

---

8. This ambiguity is theologically important in Amos 9:12, where the LXX reads "Edom" as "humanity," a reading picked up at the Council of Jerusalem in Acts 15:17. This, along with other textual variants, is a key argument used in Acts for allowing Gentiles into the nascent church (see, e.g., D. M. King, "The Use of Amos 9:11–12 in Acts 15:16–18," *ATJ* 21 [1989]: 8–13).

9. See H. van Dyke Parunak, "Transitional Techniques in the Bible," *JBL* 102 (1983): 525–48.

10. The literature on the concept is extensive. Among more recent works, see R. H. Hiers, "Day of the Lord," *ABD*, 2:82–83; K. J. Cathcart, "Day of Yahweh," *ABD*, 2:84–85; Raabe, *Obadiah*, 190–92; R. Rendtorff, "Alas for the Day: The 'Day of the Lord' in the Book of the Twelve," in *God in the Fray: A Tribute to Walter Brueggemann*, ed. T. Linafelt and T. K. Beal (Minneapolis: Fortress, 1998), 186–97; J. D. Nogalski, "The Day(s) of Yahweh in the Book of the Twelve," *1999 Seminar Papers* (Atlanta: Scholars Press, 1999), 617–42.

lex talionis, it is also known as "an eye for an eye," based on its three occurrences (Ex. 21:23–25; Lev. 24:19–20; Deut. 19:18–21). This is not the only place where Edom is the subject of this type of talion statement (Ezek. 25:12–14; 35:6, 11, 15). The same idea is repeated in the last clause of Obadiah 15. Any advantage that Edom sought from her betrayal does not benefit her after all, but rather costs her.

SHAME AND HONOR. These two concepts, important social constructs in many traditional societies, are described as follows: "If honor signifies respect for being the kind of person and doing the kinds of things the group values, shame signifies, in the first instance, being seen as less than valuable because one has behaved in ways that run contrary to the values of the group."[11] Intrafamilial violence is one of these contrary values in the ancient Near East, and so leads to Edom's shame. Shame also results from defeat (Jer. 2:36; Ezek. 7:18), losing God's protection (Deut. 32:5) as a result of treachery (Ps. 25:3). Socially unacceptable practices also are shameful in the later Mediterranean culture of the New Testament (e.g., 1 Cor. 15:34; Eph. 5:12; 2 Peter 2:2).

Family ties. A powerful Hebrew term indicating relationships is *ḥesed*, usually translated "love, loving-kindness, mercy." Most often used to describe the close, covenant relationship that God enjoys with his people (commonly in the Psalms, where over half of its 246 occurrences were found; e.g., Ps. 6:4; 103:4, 8, 11, 17), it also indicates interpersonal relationships as well. This can include king-subject (e.g., 1 Kings 2:7), friendship (e.g., 1 Sam. 20:8), and family relationships (e.g., Gen. 20:13). It is a central ideal for the concept of positive interpersonal regard and mutual support and is aptly rendered in a recent Hebrew dictionary by "loyalty."[12]

Ḥesed not only has a favorable connotation, but it also connotes permanence and stability—fundamental elements of relationships either of covenant or kin. People enter into covenants in order to establish and maintain this type of relationship, and this term depicts the ideal family life, both of which result in *šālôm* ("well-being") for those so related.[13] This is the relationship that Edom should have had with its brother, Israel. The concept also transcends time, not

---

11. David A. deSilva, *Honor, Patronage, Kinship & Purity: Unlocking New Testament Culture* (Downers Grove, Ill.: InterVarsity Press, 2000), 25.

12. See *DCH*, 3:277–81.

13. See the discussion by D. A. Baer and R. P. Gordon, "חסד," *NIDOTTE*, 2:211–18 and the accompanying bibliography.

being restricted to the ancient world. Loving-kindness resulting in relational peace is also desired for people in the New Testament since it is characteristic of God himself (Gal. 5:22; 2 Tim. 2:22; cf. 2 Cor. 13:11).

It is in this context that breach of covenant is treated so seriously. While Edom does breach the relationship with Judah, she even goes a step further. Judah is not a mere neighbor, nor even simply a covenant partner. She is actually family, distant kin through the Jacob–Esau relationship. While one might expect such despicable actions from one's enemies, one does not expect them from one's relative! The shock of Cain's betrayal of Abel in Genesis 3 is echoed by the treachery of which Edom is accused. Honorable behavior has been replaced by acts that should bring shame to the perpetrator.

An eye for an eye. This concept derives from the polar opposite of the relationship that should exist within a family group. What should be the result if kinship love is shattered and harm is caused to a family member? An appropriate response under law is the goal of a legal system. Precedent or procedure delineates the responses that had previously been made to a given situation, showing what might be appropriate in case the situation should arise again.

Mesopotamian law (e.g., the laws of Hammurabi from the eighteenth century B.C.) contains such responses. For example, if a man destroys the sight of another similar person (i.e., one of the same social rank), his sight can be destroyed (law 196).[14] These laws are not equitable, however, since a similar injury caused to someone of lower status than the offender results in a lesser punishment (laws 198, 199, 201). Also, if a lower social class injures one above his station, penalties are much more severe (e.g., a slave who strikes a gentleman on his cheek loses his ear [law 205], while one striking an equal is just fined [law 204]).

In the Bible, there are several mentions of such laws concerning "an eye for an eye," not only in the Old Testament (Ex. 21:24; Lev. 24:20; Deut. 19:21) but also in the words of Jesus (Matt. 5:38). Though not always showing equity, this biblical type of talion law is not harsh and punitive in purpose. While one can respond proportionately to a wrong, one is not required to respond with "an eye for an eye" and can exact a lesser punishment, or none at all. This type of law does not allow the injured party to exact a greater punishment, however, so the law is limiting. This is, therefore, an example of what could appear to be cruel in fact being a grace.[15] Even when wronged, one can chose to respond showing the appropriate familial loving-kindness that they themselves did not receive.

---

14. M. E. J. Richardson, *Hammurabi's Laws: Text, Translation and Glossary* (Semitic Texts and Studies 2; Sheffield: Sheffield Academic Press, 2000), 105.

15. See further Baker, "Aspects of Grace in the Pentateuch," 12–18.

SHAME AND SHAMING. It is ironic that Western society has by and large forgotten this concept, while many in the church misuse it. Decisions in business or politics are rarely made on the basis of what is either the honorable or shameful thing to do, since these are only derivable from an outside source of authority or expectation. Since much of Western society is pluralistic, it is felt that it must also be so as regards values. If there is no absolute right and wrong, there are no valid, external criteria to determine shame or honor. It is here that the church needs to return to its biblical heritage, demonstrating that moral absolutes derive from the will of the Creator (e.g., Gen. 2:17), and that how one responds to them not only should bring honor or shame, but also can have a radical impact on the very quality of life itself.

Rather than using honor and shame appropriately, too many in society at large, and even in the church, use them in an illegitimate manner, as a club to force desired actions. If one does not behave "appropriately," one is shamed into thinking that it is not one's actions but one's very being that is faulty. If one does not live by the guidelines established by the church, though not necessarily by Scripture, one is not a Christian. "If you do not give to this ministry until it hurts, you have no faith." This is coercion by demeaning, an invalidation of loving-kindness and too often a denial of the very image of God in the other.

Variations of violence. Physical assault on another human being is the very opposite of demonstrating familial love. It is both harmful and inappropriate, as reflected in its prohibition and punishment in many national penal codes as well as in Scripture (e.g., Gen. 4:15; Ex. 21:12, 15, 18, 20, 26). This is not all that is included in the list of Edom's sins in this passage, however. For them the assault is more psychological, starting with neglect and continuing through verbal taunting, culminating in misappropriation not only of goods but finally of freedom. All of this kind of behavior, whether done by the state or by one's trusted caregivers, leaves scars on the victim that are at least as deep as those left by physical abuse, even though they cannot be seen. These scars are also long-lasting, changing the psyche even after the body has healed.

Judah's neighbors recognized the psychological power of verbal abuse when they sought to demoralize the builders of Jerusalem's wall in order to make them stop (Neh. 2:19; 4:1–3). Jesus' opponents also sought to discourage and discredit him through mockery (e.g., Matt. 20:19; 27:29, 31, 41). This type of psychological warfare is defined by the U.S. Department of Defense as "the planned use of propaganda and other psychological actions having the primary purpose of influencing the opinions, emotions, attitudes, and behavior of hostile foreign groups in such a way as to support the achievement of national objectives."[16] It can be an effective strategy when used against military forces or against the civilian populations. It has been employed throughout history by such figures as Tokyo Rose during the Second World War.[17]

The use of this particular approach to military engagement might be ethically questionable, but its employ in domestic situations or even in the church is troubling. This means of interaction seeks to attack another's self-confidence and ultimately his or her self-esteem, just as Edom attacked Israel with her words and actions. Among Erik Erikson's stages of personality development, the first, usually reached at infancy, is defined as establishing trust.[18] Problems at this stage color further development and maturation.

The very first temptation in Scripture aims at this level. "Did God really say ... ?" is the serpent's question to the woman in the garden (Gen. 3:1); that is, "Can you trust your God and Creator?" This is an especially insidious "catch–22" when it is a parent who is emotionally abusing a child. They wound young hearts with verbal daggers such as "You never will match up to your brother!" or "I should never have had you in the first place!" Such a child is in a difficult situation, not knowing whether to doubt their own worth or the words of their primary authority figure. This type of abuse is unconscionable since it denies the integrity and worth of a child of God (see Ps. 3:2–3; Isa. 29:16; Matt. 6:26).[19]

Unfortunately, this type of abuse and coercive attack is not rare even in the church. Rather than providing a place where one can find care and nurture, too often church leaders set their own unbiblical standards to which people must conform if they are to feel welcome or even part of God's family. People are shamed if they do not conform or if they do not attain the standards set. No matter how well people do, they never are "good enough," do not live up to "Christian standards," and are often worn out from the

---

16. "Glossary: Department of Defense—Military and Associated Terms: Propaganda and Psychological Warfare Studies," *Joint Chiefs of Staff Publication* 1 (1987), taken from http://www.africa2000.com/PNDX/glossary.html (accessed in 2000).

17. See, for the other side of the story, A. B. Gilmore, *You Can't Fight Tanks with Bayonets: Psychological Warfare against the Japanese Army in the Southwest Pacific* (Lincoln: Univ. of Nebraska Press, 1998).

18. E. Erikson, *Identity and the Life Cycle* (New York: Norton, 1980).

19. See, e.g., G. Ketterman, *Verbal Abuse: Healing the Hidden Wound* (Ann Arbor: Servant, 1992).

striving.[20] Additionally, abuse of power in the church has gone beyond just the verbal to physical and sexual as well. This also leaves severe psychological scarring when an authority one respects and trusts becomes both debased and debasing.[21]

It is vital for the church to teach that authority at all levels—government, the church, school, or home—is not only worthy of respect, prayer, and obedience (e.g., 1 Tim. 2:1–2; Heb. 13:17; 1 Pet. 2:13–14), but is also accountable to God, the absolute authority who places men and women in leadership as he did the judges and kings in Israel. There is no absolute ruler over the church except God himself, and one who seems to be taking over this position by word or action needs to be strictly held to account. There also needs to be education within the church as to what constitutes violence and abuse, what its results are, and what the logical consequences of it should be. Often the behavior is not recognized as being hurtful, so discussion and teaching need to start addressing the issue. The state has taken some initial strides in this area, and it is a shame if the church should be lagging behind.

---

20. See, e.g., D. Johnson and J. VanVonderen, *The Subtle Power of Spiritual Abuse* (Minneapolis: Bethany, 1991); R. M. Enroth, *Churches That Abuse* (Grand Rapids: Zondervan, 1992); J. and D. Ryan, *Recovery from Spiritual Abuse* (Downers Grove, Ill.: InterVarsity Press, 1992); K. Blue, *Healing Spiritual Abuse: How to Break Free from Bad Church Experiences* (Downers Grove, Ill.: InterVarsity Press, 1993); R. Enroth, *Recovering from Churches That Abuse* (Grand Rapids: Zondervan, 1994); L. B. Smedes, *Shame and Grace: Healing the Shame We Don't Deserve* (San Francisco: Harper & Row, 1994).

21. See M. A. Fortune, *Is Nothing Sacred? When Sex Invades the Pastoral Relationship* (San Francisco: Harper & Row, 1989); E. A. Horst, *Recovering the Lost Self: Shame Healing for Victims of Clergy Sexual Abuse* (Collegeville: Liturgical, 1991); P. Mosgofian and G. Ohlschlager, *Sexual Misconduct in Counseling and Ministry* (Dallas: Word, 1995).

Obadiah 16–18

16 Just as you drank on my holy hill,
     so all the nations will drink continually;
 they will drink and drink
     and be as if they had never been.
17 But on Mount Zion will be deliverance;
     it will be holy,
 and the house of Jacob
     will possess its inheritance.
18 The house of Jacob will be a fire
     and the house of Joseph a flame;
 the house of Esau will be stubble,
     and they will set it on fire and consume it.
 There will be no survivors
     from the house of Esau."

The LORD has spoken.

ATTENTION NOW TURNS from Edom, the oppressor of God's people, to the people of Judah themselves. Here we see another surprising twist (cf. comments on vv. 11, 15). Judah desires to hear words of comfort that her time of suffering is over (Isa. 40:1–2) and that she will be restored to her former position. Restoration is indeed promised (vv. 17, 19–21), but there is a subtle reminder that Judah's suffering has also been her due. Her oppressors are indeed wrong and bear the consequences, but Israel herself is not without sin.

Verse 16 continues to address an unidentified "you," still using second-person forms. This provides a tie with the previous context and explains why numerous interpreters see Edom still as the addressee.[1] But a problem with

---

1. E.g., LXX; Vulgate; Calvin; Keil; F. E. Gaebelein, *Four Minor Prophets* (Chicago: Moody Press, 1970), 36; P. C. Craigie, *Twelve Prophets* I (DSB; Philadelphia: Westminster, 1984), 205–6; D. Stuart, *Hosea–Jonah* (WBC; Waco, Tex.: Word, 1987), 420; Finley, "Obadiah," 370–72; J. Niehaus, "Obadiah," *The Minor Prophets: An Exegetical and Expository Commentary*, ed. T. E. McComiskey (Grand Rapids: Baker, 1993), 2:535–36; W. W. Wiersbe, *Be Concerned* (Colorado Springs: Chariot Victor, 1996), 82; E. Achtemeier, *Minor Prophets* I (NIBC; Peabody: Hendrickson, 1996), 249.

this interpretation is that this verse contains only one of two *plural* forms out of forty second-person forms in the book.[2] The other plural has as its subject the nations (v. 1), but since they are part of the other half of the comparison in verse 16, they cannot be the subject here. Since Edom is in every other instance addressed by a singular, the grammatical subject here must be someone else. Judah best serves as that subject.[3]

The rhetorical function of a marked shift of grammatical number would have attracted the attention of the original hearers, since such a shift indicates that a change is on its way. The surprise comes when they realize that they, the people of God, are the ones now addressed. Instead of Mount Esau as the subject (vv. 8, 9, 21), attention is now brought to "my holy hill," specifically named "Mount Zion" in the next verse. It is holy since it holds the temple, the residence of God himself (cf. Isa. 56:7; Ezek. 20:40; cf. Ps. 15:1; 43:3). Association with this site is much stronger for Judah, since Zion is its capital, than it is for Edom, whose only explicit foray within its gates is in this prophecy (Obad. 13). To find oneself the topic of conversation in the middle of a condemnation of the enemy must have brought Judah up with a start. A similar rhetorical function occurs in Amos 5:1–2, where the rhythmic cadences of the funerary chant attract the attention of passers-by. When stopping to see who has died, they are informed that the funeral is for them.

Obadiah makes a comparison between Judah, who had already drunk, and all of the nations, who will drink. "Drinking" can be used literally for the consumption of liquid, especially wine and strong drink (e.g., Gen. 9:21; 1 Sam. 1:15; Jer. 35:5, 6, 8, 14), so it can easily accompany revelry and carousing (cf. Ex. 32:6; 1 Sam. 30:16). This is how those who see Edom as the subject take the verb here: a drunken celebration of the fall of Jerusalem (cf. v. 13). But this literal use does not fit the rest of the verse, where all nations drink continually and to oblivion, since they are not directly involved in Jerusalem's downfall. These last two occurrences show the metaphorical aspect of the verb, where the (cup of the) wrath of God, his judgment, is drunk (e.g., Job 21:20; Isa. 51:17; Jer. 25:16, 28; Hab. 2:16).[4]

---

2. See note on Obad. 13 concerning another possible second-person plural form.

3. So D. J. Clark and N. Mundhenk, *A Translator's Handbook on the Books of Obadiah and Micah* (Helps for Translators; London/New York: United Bible Society, 1982), 27; Armerding, "Obadiah," 353; J. Limburg, "The Book of Obadiah," *Hosea–Micah* (Interpretation; Atlanta: John Knox, 1988), 133; Wolff, *Obadiah and Jonah*, 64–65; Ben Zvi, *Historical-Critical Study*, 181–82; Raabe, *Obadiah*, 203–4.

4. For a detailed analysis of the concept of drinking and the cup of the wrath of God, see Raabe, *Obadiah*, 206–42.

If the first of these verbs of drinking in this verse is literal and the following two are metaphorical, there would then be a contrast between Edom and the nations. This goes against the use of the comparative adverb "just as." If the first verb is also metaphorical, however, it refers to Judah having already suffered God's wrath for disobedience. As they suffer, in like manner the nations, of which Edom is a part, also suffer. The adverb then serves its regular comparative function.

From the context, the fourth verb in the sentence also deals with drinking, but an exact rendition is problematic.[5] The final result for Edom is oblivion. Just as some alcoholics drink nonstop until they are psychologically gone, so the nations will experience the wrath of God until they are physically gone. Judah survives her ordeal. She is exiled, but she will return from her exile (cf. Ezra, Nehemiah). The nations, in contrast, will not survive.

This contrast, shown by "but," is spelled out in verse 17. Where "their fugitives" (*pĕlîṭāyw;* v. 14) had fled, there will now be deliverance and escape (*pĕlêṭâ;* Gen. 32:8; 45:7; Joel 2:32) from that wrath. Judah has already been there and does not need to return.

The next clause, "and it will be holy," is problematic since its referent is unclear. It is difficult for "Mount Zion" to be the subject since it is in a prepositional phrase. Also Hebrew has a noun "a holy place/thing" (*qōdeš*) rather than a predicate adjective (so NIV; *qādôš*). As deliverance is on Zion, so a holy place, a sanctuary, a rebuilt temple will also be on it in due course.[6]

God's holy city will be restored, and so will be his people, "the house of Jacob." "House," in addition to its literal, physical usage, also refers to those who live in a house, a family (e.g., Gen 7:1; 17:27), or descendants of a family group, a dynasty (e.g., Isa. 7:2). The name "Jacob" is a reminder of Obadiah 10, where Jacob suffers under Edom. In contrast, now it will be restored to its original patrimony. While verse 10 refers to the southern kingdom of Judah, here the entire nation of Israel, both the north and the south, is meant, as shown by the use of the phrase in other passages (e.g., Gen. 46:27; Ex. 19:3), and also its parallel with the "house of Joseph" in Obadiah 18, a designation of the northern tribes (e.g., Gen. 46:27, where this is part of the "house of Jacob"). What each Israelite originally possessed returns to his control, not this time through inheritance from

---

5. The verb used here is *lʿʿ*, and it refers to some kind of rash or incomprehensible speech (Job 6:3; Prov. 20:25), which could indicate the slurring caused by intoxication. A homonym meaning "to lap, slurp" has also been suggested for this verse; for a suggested emendation for Job 39:30, based on cognates in Arabic and Syriac, see לעע in BDB; *HALOT;* *DCH;* Wolff, *Obadiah,* 65; Raabe, *Obadiah,* 205.

6. Cf. TEV; see also Clark and Mundhenk, *Translator's Handbook,* 31; Wolff, *Obadiah,* 59; Raabe, *Obadiah,* 242–43).

a father (cf. Gen. 15:4), nor through dispossessing others, as is often done through military action (e.g., Deut. 2:12; Isa. 54:3; Amos 9:12, of Edom).[7]

In verse 18, the sweeping changes that affect Edom are pictured in a metaphor of fire and flame flashing through a dry stubble field. The nation, called alternatively "Jacob" and "Joseph" (see comment on previous verse), acts as a single unit, as indicated by the singular verbal form here in contrast to the plural of the last verse. Tinder dry conditions of a harvested field are familiar to the audience, and the effect of a fire on it is undoubtedly well known, so the image is immediately appreciated (see also Ex. 15:7; Isa. 5:24; Nah. 1:11). The reunited twelve tribes will at a future date be a fire that consumes the "house of Esau."

While the name "Esau" is familiar in this book (vv. 6, 8, 19, 21), the combination "house of Esau" occurs nowhere else in the Bible. It was minted by Obadiah to provide a formal counterpart to the other two houses in the verse and as a play on the fraternal relationship between Esau and Jacob. Here is another example of talion, where what goes around comes around (see comments on v. 15): Edom will suffer what Judah has suffered at her hand.[8] The next sentence expounds the metaphor using plural forms ("they will set *them* on fire and burn *them*") rather than the singulars of the NIV. Each individual Edomite, any potential survivor, is annihilated. Unlike Judah, which has survivors, even if Edom betrays them (Obad. 14), Edom herself has none.

The readers/hearers are again reminded in a prose statement why they can depend on the sayings here recorded—"because" (not in the NIV) they are from Yahweh himself. This fourth mention of the divine speaker marks the boundary of the third message as the previous mentions also did (vv. 1, 8, beginning points; vv. 4, 18, ending points).

Bridging Contexts

LOGICAL CONSEQUENCES. As parents, we want to protect our children. When danger looms, we jump in to save them from harm. As they mature, however, there needs to be a point where parents step back and let the chips fall where they may, especially if the impending

---

7. An alternate reading, "they shall dispossess those who dispossessed them," based on the Hiphil rather than the MT Qal form, has impressive textual support (LXX, Vulgate, Syriac, Muraba'at). It would also fit the context of Obadiah where talion is a key motif.

8. This is similar to Ezek. 25:14, where the same image of reciprocal retaliation appears, though without the motif of burning.

harm is due to their own bad choices. The maturing process does not mean just getting older, but also getting wiser, and this involves not only the ability to make one's own decisions, but also the ability to live with the consequences. When parents step in too quickly with car repair payments, erasing all debts, or providing bail, children do not learn the logical consequences of reckless driving, profligate spending, or illegal behavior. The result of this parental intervention is partially shown by high teenage driving accident death rates,[9] record high consumer debt among all age groups, and a sixfold increase in violent crime arrests among teenagers over the three decades up to 1994.[10]

Nations need accountability as well, and Edom receives that because of her bad choices. She was using her relative power to show active hostility against neighbor Israel when that nation was being beaten down by Mesopotamian forces. While Edom might not have been able to disturb Israel significantly in one-on-one interactions, she acts much like the cowardly bully who is antagonistic only when there is overwhelming power displayed against the weaker victim.

What logical consequences face the church and the nation today? Does a lack of moral integrity among church leaders not have the consequent result of showing that morality is irrelevant? Does a high jail term of forty years for Jim Bakker's financial fraud but governmental support for abortion not have the consequence that we treat money as more important than people? Does governmental financial support of unwed mothers and a tax penalty against married couples, as compared to domestic partners, not logically support parenting without marriage? Does even the use of euphemistic words such as "ethnic cleansing" and "racial profiling" instead of "genocide" and "racism" not logically lead to downplaying the severity of these, and other, issues that are of extreme importance for human life and dignity?

While this list cannot be exhaustive or even adequately representative, it illustrates that the church, like all individuals, needs to examine its words and actions as carefully as possible for potential results before they are spoken or done (cf. Prov. 6:1–5; 17:27, 28; 29:20).

Some today in the climate of ethical relativism question the morality of saying that God will punish in wrath.[11] This is not a scriptural perspective,

---

9. "Sixteen- and 17-year-olds represent only about 2 percent of all drivers, but they are involved in nearly 11 percent of crashes. Traffic accidents are the leading cause of death for teens, costing 5,805 lives in 1996" (*US News and World Reports* [Dec. 29, 1997], available at http://www.usnews.com/usnews/issue/971229/29driv.htm).

10. See information on the www.crime.about.com website.

11. See John Barton, *Joel and Obadiah* (OTL; Louisville: Westminster John Knox, 2001), 154.

however. All peoples are expected to have a moral code by which they live and by which they are judged (cf. Amos 1:3–2:3 and other prophetic oracles against foreign nations). As they seek to annihilate Israel and Judah, so they are themselves eradicated (e.g., Isa. 17:14; Jer. 46:28; Zeph. 1:18).

ACCOUNTABILITY. The old adage that "might makes right" is blatantly and biblically false, as evident from bullies, whether in school playgrounds or in international affairs. While the stronger might be able to get away with things for a while, all recognize that there is wrong that is intrinsically wrong, even if someone in power is able to get away with it. This is evidenced as I write by the extradition of the former Serbian leader Slobodan Milosevic to stand trial before the International War Crimes Tribunal in The Hague, in a similar way to the trials of Nazi war leaders in Nuremberg half a century ago. It is not true that "what is right is what I can get away with."

The church needs to be constantly aware of this problem as it takes its stand as the prophetic conscience of the state. While Israel is a theocracy, with the idea of the prophets holding kings responsible to the national constitutional foundation of the covenant, so today's state needs a prophetic voice. While the U.S. constitution calls for a system of checks and balances between the branches of government, the church needs to be ready and willing to bring a theological perspective to bear on what is constitutionally a secular enterprise. Both foreign and domestic policy need to be scrutinized biblically, and decision-makers need to be held accountable to standards derived from concepts of equity and justice rather than just national economic well-being.

Obadiah 19–21

[19] People from the Negev will occupy
    the mountains of Esau,
  and people from the foothills will possess
    the land of the Philistines.
  They will occupy the fields of Ephraim and Samaria,
    and Benjamin will possess Gilead.
[20] This company of Israelite exiles who are in Canaan
    will possess the land as far as Zarephath;
  the exiles from Jerusalem who are in Sepharad
    will possess the towns of the Negev.
[21] Deliverers will go up on Mount Zion
    to govern the mountains of Esau.
  And the kingdom will be the LORD's.

THE BOOK CLOSES with a different style, in contrast to the preceding sections. It is completely in the third person and has long sentences with little verbal variation. It mainly consists of a list, with little expansion. Some also detect numerous secondary expansions or glosses. Because of the stylistic differences, some suggest that this derives from a different hand.[1] While this may be so, there has not been sufficient study of ancient writing techniques from Israel or its surroundings to be able to categorically say what is appropriate for the period and what is not. Most claims are based on contemporary Western practices rather than being grounded in this period. More than one hand is possible, but a better established, objective methodology for determining such things needs to be developed.

Whatever the prehistory of the text, this last section had numerous ties with the preceding context. The opening Hebrew grammatical form (*waw*-consecutive) regularly indicates continuation from the previous passage.[2] The specific verbal form (*waw*-consecutive + perfect), which occurs twice in

---

1. See Allen, "Obadiah," 168–70; Raabe, *Obadiah*, 16–17.

2. "This name best expresses the prevailing syntactical relation, by *waw consecutive* an action is presented as the direct, or at least temporal *consequence* of a preceding action" (GKC § 49a, n. 1); cf. B. K. Waltke and M. O'Connor, *An Introduction to Biblical Hebrew Syntax* (Winona Lake, Ind.: Eisenbrauns, 1990), 477.

verse 19, while odd in this location, parallels the same form of the same verb in verse 17a, and "Mount Esau" occurs twice here (vv. 19, 21), echoing verse 8. Mount Zion (v. 21) picks up from verse 17. Finally, Yahweh ends the book, just as he began it.

Conceptually, these concluding verses relate to the preceding section, expanding and explaining what is meant by it (esp. v. 17). While this does not prove that the work comes from one hand, it is hard to imagine the two parts existing as autonomous entities completely separate from each other. At the very least, one of the sections is written with full knowledge of, and dependence on, the other, and this is how it is presented to its hearers/ readers.[3]

A glance at the textual apparatus of the standard Hebrew text and a study of the commentaries indicate that interpretations of these verses are divergent and many.[4] Taking the text at face value, paying attention to the various syntactic features, moves toward providing an understandable text, and William of Occam's principle that the simplest of several principles is the best will be followed here.

Verse 19 lists various people who possess, or dispossess (see v. 17 for a discussion of the verb), peoples or places. The first verb has two subjects, (lit.) "the Negev" and "the foothills," each acquiring a direct object, "Mount Esau" and "the Philistines" respectively, both marked by the regular Hebrew accusative indicator. The verb is implied rather than duplicated for the second pair (though the NIV makes it explicit).

The form of the first clause exactly parallels that of the second half of verse 17. The "Negev" is a synecdoche representing its inhabitants (cf. NIV "the people of"), as did all of the geographical names functioning as verbal subjects, since people rather than locations possess land. The Negev is a dry region geographically adjacent to Edom to its west (cf. Num. 21:1; Judg. 1:9), in the vicinity of Arad and Beersheba. It is the part of Judah most easily able to convey inhabitants to its neighboring territory. Mount Esau/Edom is the only territory among those listed that is not included within Israel's traditional territorial boundaries (Deut. 2:4–5). Rather than retaking what was originally hers, Judah is applying talion, repaying Edom for her inappropriate actions (vv. 10–14; cf. the tie with Amos 9:12, see comments on Obad. 17).

The "foothills" ("Shephelah") lay to the east of the Mediterranean coastal plain and are the western approach to the central highlands of Judah. At times they are designated as having two parts, that of Israel in the north

---

3. Ben Zvi, *Historical-Critical Study*, 197; Raabe, *Obadiah*, 18.
4. See Raabe, *Obadiah*, 256–58, for a discussion of various proposals.

(Josh. 11:1–3, 16) and that of Judah in the south, occupying a strip of about ten by fifty miles running southwest from Gezer (Deut. 1:7–8; Josh. 10:40; 11:16; 12:8; Judg. 1:9). It was the natural location to move against the Philistine pentapolis, which lay on the coastal plain immediately to its west, dispossessing its people and retaking land that was part of Judah's traditional territory (e.g., Ex. 23:31; Num. 34:6; Josh. 15:45–47, where they were listed as belonging to the foothills; implied in Gen. 15:18–21). This same promise is made in Zephaniah 2:4–7. While some of its cities were previously conquered by the Babylonians, they are still inhabitable and inhabited during Obadiah's period. The Philistines, while facing frequent wars with Israel (e.g., 2 Kings 18:8), Assyria, Egypt (Jer. 47:1), and Babylon, did not disappear as a result of any of these conflicts. By the time of the Persian acquisition of the territory in 539 B.C., the Philistine population was assimilated with its occupiers and neighbors, and by the conquest by Alexander the Great in 333 B.C., all that remained was the name "Palestine."[5]

The second Hebrew verb in verse 19 does not supply an expressed subject in relation to the first two direct objects, "the fields of Ephraim and Samaria."[6] These territories are farther north, in what was previously Israelite territory. Ephraim's tribal territory stretched from the Mediterranean just north of the Philistine territory into the central highlands. As the major tribe in the north, its name is synonymous at times with the entire northern kingdom (e.g., Isa. 7; Jer. 31:9, 18, 20).[7] Though the text does not indicate those who take this territory, the logical repossessor of this territory is the "house of Joseph" or the broader "house of Jacob" (Obad. 18). The former is appropriate since Ephraim is one of Joseph's two sons (Gen. 41:52; 46:20).

"Samaria" was the former capital of Israel and was conquered, along with the whole northern kingdom, by the Assyrians in 722 B.C., showing that Obadiah was written after that date (see introduction). This northern territory did regain some measure of autonomy under the Persians after 539 B.C., but it maintained a distinction from Judah in the south (cf. 2 Kings 17:29, where the Samaritans were condemned for syncretistic worship practices; see numerous New Testament passages, including Matt. 10:5).

The third direct object ("Gilead") will be dispossessed by Benjamin. Gilead lies northeast of the Dead Sea and of the territory inhabited by Benjamin, whose tribal territory lies just north of Jerusalem and south of that of Ephraim

---

5. See Raabe, *Obadiah*, 259–60; *NEAEHL*, sub "Ashdod," "Ashkelon," "Gaza"; Katzenstein, "Philistines (History)"; Dothan, "Philistines (Archaeology)."

6. See *HALOT*, sub שָׂדֶה 2.

7. S. Herrmann, "Ephraim (P), Ephraim in the Bible," *ABD*, 2:531; J. D. Purvis, "Samaria (Place)," *ABD*, 5:914–21.

(Josh. 18:11–28).[8] Benjamin has several historical ties with the area (e.g., Judg. 21:8–14, where Israel battles Jabesh Gilead and Benjamin stole their women for wives; 1 Sam 11:1–11, where Saul, a Benjamite, defeats the Ammonites on behalf of Jabesh Gilead; 2 Sam. 2:8–11, where one of Saul's sons becomes king over the area) and is the closest to reclaim this area that was originally part of the territory of Reuben, Gad, and half-Manasseh (Josh. 13:8–13). Other prophets also mention its restoration to Israel (Jer. 50:19; Mic. 7:14; Zech. 10:10).

Verse 20 is the most difficult in the book to interpret. The number of geographical and ethnic terms indicates that it is a continuation of the register of reoccupation from the last verse, but the form is distinct from what precedes, and much of the interpretation is tentative at best. A literal translation of the Masoretic Text is: "Now the exile(s) of this army/fortress *are* for the Israelites who *are* Canaanites as far as Zarephath, and the exile(s) of Jerusalem who *are* in Sepharad, they would possess the cities of the Negev"; this appears to have several textual difficulties.

The opening Hebrew letter of the verse (w^e) is a conjunction that can join sentences when attached to an initial verb, but tends to separate them while attached to a noun starting the sentence (as here). These "circumstantial" forms indicate a period contemporaneous with the preceding period.[9] At the same time that the (re)possessions of verse 19 are taking place, the activities of verse 20 are going on. The two halves of the verse each begin with the same term, *gālut* (NIV "exiles"). It can mean either the people involved (as per the NIV; Isa. 20:4; 45:13; Jer. 24:5; 28:4; 29:22; 40:1; Amos 1:6, 9) or the state of exile (2 Kings 25:27; Jer. 52:31; Ezek. 1:2; 33:21; 40:1). The former understanding is preferable here since the term is the subject of the only verb in the sentence, which is plural. Exile to Babylon either in 597 B.C. (2 Kings 25:27//Jer. 52:31; Jer. 24:5; 28:4; 29:22; Ezek. 1:2; 33:21; 40:1) or 586 B.C. (Jer. 40:1) is the most common referent of the noun, though two other earlier groups are also referred to by the term—an unidentified group who is taken by the Philistines and by Tyre and is handed over, probably as slaves, to Edom (Amos 1:6, 9), and a group from Cush/Ethiopia exiled by the Assyrians (Isa. 20:4). The Babylonian exiles seem the best subjects for this verse.

The meaning of the remaining geographic/ethnic terms in the verse is fairly clear, even though their function might not be. "Canaanites" (without a definite article, similar to "Philistines" in v. 19) reside along the eastern Mediterranean from what is now south Syria and Lebanon (including

---

8. M. Ottosson, "Gilead (Place)," *ABD*, 2:1020–22; K.-D. Schunk, "Benjamin (Person)," *ABD*, 1:670–73.

9. F. I. Andersen, *The Sentence in Biblical Hebrew* (The Hague: Mouton, 1974), 77.

Byblos), Sidon (cf. Gen. 10:15; 1 Chron. 1:13), and Tyre in the north, down into Israel including the Galilee, comprising most of the territory settled by Israel during the Conquest. Egyptian texts extend Canaan as far south as Gaza, and numerous biblical and extrabiblical texts refer to its northern extensions (e.g., Josh. 13:4; Judg. 1:31–32; cf. Matt. 15:22 where "Canaan" parallels "Syrophoenician" in Mark 7:26).[10] Composed of a mixture of ethnic groups, it is in constant tension with Israel since both occupy the same land.

"Zarephath" is a coastal town between Tyre and Sidon, so it is part of Canaan. It served as a refuge for Elijah when the famine he announced showed the superiority of Yahweh over Baal, Canaan's storm god (1 Kings 17:8–24; Luke 4:26). Hearers/readers would call this episode of God's deliverance to mind when they encounter the location in this prophecy. The town appears to have marked the northernmost boundary of the Canaanites in this listing.

"Jerusalem" is the capital of Judah. Its name first appears in Egyptian execration texts from the early second millennium B.C., as well as in the Amarna letters from some four hundred years later as one of the Canaanite city states.[11] First encountered in the Bible as a Canaanite site (Josh. 10:1–4), it was captured by Judah in the period of the Conquest (Judg. 1:8), but must have been resettled, since David retook it (2 Sam. 5:6–7). It was David's capital, identified as "the city of David" (2 Sam. 5:9; 1 Chron. 11:7). It continued as the capital of Judah throughout the divided monarchy, being captured and looted by the Babylonians in 586 B.C.

"Sepharad" is an enigma, with numerous suggestions as to its location. Early versions identify it with Spain; a few more recent commentators suggest Hesperides, a site in North Africa; a city located in western Media (what is today Iran; cf. Neo-Assyrian texts); or Sardis in western Turkey. Since Assyrian and Babylonian exiles from all their captured territories, including Jerusalem, were widely scattered (see 2 Kings 16:9; 17:6; 25:5–21; 1 Chron. 5:26; Isa. 20:4; Amos 5:27), any of these sites is a possibility, though the latter two suggestions appear to have more merit. Since many of the exiles are said to be taken to the east, option 3 is attractive, though many recent scholars prefer Sardis because of strong ties between Persia and the Lydians, whose city Sardis is.[12]

What is of primary importance for the passage, however, is not the starting point but the destination of the returnees. They come back to the

---

10. P. C. Schmitz, "Canaan (Place)," *ABD*, 1:828–31.

11. *NEAEHL*, 2:698, and a detailed study and detailed bibliography of the history and archaeology of the site, 2:698–804.

12. See Raabe, *Obadiah*, 266–68, for discussion and bibliography.

ancestral holdings of Israel, including the southern cities of the Negev, just as others of their brothers settle to the far north, in Zarephath. This anticipates the return under Zerubbabel and Ezra (Ezra 2; 8). Though the Negev is not mentioned in connection with this return, both Jerusalem and the towns of Judah are (2:1). This implies the inclusion of the Negev towns as well.

While the identifications are relatively straightforward, the grammatical structure into which they are placed is not. The second word of the sentence ("company" in NIV) is textually defective if not corrupt. "Company of" (*haḥêl*) reflects a form of a word that has already been encountered twice as "wealth" (vv. 11, 13, *ḥêlô*, "his wealth," derives from *ḥayil*, "wealth; troop, company"). *Haḥêl*, is interpreted as a definite article ("the") plus a masculine singular construct form of the noun. If so, the form is written defectively, meaning lacking a vowel letter (as the first word in the verse is missing one) since the construct form of the suggested noun always has a middle "y," which is not found here.[13] This suggestion is a possibility, but a difficulty is that a construct form does not generally occur with a definite article as this word appears to do.[14] The article is fairly certain, since the Hebrew practice of also attaching one to a following demonstrative pronoun is followed (*hazzeh*; i.e., "the this"). If this is the correct interpretation, in spite of the errant definite article, the demonstrative pronoun points back to those mentioned in verse 19, giving those identified there as the Benjamites, those of the foothills and of the Negev the more general title "Israelites." Raabe suggests that "Israelites" is added to make sure that the careless reader does not think that the Philistines, who also suffered exile (Amos 9:7), are included in those returning in Obadiah 20.[15]

The Hebrew describes the Israelites as "who are Canaanites." This is a puzzling, and unique, identification, which is most usefully reread as "who dispossess the Canaanites," the exact form of the only existing verb in this verse.[16] This interpretation is consistent with the activities of these two verses. It also provides a semantic, as well as structural, parallel to the second half of the verse. Another possibility, adopted by the NASB, adds a single prefixed preposition of one letter, resulting in "who are *among* the Canaanites as far as Zarephath." The exiles thus intermix with, but are not identical to, the

---

13. *DCH*, 3:213, which lists forms from extrabiblical as well as biblical sources, does not list any defective forms of the noun.

14. Waltke and O'Connor, *Biblical Hebrew Syntax*, 156–57.

15. Raabe, *Obadiah*, 264.

16. The MT reading *ʾăšer* was read as *yiršû*, the transposition of two letters and the substitution of two for one (so KJV, NIV, NRSV, REB, NJB, NJPS).

Canaanites. This indicates that the returning exiles do not in fact have very far to return; their exile is relatively local. This reading makes the entire first part of the verse the subject of the verb, which occurs toward the end.

Attention in verse 21 finally is directed back to the center of Judah. Jerusalem (here "Mount Zion") is its capital and, as such, is the former site of the thrones of its kings and also of its God. "Deliverers" or saviors (cf. Deut. 22:27; Judg. 3:9, 15; Isa. 19:20) first ascend on the mountain to liberate it, and from there they serve as governors or rulers (cf. "judges," Judg. 2:16–18 and *passim*) over Mount Esau, Obadiah's unique term for Edom (Obad. 8–9, 19). Freedom from oppression is won for beleaguered Israel, and one of the oppressors, Edom, is herself subjugated.

The new rule surpasses the former one for justice and equity, as well as a sure control over the territory, since this time Yahweh himself exercises kingship. The NIV's "kingdom" is ambiguous, more readily indicating the territory over which the king exercises sovereignty ("realm"). This term, however, refers to the act of ruling and the status of one as king.[17] While all of the earth is Yahweh's territory (Ex. 19:5), he now retakes his position as sovereign (cf. Ps. 22:27–28), not only over Judah and Israel but also over Mount Esau, and indeed over all of the nations. While Israel is yet in exile, her King promises that he is on his way back to his throne.

EXILE AS FOREIGN POLICY. The Assyrians and Babylonians pursued a foreign policy of deportation in order to control their subjects. When they defeated a people and placed them into a vassal relationship with their conquering overlords, parts of the population, especially the nobility and the skilled artisans, were uprooted from their native land and resettled elsewhere.

While this policy may have some punitive effect for opposing their power, these enemy nations had other means for punishing the ringleaders. This is visible on the famous limestone wall reliefs of the capture of Lachish from Sennacherib's palace at Nineveh. There the common folk are being led away from the city into exile, while the leaders are impaled on stakes outside the city walls, and others are flayed.[18] One of the main reasons for this policy is

---

17. HALOT, sub מְלוּכָה.

18. Currently housed in the British Museum and widely published. See, e.g., J. B. Pritchard, *The Ancient Near East: An Anthology of Texts and Pictures* (Princeton: Princeton University Press, 1958), plate 101. See also the written record of Sennacherib's third campaign, against Jerusalem, in which he boasts of deporting some and killing and impaling others (*COS*, 2:303).

to stem any underground insurgency against their overlordship. If those with leadership abilities are resettled among strangers far away from their homeland, it is difficult to conspire with those of like mind to restore the homeland. Also, any conspiracy is difficult to bring to fruition if the conspirators are so far removed from their homeland that it is doubtful that they ever see it again.

The plan of Yahweh is to stem and reverse this harsh practice. When the Babylonians fell to the Persians in 539 B.C., their vassals reverted to new masters. The Persians, however, had a different foreign policy as regards their subjects. They allowed them to return home, rebuild their religious and economic infrastructure, and thus not only be psychologically better off but also financially so. This made it easier for them to supply the tribute on which any empire depends.

This new policy is reflected in 2 Chronicles 36:23 and Ezra 1:2–4, which records Cyrus's release of the people to return to Jerusalem. An actual inscription from Cyrus has been found and published. Although a self-vaunting propaganda piece, it does confirm the biblical account, not by mentioning the name of "the LORD, the God of heaven" as the one giving him rule (2 Chron. 36:23; Ezra 1:2), but he does claim leave from Marduk, the chief Babylonian deity: "I returned the gods to the sacred centers . . . whose sanctuaries had been abandoned for a long time. . . . I gathered all the inhabitants and returned (to them) their dwellings."[19] It is this practice of returning exiles to their homelands, which is reflected in Obadiah (see also Amos 9:12). There it is promised, but in Ezra and Nehemiah, and in Haggai and Zechariah, it is coming to pass.

REFUGEES, EXILES, AND **the homeless.** The exile of Israel from her homeland looms large in the theology of the Old Testament. It is distressing to realize that exile was a deliberate domestic policy of the Assyrian and Babylonian leadership. "How could someone be so cruel?" As a practical construct, however, it has little impact on us. What is closer to home, since it is so frequently in our news magazines and papers and on our television, is the problem of refugees. While often couched in neutral sounding euphemisms such as "ethnic cleansing," this same practice of uprooting or eradicating those who are religiously, ethnically, or in some other way different is used as a deliberate policy by nations or groups such as Serbia, Somalia, and Sudan.

---

19. *COS*, 2:315.

By definition of the 1951 Convention Relating to the Status of Refugees, a refugee is a person who "owing to a well-founded fear of being persecuted for reasons of race, religion, nationality, membership in a particular social group, or political opinion, is outside the country of his nationality, and is unable to or, owing to such fear, is unwilling to avail himself of the protection of that country." The numbers are staggering, even though they are not in the forefront of the minds of most of us, since they are the results of conflicts about which we know little since they do not impinge on our "national interest." As of January 2000, the total number of refugees exceeded twenty-two million, which is the equivalent of one in every twelve people in the United States, one in every 2.7 people in Britain, and one in every 1.3 people in Canada.[20]

Even this geographic dispossession may not seem like a big deal to many of us, because Western culture is becoming increasingly mobile. Our ties are formed around our place of work or the immediate family, and any sense of connection to extended family or a specific location has been eroded. Through much of history and in much of the rest of world, however, this has not been the case. Connections and roots in a community are what provide meaning and support, and a severing of these roots deprives people of what gives them identity. In many cultures one is not complete when alone; selfhood ties to community. Deprivation of the latter has profound effects on the former.

Another kind of dispossession that is more prevalent in the English-speaking world is homelessness. Those in the United States who must, at least temporarily, sleep on the streets or in shelters at some time during their lives are estimated to be as high as twelve million.[21] While common causes of homelessness include poverty and mental illness, a decade-old Ford Foundation study indicates that among homeless women and children, 50 percent are in such a state because they are fleeing domestic violence and abuse.[22]

---

20. Refugee numbers are derived from *Refugees by Numbers: 2000 Edition* (United Nations High Commission on Refugees).

21. Based on a study by B. Link et al., "Life-time and Five-Year Prevalence of Homelessness in the United States: New Evidence on an Old Debate," *American Journal of Orthopsychiatry* 65/3 (July 1995): 347–54, with statistics extrapolated in "How Many People Experience Homelessness?" National Coalition for the Homeless Fact Sheet #2, 2/99 (http://nch.nationalhomeless.org/numbers.html).

22. J. Zorza, "Woman Battering: A Major Cause of Homelessness," *Clearinghouse Review* 25/4 (1991): 421–29. While these figures do not reach the high public profile of war statistics, they are as least as horrific, since the domestic murder of women by their partners during the period of Vietnam War involvement by the U.S. equaled the number of American battle deaths during that conflict (M. M. Fortune and C. J. Adams, *Violence against Women and Children: A Theological Sourcebook* [New York: Continuum, 1995], 502, cited in E. A. Heath, "The Levite's Concubine: Domestic Violence and the People of God," *Priscilla Papers* 13/1 [1999]: 10).

This is not a phenomenon which is happening "out there"; domestic violence is also prevalent in the church.[23] Although there are no demographic studies done of homelessness among Christians, they most likely join this population for the same reasons as do others, and in proportional numbers. The church must take a public stand on behalf of these modern-day exiles and demand the cessation of practices, especially within its own community, that lead to this situation.

A traditional conservative approach to this sort of issue is one of quietism: Our interest is to be directed toward things above, not to things of this earth. Social involvement is seen as part of the liberal agenda, and evangelicals must steer clear of that. But both the Old and New Testaments affirm that "the earth is the LORD's," all things and everyone included (Ps. 24:1; 1 Cor. 10:26), and humanity has been mandated to look after it (Gen. 1:29; 9:1). The Sinai covenant is a means for society's supporting the helpless, widow, orphan, and alien. If they do not, Yahweh himself will be their support (Ex. 22:21–24; Deut. 10:18). As Yahweh takes the part of his exiled people in Obadiah, will he not do the same for his dispossessed creatures today?

---

23. J. Alsdurf and P. Alsdurf, *Battered into Submission: The Tragedy of Wife Abuse in the Christian Home* (Downers Grove, Ill.: InterVarsity Press, 1989); N. Nason-Clark, *The Battered Wife: How Christians Confront Family Violence* (Louisville: Westminster John Knox, 1997); C. K. Kroeger and J. R. Beck, ed., *Healing the Hurting: Giving Hope and Help to Abused Women* (Grand Rapids: Baker, 1998); P. Hegstrom, *Angry Men and the Women Who Love Them: Breaking the Cycle of Physical and Emotional Abuse* (Kansas City: Beacon Hill, 1999).

Introduction to Malachi

MALACHI IS THE last of the twelve Minor Prophets, closing the collection of the "Prophets" and, in the Protestant canon, the entire Old Testament. In the Jewish canon the books of the "Writings" follow it. Malachi is unique in the Old Testament because of its form—a dispute or diatribe between God and those of his people who have become apathetic or even antagonistic to him. He dialogues with both people and priests, showing particular concern for their unfaithfulness. The prophecy closes with a look forward to the Day of the Lord, a time of judgment for those who misbehave.

Several elements of the book are most familiar to Christians. "I hate divorce" (2:16a), God says, so many people and churches take this as an absolute statement holding for all time and in every situation. A lack of care in reading a statement like this in its context has led to women and children being sent back into abusive relationships, too often to their death. Malachi 3:10–12 is often quoted in the context of teaching concerning tithing and giving to God's work, though not in a way that is based on the meaning in the context of this book. The last two verses of chapter 4 are also known through their allusion to Elijah coming to usher in the Day of the Lord (4:5–6). Jesus interprets this as anticipating the ministry of John the Baptist, his forerunner (Matt. 11:14; 17:12–13).

Malachi the Person

IN HEBREW, the name *mal'ākî* is translated either as "my messenger/angel," where the *-î* ending is the first person common singular suffix, or as "messenger/angel of Yahweh," where the ending is an abbreviation for Yahweh.[1] Since passages refer to a prophet as a "messenger of Yahweh" in the Old Testament (Hag. 1:13; cf. Mal 2:7, where the term refers to a priest),[2] the name of this book could be a title rather than a proper name, though the latter interpretation appears more convincing. Whichever interpretation one adopts, there is a play on the name in 1:1 and the role of a messenger in 2:7 and 3:1.

The text provides no direct information concerning Malachi (the same also holds for Obadiah). From the book's content, one can perceive that he

---

1. Andrew E. Hill, *Malachi: A New Translation with Introduction and Commentary* (AB 25C; New York: Doubleday, 1998), 16.
2. See David Baker, "God, Names of," *DOTP*, 362–64.

is a steadfast follower of God, who is able to stand up against at least verbal opposition even from his own people (cf. Jer. 20:7).

Geographical Setting

THE TWO NAMED protagonists in the prophecies are Jacob and Esau. While referring to two historical brothers (Gen. 25:21–28), the names also designate two nations that descended from them: Israel (Gen. 32:28; Ex. 1:1) and Edom (Gen. 25:30; 36:1). Edom is the subject of numerous other prophecies of judgment, especially that of Obadiah (see introduction to Obadiah; cf. also Isa. 11:14; 63:1–6; Jer. 25:21; 49:7–22; Ezek. 25:12–14; Joel 3:19; Amos 1:6, 9, 11). It is located in the Transjordanian highlands southeast of the Dead Sea (cf. the mountains of Mal. 1:3).[3]

In the postexilic period, Jacob, or Israel, is limited geographically. From evidence available from the list of returnees from the Babylonian exile under the Persians (Ezra 2:1–34; Neh. 3:1–32; 7:6–38) as well as archaeological findings, the Persian district of Yehud/Judah was centered on Jerusalem (Mal. 2:11) and ranged only from just south of Ein Gedi on the Dead Sea to north of Jericho, and from the Jordan River to On, about ten miles inland from Joppa.[4] Idumea bound it to the south and Samaria to the north. Although the northern nation of Israel was long exiled by this time, its name was used as a synonym of Judah (2:11).

The last geographical reference is Mount Horeb (4:4), an alternative name for Mount Sinai (Ex. 33:6; Sir. 48:7). Though the exact location of the mountain is debated,[5] it is the place where Israel became a nation, since there they received their "constitution," the law of Moses (Ex. 19–24), as well as various other instructions on how to live as a people under the authority of God (Ex. 25–Num. 10:10).

---

3. See, e.g., J. B. Pritchard, *Harper Atlas of the Bible* (New York: Harper & Row, 1987), 35. For studies of the Edomites, see J. R. Bartlett, "The Moabites and Edomites," in *Peoples of Old Testament Times*, ed. D. J. Wiseman (Oxford: Clarendon, 1973), 229–58; J. R. Bartlett, *Edom and the Edomites* (JSOTSup 77; Sheffield: Sheffield Academic Press, 1989); A. Lemaire, "Populations et territories de la Palestine à l'époque Perse," *Transeuphratène* 3 (1990): 45–54; K. G. Hoglund, "Edomites," *Peoples of the Old Testament World*, ed. A. J. Hoerth et al. (Grand Rapids: Baker, 1994), 335–47; D. V. Edelman, *You Shall Not Abhor the Edomite for He Is Your Brother: Edom and Seir in History and Tradition* (Atlanta: Scholars, 1995).

4. See Y. Aharoni and M. Avi-Yonah, *The Macmillan Bible Atlas* (New York: Macmillan, 1968), 171; Charles E. Carter, *The Emergence of Yehud in the Persian Period: A Social and Demographic Study* (JSOTSup 294; Sheffield: Sheffield Academic Press, 1999), esp. ch. 2.

5. See C. Houtman, *Exodus* I (HCOT; Kampen: Kok, 1993), 116–22.

Chronological Setting

UNLIKE SEVERAL OLD TESTAMENT prophetic books (e.g., Isa. 1:1; 6:1; Jer. 1:2; Ezek. 1:1; Dan. 1:1; Hos. 1:1; Amos 1:1; Hag. 1:1), Malachi, like Joel, Obadiah, Jonah, Nahum, and Habakkuk, does not begin with a time indicator. Any dating suggestions must arise from contextual and internal evidence. Regarding the former, Malachi's location at the end of the prophets and immediately after the postexilic prophecies Haggai and Zechariah strongly suggests a postexilic date for this book.[6]

Internally, the first event that might be datable is the destruction of Edom (1:3–4). This may refer to the campaigns of the Babylonian king Nabonidus in the several years following 552 B.C., when numerous cities were besieged and destroyed.[7] The nation was not obliterated, however, and some sites were rebuilt and reinhabited. Another, less precisely datable suggestion is the time of the usurpation of territory by the Nabateans, who forced the Edomites to resettle in Judah during the later Persian period, which ends with the arrival of Alexander of Macedon in 333 B.C.[8] The fact that the Edomites are presented as being hopeful of restoration (1:4) testifies against the latter events being the setting of the prophecy.

An operational altar and sacrificial system in a functioning temple in Jerusalem are evident (1:6–14; 2:13; 3:1; 4:10), requiring a date subsequent to the building of the Second Temple as recorded in Ezra (1; 3:2–3, 8–10). Cyrus, the king of Persia, allowed the Israelites to return and start the building project, but it stalled until reinstituted under Darius in 520 B.C., at the encouragement of Haggai and Zechariah and under the leadership of Zerubbabel and Joshua, the priest. It was finally completed in 516–515 B.C.

---

6. For discussions of the chronological ordering of the Minor Prophets, see R. Rendtorff, *The Old Testament: An Introduction* (Philadelphia: Fortress, 1985), 215; P. R. House, *The Unity of the Twelve* (JSOTSup 97; Sheffield: Sheffield Academic Press, 1990); J. Nogalski, *Literary Precursors of the Book of the Twelve* (BZAW 217; New York: de Gruyter, 1993); idem., *Redactional Processes in the Book of the* Twelve (BZAW 218; New York: de Gruyter, 1993); J. D. Nogalski and M. A. Sweeney, ed., *Reading and Hearing the Book of the Twelve* (Atlanta: Society of Biblical Literature, 2000).

7. See Bartlett, *Edom*, 157–61; idem, "Edom," *ABD*, 2:293.

8. Ibid. For more on the Nabateans, see P. C. Hammond, *The Nabataeans: Their History, Culture, and Archaeology* (Studies in Mediterranean Archaeology 37; Philadelphia: Coronet, 1973); J. I. Lawlor, *The Nabataeans in Historical Perspective* (Grand Rapids: Baker, 1974); A. Negev, *Nabataean Archaeology Today* (New York: New York Univ. Press, 1986); D. F. Graf, "Nabataeans," *ABD*, 4: 970–73; idem, *Rome and the Arabian Frontier: From the Nabataeans to the Saracen* (Aldershot: Ashgate, 1997); J. Taylor, *Petra and the Lost Kingdom of the Nabataeans* (Cambridge, Mass.: Harvard Univ. Press, 2002).

Several other historical, theological, and philological points have been brought to bear on the dating question. Malachi 1:8 mentions a *peḥâ* ("governor," which some suggest is Nehemiah),[9] a proposed Akkadian loanword (*bēl piḫāti*).[10] The term does refer to an official in other Old Testament texts, including a functionary from Assyria (2 Kings 18:24), and indicates a governor or delegated ruler during the Persian period (e.g., Ezra 8:36; Neh. 5:14; Jer. 51:28; Hag. 1:1). The term, even if borrowed, does not help chronologically, however, since it is used of functionaries from as early as the Old Babylonian period.[11]

Verhoef suggests that the excitement of renewed temple worship evident in Haggai and Zechariah has by the time of Malachi been replaced by rote uncaring (1:6–14; 2:1–9; 3:6–12).[12] While this may be the case, it is not necessary to prove a lengthy time lapse, since, for example, there is religious apathy among the priests and Levites at the same time that Hezekiah and the people were enthusiastic about restoring a vibrant Yahwism (2 Chron. 29–30). Since religious fervor on the part of some and spiritual aridity on the part of others in our congregations happens all the time, it should not serve as a criterion for establishing a date for Malachi, whose fellow worshipers are not much different from our own.

A number of the sins condemned in Malachi also concerned Ezra and Nehemiah, suggesting that they are contemporaries. These include:

- perversion of the sacrificial system (Mal. 1:6–2:9; cf. Neh. 13:4–9, 30)
- misuse of the Sabbath (Mal. 2:8–9; 4:4; cf. Neh. 13:15–22)
- intermarriage with foreigners (Mal. 2:11–15; cf. Ezra 9–10; Neh. 10:30; 13:1–3, 23–37)
- cheapening of the tithe (Mal. 3:8–10; cf. Neh. 10:32–39; 13:10–14)
- social exploitation (Mal. 3:5; cf. Neh. 5:1–12).

The implications of these similarities have been interpreted differently, particularly regarding the relative dates of the events. Some suggest that Malachi preceded Ezra and Nehemiah, since the latter put a stop to the

---

9. H. Wolf, *Haggai and Malachi* (Chicago: Moody Press, 1976), 58; G. L. Klein, "An Introduction to Malachi," *CTR* 2 (1987): 24–25.

10. See BDB; *HALOT*.

11. See *AHw*, 120; Jeremy Black et al., *A Concise Dictionary of Akkadian*, 2nd (corrected) ed. (Wiesbaden: Harrassowitz Verlag, 2000), 274.

12. P. Verhoef, *Haggai and Malachi* (NICOT; Grand Rapids: Eerdmans, 1987), 157.

undesirable practices.[13] Others suggest that Malachi is dated to the time of Nehemiah's second visit to Jerusalem (Neh. 13:6–7), since it is at that period he addressed these issues.[14] Unfortunately, dating by categories of sin is not very productive, since specific sins are also not restricted to certain times, and sin is not known to stay eradicated, even if preached against. This is clear throughout the prophets (and indeed throughout human history!), where the same breaches of covenant are condemned again and again by prophetic contemporaries and different prophetic generations.

Evidence is not sufficient to provide a definitive date for the prophecy. Its canonical position at the end of the corpus of prophets places it in the postexilic, Persian period, so Malachi could well be a contemporary of Nehemiah.

The Persians pursued a more enlightened policy toward their subject nations than did the preceding Assyrian and Babylonian empires, who took both Israel (722 B.C.) and Judah (586 B.C.) into exile. These two empires displaced major parts of captured populations, resettling them in various parts of their far-flung territories and importing others to take their place (e.g., 2 Kings 17:23–24; 25:7, 11–21). This hindered any possibility of developing an underground movement to throw off the Mesopotamian overlords, since the leaders of a nation found themselves far removed from any grass-roots support from among their people from which they might develop a guerilla and resistance movement.

Persia, however, reversed this policy among the nations that they inherited when they conquered the Babylonian empire. It allowed subject people to return to their ancestral lands and reestablish their religious practices (e.g., 2 Chron. 36:22–23; Ezra 1:1–4). This the Judeans did, rebuilding the temple and the city walls and establishing their own province under Persian rule (Ezra, Nehemiah, Esther). It is within this context that Malachi prophesies.[15] His audience has lost the enthusiasm of those who were first allowed to

---

13. E. Sellin and G. Fohrer, *Introduction to the Old Testament* (Nashville: Abingdon, 1968), 470. See Klein, "Introduction," 23–24.

14. G. L. Archer Jr., *A Survey of Old Testament Introduction*, rev. ed. (Chicago: Moody Press, 1974), 440.

15. For fuller discussions of the historical background of the Persian period, see K. G. Hoglund, *Achaemenid Imperial Administration in Syria–Palestine and the Missions of Ezra and Nehemiah* (Atlanta: Scholars Press, 1992); J. Berquist, *Judaism in Persia's Shadow: A Social and Historical Approach* (Minneapolis: Fortress, 1995); David L. Petersen, *Zechariah 9–14 and Malachi* (OTL; Louisville: Westminster, 1995), 3–23; Hill, *Malachi*, 51–76; P. Briant, *From Cyrus to Alexander: A History of the Persian Empire* (Winona Lake, Ind.: Eisenbrauns, 2002). For life in Judah during the Persian period, see esp. Carter, *The Emergence of Yehud*; J. Kessler, *The Book of Haggai: Prophecy and Society in Early Persian Yehud* (VTSup 91; Leiden: Brill, 2002).

return to Judah with the task of rebuilding not only a temple but a nation (see the enthusiastic response from diverse areas within the society of the returnees to the call for help in rebuilding the city wall, Neh. 3).

Though not necessarily reflecting all of Judean society, the vocal group with which Malachi is in dialog is at best apathetic to the law of Moses and the practices expected of God's people. Even the priests, those who led Israel in her religious and social practices, helped them discern between right and wrong, acceptable and unacceptable, and taught this to the people (cf. Lev. 10:10–11), were not practicing what they were supposed to preach. Malachi has to enter into debate with them and the people as a whole to even get them to see that what they are doing, or not doing, is irresponsible in light of the covenant with God that constituted them as a nation. They do not realize that their apathy is, in fact, unfaithfulness to that covenant and is placing its very continuation in jeopardy.

Literary Context

CANONICAL AND HISTORICAL context place Malachi closest to Haggai and Zechariah, both of which are also prophecies to a people recently returned from exile. There is a marked contrast between these books in terms of literary form and aim, however. Haggai is in the form of a narrative, tracing the ministry of the prophet as he exhorted and encouraged the disheartened people to action over the course of four months. The goal was to rebuild the ruined temple.

The first part of Zechariah shows much the same chronological framework and seeks the same goal, though in the form of vision reports. Zechariah 9–14 is different in form, language, and concern from the previous eight chapters and shows some similarity to Malachi in that it twice contains material identified as an "oracle" (*maśśāʾ*; 9:1; 12:1; cf. Mal. 1:1).[16] The contents of these two books are dissimilar, however, for Zechariah sought to encourage a flagging people through announcing judgment on her enemies and the mighty presence of God working on their behalf. Malachi, by contrast, challenges an apathetic and antagonistic people through warnings of the mighty presence of God working punishment against them.

In sum, while sharing historical context with Haggai and Zechariah, Malachi presents a different literary character and content. It also has its

---

16. Petersen (*Zechariah 9–14 and Malachi*, 2–3) argues that the shared formal indicators support an interpretation that Zech. 9–14 and Malachi have been integrated into one textual unit by an editor.

own rich vocabulary, some of which it shares with Haggai and Zechariah,[17] but some of which is unique within the Old Testament.[18] Malachi is not an island, however, but does share terms and concepts with other prophecies. A major shared theme is the Day of the Lord, referring to both judgment and deliverance for Israel and the nations (3:1–4:6).[19] Other terms and constructions are also shared, though this does not necessarily indicate literary dependence or, if there is such dependence, which way it went—that is, which book relies on which.[20]

---

17. See Y. Radday, *An Analytical Key-word in Context Concordance to the Books of Haggai, Zechariah and Malachi* (Wooster: Biblical Research Associates, 1973); Y. Radday and M. A. Pollatschek, "Vocabulary Richness in Post–Exilic Prophetic Books," *ZAW* 92 (1980): 333–46.

18. Hill (*Malachi*, 413–41) lists 38 unique terms and nominal constructions.

19. See *ABD*, 2:82–83.

20. See Hill, *Malachi*, 401–12, for a list of shared forms.

Outline of Malachi

Annotated Bibliography on Malachi

Baldwin, Joyce G. *Haggai, Zechariah, Malachi*. TOTC. Downers Grove, Ill.: InterVarsity Press, 1972. A useful, though brief, work by an experienced commentator.

Floyd, Michael H. *Minor Prophets: Part 2*. FOTL 22. Grand Rapids: Eerdmans, 2000. Especially useful for bibliography and structure.

Hill, Andrew E. *Malachi: A New Translation with Introduction and Commentary*. AB 25D. New York: Doubleday, 1998. Probably the best Malachi commentary currently available for exegetical study.

Hugenberger, Gordon P. *Marriage as Covenant: A Study of Biblical Law and Ethics Governing Marriage, Developed from the Perspective of Malachi*. VTSup 52. Leiden: Brill, 1994; rep. Grand Rapids: Baker, 1998. A useful study of the vexing ethical issue of divorce.

Kaiser, Walter C. Jr., *Malachi: God's Unchanging Love*. Grand Rapids: Baker, 1984. Accessible exegesis and application.

Merrill, Eugene H. *An Exegetical Commentary: Haggai, Zechariah, Malachi*. Chicago: Moody Press, 1994. Useful for study of the Hebrew text and biblical context. Reprint: Dallas, Tex.: Biblical Studies Press, 2003.

Petersen, David L. *Zechariah 9–14 and Malachi*. OTL. Louisville: Westminster, 1995. A useful commentary from a mainline interpretational perspective.

Pohlig, James N. *An Exegetical Summary of Malachi*. Dallas: Summer Institute of Linguistics, 1998. A helpful synopsis of various translations and interpretations of others on every word of the text.

Stuart, Douglas. "Malachi." Pages 1245–396 in *The Minor Prophets: An Exegetical and Expository Commentary*, ed. T. E. McComiskey. Grand Rapids: Baker, 1998. A full exposition with an especially complete bibliography.

Verhoef, P. A. *Haggai and Malachi*. NICOT. Grand Rapids: Eerdmans, 1987. A good, verse-by-verse commentary showing the breadth of perspectives.

Malachi 1:1

AN ORACLE: The word of the LORD to Israel through Malachi.

THIS HEADING IDENTIFIES aspects of the book: what it is, whom it is from, and whom it is to. The genre is an "oracle" (*maśśā²*), the identity of two other prophetic books (Nah. 1:1; Hab. 1:1) and of portions of larger prophetic collections (Isa. 13:1; 15:1; 17:1; 19:1; 21:1; 22:1, 11, 13; 23:1; 30:6; 46:1–2 [wordplay]; Zech. 9:1; 12:1; cf. 2 Chron. 24:27; Isa. 14:28; Jer. 23:33–40; Lam. 2:14; Ezek. 12:10). Its Hebrew root (*nś²*) means "raise, lift," with a related noun meaning "burden, load."[1]

Divine origin and authority derive from a *maśśā²* being "the word of the LORD," a general designation of laws (Isa. 2:3) and prophecies (e.g., Isa. 28:13, 14; 38:4; Jer. 1:2, 4) as of divine origin. "LORD" (*yhwh*), the personal, covenant name of Israel's God (see comments on Joel 1:1), is the most common designation of God in Malachi (forty-six occurrences); "God" (*²elōhîm*) occurs only seven times. The message claims divine authority through its oracular nature.

The prophecy is directed toward "Israel" (cf. 1:5; 2:16). From its use in 2:11, this term is synonymous with Judah. This identification also fits the prophecy's historical context, since the northern kingdom of Israel was exiled in 722 B.C., no longer existing by this period. Some Israelite remnants returned from exile under Cyrus (cf. Ezra 1:2–4), and so they also heard and appropriated this message. The united nation, Israel and Judah combined under the name of the former, is intended in 4:4, but there the modifier "all Israel" indicates this inclusivity.

The intermediary or messenger is "Malachi," who is not further identified. He fulfills a scribal function similar to that of Moses at Sinai (Lev. 7:38). This similarity of role supports seeing *mal²ākî* as a proper noun rather than as a title, since scribes regularly placed their names on documents for which they

---

1. BDB, 669–73; *HALOT*. There is evidence of an understanding of the homonyms, since Isa. 22:1, 25, for example, seems to play on the two meanings of the noun, making an inclusio for the passage. Cf. also the discussion of Jer. 23:33–40 below.

claimed responsibility.[2] The message is sent "through," that is, "by the hand of," the prophet, signifying power designated by another rather than one's own actual power and authority (e.g., Gen. 38:20; Lev. 16:21; Isa. 19:4); this word is used of messages from God or others (e.g., Ex. 9:35; 35:29; 38:21; Lev. 8:36; 1 Kings 12:15; 16:7; Hag. 1:1).[3] Just as Moses, the lawgiver to Israel at Sinai (cf. Lev. 7:37–38), did not receive his legitimation through his person but rather through Yahweh, his sender, so it is for this prophet. Both message and messenger receive a divine imprimatur.

ORACLES. The nature of an oracle (*maśśāʾ*) as well as a play on the dual meaning of the word is best seen in Jeremiah 23:33–40. Comparing English translations shows this wordplay. The NIV uses "oracle" consistently throughout the passage, while NRSV, following the LXX, uses "burden," rendering verse 33: "When this people, or a prophet, or a priest asks you, 'What is the burden of the LORD?' you shall say to them, 'You are the burden....'" The nature of an "oracle" becomes apparent in verse 36: "But you must not mention 'the oracle of the LORD' again, because every man's own word becomes his oracle and so you distort the words of the living God, the LORD Almighty, our God" (NIV).

A true oracle derives from Yahweh and is not a human product. The means of reception (a dream, vision, or oral communication) is not the issue. This is congruent with the Latin etymology of the English "oracle" as "a divine utterance," which itself derives from the Latin verb "to pray" (*oro*), since revelation is at times requested from the divine. What is central is the origin, not the means, of the message.

THUS SAYS THE LORD. The prophet stood between God and the people as an intermediary, a spokesman charged with faithfully delivering the message to the people. In an earlier period God spoke directly to folks such as Adam and Eve in the Garden of Eden (Gen. 3:9–19) and Moses on the mountain (Ex. 9–24:2), but during most of the Old Testament period, he spoke through the prophets. Many Christians

---

2. See David W. Baker, "Scribes as Transmitters of Tradition," in *Faith, Tradition and History: Old Testament Historiography in its Near Eastern Context*, ed. A. R. Millard, J. K. Hoffmeier, and D. W. Baker (Winona Lake, Ind.: Eisenbrauns, 1994), 65–78.

3. See Waltke-O'Connor, §11.2.1b.

see the preacher as fulfilling the prophetic role, or at least that of the priest, teaching people the revelation of God (Lev. 10:9).

Whichever model is adopted, it is vital to note the difference between the source of the message (God) and its conduit (the preacher). As a preacher, it is too easy to slip into a feeling that the authority lies in me rather than in the Word with which I am entrusted. Lack of diligence in studying the Word, lack of fervor in prayer over the Word, and lack of pastoral contact with the people and their hurts and desires—so that I am unaware of the specific needs they have—make it easy to no longer speak God's message to the people, but my own message, with no real concern for God whatsoever. Claiming to present God's word when it is not his at all not only affects us and our ministry, as it did with the seven sons of Sceva (Acts 19:13–16), but it damages the church and the honor of the name of God.

Jim Jones (1978) and David Koresh (1993) are but two of a regrettably steady stream of those doing this with deadly results, not only to physical life but to eternal life as well. There is, after all, only one person who speaks with his own divine authority (Matt. 7:29; 28:18), and claiming that same authority for ourselves is arrogant folly for us, while at the same time it demeans Christ.

Malachi 1:2—5

"I HAVE LOVED you," says the LORD.
"But you ask, 'How have you loved us?'
"Was not Esau Jacob's brother?" the LORD says. "Yet I have loved Jacob, ³but Esau I have hated, and I have turned his mountains into a wasteland and left his inheritance to the desert jackals."

⁴Edom may say, "Though we have been crushed, we will rebuild the ruins."

But this is what the LORD Almighty says: "They may build, but I will demolish. They will be called the Wicked Land, a people always under the wrath of the LORD. ⁵You will see it with your own eyes and say, 'Great is the LORD—even beyond the borders of Israel!'

Original Meaning

ISRAEL IS BEING belligerent, disputing with God. The book's structure shows this through their repeating God's statements or questions and countering with their own questions. This section recalls the strained relationship between Jacob, Israel's forefather, and his brother, Esau. What irony that the first statement God makes, and which they dispute, is that he loves them.

Yahweh frequently speaks in this book, with most uses of the verb "to say" (ʾmr) referring to him. The literary form used here is a dialog between God and an unidentified "you." Grammatically straightforward, the statement is theologically profound: Yahweh loves Israel. Opening the prophecy in this way indicates that love is a key theme of the book. The verb form commonly indicates completed action, but with a verb indicating a state of being rather than an action, it indicates "an ongoing emotional response."[1]

The usual English rendition "I have loved you" (e.g., KJV, NIV, NRSV, NLT) is adequate as long as one sees the love as continuing (e.g., "I have loved you and still do"; cf. GNB, "I have always loved you") rather than indicating a past action that continues no longer (i.e., "I have loved you, but don't any more"). In spite of the cantankerous nature of those to whom God is speaking and the natural human reaction of wanting to sever the relationship with people

---

1. Ibid., 493.

who are so contentious, Yahweh states his continuing commitment to covenant relationship. He previously established this covenant with his people at Mount Sinai, even though they repeatedly broke it and suffered punishment by exile as a result. Like a parent for a rebellious child (Hos. 11:1–4), Yahweh still loves them.

Israel in turn speaks to Yahweh, using the same verb for speaking, here preceded by the adversative conjunction "but," indicating that they take exception to what he just said. The confrontational nature of the dialog is clear from its very start. The addressee is an unidentified "you," though the rest of the verse indicates who this is. The speaker questions Yahweh, asking about how Yahweh shows his love in an exclamation of surprise or incredulity. The disputation form of a charge and countercharge is clear from the beginning. In other words, the speaker disputes God's love based on the sad situation in which they find themselves, having returned from exile to a ruined and as yet unrestored land (see Haggai and Zechariah, where divine promises are as yet unfulfilled visibly).

Addressing his dialog partner's immediate concern, God recalls an aspect of Israelite prehistory. He asks a rhetorical question to which the hearers are sure to know the answer: What was the relationship between Jacob and Esau (cf. Gen. 25:19–26)? This question is an authoritative declaration of Yahweh ("says the LORD"), functioning rhetorically by continuing to draw the hearers into dialog. Hill suggests that its placement here emphasizes the next clause, which can thus serve as the central thesis statement of the prophecy.[2] God reminds the hearers of the special relationship of covenant affection he has had with Jacob. The final verb of Malachi 1:2 is of the same root ("love") as the first, but the form differs, indicating a continuity with what precedes, translated as "yet" (cf. Gen. 32:31; Judg. 1:35).

The logic of the verse indicates that the unidentified "you" who is loved at its start is the same as "Jacob" loved at its end. God through his prophet addresses his people, the descendants of twelve sons of Jacob, whose changed name "Israel" (Gen. 32:28) became that of the nation as a whole.

An emphatic contrast opens verse 3, which was unhelpfully separated off when the Hebrew scribes divided this text into verses. The word order (in the form of a small chiasm in Hebrew: verb–object–object–verb) shows emphasis: "now as for Esau." The contrast culminates in the second verb, "I have hated" (*śānē'tî*), the exact same verbal form as the first verb in the sentence, but polar opposite in meaning. Its meaning derives from context, which in this text does not concern a strong emotional aversion, a major meaning element of the English term "hate." In the covenant context, one

---

2. Hill, *Malachi*, 150.

loved is a covenant ally, while one hated is outside this covenant relationship, an enemy (cf. Ex. 1:10).

This statement pair (love–hate) concerns election rather than emotions (cf. 2:16): Jacob (and his line) is chosen by God while Esau (and his line) is peripheral to the story of God's continued activity in the Bible. The contrast also brings to bear the friction between the two brothers prophesied to their mother Rebekah (Gen. 25:23). This terminology is also used in the context of marriage, where one wife might be loved and the other "hated" (e.g., Gen. 29:31, 33; Deut. 21:15–17)—a theme picked up, though without this terminology, later in the prophecy (Mal. 2:14–16).

God's "hate" for Esau is expressed in geographic terms. Esau is the progenitor of the Edomites (Gen. 36), settlers in the mountain fastness of the Transjordan. It is proud in its secure location, strategically impregnable, so they thought, to enemy attack (see comments on Obad. 3). Rather than a place of refuge, it will be a "wasteland," ruined by warfare (cf. Lev. 26:33; Josh. 8:28; Isa. 1:7), where wild animals roam instead of its original human inhabitants (Ex. 23:39). Its "inheritance," like that of its Israelite cousins, is described in terms of land (e.g., Gen. 12:1; Num. 26:53–56), which also will experience animal incursions. Jackals are found in deserted ruins (Jer. 9:11; 49:33), not in watered, habitable spots. "Hatred," lack of a covenant relationship, results in a lack of habitation.

There is a possibility that Edom "may" respond in defiance (v. 4), claiming that even God cannot keep them down. Judah is still being addressed, receiving this possible scenario from the prophet. Though Edom has been devastated and destroyed (cf. Jer. 5:17), they claim ability to rebuild under their own power from any destruction God might cause.

Yahweh responds in the words of a complete messenger formula ("this is what the LORD Almighty says"), since the prophet acknowledges that he is simply the conduit for the words of God (v. 1). This complete citation form, unique here in the book, indicates a significant new section of this dialog. Yahweh now speaks with an accompanying epithet "Almighty" (*ṣᵉbā'ôt*; KJV, NRSV, "of hosts"). This is a military term (e.g., 1 Sam. 17:45; Jer. 51:3), accentuating Yahweh's ability to bring the promised destruction; if he has the will, he also has means.

Yahweh does not deny Edom's attempt to take things into her own hands. He rather denies its effectiveness through the use of an antithesis between what they will do ("rebuild") and what he will do ("demolish"). The latter is used of cities and strongholds (2 Sam. 11:25; Ezek. 26:12; Mic. 5:10). Nothing Edom might attempt can be proof against God. As a result of divine destruction, Edom will no longer be known for pride (Obad. 3), but its "land" (lit., its "border") will be renowned for moral wickedness (cf. Mal. 3:15, 19; Ezek. 18:27).

A second unfortunate designation is somewhat hidden by the NIV, since the Hebrew starts the next clause of verse 4 by talking of "*the* people," those recognized as being under God's wrath, his judgment or curse (cf. Num. 23:7–8; Ps. 7:12). The seriousness of this state is emphasized since it is endless (Gen. 13:15; Isa. 30:8; Zeph. 2:9; cf. Mal. 3:4).

In verse 5, Yahweh makes another declaration to Judah (see v. 2). Malachi emphasizes that it is Judah's own eyes that will see God's love by starting this verse with "with your own eyes"; that is, you and no one else will see, and you will not have to take the word of anyone else. It is possible to interpret what is seen ("it") as God's "hatred" for Edom (cf. "the destruction," NLT), but that does not seem to be a proper lead-in to the following doxology. It is not Edom's power but rather God's love that is questioned and needs demonstration. This love for Judah is shown by God's dealing severely with Edom, Judah's enemies. The structure of the contrast (i.e., love–Jacob–Esau–hate) emphasizes its first element over the last.[3]

Because of their seeing, "you [Judah, emphasized again by the front placement of the pronoun in the clause] will say." Now the tone completely reverses the skepticism of verse 2. There Judah questioned, now Judah praises. This doxology, or hymn of praise to the Lord, is an inversion of the first words of the question Judah directed toward him. Some scholars see this doxology as extolling God's greatness (cf. the same wording in Ps. 35:27; 40:17) not only over nations such as Edom (and Judah) but also over circumstances, because (cf. NIV) it is evident even "beyond the borders" of his people. God's fame is spreading abroad (NASB, NLT, NRSV). God will be universally known.

This wide-spreading fame of God does not fit the context, however, since it does not address the point of Judah, who is questioning whether God loves them. Another interpretation fits the context better, therefore, addressing the challenge raised in verse 2. "Border" can denote a country's territory (see comment on v. 4), and this sense fits here as well: God's power is *over* the territory of Judah/Israel.[4] The term "Israel," once designating the combined nation of twelve tribes and later the northern kingdom, here means the much smaller remnant of Judah after their return from exile. Judah, who questions

---

3. S. D. Snyman, "Antitheses in Malachi 1,2–5," *ZAW* 98 (1986): 437–38.

4. Verhof, *Haggai and Malachi*, 206; Hill, *Malachi*, 161. The preposition "over" (*mēʿal*) is used as "on, over" in several places (e.g., Gen. 7:17; Ps 148:4). Waltke-O'Connor §11.3.2 suggest the combination proposition be translated "within," also supporting this interpretation.

God's love, will experience it through his greatness wherever in their land they might live. They are loved, even if they do not respond in kind.

Bridging Contexts

ESAU AND JACOB. Paul, like Malachi, also engages in a disputation, only his is on the subject of God's sovereignty (Rom. 9:14–23). The question he counters is, "Isn't God being unfair in saving some and not others?" He uses this disputation passage concerning God's love for Jacob and hatred of Esau (Mal. 1:2–3) in his own dispute over God's election (Rom. 9:13). Paul looks at the passage from both sides. God's love for Jacob indicates God's great mercy and compassion (9:15, citing Ex. 33:19), not any merit on Jacob's part. From the negative side, Paul doesn't follow through on Esau but on Pharaoh, whose heart he "hardened" in order to display his power (Rom. 9:17, citing Ex. 9:6).

This passage in Romans weighs heavy in the discussion between Calvinists and Arminians on the subject of sovereignty and free will. The topic is beyond the scope of adequate address here, but it should be noted how Paul ends this dispute section. He comes out on the side of God's grace, noting that if it were not for this grace, forgiveness, and love, we would all be "hated" (Rom. 9:29). He is probably using the words "love" and "hate" in the same covenantal way that Malachi did.

Covenant love. "Love" has a range of meanings, from the physical/sexual (Gen. 24:67; 2 Sam. 1:26; Song 1:1, 3, 7) through the relational with family (Gen. 22:2; 25:28) and friends (Lev. 19:18; Jer. 20:4) as well as one's God (Ex. 20:6; Deut. 6:5). This close emotional tie also leads to commitments at various levels, including marriage, but also more broadly in the context of a covenant. It is this progression from emotion to formal commitment that takes place in the relationship between David and Jonathan. They had the emotional bond of love (1 Sam. 18:1, 3; 20:17), which deepened to a sociopolitical commitment when Jonathan willingly gave up his princely robe, tunic, and weapons, symbolically handing his future rule over to David in what is specifically termed a "covenant" (1 Sam. 18:3–4). "Love" is a technical term used in covenant documents, indicating the expected relationship between covenant parties (cf. Deut. 7:8).[5]

"Hate" has the same range of meanings, though at the opposite end of the spectrum. It denotes strong emotional dislike to such an extent that one even goes as far as turning one's back on the expected bonds of family (e.g., Gen.

---

5. See W. Eichrodt, *Theology of the Old Testament*, 2 vols. (OTL; Philadelphia: Westminster, 1961, 1967), 1:250–58.

37:4, 5, 8; Luke 14:26) or clan (Lev. 19:17). It is also used of a covenant relationship. This is most clearly seen in divorce documents where the divorced party, the one deemed outside any continuing covenant, is designated the "hated one" (see also Hos. 9:15).[6]

In the light of this technical terminology, how should one understand God's "love" of Jacob and "hatred" of Esau. They are both statements of election, or lack of it, in relation to God's covenant with Israel and should not be viewed in an absolute way. Esau does not have part of the Mosaic covenant at Sinai, of which Jacob (Israel) is a partner. Esau is punished, driven from her inheritance (v. 3) because of her wickedness (v. 4). That Esau is not "hated" in a universal sense is seen by her inclusion, along with all of humanity, in an even earlier, and more foundational, covenant between God and Noah and all of his descendants (Gen. 9:9–10).

The inclusion of the Edomite/Esau genealogy in Genesis 36 shows the same thing. Jacob is the main recipient in his generation of the covenantal promises, and so is "loved" in relationship to the promises spelled out first to his grandfather, Abram, in Genesis 12:1–3 (cf. 15:1–21, esp. v. 17, where the promises are first called a "covenant"). Esau is not ignored, however. Amos speaks of some Edomites being included in greater Israel, a theme that Acts 15:13–18 picks up.[7] Obadiah pictures Esau's descendents, the Edomites, as unfaithful parties of a covenant in their national history (Obad. 7). Another indication that God's "hatred" of Esau is not permanent and absolute is that the same term also applies to Israel (e.g., Jer. 12:8; Hos. 9:15).

THE LOVE OF GOD. It is significant that the relationship between God and his people, Israel, and between God and others of his creatures is expressed in terms of "love."[8] There are other models that could be chosen to express this relationship, even within the conceptual model of a covenant. Since, for example, the covenant form God uses to describe his relationship with Israel is that of vassal (Israel) and great King (Yahweh), the terminology of choice could equally be one of

---

6. E. G. Kraeling, *The Brooklyn Museum Aramaic Papyri* (New Haven, Conn.: Yale Univ. Press, 1953), 7:34, 39.

7. See D. M. King, "The Use of Amos 9:11–12 in Acts 15:16–18," *ATJ* 21 (1989): 8–13.

8. Yahweh, but not "God," is the subject of the verb "love" some 34 times in the Old Testament, 24 of these with human objects (mostly Israel or Israelites, e.g., Deut. 4:37; 7:8, 13; 10:15; 23:5; Neh. 13:26; Mal.1:2[3x], but also others [e.g., Deut. 10:18, aliens; Isa. 48:14, Cyrus; Ps. 146:8; Prov 15:9, righteous]).

---

power or coercion. Instead, it is expressed in terms of love, with all of the risk that such a basis for a relationship entails.

When one opens up to a love relationship, one also opens up to the possibility of hurt. This is poignantly expressed by one who writes: "God is love. That is why he suffers.... The tears of God are the meaning of history."[9] God maintains that covenant love with his chosen people even though they regularly "unchose" him, "hating" him by entering into a covenant relationship with others.

This love is not exclusive to Israel, however, because God loves the entirety of his creation (e.g., John 3:16; 2 Cor. 13:11, 14; Eph. 2:4). This love is covenantal and certain because of the nature of the divine lover, who does not waver in his commitments (Num. 23:19; 1 Sam. 15:29; Hos. 11:8–9; Titus 1:2; Heb. 6:18). Even though his lovers abandon and "hate" him and "love" another (John 3:19; cf. 15:18–25), he cannot do so to them.

This kind of covenantal, committed love must serve as a model to the church, since we are to love each other as God, in the person of Jesus his Son, loves us (John 13:34; 1 John 4:7–12). This will be actualized not in a vapid, fickle sentimentality, since that is fleeting and self-centered at its foundation. Rather, it is based on a realization of mutual need for the other for the benefit of both parties.

This kind of love must also be open to discipline, which is incompatible with love seen only as emotion. True covenant love must be willing to show itself, if necessary, as "hate," that is, expelling the other from the relationship (Matt. 18:15–17). This is not absolute abandonment but is done so that the person expelled might experience the loss of the compelling love of the covenant relationship, with the goal that he or she seeks reconciliation and restoration. After all, Jesus commands love toward those who "hate" us, no matter how this is shown (5:43–44).

---

9. N. Wolterstorff, *Lament for a* Son (Grand Rapids: Eerdmans, 1987), 90.

Malachi 1:6–14

"A SON HONORS his father, and a servant his master. If I am a father, where is the honor due me? If I am a master, where is the respect due me?" says the LORD Almighty. "It is you, O priests, who show contempt for my name.

"But you ask, 'How have we shown contempt for your name?'

⁷"You place defiled food on my altar.

"But you ask, 'How have we defiled you?'

"By saying that the LORD's table is contemptible. ⁸When you bring blind animals for sacrifice, is that not wrong? When you sacrifice crippled or diseased animals, is that not wrong? Try offering them to your governor! Would he be pleased with you? Would he accept you?" says the LORD Almighty.

⁹"Now implore God to be gracious to us. With such offerings from your hands, will he accept you?"—says the LORD Almighty.

¹⁰"Oh, that one of you would shut the temple doors, so that you would not light useless fires on my altar! I am not pleased with you," says the LORD Almighty, "and I will accept no offering from your hands. ¹¹My name will be great among the nations, from the rising to the setting of the sun. In every place incense and pure offerings will be brought to my name, because my name will be great among the nations," says the LORD Almighty.

¹²"But you profane it by saying of the Lord's table, 'It is defiled,' and of its food, 'It is contemptible.' ¹³And you say, 'What a burden!' and you sniff at it contemptuously," says the LORD Almighty.

"When you bring injured, crippled or diseased animals and offer them as sacrifices, should I accept them from your hands?" says the LORD. ¹⁴"Cursed is the cheat who has an acceptable male in his flock and vows to give it, but then sacrifices a blemished animal to the Lord. For I am a great king," says the LORD Almighty, "and my name is to be feared among the nations.

MALACHI NOW ADDRESSES the issue of sacrifice, which should be a loving response to love received (cf. 1:2–3) but instead has degenerated into something else. Malachi 1:6–2:9 opens with another disputation dialog but continues with different literary genres, including accusation and command. This section as a whole has been identified as a "prophetic exhortation"[1] directed to the priests (see 1:6; 2:1). The temple was rebuilt under Ezra, but Israel and its religious leaders soon fell again into their misguided ways. These were precipitating factors in the earlier disruption of the nation and the destruction of the Solomonic temple in 587/586 B.C., but human nature forgets previous lessons learned, necessitating reteaching.

God expected sacrifices and offerings to be taken from his good gifts and returned to him. They represented one's love, loyalty, honor, and, at times, sorrow for sin and wrongdoing (see Lev. 1–7). They showed an inner commitment to the covenant relationship between God and people, not arising from duty but from devotion. When duty replaces devotion, however, human nature is such that it seeks minimum steps, barely enough to meet an obligation. This contrasts with a true love relationship, seeking to do the maximum for the beloved. Israel, and in particular her priests, are seen here having lost their first love.

Malachi 1:6–14 begins with statement of the problem. Two propositions, undoubtedly well-known truisms to the audience, draw the audience in by starting where they are and then moving to someplace new (v. 6). The first concerns family relationships: children honoring their parents. The particular verbal form used for "honor" (*kbd*) indicates an ongoing practice, not a one-time event. Expectation of filial honor was inbred in Israel, for it was one of the Ten Commandments (Ex. 20:12; Deut. 5:16), their national charter document. Honoring involves treating someone with respect, lifting them up, and showing that they have worth. In a family situation, this includes obedience and support. Its opposite is disobedience (Deut. 21:18), neglect, or mistreatment, whether physical or verbal (e.g., Ex. 20:17; Lev. 20:9; Deut. 27:16). Though mentioning sons and fathers explicitly, daughters and mothers are not exempt from these same relational expectations.

The second proposition involves relations between servants/slaves and masters. The verb "honor" of the previous clause does double duty as the implied verb here. In the economic relationship of master-slave, well known

---

1. Michael H. Floyd, *Minor Prophets: Part 2* (FOTL 22; Grand Rapids: Eerdmans, 2000), 589.

in Israel even if not an aspect of the life for everyone, there must also be honor and respect. Obedience to authority is expected, since it defines the relationship.

Building on the foundation of these two well-known and acknowledged relationships, God makes the next step in his syllogism, again using statements against which his hearers have no quarrel: God is their "father" (e.g., Deut. 32:6; Job 29:16; Isa. 63:16[2x]; 64:8) and "master" (Ex. 23:17; 34:23; Deut. 10:17; Mic. 4:13). These are in the form of hypotheticals, indicating a real condition ("now if I am father/master [and you know that I am], then ..."). The hearers can follow the argument and so await its conclusion: "A son honors his father, as you well know. I am your Father, a relationship you know to be true. Therefore, you should honor me."

God then demands to know, in the second part of the conditional clause in verse 6, where his expected honor is to be found. This implies that the third stage of the syllogism is reversed from the expected and that there is none of the expected honor. The rhetorical snare into which the hearers have naively entered has snapped shut.

The first verb in verse 6 (*kbd*), as noted above, applied to the two clauses. Its cognate noun, "honor" (*kābôd*), is something that Malachi sees as lacking in the personal relationship between father and son. A new noun, "respect," is lacking in the master-slave relationship in the second clause. "Respect" is from the root "to fear, be in awe" and refers to the terror-inspiring mighty acts of God (e.g., Deut. 4:34; 26:8) or, as here, to the emotional response of reverence and awe engendered by such actions (e.g., Ps. 76:12; Isa. 8:13; Mal. 2:5)—an even more powerful reaction than what derives from the NIV's "respect." God expects an appropriate response from his people to their Father who is the very Creator and Sustainer of the universe, but this is not forthcoming. Noting again that God is the One who is speaking ("says the LORD Almighty"; cf. v. 2) emphasizes the truth and solemnity of these words.

Instead of respect, God receives "contempt" (cf. 1:7, 12; 2:9); he is despised and treated lightly, not even worthy of notice (cf. 1 Sam. 10:27; 17:42). "Contempt" elsewhere indicates disobedience to covenantal authority (e.g., Num. 15:31; 2 Sam. 12:9; Ezek. 16:59), as is the case here. Ironically, those exhibiting this contempt are the "priests," whom Yahweh addresses. In this literary context, which has placed Jacob and Esau in opposition (Mal. 1:2–3), despising most likely recalls to the episode of Esau's despising his birthright (Gen. 29:29–34). As Esau considered his family position not worth keeping, the priests, charged with representing the people before God as ministers of sacrifice, and God before the people as teachers of the law (e.g., Hag. 2:11–13), treat him as unworthy of adequate representation in sacrifice (Mal. 1:7–8) or teaching (cf. 2:8).

Their contempt is for God's "name," that is, his reputation, as in the English phrase, "He has a good *name*" (cf., e.g., Gen. 12:2; 2 Sam. 7:9; Isa. 63:12, 14; Jer. 32:20). Rather than maintaining the reputation of the holy God, his own ministers besmirch it. They in turn respond to the charge as they did previously, disputing the statement and denying such wrongdoing by demanding examples.

In verse 7, God duly provides the demanded answer. Priests, charged with bringing right sacrifices, are instead bringing "defiled" sacrifices. The verbs describing both the priestly actions and the nature of the food are participles, indicating a continuing state of unacceptability rather than a single action. This is a habitual practice of the priests. For the third time (cf. 1:2, 6) the accused reply in astonishment at a statement. God substantiates his claim, calling the altar "the LORD's [Yahweh's] table," a phrase unique to Malachi (cf. 1:12). It, like Yahweh's name (1:6), is treated lightly, as something not due serious consideration.

This uncaring attitude is shown in sacrifice (v. 8), a fundamental priestly function (see Lev. 1–7). Their role is to be "boundary setters," establishing for and teaching the people about clean and unclean, acceptable and unacceptable (Lev. 10:10–11).[2] God gave them specific instruction regarding acceptable sacrificial animals, those "without defect" (see Ex. 12:5; 29:1; Lev. 1:3), further defined as those "without . . . blemish" (Lev. 22:21; Num. 19:2). But rather than obeying these injunctions, they have been accepting inferior animals: the blind, lame, or sick. The first two are specifically forbidden for sacrifice (Deut. 15:21; cf. 17:1; Lev. 22:22).

The priests are then challenged through rhetorical questions. They know that what they are doing is "wrong." This word can indicate things that are contemptible, of little worth (cf. Num. 13:19; Jer. 24:2), which would fit the context of these useless animals. The context of defilement (see Mal. 1:7), however, supports a stronger reading of the word, which can denote moral depravity and wickedness (e.g., Gen. 6:5; 13:13; Isa. 32:7). These priests are not simply "cheap," they are being wicked. With irony, Malachi asks if such "gifts" are suitable for their secular state governor. Let them try to get away with such a disrespectful act toward one who is placed in authority over them by a foreign overlord (e.g., Isa. 36:9; Ezek. 23:23; Hag. 1:1; Esth. 3:12); here they are trying to do this with the Creator and Ruler of the universe!

Malachi asks two rhetorical questions about the governor's acceptance of such inferior gifts. The desire to please those important to us, especially those with authority or the ability to benefit us (e.g., Gen. 33:10; Ezek.

---

2. See, e.g., R. D. Nelson, *Raising Up a Faithful Priest: Community and Priesthood in Biblical Theology* (Louisville: Westminster John Knox, 1993); Duke, *DOTP*, 646–55.

43:27; Mic. 6:6), often motivates actions. The second clause uses a Hebrew idiom "raise the face," which indicates acceptance and a positive response. These positive reactions are desired, but these inadequate gifts will not bring that about.

In verse 9, the discussion moves up a notch ("now"), from the lesser (the governor) to the greater (God). Yahweh suggests that the priests should just try this presumption on him! Sacrifice should solicit God's pleasure (cf. Jer. 14:12), imploring his graciousness (lit., "appease/flatter the face"; cf. Ex. 32:11; 1 Sam. 13:12; Zech. 7:2; 8:21, 22)[3] and acceptance (using the idiom of Mal. 1:8). The rhetorical question in 1:9 strongly challenges the acceptability of this behavior, emphasized further through the double use of the strong name "the LORD Almighty" ("Yahweh of Hosts") in both this and the preceding verses (see comment on 1:4).

The rhetoric ratchets up even further in verse 10 when Yahweh desires that the entire temple complex be closed. The verse begins with an interrogative pronoun in a question (cf. KJV: "*Who* is there even among you?"), which can be well rendered in English as a desired action (NIV, "Oh, that one ..."). God wishes that one of the priests (the "you" of the context) might stop the cultic activity that is their calling. Temple personnel were charged with opening the temple doors so people could worship (1 Sam. 3:13; cf. 2 Chron. 29:3). The word "temple" does not occur in the actual Hebrew text (it is supplied by NIV; cf. 3:1, where it does occurs), but is implied by the context. Note that the form of "door" here is a dual, indicating the large, double-wide temple doors (1 Kings 6:34; Ezek. 41:23, 24). Only those who did evil willingly shut them (e.g., Ahaz, 2 Chron. 28:24, so people would worship at his pagan shrines).

It is ironic that the only other request in the Bible to close these doors was to preclude unauthorized killing by an enemy (Neh. 6:10). In Malachi, they are closed to prevent the unauthorized killing of unacceptable animals for sacrifice by those whose duty it is to see this is not done. In one way, God is calling for the doors to close to protect the priests themselves from doing further unacceptable acts. Any such offerings are "useless," having no effect. Israel's own King David was aware that sacrifices costing nothing (an oxymoron) avail for nothing (2 Sam. 24:24). This is what the priests, who should know better, have forgotten.

As no governor accepts second-rate gifts (v. 8), neither does God, even if the priests brings them personally ("from your hands"). The Hebrew term for these gifts (NIV, "offering") is both secular (e.g., the gifts of homage one

---

3. Hill, *Malachi*, 182, notes the ironic sound play on attempting to placate God (*ḥallû*) through sick (*ḥōleh*) animals (v. 8).

brings to a potentate like a ruler, 1 Sam. 10:27) and religious (e.g., offerings to God, Gen. 4:3–5; particularly the grain offerings of Lev. 2). God takes pleasure, even delight (cf. Mal. 2:17; 3:1, 12), in accepting good gifts from his people, but as Samuel reminded them generations previously, God desires obedience more than sacrifice (1 Sam. 15:22). This implies that if he can't have the former, forget about the latter. As in Samuel's time, obedience is not accompanying the sacrifice. Yahweh does not voice his displeasure so much against the sacrifices themselves as against the priests.

In verse 11, God does not hesitate to declare his universally acknowledged character, his "name" that, when magnified, indicates that his fame and reputation are held in high regard (see comments on v. 6). The "name" unifies this verse, occurring at its opening, middle, and closing. This exaltation of God's name is not localized among his people but extends "among the nations," a term often used in direct contrast with Israel among whom God's exaltation is expected but is not forthcoming (Ex. 34:24; Lev. 18:24; Ezek. 5:6–8).

Repetition emphasizes the unexpected location of God's recognition. His reputation is known from east to west, shown by the idiom of the rising and setting sun (Ps. 50:1; 113:3; cf. Isa. 45:6; 59:19), throughout the entire perceived world. "Incense and pure [ceremonially acceptable] offerings" are to be brought in honor of God ("to my name"), in contrast to what Judah itself is bringing. These come "from every place," or (in a universal but unspecified sense) "from any place." This is likely an intentional irony on the part of the author. The "place" par excellence is the holy city, Jerusalem, with its temple (Deut. 12:5; 1 Kings 8:30; 2 Kings 22:16; Isa. 60:13), which has lost its exalted place because of the wicked priestly actions. As the Lord's glory left its rightful place in Ezekiel's temple (Ezek. 9:3; 10:4, 18–19; 11:23), so true worship of the Lord departs from there in Malachi, ending up with the rest of the world instead of with the people for whom the temple had been provided (cf. Jer. 7:2–12).

In verse 12, many of the terms and concepts of verses 6–11 are presented again with some variation. In emphatic contrast with the rest of the world who worship God correctly, the author returns to the priests (lit., "now, as for you"), who do not do so. While foreigners magnify God's name (v. 11), Israel's own priests "profane" it just as surely as if they offered child sacrifices (Lev. 18:21; 20:3). This is not through a one-time event but through a long-enduring state, as is shown by another participle (see comment on 1:7). The priests profane God's name not only by action (v. 8) but also by attitude, casting aspersions on the integrity of the sacrificial system. They claim the altar is "defiled" and its food "contemptible," reversing the noun-modifier combinations of verse 7.

Another variation is in the designation of God, here "my Lord" (ʾ*ªdō-nāy*; cf. "LORD" [*yhwh*] in v. 7). This may be simply a literary variation, or, as Hill suggests,[4] a claim that Yahweh is in fact Lord of all altars, whether domestic or foreign (cf. v. 11). "Lord" is an honorific title used of someone to whom one shows deference in some way, whether because of age, power, or social position. It is a common form of polite greeting, much like English "mister," which derives from "master."[5] It is also used in sociopolitical contexts by the vassal addressing his overlord.[6] This variation here seems to diminish God; he is only addressed as if he were a human, not a divine ruler.

The last clause of the verse is problematic. The Hebrew reads literally, "and as for its fruit, its food is contemptible." Some handle the problem text-critically, taking the first word ("fruit") as a variant repetition of the second and so deleting it as a secondary addition (e.g., NIV, NEB, NRSV).[7] This word is only used once elsewhere in the Old Testament, in an idiom "fruit of the lips," metaphorically indicating commendatory speech (Isa. 57:19), a metaphor not fitting here. If the noun is to be kept, it appears to make the second noun, "food," redundant, so several interpreters delete that word.[8] Others take the approach, however—more sound on text-critical grounds— of trying to understand the text as it stands, with the second noun as an explanation of the rarer first noun (KJV, ESV, ASV, NJPS).[9]

In verse 13, the priests continue to respond to God's challenges in what appears to be a manner indicating *ennui*. The introductory exclamatory word indicates immediacy, allowing it to be contemporized as "Hey, what a drag!" The second word (NIV "burden") is a composite pronoun + noun.[10] This noun occurs only five times in the Old Testament, indicating that the flippant priestly response equates their temple service to the hardships endured by their ancestors during the desert wanderings (Ex. 18:8; Num. 20:14) and under their Assyrian and Babylonian overlords (Neh. 9:32; Lam. 3:5). They complain because they consider themselves so put upon.

---

4. Hill, *Malachi*, 190.

5. See *HALOT*, 13 (A, 2–3).

6. See, e.g., *COS*, 3:78–81.

7. See also Peterson, *Zechariah 9–14 and Malachi*, 176.

8. E.g., R. L. Smith, *Micah–Malachi* (WBD 32; Waco, Tex.: Word, 1984), 308. A. B. Ehrlich, *Randglossen zur hebräischen Bibel: textkritisches, sprachliches und sachliches* (Leipzig: J. C. Hinrichs, 1908–14), 358, deletes the entire final clause.

9. Also Hill, *Malachi*, 171.

10. *mattᵉlāʾâ* appears to consist of the pronoun *mâ* assimilated to the rare noun *tᵉlāʾâ*. The former is usually an interrogative pronoun, but here it is used emphatically indicating an exclamation (Williams, §127; Waltke-O'Connor, §18.3–4).

The attitude is also expressed nonverbally, with the people sniffing contemptuously (NASB; NIV; NJB)[11] or snorting (ESV)[12] at the very idea of having to bring acceptable sacrifices. Their inner contempt is exemplified and continued by their outward actions: bringing unacceptable animal sacrifices instead.

Two of the categories of infirm animals ("crippled" and "diseased") echo those of verse 8, but the third ("injured") derives from a verb meaning "to steal, pilfer, take by clandestine means" (Lev. 19:3; Judg. 9:25; Job 24:2).[13] This may be the intention here, that the priests are bringing sacrifices that are valueless, either because of their physical deformity or their acquisition by perfidy rather than by purchase, thus costing the priests or those who bring them nothing. They are thus a sacrifice that is no sacrifice. Others suggest that this third term indicates some physical deformity observable by the priests but ignored by them, in line with the other two descriptors (NIV; NCV; NEB; NLT combines suggestions, "stolen and mutilated").

Ironically, the nation called to administer justice to those who are robbed (cf. Jer. 21:12; 22:3) is represented before God by offerings taken by robbery. This representation is the last link in the litany of wrongdoing ("you said . . . and then you sniffed . . . and then you brought . . . and then you [even] offered [them as] the sacrifices"). The boredom and lifelessness of the empty ritual is matched by the plodding grammatical construction.

In the final verse of this section (v. 14), Yahweh evaluates the entire shoddy situation, beginning with a coordinating conjunction (w^e), tying it to the preceding context. This can be left untranslated (NIV, NLT, NRSV) or be seen as giving emphasis (i.e., "now").[14] Yahweh states that the miscreant is "cursed," a passive participle (cf. 2:2, where "curse" occurs three times; 3:9). The participial form indicates an enduring circumstance rather than a particular action, while this passive form concentrates attention on the commencement of the new state, that is, "now, from this point onward, X will be cursed."

This passive form occurs forty times in the Old Testament, the largest concentration of which is in two chapters each in Deuteronomy and Jeremiah.[15] In Deuteronomy and Jeremiah 48 the context is punishment following a

---

11. See BDB, 656.

12. Paul L. Redditt, *Haggai, Zechariah, and Malachi* (NCBC; Grand Rapids: Eerdmans, 1995), 166.

13. For this interpretation here see *HALOT*; NASB; NJPS; NRSV.

14. Translating with an adversative "but" (Williams, §432; KJV; NASB) does not fit with the context, since this verse is climactic rather than antithetical to the preceding context.

15. Deut 27:15, 16, 17, 18, 19, 20, 21, 22, 23, 24, 25, 26; 28:16[2x], 17, 18, 19[2x]; Jer 20:14, 15; 48:10[2x].

breach of obligations to God, specifically the covenant in Deuteronomy. This is also the context in Malachi, where failure of required sacrifices results in those responsible being outside the protection and community of the covenant.

The wrongdoer is a "cheat," someone acting in cunning deception with harmful intent (cf. Gen. 37:18; Num. 25:18). Once again, the participle here, as in two of the three following clauses, indicates a consistent pattern of action rather than a singular instance.

The next three clauses explain the nature of the deceptions.[16] Each clause describes subsequent steps in a process. The situation concerns one who has an acceptable sacrificial animal in his possession. The animal is in his *ʿēder* (NIV "flock"), a general term for a collection of domesticated animals, cattle as well as sheep and goats. The sacrifice results from having made a "vow" (another participle). In the handbook of sacrifices in Leviticus 1–7, a vow is mentioned only in conjunction with the fellowship or peace offering (7:16), which can be from either the herd (3:1–5) or the flock (3:6–16). In Malachi, only a male is offered, while the levitical legislation does not specify its gender. This may indicate that this offerer is especially prideful of his more prestigious gift.

What this person "sacrifices" (another participial form), however, is not quality but something completely unsatisfactory, described by an adjective ("blemished") used elsewhere for a polluted spring (Prov. 25:26) or a mutilated animal brought as a sacrifice (Lev. 22:24–25). Neither of these is efficacious for their purposes of drinkable water or a sin offering. The present sacrifice isn't efficacious either; in fact, it is not even a "sacrifice" with the English connotation of the term as something that costs the giver.

The "sacrifice" is directed toward "the Lord" (*ʾădōnāy*). The attempted deception denies the lordship of the recipient, which is not acceptable, as the following sentence states. Here the difficulty of customarily translating the personal name of God, Yahweh, as "LORD" becomes apparent since many English readers miss the distinction between "the Lord" to whom offerings are brought and Yahweh Almighty who is speaking. In contrast to the governor of verse 8, who is a "lord" with only delegated authority and derived power, Yahweh is a "great king," wielding his own supreme authority and personal power.

Foreign overlords such as the Assyrian kings called themselves by the title "great king" (2 Kings 18:19, 28//Isa. 36:4, 13; Jer. 25:14), but they were

---

16. The first clause begins with the conjunction *waw*, which could be a *waw explicativum*, resulting in a translation "cursed is the cheat, *that is*, anyone who . . .'; cf. D. W. Baker, "Further Examples of the *Waw Explicativum*," *VT* 30 (1980): 129–36.

feeble compared to this great King. His "name" (see comments on Mal. 1:6), which is also said to be "great" (1:11[2x]), is now described as awesome, something dreadful and "to be feared" (cf. 3:23; see the discussion of Joel 2:11) among the nations. Once again these pagan foreigners show the correct attitude toward God in implied contrast to God's own people, who show themselves unworthy of this description, since they do not reverence him appropriately.

The section closes, in other words, in response to the rhetorical question regarding lordship in verse 6. Yahweh is in fact the only true "Lord" and should be treated as such. Also, his reverence, which is questioned there, is proclaimed here.

DISPUTING WITH GOD. Two other Old Testament books contain what may seem to be a similar literary genre to that in Malachi, namely, disputations. Both Job and Habakkuk portray individuals in heated discussion with God, with no ill results. Why then does God get upset with the disputants in Malachi?

A major difference lies in the personnel involved. In Habakkuk it is the prophet alone who raises his own questions and concerns, and in Job, he alone is in dialogue with God. Both raise questions based on their own personal experience, trying to understand rather than to attack. In Malachi, it is a group, a large portion of the population, apparently representing a sizable portion of Judean society, who are attacking the very concept of God's authority. Moreover, Job and Habakkuk discuss their own personal theological understandings, parts of their worldview challenged by the realities of their actual life. Job was concerned about God's justice in letting the innocent suffer (Job 3), while Habakkuk had the opposite problem—God's not punishing the wicked (Hab. 1:2–4, 12–17).

Malachi faces a problem of pettiness rather than profundity. Like small children, his contemporaries challenge whatever an authority figure says. God has no problems with the former two disputants because they are majoring on important issues, struggling with doubts and concerns.[17] He has less time for Malachi's crowd who manufacture ephemeral issues from the air.

---

17. See, e.g., Os Guinness, *In Two Minds: The Dilemma of Doubt and How to Resolve It* (Downers Grove, Ill.: InterVarsity Press, 1976); A. E. McGrath, *The Sunnier Side of Doubt* (Grand Rapids: Zondervan, 1990).

Feeding versus worshiping God. In the ancient Near East, particularly Mesopotamia, humanity was created to serve the gods.[18] Among their tasks was providing them nourishment, both food and drink. This was done through sacrifices. In this way, the people understood the altar as being literally the table of the gods, where they came to eat (cf. the starving gods crowding around Utnapishtim's post-deluvial sacrifices "like flies").[19]

This is different from the Old Testament concept of sacrifices and altars. There, God is in no way reliant on humanity for sustenance. Sacrifices serve a completely different purpose, and generally altars are not called "table," or more specifically a "table of God" (cf. Ezek. 41:22; 1 Cor. 10:21). In the tabernacle, "table" refers to the golden table in the Holy Place with its special bread (e.g., Ex. 25:23–30; 37:10–16) or other tables for sacrifice preparation (Ezek. 40:38–43), but these are consistently distinguished from the altar. One reason for the Israelites avoiding the term in their worship is probably to avoid mixing the pagan concept that God is dependent on his creation for food into Yahwism.

God demanding and refusing sacrifice. Malachi is not alone in rejecting sacrifices. Amos had a statement from God who said: "I hate, I despise your religious feasts; I cannot stand your assemblies. Even though you bring me burnt offerings and grain offerings, I will not accept them. Though you bring choice fellowship offerings, I will have no regard for them" (Amos 5:21–22). This appears puzzling, since God himself established the feasts and assemblies (Lev. 23; Num. 28–29), the burnt, grain, and fellowship offerings (Lev. 1–3). Is he changing his mind, now saying that he demands a different way of worship?

That is not what God demanded through Amos, since he went on to say in Amos 5:24: "But let justice roll on like a river, righteousness like a never-failing stream!" Through Amos, God was saying that he indeed wants the vertical relationship of worship directed toward him, but it is of no avail without the horizontal relationship, namely, justice and righteousness in dealing with fellow Israelites. When vertical religion becomes meaningless rote that has

---

18. In Mesopotamia, some among the divine had to labor to supply the needs of the gods. When they complained about this onerous task, humanity was created to relieve them of it. See the Sumerian story of Enki and Ninmah (*COS*, I 1.159:516–7), the Assyrian Atraḫasis Epic (ibid., 1.130:450–451), and more briefly, the Enuma Elish creation story (ibid., 1.111:401); see also John Walton, *Ancient Israelite Literature in its Cultural Context: A Survey of Parallels between Biblical and Ancient Near Eastern Texts* (Grand Rapids: Zondervan, 1989), 29–30. The situation is less clearly drawn in Egyptian texts, where humanity is called "god's cattle" (*COS*, I 1.35:65).

19. *COS*, I 1.132:460. For the association of "table" with a temple, see *AHw*, 846 *paššuru(m)* 3.

no impact on interpersonal ethics, it is only religion and not worship, so get rid of it. Jesus demonstrated the same priorities, desiring mercy more than sacrifice (Matt. 9:13; 12:7, quoting Hos. 6:6).

Malachi shows the same approach to religious observance. Worship shows an appreciation of the value of the one being worshiped in the eyes of the worshiper. Part of worship is bringing gifts of love, as a token of thanksgiving, but one must also mend the relationship if it has been damaged in any way. Based on the value of the sacrifices that Judah brings, God knows that the people do not value him or his relationship with them more than just as a token. It is not that God does not want sacrificial gifts of love; those are exactly what he does want. What he does not want is perfunctory, meaningless ritual, bringing offerings that are neither sacrificial, since they cost little to those who bring them, nor loving (also Isa. 29:13, cited in Matt. 15:8–9).

Israel denigrates other aspects of worship as well, including the temple. In Jeremiah 7:4, the prophet condemns the people for treating the temple like a good-luck charm or a rabbit's foot. They think that simply because they control the temple, they also control the God of the temple. While God is not condemning the temple as being bad in its own right, he says that it has no efficacy if the people are living as if the temple and its inhabitant are not even there. He calls them to get their ethics right before they can hope to be able to get their worship right (7:3–11).

AUTHORITY. Many of us who were working toward maturity in the 1960s remember "authority" as a dirty word, showing it much the same disdain as Malachi's contemporaries. Anyone or anything that smacked of telling us what we could or could not do was repressive and to be overthrown. Proponents of free love and free drugs attempted overthrow authority through relatively peaceful means, while proponents of "free hate," if you will, used violent means—the bombs of the Students for a Democratic Society and the guns of the Baader-Meinhof group.

Activists from that era have now exchanged tie-dyed t-shirts for business clothes and peace rallies for boardrooms, but a suspicion of authority remains, perhaps mutating to a postmodern view that there is personal liberty at every level, even regarding how we read a text or understand a conversation. How should a freedom seeker understand and appropriate descriptions of God as Father and Master (v. 6), words sounding with authority? Should we not argue against it, just as Malachi's audience did in his day?

To a large extent, we gain our understanding of God first of all through our experiences on the human level of the everyday. Our appreciation of God is most strongly shaped by our experience of our parents, most specifically the father. In a childhood where paternal authority is actualized through abuse, whether sexual, physical, or emotional, our view of God is skewed to seeing him as harsh and nonresponsive. We build a metaphor, taking our experience as the vehicle that carries the applied meaning to the object I am trying to describe by comparison (technically the "tenor"), in this case, God. God, whom I am trying to understand and define, is like my father, and since I know my father to be mean, so must God be.

When we do this, we build the metaphor in the opposite way than it should be built. The vehicle, the provider of meaning, is in the divine realm, not the human, since the former is perfect and untainted by the sin found in the latter. We should say that instead of understanding God by looking at my earthly father, in order to see a true understanding of fatherhood, we must look to God. His fatherly love, which is the model we need to understand as ideal, is not a "love" that demands sexual satisfaction of his children or power through their intimidation, seeking his own self-gratification. Rather, it is a love exhibited in self-sacrifice of that which he most cherishes for the complete good of the beloved (1 John 4:9; John 3:16; Eph. 1:3–10).

Authority should also be understood in the same way, from the top down rather than from the bottom up. Human authority can be oppressive and self-seeking, while divine authority is liberating (Matt. 11:28–30) and other-seeking (Heb. 12:5–11). Malachi's peers seem not to understand the difference. His instruction and discipline are for the good of their recipients and not for the good of their Giver (Ps. 1; Prov. 8:33). His instructions are not to limit human freedom but rather to allow the freedom to be truly human, living to the fullest benefit of ourselves and our fellow human beings. The Ten Commandments are not restrictions but rather the foundations of what it is to be human.

Turning the metaphor in this direction, from God to us, should also affect how we wield authority, whether like a sword or like a rein. Parents are charged to not exasperate their children but instead to use godly discipline (Eph. 6:4). Modeling a lack of self-interest and true love shows we understand the metaphor rightly. It also shows the truth of the saying: Authority is like soap: "The more you use, the less you have!"

Mixed religion. Israel's prophets repeatedly remind Israel that they are a peculiar people, unlike their pagan neighbors in both belief and practice. Distinctions seem to be harder to maintain in today's church, which operates in a pluralistic society. Israel contended with Canaanite enclaves among a predominately Israelite society, but the church faces the opposite situation, being solitary bastions amid either a secular society or one where many religious voices compete for a hearing. Without a biblically based and clearly articulated theology and worldview, with an inadequate understanding of what difference being a follower of Christ means in the way one lives daily life, the edges between church and society have become porous.

One way, among many, where this is evident is in the secularization of the church. While the church is called to be salt and light (Matt. 5:13–16), it too often becomes diluted and dim, advocating conformity to society rather than confrontation. Comfortable accommodationism often finds writers who address these issues uncomfortable for us to read since they challenge our complacency and call us back to accountability.[20] Ignoring these voices, however, can lead to stagnation and the loss of theological vitality. God can become so secularized in our view that he needs us to provide for him just as Mesopotamian gods needed humans to provide their sustenance. The church then, in a real way, becomes pagan.

Second best is good enough. From our own perspective, none of us has enough time or money. There are so many demands in so many areas that we have to do what we can just to get by. We are not the first to take this approach, and unfortunately, we will probably not be the last. Judah also tried to get by with "good enough" in their worship. They brought the required animals, but they were only second-rate (vv. 8, 13), because anything more might cost too much; God's people might have to change their standard of living. If they can cheat on their taxes, surely they can do the same in their tithes!

The same approach is not unknown today. Our worship demands so much time in technical preparation, with its Powerpoint presentations and multimedia, that it is all we can do to get it done between services. Worship leaders seem to have no time for anything else! There is nothing wrong with technology; God is not a Luddite. However, where is God amidst the technology? What is the benefit of Powerpoint without the presence of the Spirit? If we have not taken time to "be still and know that I am God" (Ps. 46:10), who is being exalted with our multimedia?

---

20. Three names come to mind as among those who address these issues. From a previous generation is Jacques Ellul (e.g., *False Presence of the Kingdom* [New York: Seabury, 1972]; *The Subversion of Christianity* [Grand Rapids: Eerdmans, 1986]), and from this generation are Tony Campolo (e.g., *Is Jesus a Republican or a Democrat: and 14 other Polarizing Issues* [Dallas: Word, 1995]; *Who Switched the Price Tags? A Search for Values in a Mixed-up World* [Waco, Tex.: Word, 1986]), and Ronald Sider (e.g., *Christ and Violence* [Scottdale: Herald, 1979]; *Rich Christians in an Age of Hunger: A Biblical Study* [Downers Grove, Ill.: InterVarsity Press, 1977]).

The same holds true in education, even, unfortunately, in ministerial training. "In light of my full-time job, pastoral responsibility at the church, and a full-time seminary load, I do not have time to get my papers done on time or with the academic excellence that I should." We offer God our second best, thinking what we are able to do is good enough. Try offering that to the boss (cf. "the governor," v. 8), suggesting that he pay for forty hours of work a week, but we will really only do thirty, because course work requires too much time. That is not good enough for him, so why should we think it is good enough for God? Should we expect him to accept our second-best offerings? "Good enough" seldom is.

Malachi 2:1–9

AND NOW THIS admonition is for you, O priests. ²If you do not listen, and if you do not set your heart to honor my name," says the LORD Almighty, "I will send a curse upon you, and I will curse your blessings. Yes, I have already cursed them, because you have not set your heart to honor me.

³"Because of you I will rebuke your descendants; I will spread on your faces the offal from your festival sacrifices, and you will be carried off with it. ⁴And you will know that I have sent you this admonition so that my covenant with Levi may continue," says the LORD Almighty. ⁵"My covenant was with him, a covenant of life and peace, and I gave them to him; this called for reverence and he revered me and stood in awe of my name. ⁶True instruction was in his mouth and nothing false was found on his lips. He walked with me in peace and uprightness, and turned many from sin.

⁷"For the lips of a priest ought to preserve knowledge, and from his mouth men should seek instruction—because he is the messenger of the LORD Almighty. ⁸But you have turned from the way and by your teaching have caused many to stumble; you have violated the covenant with Levi," says the LORD Almighty. ⁹"So I have caused you to be despised and humiliated before all the people, because you have not followed my ways but have shown partiality in matters of the law."

Original Meaning

THE PREVIOUS SECTION addressed priests (1:6), most directly their acceptance of the unsuitable offerings being brought to God. In this passage Malachi continues to address the priests (2:1), but his indictment is wider: Sacrifice is not mentioned, but other priestly functions such as instruction and legal interpretation are now brought under condemnation. It looks as if nothing the priests do is being done appropriately.[1] The implications of Judah's wrongdoings are expanded, and the resulting punishment spelled out.

---

1. This section also relates to the previous one through shared vocabulary, such as "And now" (w⁽ᶜattâ; 1:9; 2:1); God's "name" (šēm; 1:6, 14; 2:2); cursing (from the root ʾrr; 1:14; 2:2[2x]); and "honor, reverence" (môrāʾ; 1:6; 2:5).

This section is described as an "admonition, warning," a word commonly translated "command, charge" (KJV; NASB; NLT; NRSV). While not stated in the form of an explicit imperative, Malachi's message here is an implicit instruction warning for the priests to be more diligent in fulfilling their obligations. The admonition could refer to the entire following text section (vv. 2–9), but most likely it refers to the levitical covenant in v. 4, which has the same designation ("admonition, warning").[2]

Yahweh strongly warns the priests in the form of a conditional sentence consisting of a double condition ("if . . . and if . . .") and the consequence. Here the conditions are negated; the priests are not doing what is desired. The first thing they lack is listening. The Hebrew verb šmᶜ has the range of meaning "hear, listen, obey." God's will regarding priestly duties has been presented numerous times previously, so they have indeed heard. What they lack is to render due honor to God through "setting their heart" toward him. This idiom, used twice in verse 2, occurs four more times in Scripture indicating an attitudinal position of caring about or understanding things of God (Isa. 42:25; 57:1, 11). The lack of this attitude results in destruction (Jer. 12:11).

If these connotations occur in Malachi, the prophet may be decrying the lack of two things: a higher level of expected response to God, namely, obedience, and a lower, less-demanding level, caring about what their attitude is. God may be saying to Judah: "You not only don't obey me, you don't even care about showing me any respect!" No honor is being given to Yahweh's name (2:2), a recapitulation and summary of the charges from chapter 1 (cf. 1:6).

The result of the noncompliance is a destructive curse (2:2), probably having in mind those curses promised for those guilty of breach of covenant in Deuteronomy 28:15–68. This curse is not only anticipated but has already arrived. The object of the curse is the "blessings" of the priests. These can either be the blessings that they are to direct toward the people (e.g., Num. 6:24–26) or the ones which they receive as a consequence of their role in the national cult (e.g., Lev. 6:16–18; 7:6–10). The latter would be an ironic punishment for the priests: If they accept substandard animals for sacrifice, their consumable portions will also be only second rate. By repeating the conditions and curses a second time, the prophet certifies they are firm and sure.

The specific nature of the curse follows (2:3). It comes about "because of you [priests]." An exclamatory particle (*kî*) opens the verse, indicating immediacy and describing the action God is about to undertake. The verb describing God's response (*gᶜr*) is usually translated "rebuke, speak disparagingly,"

---

2. Hill, *Malachi*, 197.

here against the "descendants" (lit., "seed"; 2:15; NASB; NIV; NRSV) of the serving priests. Some suggest a textual variant for the verb (*gdʿ*, "cut off"; cf. NIV text note), since a simple verbal response seems too light a punishment for the context. The term *gʿr*, however, is also used in Deuteronomy 28:20, where it is among the covenant curses on Israel.[3] Some suggest that "seed" is literal (i.e., agricultural seed), cursed to impede its growth and so produce a famine.[4] While there are such curses against grain listed (e.g., Deut. 28:18b, 23–24, 38–40, 42, 51), there are also ones against offspring (28:18a, 32, 41, 53–57). The priests' own physical descendants must be the subject of the curse since they as a group were prohibited from owning land (Num. 26:62), so they could not produce their own grain. For this they were dependent on their portion of the sacrifices of the people (Josh. 13:14; cf. Lev. 6:16–18, 23).

God's response is not simply verbal, however, since he acts in such a way as to make the recipients unclean and unable to partake in the cult. This involves the "offal" (better "dung" or the undigested food remaining in the stomach of a sacrificed animal), which was not fit for most sacrifices. It was rather removed to an unclean spot outside the Israelite camp (Ex. 29:14; Lev. 4:11; 8:17; 16:27). This will be spread or scattered (cf. Lev. 26:33; 1 Kings 14:15) over the priests' faces.[5] Whether literal or (more likely) metaphorical, this is a clear and public display of their disgrace and inability to carry out the sacrificial functions of their office, just as unclean bones scattered around altars rendered them unsuitable in another context (Ezek. 6:5).

The offal is identified with "your festivals," each of which includes sacrifices (e.g., 1 Kings 12:32, 33; Ezek. 45:17; Amos 5:21–22). Here the broader term ("festival") is used in place of one of its constituent elements ("sacrifices"), a literary device known as metonymy in which a whole is identified by one of its parts. Rather than being pleasing to God (cf. the "lifted [*nśʾ*] face" in 1:8), the priests themselves will be "carried off [*nśʾ*] with it," apparently referring to the offal. The punishment relates directly to who the priests are in their official capacity. As priests represent the people before God, they need to be holy and consecrated to God (cf. Lev. 8:1–9:14). Now no longer able to perform their functions, which require ritual purity, the priests are expelled from the camp, as is the unclean offal (so NIV).

Verse 4 reflects either events subsequent to the priests' humiliation ("*and you will know* ..."; KJV; NIV) or the consequence or result of the preceding ("*so you will know* ..."; NASB; RSV; NLT). This verse also may be volitional, an

---

3. Wolf, *Haggai and Malachi*, 79.

4. W. C. Kaiser Jr., *Malachi: God's Unchanging Love* (Grand Rapids: Baker, 1984), 56–57.

5. There is a sound play between this and the preceding word: *hazzeraʿ wᵉzērîtî*.

implied command that the priests should now know as a result of what befalls them ("Know, then . . ."; NRSV).[6] The phrase "you will know" is often used where God expects his people to respond to an experience of either his goodness (e.g., Ex. 6:7; 16:6, 8, 12), or his judgment (e.g., Ex. 7:17; 8:22; 11:7; Num. 16:28, 30). Knowledge here is not simply an intellectual exercise. The priests can be sure that the events accompanying this admonition or charge (Mal. 2:1) are not simply random but are sent by God himself, just as he sends the curse (2:2; 3:1, 23; cf. 2:16).

The charge's purpose or result[7] concerns a "covenant," an important word in this prophecy (cf. 2:5, 8, 10, 14; 3:1, 2). The covenant here is between God ("*my* covenant," v. 5) and Levi (2:8; 3:3), and, by implication, his descendants, the priests.[8] Levi was the ancestor of the tribe set apart for sanctuary service (Num. 3–4), of which Aaron and his descendants are specifically designated as priests (Lev. 8). This particular covenant is mentioned only here and in Nehemiah 13:29 ("covenant of the priesthood and of the Levites"). There, like here, ritual defilement endangers it. Since a covenant is an arrangement of mutual obligation, it is best to see this as referring to the priestly and levitical obligations that are part of their heritage as a special group in God's sight and service (see Num. 1:47–54; 3:5–13), even if these are not specifically termed "covenant" elsewhere. This is then equivalent of the "admonition" to obedience mentioned here and in verse 1. From the human perspective of the priests, the admonition/covenant involves cultic purity and ritual ministry, while from the perspective of Yahweh Almighty, it involves the blessings enumerated in the next verse.

The priests, as beneficiaries of the covenant relationship, are again reminded in verse 5 that while the covenant is with Levi, it originates with God alone ("*my* covenant"). The covenant consists of "life," given and protected by God (Job 10:12; Ps. 21:4; 64:1; 66:9; 103:4; Lam. 3:58), and "peace," wholeness and tranquility as granted by God (šālôm; 2:6; Lev. 26:6; Num. 6:26; Isa. 9:5, 6; 26:12; Jer. 29:7) to Levi. These two terms of favor occur together only here and in Proverbs 3:2, where they result from keeping God's law and admonitions (3:1), much as they do here. Levi does the wise and expected thing demanded by the covenant: showing a respect from the subject (Levi) toward his overlord (Yahweh, the master; cf. 1:6).

One text in particular mentions a covenant with a member of the priestly line. Phineas executed a couple for violating the Israelite camp, averting a punishing plague that had already killed 24,000 people (Num. 25:6–9). God

---

6. See Hill, *Malachi*, 203.

7. The preposition *lᵉ* plus the infinitive of the verb indicates either purpose or result.

8. Cf. a similar construction of covenant "with" others (Gen. 9:12, Noah; 17:4, Abram).

entered a special covenant relationship with him because of his "passionate zeal" for God, a covenant described as a "covenant of peace" (25:12). This covenant, bringing life in the midst of judgmental death, may well be the referent for this covenant to which faithful priests, of which there are a woeful few, are called in Malachi.

God's name (2:5; cf. 1:6[2x], 11[3x], 14; 2:2; 3:16, 20) does the same for the founder of the line of priests and Levites. A second term for reverence ("stood in awe") emphasizes this attitude, contrasting with that of the priestly contemporaries of Malachi. The two sides of the covenant are depicted here: God from his side gives his blessings (life and peace) and, from the other side, Levi gives appropriate honor (implying obedience) to his master. All three of these nouns are thus constituent of the covenant.

While priests played an active role in the cult, religious instruction of the people was another of their important functions. Called here "true instruction" (2:6), it contrasts with something wickedly "false."[9] Truth characterized the speech of the priestly ancestor Levi. His very lifestyle, or customary behavior ("walk"; cf. Ps. 6:12; 15:2; Isa. 33:15), exemplifies covenantal peace and integrity or uprightness (Ps. 45:7; 67:5; Isa. 11:4).[10] His walk is "with me [God]," showing the mutuality of a covenantal relationship, since Malachi 2:5 expresses the other side of the relationship: God's covenant is "with him."

As a result of this positive lifestyle,[11] "many" (cf. v. 8) completely change their own negative lifestyle. This former way of life was characterized by "sin" (cf. Mic. 7:18, 19; Zech. 3:4, 9), a noun including in its meaning the guilt (Gen. 15:16; Jer. 50:20; Zech. 3:4) and punishment (Gen. 4:13; Ezek. 44:10, 12) deriving from these unacceptable actions. These folk "turned" or repented (cf. 3:7; Ezek. 18:8) of this lifestyle, returning to the position of covenant fellowship they had enjoyed some time previously. "Many" seems to be a technical term in Malachi, indicating the masses of lay Israelites in contrast to the priests.[12]

The ideal established by Levi is that his descendants, the priests, should live what they speak (2:7). Priestly lips, eschewing falsehood, are to produce "knowledge," and their mouth, "instruction" (see 2:6, with the two nouns

---

9. This term is in the same semantic field as bloodshed and lies (Isa. 59:3; Mic 3:10; Hab. 2:12; Zeph. 3:13), robbery (Isa. 61:8), wickedness and deception (Hos 10:13), sin (Job 11:14), and evil (Ps 37:1).

10. The noun *mîšôr* derives from the root *yšr*, indicating that which is physically (Ps. 26:12; Isa. 40:4; Zech. 4:7) or morally (Ps 45:6; Isa. 11:4) straight or smooth ("upright").

11. Cf. Amos 9:1 for a similar resultative use of the coordinating copula *wᵉ*—.

12. Hill, *Malachi*, 209–10, indicating this use also in Qumran. This could be parallel to the more common "people of the land" (cf. v. 9; also Jer. 1:18, where it is contrasted to officials and priests, translated "laity" in the LXX), which occurs almost fifty times in the OT.

in reverse order). Their calling as teachers is a lofty one. The verbs strengthen the situation as recorded in the previous verse. There the verbs designated existence/nonexistence, but here there is active care and superintendence on the part of the priests (cf. Gen. 41:35; Eccl. 3:6), and a purposeful searching on the part of the people (cf. 1 Kings 10:24; Amos 8:12). Who does the actual seeking is debated. The NIV adds the subject "men" to the clause (cf. NASB, "people"; NKJV, NLT, NRSV), which is not in the Hebrew (which simply reads "they seek"). The nearest antecedent masculine plural noun that can serve as subject of the verb is the "many" of verse 6.[13]

The particle *kî* at the beginning of verse 7 ("for") may be used for emphasis ("indeed"), though it could also be simply a logical connecter ("because, for"), as later in the verse (NIV "because"). There it introduces a clause that explains the need for priestly knowledge and instruction, namely, because the priest is "the messenger of the LORD" (cf. 3:1), one charged with the transmission rather than the origination of the message. Elsewhere this description applies to prophets (e.g., 2 Chron. 36:15; Isa. 44:26; Hag. 1:13) and heavenly messengers (angels; Gen. 28:12; Isa. 63:9; Hos. 12:5); only here is it used of the priests.

The priests are in stark contrast to this ideal, however. The verb in verse 8 is preceded by a conjunction indicating a contrast plus an independent personal pronoun ("but, as for you"), so there is an explicit antithesis between the priests addressed by Malachi ("you") and the dutiful priest of verse 7. These priests err, turning aside (*sûr*) from the path just as Moses turned aside (*sûr*) from his journey to see the burning bush (Ex. 3:3—4). Here the path is metaphorical, referring to God's instructions and will (Mal. 2:9; 3:1), which the priesthood purposefully abandon and ignore (3:7).

Not only do the priests of Malachi's day pervert themselves, they do so to those in their charge, in contrast to Levi. He restored "many" (2:6), while they "have caused many to stumble." These common folk (the "many"), rather than finding the truth they seek, are mislead. While God seeks to lead his own on smooth paths so they may not trip (Jer. 31:9), the priests, their teachers and guides, actually impede their way (cf. Jer. 18:15; Hos. 5:5). Restoration is by means of "true instruction" (v. 6; cf. 7), while stumbling is caused (lit.) "in regards to the instruction/law."

There is diversity of opinion regarding the identification of the "teaching" (*tôrâ*). The NIV and others supply an identifier "your" that does not occur in the Hebrew. This, coupled with an understanding of the preposition (*b^e*-) functioning instrumentally, interprets the faulty priestly instruction as the means by which people are made to stumble. A problem with this

---

13. See Hill, *Malachi*, 211—12.

interpretation is that, apart from uses in Proverbs where "teaching" derives from the mother (e.g., Prov. 1:8; 6:20), in all other instances the word *tôrâ* refers to Yahweh's instruction, never to that of the priests (e.g., 23 times in Ps. 119). A better interpretation, more closely following the actual text, is that *tôrâ* has its customary meaning of God's law or instruction in which the common people stumble because of the priestly perfidy.[14] They cannot keep it aright because they have not been properly taught how to do so.

In other words, the descendants of Levi have destroyed the special levitical covenant of blessing (Mal. 2:4–5) as surely as the Flood destroyed human life (Gen. 6:17; 9:11, 15), but like the remnant that remains and allows the reestablishment of life (8:1; 9:1), so the special place of Levi and his descendants will also be reconsecrated (Mal. 3:2–4). The covenantal relationship is seriously jeopardized, but not abrogated. For the fourth time in this section, the speaker is "the LORD Almighty" (cf. 2:2, 4, 7), God's title of power, highlighting the seriousness of the charges being laid.

The results of the gross dereliction of duty are spelled out in verse 9, with heightened emphasis through changed word order. The word "and" (*wᵉ*) joined with *gam* ("so") is emphatic, especially with the following pronoun, which also provides an explicit contrast or antithesis between what God ("I") now does and what the priests ("and you") have done (v. 8). Yahweh renders the priests despised or contemptible as they in their turn did to the altar (1:7, 12; cf. Isa. 53:3). They are also humiliated or made low and worth little (cf. 2 Sam. 6:22; Ezek. 29:15). This degradation takes place "before all the people." Those in whose presence the humiliation occurs are most likely the same as the "many" of verses 6 and 8.

The prophet reiterates the reasons for bringing judgment by picking up terms used previously in the section. The linking form "because" ("inasmuch as," NRSV) is unique, though the causal meaning is evident from the context. The priesthood was to preserve (v. 7) knowledge, but it had not kept (NIV "followed") God's ways; God's ways and his will are to be protected, but the priests have abandoned them (cf. v. 8).

The last clause (lit., "and ones raising faces in the law") is difficult, with several possible interpretations, though all of its vocabulary is reused from earlier verses. The conjunction can be contrastive and disjunctive ("but"; see LXX; KJV; NASB; NIV; NLT; NRSV). If so, the contrast is with the previous action, following God's ways. Usually taken as an idiom, there are several other instances where "to raise the face" indicates showing partiality, diverting from an expected action (Gen. 32:21; Lev. 19:15; Deut. 10:17), in this case

---

14. Ibid., 215.

perverting the application of the law (*tôrâ* found in vv. 6 and 7, with this exact form in v. 8).

Another interpretation reads the syntax differently, seeing the negative term *ʾênkem* (used in "*not* followed") as covering this last clause as well.[15] This necessitates reading the idiom positively, since both clauses are then parallel (see v. 8, where "way" and "teaching" are also parallel), describing actions that the priests do not take. Priests are thus accused of not keeping to, nor in any way favoring, God's instruction (cf. 1:8–9). The last action could also have an implicit direct object (i.e., the people mentioned earlier in the verse); the priests not only do not favor the law themselves, they do not show it to their congregation in a favorable light either, leading themselves and others astray (i.e., a conceptual repetition of 2:8).

COVENANTS IN THE **Old Testament and its world.** Covenants or treaties were tools of diplomacy in the ancient Near East. Two or more sovereign nations allied themselves through a *parity treaty*, in which each party is of equal stature. A current example of this type of treaty is NATO, which exists for the mutual protection of each of its members. This is one of the purposes of a such a treaty in Bible times—for example, the treaty between the Syrian state Amurru and the king of the Hittites living in what is today Turkey.[16]

Another type of treaty is the *vassal treaty* or *suzerainty treaty*, done between two parties of different stature or power: the dominant party, usually represented by their "great king" (often called "my lord"), and the lesser party, whose representative often refers to himself as "your servant."[17] It is theologically significant that this covenant model was commonly used to depict the relationship between God and Israel (e.g., Gen. 15:18; 17; Ex. 2:24), and also, more broadly, between God and all of humanity (Gen. 9:8–10).

---

15. Ibid., 217.

16. See *COS*, 2:94, 97.

17. See, e.g., G. E. Mendenhall, *Law and Covenant in the Israel and the Ancient Near East* (Pittsburgh: Biblical Colloquium, 1955); D. J. Wiseman, *The Vassal-Treaties of Esarhaddon* (London: British School of Archaeology in Iraq, 1958); M. G. Kline, *Treaty of the Great King: The Covenant Structure of Deuteronomy: Studies and Commentary* (Grand Rapids: Eerdmans, 1963); K. Baltzer, *Das Bundesformular*, 2nd ed. (Neukirchen-Vluyn: Neukirchener Verlag, 1964); D. R. Hillers, *Covenant: The History of a Biblical Idea* (Baltimore: Johns Hopkins Univ. Press, 1969); P. R. Williamson, *DOTP*, 139–55.

A major constituent of covenants in biblical times, and the reason why they were made in the first place, was the obligations or stipulations laid on each party. In order for the covenant to function, there were expectations on both sides. If these were breached, the covenant was in jeopardy, or at least open to some of the sanctions spelled out as part of the covenant document (e.g., Deut. 28:15–68). If the stipulations were kept, however, blessings were called down on the parties (28:3–14), and the relationship flourished.

The life of the Israelite nation is presented as a model of this blessing/curse progression, which looks almost like a sine wave, with blessing on the top of the wave and curse at the bottom (see Judg. 2:10–22). Here Malachi contrasts the two extremes, using faithful Levi as the top and the current priesthood as the bottom. Using their theology of history, he is calling the Judean priests to move back to the top, to the blessed position they once enjoyed but lost through their departure from the obligations placed on them.

One use of Israel's covenant with God was to provide a teaching tool. Each new generation had be enculturated into society, and for Israel a foundational element of that covenant was knowing what it was to be God's people. The existence of the covenant relationship and its responsibilities was passed down from parent to child through their teaching by word and example (Deut. 6:1–9). The new covenant also has its reminder, as Jesus indicated when initiating communion in his memory (Luke 22:19–20; 1 Cor. 11:24–25). It serves not only as a reminder of Christ's sacrifice, but also teaches us of our responsibilities as members of his new covenant.

MODELING AS A **teaching tool.** We teach by our words, but we also teach by our lives. This is exemplified in a recent television advertisement that shows a young boy literally following in his father's footsteps, wearing the oversized shoes of his dad, snoozing against a tree like his dad, and reaching for the cigarette pack of his dad. Too often our message becomes muted because our life gets in the way: "I can't hear you because I see you." Jesus notes the same dichotomy between words and actions in his teaching (Luke 6:46).

This truth is to be before the minds of the faithful priests in Malachi's day, and it must be before ours as well, whether as professional teachers and preachers, or even as parents, aunts, or uncles. Malachi 2:6 explains several aspects of this teaching model. The priests are praised for passing on God's truth, but of the manner in which this is done, no words are mentioned. The truth in the context of Malachi included correct ritual practices for maintaining and regaining holiness. Religious instruction is also in our purview as teachers, but since "all truth is God's truth,"[18] we should be mindful that teaching extends beyond religion to encompass all of life.

The teaching model presented by Malachi is to be through lifestyle, both negative (avoiding sin) and positive (living righteously according to God's covenant). We hear the phrase that one must "talk the talk and walk the walk," a concept that has its home here as well as in other places in the Bible (e.g., Ps. 119:1; 1 John 1:6–7). It is through living correctly rather than just mouthing the right words that people are led away from lives of sin (cf. Dan. 12:3).

This also happened following Pentecost in the life and experience of the newly born church, God's new covenant people. Many were drawn to new life through Peter's preaching (Acts 2:41), but many more came through the lived message of Christ's followers (2:43–47). Later, when Paul wrote to Titus, he explains at least part of his understanding of what "sound doctrine" is by explaining it as matters of daily life rather than as objective propositions of belief (Titus 2:1–10). This extends beyond teaching to daily life, since it is the inward heart as well as the outward actions that reflect our relationship with God (e.g., 1 Sam. 16:7; Ps. 51:16–17; Mic. 6:8; Matt. 12:34–35).[19]

This model also has negative implications. Many lives of faithful service have been ruined over a fleeting indiscretion, ruining the person's witness. What takes so long to attain is so quickly lost. This is at heart the message of the definition of "integrity," an unbroken wholeness where, in the matter under discussion, there is no gap at all between words and deeds. This must characterize the life of the Israelite priest as well as that of each Christian as a member of a kingdom of priests (Ex. 19:6; Rev. 1:6). This also sheds light on the saying attributed to St. Francis: "Preach the Gospel, and sometimes use words."

---

18. Taken from the title of the book by A. F. Holmes, *All Truth Is God's Truth* (Grand Rapids: Eerdmans, 1977).

19. The three aspects of life—inward, outward, and upward—are developed by R. Foster, *Celebration of Discipline: The Path to Spiritual Growth* (San Francisco: HarperSanFranicsco, 1988); idem, *Prayer: Finding the Heart's True Home* (San Francisco: HarperSanFranicsco, 1992); cf. T. Wardle, *Healing Care, Healing Prayer* (Siloam Springs, Ark.: Leafwood, 2001); K. L. Ladd and B. Spinka, "Inward, Outward, and Upward: Cognitive Aspects of Prayer," *JSSR* 41 (2002): 475–84; Terry Wardle, *The Transforming Path: A Christ-Centered Approach to Spiritual Formation* (Siloam Springs, Ark.: Leafwood, 2003).

Malachi 2:10–16

HAVE WE NOT all one Father? Did not one God create us? Why do we profane the covenant of our fathers by breaking faith with one another? [11]Judah has broken faith. A detestable thing has been committed in Israel and in Jerusalem: Judah has desecrated the sanctuary the LORD loves, by marrying the daughter of a foreign god. [12]As for the man who does this, whoever he may be, may the LORD cut him off from the tents of Jacob—even though he brings offerings to the LORD Almighty.

[13]Another thing you do: You flood the LORD's altar with tears. You weep and wail because he no longer pays attention to your offerings or accepts them with pleasure from your hands. [14]You ask, "Why?" It is because the LORD is acting as the witness between you and the wife of your youth, because you have broken faith with her, though she is your partner, the wife of your marriage covenant.

[15]Has not the LORD made them one? In flesh and spirit they are his. And why one? Because he was seeking godly offspring. So guard yourself in your spirit, and do not break faith with the wife of your youth.

[16]"I hate divorce," says the LORD God of Israel, "and I hate a man's covering himself with violence as well as with his garment," says the LORD Almighty.

So guard yourself in your spirit, and do not break faith.

THIS SECTION CONTINUES the covenantal idea of the previous sections, highlighting in particular the concept of faithfulness illustrated through the covenant of marriage. God condemns the priests on two counts: unfaithfulness and crocodile tears when God reprimands them for it. They are not alone in receiving condemnation, however, since Malachi includes not only himself, but the entire nation, and even all of humanity, in the sweep of his charges. Lack of covenant faithfulness spreads through many aspects of the life of the covenant people.

Structurally, Wendland suggests a chiasm for this section.[1] A modification of it shows the arrangement of the passage:

A A fatherly God, who is one, created us, his people (v. 10a)
  B Why break faith with our covenant brothers? (v. 10b)
    C Breaking faith by pagan marriage, damaging the sanctuary (v. 11)[2]
      D Result: cut off even if he brings offerings (v. 12)
      D' Result: tears because of unaccepted offerings (v. 13)
    C' Breaking faith through divorce (v. 14a)
  B' Damaging marriage covenant and marriage partner (v. 14b)
A' The One made the family one (v. 15a)
  B'' Don't break faith with your wife (v. 15b)
  B''' Summary: Don't break faith through divorce and violence (v. 16)

The desired state of covenant relationship (the A elements) bracket the result of breaking this relationship: tears and separation (the D elements).

In verse 10, God, through the prophet, returns to a dialogic disputation with Judah through a series of three questions. The first two are rhetorical, drawing the hearers in by demanding an affirmative response. The initial Hebrew interrogative ("Is it not so that . . .") renders the questions even more emphatic than those previously encountered, where God delivers a declarative statement that is challenged.[3] Here the challenge is hurled directly in the face of the hearers. In each of the three questions, the author joins himself with the rest of the people by the use of first person plural ("we," "us"). He does not just point his finger at others, but acknowledges his own complicity in their wrongdoing.

The first question concerns a common kinship—"one father." The referent is ambiguous. This word often refers to Abraham, the father of the Israelite people (Isa. 51:2; cf. Matt. 3:9), though most likely it here refers to God as Father (cf. Isa. 63:16), especially with the parallel location of "father" and God" in these first two questions.[4] God is "Father" elsewhere in Malachi (1:6), and his fatherhood is associated elsewhere with

1. E. Wendland, "Linear and Concentric Patterns in Malachi," *BT* 36 (1985): 116; cf. Gordon P. Hugenberger, *Marriage As Covenant: A Study of Biblical Law and Ethics Governing Marriage, Developed from the Perspective of Malachi* (VTSup 52; Leiden: Brill, 1994), 25.

2. The object of God's covenant love; see comments on 1:2 regarding "love."

3. Cf. Waltke-O'Connor, §18.2g, where rhetorical questions "give information with passion"; BDB, 210 ("an impassioned or indignant affirmation").

4. This interpretation is that of the NIV, with its capitalization of "Father," while the alternate is indicated through the lower case option given in a marginal note.

his creative activity.[5] Whichever interpretation is adopted, the hearers agree that they are united, both ethnically and religiously. The unity is even more elemental in the second question concerning the Creator God. Here not only Israel, but all humanity finds unification. These two questions are formally united in Hebrew by their parallel rhythmic and content structure.[6] They combine to indicate that Israel's unity and very national existence are only attributable to a single source, God himself.

In light of these undeniable truths, the prophet asks the third question: If we are so clearly united, why does Israel belie this unity by their actions? This is done by "breaking faith, being unfaithful," a strong verb (*bgd*) that indicates treachery toward one who should expect fidelity (e.g., spouse, Ex. 21:8; Jer. 3:20; kin, Jer. 12:6; allies, Judg. 9:23; God, Jer. 5:11; Hos. 5:7; 6:7). This is a key theme of this passage, occurring here five times (Mal. 2:10, 11, 14, 15, 16), with its particular application to the marriage bonds. The breach is between "one another" (lit., "a man against his brother"; cf. 3:16), a reciprocal disruption of relationships.

This breach has a serious result for God's people: Their covenant with God is "profaned" or desecrated through breaking its provisions. The verb (*ḥll*) describes what happens when polluting objects or acts affect holy things dedicated to God (Sabbath, Ex. 31:14; Ezek. 20:13; God's name, Amos 2:7; God's table, Mal. 1:12), making them unsuitable for further sacred service. In this case, it is the ancestral covenant (cf. Deut. 4:31) that is breached through severing a foundational family bond. Some suggest this refers to some universal understanding of covenant agreements among all peoples (e.g., Amos 1:9)[7] or to the patriarchal covenants of Genesis (Gen. 9; 14:13; 15:18; etc.).[8] But most likely it refers to the Sinai covenant, in anticipation of which the Fatherhood of God is first encountered (Ex. 4:22–23; cf. Isa. 63:16).[9] That foundational document for Israelite national unity is voided if interpersonal relationships are not considered worthy of being fostered.

---

5. Cf. Deut. 32:6, though the creation verbs there (*qnh*, *ʿśh*, *kwn*) are different from the one used here (*brʾ*).

6. In Hebrew, each of the first two questions has nine beats and differs from the other in only four consonants and two vowels: *hᵃlôʾ ʾāb ʾeḥād lᵉkullānû / hᵃlôʾ ʾēl ʾeḥād bᵉrāʾānû*.

7. Cf. J. M. P. Smith, *A Critical and Exegetical Commentary on Haggai, Zechariah, Malachi, and Jonah* (ICC: Edinburgh: T. & T. Clark, 1912), 48.

8. E.g. Joyce G. Baldwin, *Haggai, Zechariah, Malachi* (TOTC; Downers Grove, Ill.: InterVarsity Press, 1972), 237; S. L. McKenzie and H. N. Wallace, "Covenant Themes in Malachi," *CBQ* 45 (1983): 552.

9. Cf. Eugene Merrill, *An Exegetical Commentary: Haggai, Zechariah, Malachi* (Chicago: Moody Press, 1994), 414; Hill, *Malachi*, 227–28.

In verses 11–12 Judah is held up as an example of this polluting perfidy. Her actions affect not only her capital, Jerusalem, but also its religious center, God's sanctuary, the holy temple (Ps. 20:2).[10] Here Judah is designated as "Israel," since she is the sole remaining element of God's chosen people after the exile and disappearance of the ten northern tribes of Israel (cf. Mal. 1:1; also 2 Chron. 11:3). Her acts are as an abomination ("a detestable thing"), a term common in Ezekiel (43x), Deuteronomy (17x), and Jeremiah (8x). Rendering the sanctuary an abhorrence starkly contrasts with God's natural reaction toward his temple, which is love (Mal. 1:3; see NIV, GNB, NKJV, NLT). This is the sole reference in the Old Testament to God's loving the sanctuary, though humans do in one case (Ps. 26:8), and God does love Zion (78:68; 87:2).

The context, however, better argues for Judah being the lover, with the next verb, "marry" (Deut. 21:13; 24:1), following naturally—love and marriage.[11] God already claimed to love Jacob at the beginning of the book (Mal. 1:2). The sanctuary, where God meets with his covenant beloved, is also viewed affectionately by God as the symbol of his covenant "love" (see comment on 1:2). It contains his covenant "love letter" to Israel in the form of the Ten Commandments, the foundation of the covenant document (Deut. 10:5). But God's beloved has spurned all of this and turned instead to someone else. If Judah is the lover, the covenant force of "love" still plays a role, since it, and therefore her covenant loyalty, is diverted to another, breaking the first commandment against other divine "lovers" (Ex. 20:3).

Regardless of who is doing the loving, the abomination concerns marriage, specifically with "the daughter of a foreign god." "Daughter" is usually understood as referring to pagan women whose deity is other than Yahweh (LXX, GNB, NLT). Such religious syncretism was a prevalent problem in the pre- and postexilic periods (cf., e.g., Ezra 10:18–44; Neh. 13:23–29). This interpretation fits well with the discussion of literal divorce that follows.

Another, less likely possibility is that "daughter" is metaphorical, referring to the worship of foreign goddesses.[12] This interpretation receives some support since the verb for "marry" here is *bˤl*, which shares its root with the

---

10. The term here rendered "sanctuary" (*qōdeš*) is literally Yahweh's "holiness" (HALOT; cf. LXX, Vulg., KJV, ASV). In construct with Yahweh, it can refer to sacrifices (Lev. 5:15; 19:8) as well as the temple (Ps. 11:4; cf. Ps. 93:5; 102:20), which is how it appears to be best understood in this context (cf. NASB; NRSV; NLT). Hill (*Malachi*, 230–31) suggests that it be left ambiguous, which may well reflect the author's intent.

11. This entails reading the Hebrew particle *˒ªšer*, taken in the NIV reading as a relative pronoun ("the sanctuary *that* Yahweh loves") instead as a causal clausal introduction ("*because* he loved . . .; BDB, 83, 8c; DCH, 1:436,8b; NEB; Hill, *Malachi*, 231).

12. Petersen, *Zechariah 9–14 and Malachi*, 198–200. Petersen also reads the particle mentioned in the previous note as "Asherah," a Canaanite goddess (199–200).

Canaanite Baal, rather than other verbs that could have been used.[13] Deities or semidivine beings are "sons/daughters of [a] god" elsewhere in the Old Testament (e.g., Gen. 6:2, 4; Job 1:6) as well as in other literature from the period.[14] Whichever interpretation is best, the wrong mentioned involves breach of the exclusive covenant between God and Israel, a covenant founded on unadulterated loyalty between Israel and her God (Ex. 20:3; Deut. 5:7).

Whoever commits the sin is "cut off,"[15] completely wiped out with his line and exterminated (v. 12; cf. Ezek. 25:7; Mic. 5:9). If this passage is referring to forbidden marriage, the noun "man" refers to males, since, according to contemporary divorce regulations, divorce was restricted to men (Deut. 24:1–4; Jer. 3:1). If the passage is referring to pagan worship, "man" can be gender neutral (NASB; NRSV, "everyone/anyone"). The separation is "from the tents of Jacob," another term for the Israelite community (Num. 24:5; Jer. 30:18). Israel's breach of her primary and foundational promise to worship God alone excludes her from the covenant, even if she continues to bring the prescribed offerings. Israel had been previously warned that empty ritual without a proper devotion of heart is worthless (e.g., Amos 5:22).

Two enigmatic verb forms occur just prior to "the tents of Jacob." These forms are both participles of verbs meaning "to awake, arouse" (ʿwr) and "to answer" (ʿnh) respectively, joined by "and." The combination is difficult to understand in this context. The legal context, as noted by Hill,[16] supports the suggestion that the phrase gives further definition to those engaging in forbidden religious practices, those who "witness and respond," that is, those who aid and abet the wrong by putting their name to its legal recognition as witnesses (see NIV text note here). This spreads culpability throughout the Judean community, since most would know of these forbidden marriages but are not speaking out against them.

These wrongdoers attempt to cover their continuing sin by surface religiosity, that is, by bringing offerings (cf. the contrast in 3:3). These, as well as the priests, the actual presenters of the offerings before God, are all complicit in God's sight. Formal ritual activity is not sufficient to atone for willing and flagrant covenant disregard.

---

13. BDB, 127; *DCH*, 2:239. See J. Barr, "The Image of God in Genesis—A Study of Terminology," *BJRL* 51 (1968–1969): 11–26, for a sample study of word selection from within a semantic field.

14. *CAD*, 2:239 (*bintu* a); *UT*, 373:481.

15. *krt* can be read as a jussive or desired action rather than as an indicative (see ESV; NASB; NIV; NLT; NRSV, in contrast to the straight future reading of LXX; KJV; ASV).

16. Hill, *Malachi*, 235.

While the NIV indicates a change of topic in verse 13 through a paragraph break, the beginning phrase (lit., "and a second thing") indicates that this section continues the theme of verses 11–12: intermarriage and divorce. For the third time in the book, humans are "doing" something (*ʿśh;* cf. 2:11, 12). Each time that this verb has a human subject, the action is evil (see also 2:17; 3:15, 19). Since Yahweh ignores the offerings, the offerer "weeps," covering the "altar with tears." The use of three terms of emotional distress ("tears," "weep," "wail") denotes extreme agitation. All three arise from a break in the relationship between Israel and her covenant God, which is supposed to be maintained by ritual purity. As long as Yahweh no longer acknowledges the efficacy of ritual, the relationship is severed.

Yahweh's distance is described in two ways in verse 13: *inattention* and *displeasure*. The phrase "no longer" implies that until this turn of events, Yahweh did look approvingly on Israel's ritual. The word "pleasure" elsewhere describes acceptable sacrifice (Lev. 1:3; 19:5; 22:19, 21, 29), as here. The "hands" bringing the sacrifice are those presenting it in verse 12 (note the change to the second person, "your hands").

In verse 14, Malachi's audience again disputes his allegations (cf. 1:2, etc.), asking the basis for his claims ("Why?"). Whereas earlier it was illicit marriages, Yahweh now proceeds to present yet another issue: abandoning their current, rightful marriages. Yahweh observes this pattern as a "witness," a legal term concerning providing evidence of which one has knowledge (Deut. 4:26; Isa. 8:2). The situation is made even more serious by the use of God's covenant name ("Yahweh") in the emphatic, preverbal position in this context of covenant breach.[17] It is God, not a mere mortal, who takes an active role in this lawsuit between two parties: "you" (the Israelite covenant breaker) and "the wife/woman."

God is not only witness to this lawsuit but also a witness to the marriage. Marriage is a covenant (Prov. 2:17; Ezek. 16:8), and although we do not have any actual marriage contracts from the period of the Old Testament, we do know that other covenants or treaties included witnesses.[18] This may well be the case also for personal covenantal arrangements such as a marriage, part of which even today is to make promises "before God and this company."

The woman involved is not just any wife, a possibility in a society where polygyny was possible, but one "of your youth" (cf. Prov. 5:18; Isa. 54:6), most

---

17. T. Muraoka (*Emphatic Words and Structures in Biblical Hebrew* [Leiden: Brill, 1985], 35) suggests that the divine subject preceding the verb flows from a religious psychology that recognizes God's dominance, an explanation that also highlights the gravity of the present statement.

18. In the treaties between nations, for example, the witnesses are the deities of the parties involved (see, e.g., *COS*, 2:95, 97–98, 105–6).

likely the first and primary wife who had special legal rights but is now abandoned. The wife is also described as Israel's "partner" and "wife of [the] marriage covenant." Both phrases are unique to this verse. "Partner" comes from a root denoting an alliance (*ḥbr*), a close and indissoluble bond (Gen. 2:24; cf. Ex. 26:6, 9, 11). "Covenant" (*bᵉrît*) likewise connotes inviolability. This may refer to the Mosaic "covenant of our fathers" (Mal. 2:10), with the point being marriage restricted to the covenant group (Deut. 7:3), or it could highlight the solemn nature of marriage, of which God is a witness (see comments above on Mal. 2:12).[19] The word "marriage" is supplied by the NIV; while it is not explicit in the text, it certainly can be implied.

In spite of the fixed nature of the marriage relationship, Israel has "broken faith" (*bgd*), the third time in this section that this verb has been used. It unites the discussion of divorce (vv. 13–16) with that of mixed marriages (vv. 10–12). Here the finger points even more emphatically, with the use of the independent personal pronoun "you" preceding the verb, and is in stark contrast to the injured party, "she," also indicated by an independent personal pronoun.

Verses 15 and 16 form a single subunit through an inclusion, a conceptual repetition at the boundaries of a section, continuing the discussion of "the wife of your youth." In verse 15 broken faith is prohibited through the use of a negative imperative form. The MT here reads the verbal form as an impersonal third masculine singular: "Don't let anyone break faith" (see KJV, NASB, NRSV). There is textual evidence for a second person ("Don't you break faith"; LXX, Vulgate, NIV, NLT), which also makes good sense in the context, especially in light of the preceding verb "guard yourself," which is second person. The plural verb indicates a distributive action where each individual responds individually rather than as a collective ("each of you guard yourself"). The locus of that care is in the "spirit," the mind or one's sense of self, though some take it as simply reiterating the reflexive nature of the verb ("yourselves," NLT, NRSV).

The exhortation to faithfulness in the second half of verse 15 is relatively clear, but the preceding elements in verse 15 are much more obscure. The first clause concerns unity (lit., "and not one he made"). It continues the previous verse through the use of the conjunction *wᵉ*, which can be simply coordinative ("and not"; KJV) or adversative ("but not"; NASB), though most English translations take it as an interrogative construction ("is/has not?"; Vulgate, Peshitta, KJV, NIV, NEB, NRSV). The word "one" itself is also unclear. Some interpreters see it as the subject of the following verb (e.g., "and no one has done," NASB; but see also NIV text note, "But the one who is our father did not

---

19. See Hill, *Malachi*, 243.

do this"), while more take "one" as the verb's object ("and has not he made one"; KJV, NIV, NJB, NLT, NRSV). The second option refers to human unity, which fits the present context of covenant unfaithfulness and marriage/divorce. This could refer to the marriage unity of the first couple (Gen. 2:24) or to the fact that man and woman are united in creation, sharing in God's image (Gen. 1:26–27, though "one" does not occur there).

The next clause does not get any easier, and its interpretation depends to a large measure on that adopted for the previous clause. The least ambiguous word is the word "spirit." The word preceding "spirit" (*šᵊʾār*) may mean "remnant, remainder" (cf. LXX, KJV, NASB) or, by emending the vowel, "flesh" (*šᵊʾēr*; NIV, NLT, NRSV). This second option would make a neat word pair "flesh/spirit," while "remnant of spirit" is obscure, though it may denote "an enlivened body," which "belongs to him." The referent for the pronoun "him" depends on the interpretation of the previous clauses. If "one" is the subject of the verb "made," it could be described more fully in this next clause with the resumptive pronoun picking it up ("to him[self]"; e.g., NASB, "But not one has done so *who* ...") or, if Yahweh is seen as the implied subject of "made," the text would read as in the NIV: "Has not the LORD made them ... they are *his*."

The next section of verse 15 contains a question and answer, though where the division between the two lies is unclear. The question being asked is either, "And what is the One [i.e., God; ESV, NRSV] doing?" or "And why unity" (cf. KJV, NIV). Regardless of which option is chosen, the object of the search is identical—"the seed of God" (a phrase found only here in the Old Testament that probably denotes "godly offspring"). These "godly offspring" likely denote those who display his character, following his covenant will;[20] this interpretation provides identification between these offspring and the vivified flesh earlier in the verse and links to the importance of the topic of faithfulness/unfaithfulness in this prophecy.

When the unity yearned for in verse 15 is breached by divorce, there is a strong reaction (2:16). This and the previous verse are related through vocabulary and theme, but they also share semantic and syntactic ambiguity. A literal translation, showing various options with their ambiguities, is: "'For/Indeed/If—he hates/one hates/I hate—divorce!/divorcing,' said Yahweh, the God of Israel, 'then violence will cover/then he will cover with violence—his clothing,' said Yahweh of hosts." This indicates that there is hardly a word that is not fraught with controversy.

The opening word (*kî*, not translated by the NIV) may indicate purpose ("for, because"; KJV, NASB, NLT, NRSV) or emphasis ("indeed, surely"). A problem with either of these options is that these functions are subordinate, with

---

20. See Hill, *Malachi*, 247–48.

the main clause generally preceding the subordinate clause, rather than following it as it does here.[21] Some, with more justification, see it functioning conditionally ("if"; LXX, NEB), which is more common when the main clause follows, as it does here.

There follows in the MT a verb literally translated as "he hated" (*śnʾ*). The preceding context suggests Yahweh is the subject of the verb, but it appears unnatural for Yahweh to speak of himself impersonally in his own direct speech, the genre of the present verse.[22] Another approach, taking into consideration the problem just mentioned, emends the form to a first person masculine singular ("I hated/hate"; NASB, NIV, NLT, NRSV, NJPS, *BHS*). Most English versions take this approach, though without support from any of the older versions. Such a severe emendation should be undertaken only as a last resort, if the current text is clearly corrupt and not understandable.

Another textual option is to reread the verb as a masculine singular participle, "one (is) hating/hates," necessitating a change of a single vowel from the MT,[23] which is the subject of the following verbs. Some read the form as a verbal adjective (i.e., "Divorce is hateful"), which does fit the context. An option preferred here is that the subject is not Yahweh but is impersonal, "one," who in this case is the husband in the marriage under discussion. It is his hating that is condemned, using a root that occurs elsewhere in the context of marriage (Gen. 29:31, 33; Deut. 21:15–17; 22:13, 16; 24:3; Judg. 14:16; 15:2; Prov. 30:23; Isa. 60:15).[24]

The term following this aversion is "divorce" (lit., "sending away"—either a masculine singular imperative or an infinitive). Some earlier versions, adopting the former option, view this as a mandate for divorce, "if one hates, send away!"[25] This supports the apparent tolerance toward divorce in the Mosaic law (Deut. 24:1–4), and has the merit of reading an unemended Hebrew text. However, this reading runs counter to the tenor of the context. Israel has just been chastised for unfaithfulness to its covenant commitments, and this very verse concludes with the same warning. It therefore appears incongruous to now completely reverse this condemnation.

---

21. Anneli Aejmelaeus, "Function and Interpretation of כִּי in Biblical Hebrew," *JBL* 105 (1986): 193–209.

22. The KJV translates as reported rather than direct speech, "For the Lord ... saith," repointing the verb as a participle; cf. Beth Glazier-McDonald, *Malachi, the Divine Messenger* (SBLDS; Atlanta: Scholars, 1987), 110–11.

23. *śānēʾ* read as *śōnēʾ*; LXX; REB; Glazier-McDonald, *Malachi*, 110–12.

24. See R. Westbrook, "The Prohibition on Restoration of Marriage in Deuteronomy 24:1–4," in *Studies in the Bible 1986: Scripta Hierosolymitana* 31, ed. S. Japhet (Jerusalem: Magnes, 1986), 387–405; Hugenberger, *Marriage*, 70–72.

25. See Baldwin, *Haggai, Zechariah, Malachi*, 241; Hugenberger, *Marriage*, 57–58.

The second option shows two sequential actions: a husband feeling aversion for a wife and consequently "sending [her] away/divorcing [her]" (cf. ESV). In this case, the divorce is not prompted by any identified fault on the part of the wife of his youth (the covenant wife [v. 14]), but lies completely at the initiation of the husband, who leaves her for someone else (v. 11).[26]

The importance of this message concerning covenant fidelity is accentuated through the speaker's self-designation in two divine messenger formulae in this verse. Both times he is named as Yahweh (*yhwh*; "LORD"), using the intimate, covenant name of relationship. The first time, the other party of the divine covenant is also identified, with Yahweh described as Israel's God, the only time he is so identified in the prophecy (cf. Zeph. 2:9). This is in contrast to his second identification with power ("Almighty"), which is a frequent description (Mal. 1:4 plus 23 other times in the book). The warnings here must be taken seriously indeed. The double identification in a single verse also emphasizes a new, less tolerant attitude toward divorce than that expressed in the Mosaic law, where it is permitted (Deut. 24:1–4; cf. Acts 10:9–23, where God's revelation of a new twist on an old law needs a threefold repetition).

The next clause (lit., "and he covers [with] violence on his garment") begins with a conjunction (*wᵉ*) whose function varies depending on the interpretation of the previous clauses. It can simply join two clauses (i.e., X *and* Y; NASB, NIV, NRSV); it can function causally, indicating that the next clause is a result of what precedes ("so [that]"); or, if it is preceded by a conditional indicator ("if"), it can introduce the result ("then/as a result of this"; cf. NEB). Hill suggests that it functions epexegetically, explaining the nature of what comes just before ("for he covers").[27]

The verb with the attached conjunction indicates an incomplete action rather than something that is a one-time event ("he covers, is covering ... with violence"). Again, no subject is explicit. It can no longer be Yahweh, if that is how the previous verses are to be interpreted, since he does not perpetrate violence. The subject must now change to the implied husband (KJV, NASB, NIV). If so, there is no compelling reason why he is not the implied subject throughout the verse, as suggested above. Another possibility is that violence is the subject as it covers his (the husband's) clothing (LXX, Vulgate; cf. Prov. 10:6, 11; Hab. 2:17).[28]

---

26. See Glazier-McDonald, *Malachi*, 111.

27. Hill, *Malachi*, 251; "thereby covers"; see also Glazier-McDonald, *Malachi*, 82. A variation of this last option is for the conjunction to function explicatively, "divorce, *that is*, covering ..."; cf. D. W. Baker, "Further Examples of the *Waw Explicativum*," 129–36. This highlights the abusive nature of divorce in the context.

28. See Verhoef, *Haggai and Malachi*, 279; Hill, *Malachi*, 252;

Violence (*ḥamas*) is a strong word used of brutal, deplorable acts that violate God's order.[29] It is unacceptable to God and hateful, whichever interpretation of the preceding clauses might have been accepted. Violence covers over "his garment," with the pronoun necessarily referring to the husband (and so providing support for seeing him as the implicit subject of earlier verbs in the verse as well). This particular expression is unique to Malachi, and there are no clear parallels to aid in understanding it, so options are almost as numerous as interpreters, ranging from literal to metaphoric. The two best options are the NLT, which moves toward the former in its reading that divorce "is as cruel as putting on a victim's bloodstained coat," a possible allusion to literal blood shed during incidents of domestic violence, and the NIV, which understands the garment figuratively to represent the offending husband, with clothes representing, if not making, the character of a man (cf. Isa. 64:6; Zech. 3:4). His violence through divorce is equivalent to wearing a bloody butcher's apron.

Two final admonitions in verse 16 conclude the section. The first harks back strongly to verse 15, where three of the Hebrew terms used are repeated ("so [1] *guard yourself* [2] *in your spirit* and do not [3] *break faith*). The resulting "envelope" surrounding the discussion of divorce highlights it by making it stand out from its immediate context, while still being part of it. The second person plural forms in both verses emphasize that this is not just a societal problem, as if unfaithfulness happens "out there." Rather, it is a problem facing each one of "you" collectively and individually. This is not just a problem of the priests and Levites (1:6–2:9) or of Judah generally (2:10–11), but of every one of the people.[30] The passage ends with a human picture of breach of relationship (in marriage) that exemplifies the breach in divine-human relationship (in cultic service).

Bridging Contexts

DIVORCE IN THE BIBLE. There are several discussions of divorce in the Bible, some of which can be seen as contradictory to each other. Deuteronomy 24:1–4 says that if a man marries a woman and later finds her unsuitable for some reason, he is allowed to divorce her.

---

29. Gen. 6:11, 13; Hab. 1:2, 3, 9; *TDOT*, 4:478–87; I. Swart and C. Van Dam, "חמס,"*NIDOTTE*, 2:177–79. Petersen (*Zechariah 9–14 and Malachi*, 194–95) prefers "wrongdoing" in an attempt to avoid a connotation of physical abuse, but abuse, whether physical assault (Judg. 9:24; Ps. 58:3; Jer. 51:35; Ezek. 7:23), verbal and psychological maltreatment (Gen. 16:5; Ex. 23:1; Ps. 27:12), or economic exploitation (Ezek. 28:16; Amos 3:10; Hab. 2:8), seems completely appropriate.

30. This plural addressee also provides a segue into the next section of the prophecy.

This verse presupposes that divorce is allowable under certain circumstances (cf. also 22:19, 29) and does not condemn the practice. The focus of the legislation in Deuteronomy is only secondarily on divorce, however. The major emphasis is on the unacceptability or the remarriage of a previously divorced couple to each other (24:4; cf. Jer. 3:1).

The existence of divorce is presupposed elsewhere as well, including a proscription against a priest marrying a divorced woman (Lev. 21:7, 14; Ezek. 44:22) and the ability of a widow or divorcée to take a binding oath (Num. 30:9). In the case of the mixed marriages between Israelites and non-Israelites after the return from the Exile, both Ezra 9–10 and Nehemiah 13:23–28 find the practice unacceptable, a sign of unfaithfulness to God. The people who heard Ezra's condemnation of mixed marriages proposed to send their pagan wives away, though the specific term for "divorce" found in Malachi 2:16 is not used there. No steps are prescribed for the current problem in Nehemiah, but simply a vow to avoid the practice in the future (Neh. 13:25). A specific priest is singled out for condemnation, and the wrong is described as a defilement of priestly obligations (vv. 28–29), so perhaps the problem there is really a breach of Leviticus 21:7. In any case, Ezra and Nehemiah both face the same situation as found in Malachi 2:11: intermarriage with a pagan.

The relationship between God and Israel is pictured as a marriage, and on several occasions the prophets speak in terms of God's divorcing Israel, his "wife" (Isa. 50:1; Jer. 3:8). From an Old Testament perspective, therefore, divorce does not seem to be absolutely banned, and in Ezra it is seen even to be encouraged. The problem arises with Malachi 2:16, which can be read as a blanket condemnation of all divorce—and this coming from the mouth of God himself. If so, this is the end of the matter, but it still leaves the historical difficulties of various other views in the same Old Testament.

A universal prohibition seems unknown to Joseph in the New Testament. In the same verse he is described as being "righteous" and also considering divorcing his pregnant fiancée, Mary (Matt. 1:19). If the ban on divorce is absolute and from God, then the author would be hard-pressed to describe Joseph in this way. In the Sermon on the Mount, Jesus picks up the law from Deuteronomy 24, not making a statement about divorce per se, which he seems to accept (Matt. 5:31–32; 19:1–9; Mark 10:1–12; Luke 16:18), but he tightens the restriction on remarriage.[31] Paul bans divorce for both husbands

---

31. The topic of remarriage is important in a pastoral context. Helpful resources from different perspectives include W. A. Heth and G. J. Wenham, *Jesus and Divorce: The Problem with the Evangelical Consensus* (Nashville: Nelson, 1984); C. S. Keener, *And Marries Another: Divorce and Remarriage in the Teaching of the New Testament* (Peabody, Mass.: Hendrickson, 1992); D. Instone–Brewer, *Divorce and Remarriage in the Bible* (Grand Rapids: Eerdmans, 2002).

and wives (1 Cor. 7:11), and when a marriage was entered into prior to one of the spouses becoming a Christian, he urges the new Christian to stay in the relationship if the unconverted spouse so desires (vv. 12–13). The implication is that if the unconverted spouse does not wish to maintain the relationship, it can be dissolved through divorce without condemnation. This therefore differs from the Ezra–Nehemiah situation, since the latter involved what were mixed marriages from the outset.

Some try to ascertain the relative order of books of Ezra, Nehemiah, and Malachi based on their respective views of divorce.[32] This is fraught with difficulty, not least being the subjectivity of what might be argued. Is a dogmatic condemnation the starting point, which is slowly eroded by accommodation to real-life, or does a growing crisis finally lead to a complete ban as the final answer? Either view is arguable from the textual evidence, though neither view is compelling based on the textual evidence.

There is a major contrast spelled out between Malachi on the one hand, and Ezra–Nehemiah on the other. The latter regulate marriages crossing boundaries of nationality and religion, leading to breaching the first of the Ten Commandments (i.e., the command against foreign gods, Ex. 20:3; Deut. 5:7), as it did in the case of Solomon (1 Kings 11:1–13). This type of marriage Malachi condemns in Malachi 2:11–12. He also condemns divorce within the boundary of Israel, however. Merrill suggests that the Israelites are divorcing their Israelite wives in order to marry outside of their people, a possibility that cannot be proven from the text.[33] This makes the prohibition contextual rather than universal.

Yet another possibility reads the divorce prohibition against its immediately following context: God's hatred of violence. Violence, mistreatment, and exploitation are not to be inflicted on one's neighbors or slaves (e.g., Ex. 21:18–27), and in some cases such actions result in freedom for the slave (21:26–27). The two actions, divorce and domestic violence, can be viewed as complementary, the latter leading to the wife's release from the marital covenant in compensation for the physical, emotional, economic, verbal, or spiritual suffering she undergoes. In this case, God's disfavor of divorce is not absolute, but he absolutely opposes domestic violence in any form, since such violence can be experienced in a variety of equally harmful ways. The only difference between them is that not all are visible.

---

32. See discussion in Merrill, *An Exegetical Commentary*, 422–23.
33. Ibid., 423.

DIVORCE AND DOMESTIC VIOLENCE. One area in which the church should hang its head in shame is its acknowledgement of, and approach to, domestic violence and abuse among its members. The Catholic Church has been tarnished of late with evidence of sexual abuse of minors by some among its clergy, with the hierarchy turning a blind eye, or even abetting the misdeeds through a lack of biblical response. Evangelicalism cannot take this as an opportunity for self-congratulation, however, since Jesus himself allows only the sinless to cast the first stone (John 8:7). The statistics are sobering: As many as one out of three to four girls and one out of five to seven boys will be sexually abused by the time they reach age eighteen.[34]

Demographically, in general the more conservative the religious leanings of the population group, the higher the rates of incest. This follows from a patriarchal view of family power dynamics since, if the father is the ultimate and final authority, whatever he says or desires cannot be questioned. On one extreme are Jewish families, where the mother plays an active role in family guidance; and on the other extreme are the Amish, where the father is the authoritative person.[35] As regards physical violence, "domestic violence is considered one of the foremost causes of serious injury to women ages 15 to 44," according to the U.S. Surgeon General.[36] Today in the West the most common contact we have in our daily lives with those who are being oppressed and exploited are with victims of abuse and violence, and we do not even know who they are.

One reason for the lack of knowledge is really a lack of acknowledgment. Rarely do churches, especially among conservative denominations, acknowledge that a problem exists in this area of domestic violence among its parishioners, even though statistics indicate that it does exist.[37] Living in denial is different from living in ignorance, a distinction Paul makes in

---

34. Exact figures are unavailable, one of the reasons being that sexual abuse is still under-reported. For studies on this difficult issue from a secular perspective see D. Finkelhor, *A Sourcebook on Child Sexual Abuse* (Beverly Hills: Sage, 1986), and other works by him. On family domestic violence in general, see D. Finkelhor et al., *The Dark Side of Families: Current Family Violence Research* (Beverly Hills: Sage, 1983).

35. Oral communication from Victoria Kepler Didato, sexual abuse therapist and expert.

36. www.mentalhealth.samhsa.gov/features/surgeongeneralreport/chapter4/sec1_1.asp.

37. A 1998 survey by the Commonwealth Fund reports that violence or abuse will affect 39 percent of women at some time during their life.

1 Corinthians 5. There it was not a matter of immorality unknown to the church, but a situation where they were well aware and even seemed to revel in (5:2). This lack of acknowledgement, coupled with a position that divorce is unacceptable at all times and under any circumstance, does a serious disservice to the gospel of Christ and also places innocent lives in jeopardy. Many an abused woman has finally gathered enough courage to approach her pastor about an ongoing pattern of physical abuse, only to be reabused emotionally. On what I feel to be an incorrect reading of Malachi 2:16, women are sent back into this abuse, "encouraged" by the misunderstanding of another passage about wives submitting to their husband (Eph. 5:22).

How should we address this problem in the light of both Malachi and Paul? First, we must remember that Malachi addresses only the husband, the wife having no opportunity to initiate divorce in Israelite society. This is also clear from the immediate context, which speaks of marrying "daughters," not sons, and wives, not husbands. Grammar also indicates that a male is the concern in verse 16. A valid reading is to see domestic violence in itself as being a divorce; if the man has done this, he has de facto broken the covenant relationship, initiating a divorce in a hateful way.

If a husband uses Ephesians 5 as a justification for his wife to submit in all things, even abuse of any form, that needs to be done in full cognizance of what 5:25 says. If husbands are able to act in this way toward their wives, that is saying that Christ raped, abused, and exploited his church. Our shock at this claim needs to be at least matched by an outrage at using Ephesians as justification for domestic violence. What a civil society recognizes as abhorrent and unacceptable, as evidenced through its laws, how can the church accept as permitted? Note also Paul's words from Colossians 3:19: "Husbands, love your wives and do not be harsh with them."

The direct victims are not the only ones harmed by domestic violence, however. The cycle of abuse is such that those raised in households of domestic violence are more likely to be abusers themselves. There are also serious consequences for the abuser. Making abuse part of one's character results in a person who is far from exhibiting the fruit of the Spirit, which includes "patience, kindness, goodness, faithfulness, gentleness and self-control" (Gal. 5:22–23). None of these traits find realization in an abuser, who also by his abuse disqualifies himself from a position in church leadership, since leaders also are called away from violence and toward gentleness (1 Tim. 3:3). Theologically significant are verses that indicate that the prayers and worship of a violent abuser are unacceptable, since God will not hear when human relationships are damaged (see Isa. 58:4; 1 Peter 3:7).[38]

38. A number of Christian resources are available on this topic. For example, J. and P. Alsdurf, *Battered into Submission* (Downers Grove, Ill.: InterVarsity Press, 1989); D. Allender, *The Wounded Heart: Hope for Adult Victims of Child Sexual Abuse* (Colorado Springs: NavPress, 1990); C. J. Adams and M. M. Fortune, ed., *Violence against Women and Children: A Christian Theological Sourcebook* (New York: Continuum, 1995); C. C. Kroeger and J. R. Beck, *Women, Abuse, and the Bible: How Scripture Can Be Used to Hurt or Heal* (Grand Rapids: Baker, 1996); N. Nason–Clark, *The Battered Wife: How Christians Confront Family Violence* (Louisville: Westminster John Knox, 1997); C. C. Kroeger and N. Nason–Clark, *No Place for Abuse: Biblical & Practical Resources to Counteract Domestic Violence* (Downers Grove, Ill.: InterVarsity Press, 2001).

Malachi 2:17–3:5

❧

YOU HAVE WEARIED the LORD with your words. "How have we wearied him?" you ask.

By saying, "All who do evil are good in the eyes of the LORD, and he is pleased with them" or "Where is the God of justice?"

3:1"See, I will send my messenger, who will prepare the way before me. Then suddenly the Lord you are seeking will come to his temple; the messenger of the covenant, whom you desire, will come," says the LORD Almighty.

2But who can endure the day of his coming? Who can stand when he appears? For he will be like a refiner's fire or a launderer's soap. 3He will sit as a refiner and purifier of silver; he will purify the Levites and refine them like gold and silver. Then the LORD will have men who will bring offerings in righteousness, 4and the offerings of Judah and Jerusalem will be acceptable to the LORD, as in days gone by, as in former years.

5"So I will come near to you for judgment. I will be quick to testify against sorcerers, adulterers and perjurers, against those who defraud laborers of their wages, who oppress the widows and the fatherless, and deprive aliens of justice, but do not fear me," says the LORD Almighty.

ISRAEL'S PATTERN OF arguing with God returns with a vengeance. Now they impugn God's personal character. This pushes God even further than in the previous disputations, since now he responds with judgment. The current chapter division appears misplaced, since it divides a section that is united by theme.

This prophetic dispute, directed to the Judean people in general ("you," including the Levites, 3:3), continues the series started at 1:2. This series was interrupted by a dialogue with the priests and Levites in 1:6–2:9 and was picked up again in 2:10–13.[1] The initial assertion is that the people have verbally "wearied" (*ygᶜ*) Yahweh. This verbal stem occurs only four times, twice here and in Isaiah 43:23–24. It indicates physical exhaustion resulting

---

1. This could be again speaking to the priests, cf. R. L. Smith, *Micah–Malachi*, 326; DCH, 4:81.

from strenuous labor (cf. the same verb in another Heb. stem, 2 Sam. 23:10; Isa. 40:30; 49:4; Hab. 2:13). Here this is applied metaphorically to Yahweh, who does not literally experience such weariness (Isa. 40:28). In this case, it is the psychological tedium of artificial worship in word but not in action (cf. Jer. 7:4–10) that has become so debilitating to him.

The people dispute this yet again by asking: "How?" (lit., "in what [way]?"; 1:2; cf. 1:6, 7; 3:7, 7). The verb in their response is literally "we have wearied," with no explicit direct object, though clearly Yahweh is to be understood. As the MT stands, the emphasis of the respondents is on the action, and their puzzlement is over how their ritual acts could be wearisome. Many translations add "him" after the verb as its direct object. This unnecessary addition seems to shift the attention more toward the object of the action and away from the action itself.

The rebuttal to Israel's question has two elements, statements the people have made that are turned around as evidence against them. The first is a claim that Yahweh has no standards of good and evil (2:17b). They make a hyperbolic claim concerning everyone ("all," NIV) who practices evil.[2] "Evil" in its previous use in Malachi refers to unacceptable sacrifices (1:8; cf. different terms for evil in 3:15; 4:1), so this statement may refer to those practicing this particular evil or to anyone who goes against the wishes of God.

The disturbing claim is that this evil is in fact "good" or "favorable" (NLT) in God's estimation. This turns the moral spectrum completely on its head. In Deuteronomy, the clause "do evil in the eyes of the LORD" (Deut. 4:25; 9:18; 17:2; 31:29), or its opposite, doing good (6:18; 12:25, 28; 13:18; 21:9), are common ways of expressing commendation or condemnation of actions, including keeping the divine covenant. This Mosaic law is foundational for prophetic messages, being the standard to which the people and their leaders are repeatedly called back. The people's claim here reverses the very polarity of the covenant, going as far as claiming that these miscreants are favorable, even "pleasing" to Yahweh, in spite of the prophet's having already denied this in the second dispute (Mal. 1:10).

The second statement begins with the interrogative adverb "where" (*ʾayyēh*), used twice before in the prophecy (1:6), both times of God asking what happened to the respect and honor due someone of his character. Now the question is turned on its head, with the people asking God about a characteristic they perceive as lacking, namely, his "justice" (NIV, NASB, NLT, NRSV) or "judgment" (KJV).[3] Yahweh demands justice of others (Zech. 7:9; 8:16), and

---

2. The verb is a participle, indicating habitual, ongoing behavior (see Waltke-O'Connor, §37.6b).

3. See Hill, *Malachi*, 264.

Job bases his entire argument on God's being just (Job 8:3; 40:8), but the speakers here claim that it is lacking in God. The same phrase "God of justice" is used of Yahweh in Isaiah 30:18, where he shows grace and compassion; has his character now changed?

These two statements can be read in two different ways: as a complaint question directed against God[4] or as a statement concerning the worldview espoused by the people. In the former, the speakers are upset that God is not acting according to their expectations by providing a sign that he has not changed in the new, postexilic context in which they now find themselves. This attitude parallels that of Habakkuk, who also was upset at God's apparent inactivity (Hab. 1:2–4, 12–2:1). The second possibility reflects a blasé, complacent attitude on the part of the people (cf. Mal. 1:13), a perspective suggesting that God does not care and does not act, so why should his people do so (Deut. 32:15; Zeph. 1:12). This can be seen as a variation of what Hugenberger aptly calls "religious relativism,"[5] which is now termed a postmodern view that there are no such things as absolute standards and values and no objective good or evil.

But in 3:1 Yahweh strongly rebuts this notion, indicating his action is imminent. His speech begins with an exclamatory interjection (*hineni*) that indicates immediacy, especially when coupled with a participle, as here (cf. 1:13; 4:1).[6] Yahweh is on the verge of sending a messenger with an implication of "just wait!" This probably picks up the same clause in Exodus 23:20, where preparation for care and safety is provided, along with an admonition to heed what Yahweh directs as regards the covenant. The messenger is Yahweh's, as shown by the word "my" (*mal'aki*, a play on the name of the prophet himself; cf. 1:1). This ambiguity suggests that the present prophecy itself is fulfilling God's promise of this verse; this coming is not a future event but one that is happening now in the presence of the hearers themselves.[7]

The messenger's task is to "prepare the way" (lit., "a way") before Yahweh. This same verb and direct object combination is used only in Isaiah 40:3; 57:14; 62:10, each passage describing the restoration of fallen fortunes by clearing out the hindering obstacles. Here it is the Israelites and their leaders who are the obstacle (cf. Mal. 3:3, 5). Similar wording occurs in Exodus 23:20;

---

4. See Glazier-McDonald, *Malachi*, 123; Hill, *Malachi*, 262.

5. Hugenberger, *Marriage*, 102.

6. Waltke-O'Connor, §37.6d; 40.2.1b. Most English translations render the interjection as an imperative verb ("see!"; "behold!" etc.), though it is in fact neither verb nor imperative.

7. Cf. Glazier-McDonald, *Malachi*, 134–35, who calls this identity a "deception."

33:2, where God promised an assisting forerunner after the Exodus.[8] There it was the people coming to their Promised Land, while here it is Israel's God coming to his chosen people. His passage will open before him, just like a contemporary head of state finds no traffic or traffic signals to slow his entourage's progress.[9] It is not in this instance the entrance of a new, conquering king, but rather the return by one already crowned to his rightful place.

The goal of the journey, the "throne room" of the returning King and the place where he belongs, is "his temple." While this term is not used elsewhere in Malachi (cf. 3:10, "my house"), cultic rituals illegally performed there were previously noted (1:7–14). The priests have misused it as if it were their own, but now its rightful owner reclaims possession. The arriving one is "the Lord" (ʾādôn). This term for a master or lord is used on a human level (e.g., of a human king in Isa. 26:13; Jer. 22:18), but much more frequently of God, especially when used with the definite article (Zech. 4:14; 6:5), as well as of the Messiah (Ps. 110:1). In the previous uses of ʾādôn in Malachi (Mal. 1:6),[10] it vacillates between the human and divine, but here "the Lord" is indeed "the LORD."

The Lord's arrival is described by a form of the verb ("will come") that signifies "a situation [that] is conceived of as beginning and continuing," translated almost uniformly into English as a future.[11] His arrival is unexpected, happening "suddenly" and by surprise (Josh. 10:9; 11:7). Every other occurrence of this word in the Old Testament is in the context of calamity, which the next verses will show is also the case here, at least for those who live as if the rightful King were gone for good.

The people are said to be "seeking" this Lord, but whether this is to be taken literally or, more likely, ironically depends on which of the two interpretations is espoused for the two questions closing 2:17. The verb "seeking" is another participle, an ironic echo of the same form in 2:15. There God truly seeks offspring, while here the people only nominally seek God or, if they are seriously questioning him in 2:17, the one whom they seek will turn out to be their judge. That which they look for is not what they really want.[12]

---

8. Parallel terms in the two passages to those in Malachi are italicized. Ex. 23:20 reads: "*See, I am sending* an *angel ahead of* you to guard you along the *way*," implying opposition from which the people will need protection, and 33:2 reads "and I will *send* an *angel before* you," whose purpose will be to remove the opposing Canaanite nations.

9. See Hill, *Malachi*, 266, for the ancient Near Eastern royal processional background.

10. See Hill, *Malachi*, 268.

11. An "incipient present non-perfective"; Waltke-O'Connor, §31.3d.

12. Cf. other cases where people get what they want but find out that they do not want it after all; e.g., wanting human wisdom and autonomy from God (Gen. 3); "if only we had died . . . in this desert" (Num. 14:2); the "day of the LORD" (Amos 5:18–20).

The next clause elucidates the identity of this "Lord," beginning with a conjunction (w*) that is either simply coordinative ("and") or explicative ("even"). Identifying "the messenger of the covenant" (an expression occurring only here in the Old Testament) with Yahweh is difficult, since then Yahweh speaks in the first person apparently about someone else in the third person.[13] Also, messengers/angels regularly reveal Yahweh, but he is rarely called one of them himself.[14] Yahweh is indeed coming (3:5), but he seems here to be represented by a semi-divine/angelic[15] or human (4:5; NIV, NRSV) messenger who prepares the way for the holy God. This may be a messianic reference,[16] being at once human and divine (cf. Heb 8:8–13; 12:24).

Like the Lord whom they seek, this messenger is anticipated by the audience, who "desires" him—in contrast to Yahweh, who does not desire them (cf. "not pleased" in 1:10) until they are purified (cf. 3:3, 12). This also counters the invalid claim (2:17) that God desires ("is pleased with") those who change good for ill. The prophet seems almost to be taking his audience to task for inexact exegesis, not fully understanding either the meaning of the term "desire" or the nature of God.

Whether the sought-after coming ones are human or divine, single or multiple, the coming is imminent, as shown by the same combination of exclamatory interjection (*hinnēh*, untranslated in the NIV) plus participle that opens the verse. The messenger being sent is on the verge of arriving, and with a result not anticipated by the people, since he comes in the multifaceted Day of the Lord. This subsection ends with a common messenger formula ("says the LORD Almighty," 1:4, 6, 8, 9, 10, 13, 14; 2:2, 4, 8, 16; 3:5, 7, 10, 11, 12, 17; 4:1, 3), reminding the hearers of the identity and power of the speaker.

Malachi opens the next subsection (3:2–4) with two parallel rhetorical questions designed to draw the hearers into dialogue. Each begins with a conjunction w* ("and, but"), tying these questions back to verse 1: As a result of the coming one, who will be able to withstand? Each question uses the interrogative pronoun "who," likely referring to those seeking and anticipating the coming one in 3:1 and doubting him in 2:17. The second verb (*md*) indicates the ability to withstand opposition (Est. 8:11; Ps. 147:17; Dan.

---

13. On this, see Verhoef, *Haggai and Malachi*, 289; B. Glazier-McDonald, "MaPak habberit: The Messenger of the Covenant in Mal. 3:1," *HAR* 11 (1987): 98; NKJV; cf. Petersen, *Zechariah 9–14 and Malachi*, 211.

14. The enigmatic appearances of Yahweh through/ in the person of angels (Gen. 16:7–14; 18:22; Judg. 13:8–23) show that the separation between God and his messenger is not absolute. Contra JB (note), which suggests their identity in this passage.

15. Cf. Petersen, *Zechariah 9–14 and Malachi*, 211.

16. This is the position of Kaiser, *Malachi*, 81–85.

11:16; Nah. 1:6), to "survive" (NCV, GNB). Most translations give the participle used here a modal thrust ("[Who] *is able* to withstand . . ."). The meaning of the first verb (*kwl*) derives from the context of the second. The root means "to contain, hold" (cf. Isa. 40:12; 1 Kings 8:27), with the understanding of enduring (NJPS, NASB, NIV, NLT, NRSV) or holding out.

What the people are facing is "the day of his coming," referred to in other prophecies as the eschatological "day of the LORD," discussed more fully below (see 4:1, 3). God's coming is a momentous occasion, whether for salvation (Isa. 40:10; 59:20; Zech. 2:10; 9:9) or judgment (Isa. 3:14; 13:5; 66:15; Mal. 4:6; cf. Ps. 96:13; 98:9, where both aspects appear). The context of this passage suggests the latter, a coming for purification that will benefit the people, though not to their liking. The second question refers to this as the time of "his appearing," when the one whose existence is questioned by the people (Mal. 2:17) will be seen by them in a divine epiphany (Ps. 102:16).

Both rhetorical questions expect a negative response, in the light of the understanding that the unrighteous are unable to stand in God's presence (Jer. 7:10; cf. Ps. 24:4). Therefore, "who is (able to) . . . ?," when addressing these people in this setting, can only be answered, "No one!"

The final clause in verse 2 supplies the reason for the inability to stand, using two metaphors that depict the coming of the covenant messenger for cleansing the unclean. He comes first as a "refiner's fire." Fire regularly accompanies divine theophanies (e.g., Gen. 15:17; Ex. 3:2; 19:18), including those in eschatological contexts (Isa. 4:5; Joel 3:3). The destructive nature of fire made it a natural accompaniment to divine judgment (Isa. 10:16–17; 66:16; Amos 5:6). Since judgment, especially for God's people, is disciplinary and purgative (cf. 3:3), it is here designated as being through fire that refines, a function also mentioned in the New Testament (e.g., 1 Cor. 3:11–15). Elsewhere the verb refers to the metallurgical tasks of smelting and refining (Judg. 17:4; Isa. 40:19; Jer. 10:9), where the metal is heated to melting so the impurities within it separate and can thus be removed, leaving a purer metal.[17] The prophets use this process metaphorically to signify eliminating sinful behavior through the hot fire of God's judgment and wrath (Isa. 1:25; Zech. 13:9).

The second metaphor derives from the realm of cloth manufacturing. The fuller (one who cleans and thickens cloth by beating and working it) uses a special lye soap to clean it.[18] The Old Testament only refers to this soap

---

17. F. E. Deist, *The Material Culture of the Bible: An Introduction* (Sheffield: Sheffield Academic Press, 2000), 211–13; P. J. King and L. E. Stager, *Life in Biblical Israel* (Louisville: Westminster John Knox, 2001), 164–76.

18. King and Stager, *Life in Biblical Israel*, 158–59. The Hebrew consonants for the soap are the same for the covenant (*bryt*; 3:1), which may explain its use here (Hill, *Malachi*, 274).

metaphorically, indicating cleansing from sin (Jer. 2:22), while the verb (*kbs*), which can indicate literal purification (Ex. 19:10, 14; Isa. 7:3), also functions in the metaphorical, spiritual realm (Ps. 51:2, 7). Though the coming messenger is not eagerly anticipated by the people, his coming is not for the purpose of destruction but rather for restoration.

The purification process continues in verse 3 with the divine representative sitting down to begin his task—a task that takes a certain amount of time (an interpretation favored by the use of the following two participles).[19] The task is twofold: refining (cf. v. 2) and purifying. While the two terms are similar, ritual cleansing is commonly associated with the second (*thr*; e.g., Lev. 13; Ezek. 36:25), appropriate to this context of necessary purification, since the contamination involves cultic ritual (1:7–14). Silver is the object purified, though here it is metaphorical, referring to impure people (cf. Ps. 66:1; Zech. 13:9).

The metaphor is explained in the following sentence. It is the Levites (lit., "the sons of Levi") who are purified. Levi has been mentioned twice earlier in Malachi in relation to a covenant of religious obligation with him (2:4, 8). His descendants, the Levitical priests (the terms "Levite" and "priests" are equivalent in Malachi),[20] have reached a state of ritual impurity that disallows them from performing their expected duties. They therefore need to be made ritually pure.

The messenger will also "refine" them (*zqq*), a rarer verb than *srp* (used in v. 2 and previously in this verse) for removing impurities from metal such as silver and gold (1 Chron. 28:18; 29:4; Ps. 12:6) or wine ("strain, filter," Isa. 25:6, NRSV). Malachi's is the only metaphorical usage of this verb in the Bible.[21] These Levitical priests, whose role was to purify the people through sacrifice, have so polluted the ritual practice and themselves that they now need purification before they can offer sacrifice on behalf of others. Those who raise themselves above the ordinances of God (Mal. 1:7–8) now need the cleansing only achieved through their own abasement (2:9).[22]

When purification is complete, the Levites will be restored to their role as those who can effectively officiate in the sacrificial cult. The verbal form continues that of the previous verbs, with the conjunction *wᵉ* playing a consequential role here ("so that" KJV, NASB, NJB, NLT; "then," NIV; "until" NRSV). Some of the narrative impact of the result clause is lost because of the

---

19. Hill, *Malachi*, 274–75.
20. J. M. O'Brien, *Priest and Levite in Malachi* (SBLDS 121; Atlanta: Scholars Press, 1990), 47.
21. See also 1QH 14.5, 8; 6.3; 4QShirᵇ 35.2.
22. Hill, *Malachi*, 276.

differences between Hebrew and English word order.[23] The ones contemptuously challenging God (1:7) are now his possession. The syntactical priority of this may also indicate the relative importance of this relationship over the function that they can again perform, bringing (*ngš*) sacrifice; relationship (belonging to God) has priority over role (serving God).

The verb *ngš* is an important word here and earlier in the book. Those repeatedly bringing defiled sacrifices (1:7, 8[2x]) and who are unacceptable even though bringing them (2:12) are now be able to do so, starting the fulfillment of God's prediction that this will happen throughout the world (1:11). The offering previously unacceptable from the hands of the priests (1:10; 2:13) is now no longer so because of the righteousness in which it is brought.

"Righteousness" (cf. 4:2) can act as an adjective describing the offerings themselves ("right/acceptable/proper offerings," NLT, RSV),[24] though the presence of the preposition *bᵉ* ("*in* righteousness") leads more toward an adverbial understanding, describing the manner in which they are brought, corresponding to the way mandated by God and reflecting more on the offerer than the offering (Deut. 33:21).[25] This indicates that Yahweh did not previously condemn the Levitical priesthood as an institution, but rather the manner in which they had been performing their role. When the manner is rectified, the role can and must be resumed—not only for the sake of the priests but also for the people.

The word "sacrifice" links verse 4 to the previous verse, now speaking specifically of the sacrifices of Judah and its capital, Jerusalem. Priestly sacrifices (v. 3) represent those of the people, but they must also precede them in time, since a defiled priest cannot perform acceptable rituals for a defiled people, but must purify himself first.[26] The sacrifice of the people will then be "acceptable to the LORD" (NIV; "welcomed" JB; "pleasing/pleasant," KJV, NASB, NEB, NRSV), a term used elsewhere of sacrifice (cf. those which are unacceptable, Jer. 6:20). This contrasts the previously unacceptable offerings (Mal. 1:9–10). Yahweh now accepts these offerings.

The acceptable offering is a return to their original intent, what they were in "the old days" ("in days gone by," NIV), a phrase that probably refers here to the patriarchal period (cf. 3:7; 1:2).[27] The second nostalgic phrase ("as

---

23. The Hebrew lit. reads: "and-they-will-become for-Yahweh ones-characterized-by-bringing-near offering in-righteousness."

24. See Verhoef, *Haggai and Malachi*, 291; Petersen, *Zechariah 9–14 and Malachi*, 206.

25. Waltke-O'Connor, §10.2.2e.

26. See the order of the sin offerings in Lev. 4, with that of the priest preceding those of the people; see also 9:2–3; 2 Chron. 29:5–16, 34; 30:3, 15–17.

27. See Hill, *Malachi*, 279.

in former years") is unique, but the adjective elsewhere refers to events preceding the prophecy of Ezekiel 38:14, the time of the judges (1 Sam. 24:13), or an indeterminate time long ago (Isa. 43:18), which leaves the referent quite open. Whenever these good old days may have been, they are missed but will now be restored.

Not only will the earlier ritual situation be restored, but Yahweh himself will come near again as he had in the past (3:5), this time "for judgment." This latter term forms an inclusio with 2:17, closing this fourth dispute with its emphatic rebuttal to the claim that there is no just God. Rather than a simple consequential conjunction ("and, then, so") beginning 3:5, we should probably read it as an emphatic *wᵉ* ("indeed, be sure that I will come near").[28]

Rather than being distant or even nonexistent, God "comes near" (*qrb*), a possible play on the other use of the term in the book when God challenges his hearers to "offer" (*qrb*) unacceptable things to their civil leaders (1:8). They were attempting to defraud their leaders, and now the judge approaches for the purpose of holding them accountable. Judgment is definite, reiterating something already identified, most probably the actions in 3:2–3, with the vocabulary of judgment both opening and closing the dispute, with the action of judgment as its center.

Judicial vocabulary continues in the next clause, where Yahweh serves as a witness to "testify" against an array of evildoers, as he does in the case of the unfaithful Israelite and his wife (2:14). The vocabulary here is reminiscent of a covenant lawsuit (*rîb*). This is a serious situation since in such lawsuits between covenant parties God fulfills the multiple roles of prosecuting attorney, witness, judge, and executioner.[29] There is an immediacy to this dispute, since God "will be quick" (*mhr*), a participle serving as an adjective describing the witness. An additional nuance of *mhr* is skill as well as alacrity ("ready," JB, NLT; Ps. 45:1; Ezra 7:6); that is, God is not only able to bear witness soon but will do so with expert authority, since he both knows the ritual expectations and knows how they have been degraded in more recent times.

Yahweh's witness is for the prosecution, being "against" (*bᵉ*) five types of miscreants, each, except the last, preceded by that same preposition. This drives home fact that God is "against" four times, hammering at the term with relentless force. The first type is "sorcerers," professional practitioners of the black arts. Strongly condemned in Israelite law (Ex. 22:18), they often

---

28. Ibid., 279.

29. For bibliography on the *rîb*, see D. W. Baker, "Israelite Prophets and Prophecy," in *The Face of Old Testament Study: A Survey of Contemporary Approaches*, ed. D. W. Baker and B. T. Arnold (Grand Rapids: Baker, 1999), 274, n. 40. Note some translations of this verse: "I will appear before you in court," NEB; "But [first] I will step forward to contend against you," NJPS.

appear in conjunction with diviners (Deut. 18:10; cf. Dan. 2:3). The latter determine the future by consulting with the gods, while the former manipulate the divine, people, and events by occult means to make the future aid their own ends.

The Decalogue soundly condemns "adulterers" (Ex. 20:14; Deut. 5:18), a sin punishable by death (Lev. 20:10) since it attacks the foundational element of society, the family. It was common enough in Israel that the prophets had to repeatedly stand against it (Jer. 23:10; 29:23; Hos. 4:13–14). The sin of "perjurers" (lit., "those who habitually lie under oath"; cf. Lev. 6:5; 19:12; Jer. 7:9; Zech. 5:4) also reiterates something condemned in the Decalogue (Ex. 20:16). This is another threat to the bonds of trust and civility that unite a society and need to be reestablished if the society hopes to survive.

The Israelite covenant protected the powerless, those unable to look after themselves. Malachi highlights four groups (laborers, widows, orphans, and aliens) in this category who are not receiving fair and just treatment. Members of the first three social categories were particularly open to exploitation (ʿšq, "defraud," NIV; "oppress," KJV, NASB, NRSV; "cheat," NJPS, NLT). The verb indicates willful misuse of power by the strong over the weak, whether physically, economically, or socially (Deut. 24:14; Isa. 52:4; Jer. 7:6; 21:12), even being used of rape (Isa. 23:12).

To summarize all these ills, Yahweh claims that the wrongdoers exhibit a lack of "fear" (KJV, NASB, NIV, NLT, NRSV), or better "respect" (NJB), for him, something ironically evidenced by the foreign nations even if not by God's own people (1:14; cf. 2:5; 3:16). This fear of the Lord is where life's wisdom starts (Prov. 9:10; 10:27) and is associated with the law (tôrâ, 2 Chron. 17:9–10; 19:7–10; cf. Mal. 2:6, 7), which is being broken by these wrongdoers. By doing these things, they are being unwise, unfaithful, and in danger of death, not because of their mistreatment of others but because of their opposition to God. Yahweh reminds them of this through the concluding messenger formula indicating his power (see comments on 1:4; 3:1), thus demonstrating how the claim of the disputants that God does not know good from evil, nor is he just (2:17), is a lie.

Bridging Contexts

THE LEAST OF THESE. In Israel, as within most societies, those with power were able to fend for themselves. They did not need the protection of an advocate apart from their own resources. But there was a subsection of society that did not enjoy this protection. For various reasons they were deprived of power and were at the mercy of others. The wage-laborer (lit., "wages of the hired [day]laborer," Lev. 19:13; Deut. 24:15) was in an economically precarious position, since he did not hold land from which to derive a living. Nor was he a slave or servant of a master of whose household he is a part, receiving care and support (Deut. 24:14; Job 7:1–2). It is ironic that even slaves, who are often viewed as being at the bottom of a nation's social structure, had a more adequate support framework than did others in the society. After all, from the point of view of their owners, slaves were an economic asset in the same way as were land and cattle, since they produced economic gain for the owner. But the same did not hold true for the itinerant day laborer, who was viewed by an employer as just one of numerous readily interchangeable pieces.

Two others of this endangered category were the widow and the orphan, often listed together in contexts concerning social responsibility (e.g., Ex. 22:22–24; Job 24:3). Their lack of support structure arose because of the loss of either husband or father. Since to a large extent deprived of land ownership and hard pressed on their own to adequately farm the land if even able to hold it, their very daily provision of food was problematic. This was particularly the case for women, who left the care and support of their birth home to join the family of the husband. If he died, their support was not as forthcoming as it was at home. Elements of this necessary support network can be seen behind the stories of Tamar and Naomi (Gen. 38:11; Ruth 1:6–10).

A fourth class of marginalized people in the Israelite society was the alien (NASB, NIV; "sojourner," KJV). This was also a landless class of people residing in Israel because they had left their own country for some reason (e.g., famine, Ruth 1:1; cf. Gen. 15:13; Deut. 23:8; war, Isa. 16:4). Though poor (Lev. 19:10), they were due legal protection under Israelite law (Ex. 20:10; 22:21). Their particular source of exploitation was deprivation of justice (Mal. 3:5). The alien was to receive adequate provision and protection under the law, but this is being denied in Malachi's day—which is ironic since Israel itself was once in this situation (Deut. 10:18–9).

In order to provide for these unfortunates, if family and neighbor were unable or unwilling to do so, Yahweh himself championed their cause. He became provider, husband, and father, in a way establishing a theological system of unemployment assistance and social security protection (Deut. 10:18; 14:28–29; 24:19–21; 26:12–15). By doing so, God mandated through legislation the kind of compassion for the unfortunate that Israel should show on their own, but apparently seldom did.

Impure priests. Since we as Christians in the main view ourselves as a "kingdom of priests" (1 Peter 2:9–10; cf. Ex. 19:6), practicing autonomy in worship and service of God, we do not have the same understanding of the importance of priesthood as those in the time of Malachi. In the prehistory of the nation of Israel, an individual had the opportunity to approach God directly in worship and even in sacrifice, without the need of an intermediary (e.g., the first man and woman, Gen. 2–3; Cain and Abel, 4:3–4; Noah, 8:20; Abra[ha]m, 12:7, 8; 13:4; 15:9–10; 22:9–10; Isaac, 26:25; Jacob, 28:18; 31:54; 33:20; 35:14). The idea of needing an intermediary seems only to have arisen at Mount Sinai, when the people were afraid of approaching a holy God directly themselves. For protection, they requested that Moses represent them (Ex. 20:18–21). It was also there that God established a place for worship (Ex. 25–26) and the priesthood to serve there (28:1–5; Lev. 8–9).

The priests had several roles within the life of Israel, not all of them limited to what we ordinarily think of as "religious." One of their roles foundational for Israelite society was to serve as "boundary setters," establishing and discerning between sacred and common, ceremonially clean and unclean (Lev. 10:10; Ezek. 44:23). Failure to maintain these boundaries had serious theological ramifications (e.g., Ezek. 22:26), as well as sociological outcomes—for example, when there was not adequate distinction in the time of Ezra and Nehemiah regarding who were suitable marriage partners (see the discussion of "Divorce in the Bible," 260–62).

The priests were also to maintain these boundaries in several ways. First, their decisions and determinations about acceptable and unacceptable were not to be kept as esoteric information for their own use but were to be taught to the people (Lev. 10:11; Deut. 17:10–11; 2 Kings 12:2; 17:26–28; Jer. 18:18; Mal. 2:7). The law was not incumbent on the priests only, but on all of the people, so they needed instruction as to what was required of them. When disputes arose about the interpretation of boundaries, the priests functioned as judges and arbiters (Ezek. 44:24; Hag. 2:11–13). This brought their teaching function in touch with practical reality.

A final role was to restore the boundaries, or at least those who transgressed them. This was done through their function as ritual performers. They took an active and central role in the sacrificial and offering system of Israel, one of whose functions was to atone for breaches of covenantal expectations and purification and restoration of those who crossed the boundaries (e.g., Lev. 1–7). In this way they ministered to every level of society, since everyone, from commoner to king, was bound by the law and was expected, through ritual means, to address wrongs they committed (e.g., Lev. 4:3, 13, 22, 27). The priests' whole role here can be summed up by the concept of "restoration." The aim was not to exclude people from the community because of their deeds or their condition, but rather to allow the means for restoration.[30]

---

30. For discussion of the priesthood, see R. D. Nelson, *Raising Up a Faithful Priest: Community and Priesthood in Biblical Theology* (Louisville: Westminster John Knox, 1993); cf. also R. Duke in *DOTP*, 646–55, and the bibliography there.

An example of what can happen when priests are unprepared is seen in the description of Hezekiah's attempts to restore faithful worship of Yahweh to a nation who abandoned it under the reign of his father, Ahaz (2 Chron. 29:22–25). He set out to purify the defiled temple, but in order to do so, he first had to call the Levites and priests to sanctify themselves, since they had become lax in their own personal relationship with the holy (29:5). Even though a number of the priests responded, insufficient numbers did so to handle the volume of sacrifices, so the Levites stepped in and helped in a role that was not theirs under the law (29:34; cf. Lev. 1:6). When word spread to the entire nation that revival had broken out, they responded in such numbers that again the limited number of sanctified priests caused a slowdown in the celebration (2 Chron. 30:3), shaming them so they finally responded (30:15). In a situation where a vision of what worship should be came to the leader and ignited also among the people, it was the "middle management," the priests and Levites, who neglected their God-given functions and who could have derailed the whole process, were it not for God's grace.

Dereliction of duty in any of these areas had profound consequences for the people as a whole. There were no set standards for what was acceptable and what was not; no one knew what standards there might be; there was no evaluation as to whether standards were being followed, and there was no restoration to a covenant relationship with God once the relationship was breached. This was a serious state of affairs when the nation was a theocracy, operating under the rule of God. A separation on the religious level also led to dissolution on the civil level, and the very existence of the Israelite state and nation was imperiled (see 2 Kings 17:7–20). This is why Malachi needs to take the matter of nonfunctional priests seriously.

RELIGIOUS WRONGS. Too many Christians today live as if they have a spiritual form of what is now called "dissociative identity disorder," previously known as "split personality disorder." They take Jesus' words in Matt. 22:21 ("Give to Caesar what is Caesar's, and to God what is God's") completely out of context by saying that life is bifurcated; part of what I do is religious, and the rest is secular, and never the twain shall meet. This works out in practice by saying that for two hours on a Sunday morning (and maybe for an hour every now and then on a Wednesday evening) I attend to spiritual things, but the rest of the time is mine. Unfortunately, there is often no discernable impact of those two to three "God" hours on any element of the remaining hours of the week; religion has nothing to do with life in practical terms.

This understanding is foreign to Israel. Even within its foundational document, the Ten Commandments, there are only possibly two of the laws that we consider to be religious: the ban on pagan gods and their images (Ex. 20:3–6). While these had religious implications, they also had a strong sociopolitical element, since each of the surrounding nations also had its own deities. The ban on turning to other gods was also a ban on turning to foreign alliances for protection or benefit instead of relying on the power of Yahweh, Israel's God.[31]

The next two commandments, against misuse of God's name and concerning the Sabbath, also are strongly "secular," dealing with the taking of oaths and resting from work. While some of the laws in Exodus dealt with religious matters (e.g., idols and altars, 20:22–26), many more dealt with nonreligious aspects of life. It is not that religion or belief was unimportant in Israel, but rather that, in their eyes, there was only religion; under the theocracy of God in the life of Israel, nothing was secular. With this kind of unified view of reality, they did not have to be taught by supernatural signs that "the earth is the LORD's," as the Egyptians had to be taught (Ex. 9:29). They sang it as part of their creed (Ps. 24:1; cf. 1 Cor. 10:26) and were aware of him in everything they encountered in it.

Israel was not consistent in their understanding, however, any more than we are in the church. They thought that minimal attempts at religiosity would satisfy God (Mal. 1:8, 13), but forgot that the "secular" needed attention as well; their own fellows had to be treated with justice and righteousness (3:5).

Conservatives within the church, especially in North America, have made this same false bifurcation between "sacred" and "secular." This is due to a large part to elements of the "fundamentalist–modernist" controversy from the beginning of the twentieth century, most particularly the "social gospel" as espoused by W. Rauschenbusch.[32] Because of a perceived tie between social concern and a more liberal theology, conservatives (mostly finding their home in the middle and upper classes) turned their back on social issues (apart from temperance). In some instances, and also for other theological reasons, some also turned their back on the entire political process, with

---

31. There are too many instances in Israel's history when they turned away from their God and imported others gods and relied on other nations (e.g., 1 Kings 16:31–33; Hos. 2:2–13). The association of foreign gods with subservience to foreign powers is shown in the reign of King Hezekiah. When he became king, he removed pagan religious shrines and idols from the land of Judah (2 Kings 18:4). This is part of what the writer termed rebellion against the Assyrian king (v. 7), who then moved his armies against Judah (v. 18).

32. E.g., W. Rauschenbusch, *Christianity and the Social Crisis* (New York: MacMillan, 1910).

several unfortunate results. The gospel became divided, separating a concern for someone's eternal destiny from a concern for their temporal well-being. It also made the only Christian message that some of the poor and oppressed heard one of liberal theology.

A healing from our "dissociative identity disorder" is much needed, and we can learn from some of our number, especially those from non-American contexts who have never been strongly affected by the split.[33] It will affect our understanding and outworking of what it is to be the body of Christ. It will also affect our understanding of missions, that they are not only an interest in real needs that exist overseas, but equally real, and at times identical, needs that exist next door, but which we have not seen. Since such needs have not been encouraged or at times even allowed to enter our church doors, they have not been noticed by our religious radar, since they are "secular" problems. We need to open our eyes, or possibly a better metaphor, we need to tear down our church walls, thus eliminating this artificial and unbiblical separation and acknowledging that this is all God's world.

---

33. Some authors who have usefully addressed some of these issues are T. Campolo, S. Escobar, J. Hollyday, R. Padilla, R. Sider, T. Sine, J. Wallis, L. Wilkinson, N. Wolterstorff, T. Yamamori, and J. H. Yoder.

Malachi 3:6–12

I THE Lord do not change. So you, O descendants of Jacob, are not destroyed. ⁷Ever since the time of your forefathers you have turned away from my decrees and have not kept them. Return to me, and I will return to you," says the LORD Almighty.

"But you ask, 'How are we to return?'

⁸"Will a man rob God? Yet you rob me.

"But you ask, 'How do we rob you?'

"In tithes and offerings. ⁹You are under a curse—the whole nation of you—because you are robbing me. ¹⁰Bring the whole tithe into the storehouse, that there may be food in my house. Test me in this," says the LORD Almighty, "and see if I will not throw open the floodgates of heaven and pour out so much blessing that you will not have room enough for it. ¹¹I will prevent pests from devouring your crops, and the vines in your fields will not cast their fruit," says the LORD Almighty. ¹²"Then all the nations will call you blessed, for yours will be a delightful land," says the LORD Almighty.

Original Meaning

THIS SECTION FOLLOWS the already familiar disputation pattern, with a slight variation in the middle element, where the dispute/rebuttal appears twice: God's statement (vv. 6–7a), Judah's dispute (v. 7b), God's rebuttal (v. 8a), Judah's dispute (v. 8b), and God's rebuttal (vv. 8c–12). It also heightens the dialogue by including four repetitions of the messenger formula (vv. 6, 10, 11, 12). It returns, with different terminology, to some of the concepts previously discussed: Jacob (1:2–5), sacrifices (1:13–14), cursing and blessing (1:14; 2:2), the nations' response (1:11, 14), and the "good old days" (3:4). In spite of blatant Israelite opposition to God, he exhibits a grace that surrounds them even as it opens (v. 6) and closes (v. 12) this section.

Verse 6 joins to the previous section through the coordinating conjunction "for" (*kî*; see comments on 2:3, 7, 16), which several English translations supply, but the NIV omits. This subordinate clause indicates the cause of the previous statements: "I did all of this *because* I am the unchangeable Yahweh" (LXX, NRSV).[1] Another option views the conjunction *kî* as indicating emphasis or strong assurance, effecting some separation from the previous section: "I did all these things. *Indeed/truly* I am the unchangeable Yahweh."[2]

The verse continues the statement of Yahweh, who distinguishes between himself ("I") and Israel ("you"), using independent pronouns to emphasize this contrast.[3] Each party in this contrast is clearly identified: "Yahweh" and "the descendants [lit., sons] of Jacob."[4] Yahweh's self-introduction, because of its emphatic, initial position and following the conjunction, is most likely a free-standing verbless clause ("I am Yahweh"; LXX, Vulgate, KJV, NLT), rather than an appositional form ("I, Yahweh, do not . . ."; NASB, NIV, NRSV).

Yahweh then states concerning himself that he has not changed, using a verb (*šnh*) meaning either "to repeat, do again" (e.g., 1 Kings 18:34; Neh. 13:21) or "to change, be different" (Est. 1:7; Ps. 77:10; NASB, NLT, NRSV). The verbal form indicates actions or states that have already taken place ("I haven't changed," NJPS),[5] but can also indicate an idea usually shown by the English present ("I do not change," most English translations). Either fits this context addressing Israel's present situation. Since her covenant God is steadfast, in spite of her own fickleness, Israel is "not destroyed" (NIV, NLT; "consumed," NASB, RSV; cf. Amos 7:2; Zech. 5:4), though that is her due.

Justifiable grounds for God's turning his back on his covenant promises include Israel's dereliction of her covenant duty (3:7), namely abandoning God's "decrees" ("statutes," NASB, NRSV, or "laws"; cf. Isa. 30:8; 49:16). Yahweh himself gave these laws through Moses (Deut. 4:40; 6:2). The term is often accompanied by the synonymous "laws" (Ex. 15:25; Josh. 24:25) and "commandments" (1 Kings 8:61; Ezra 7:10), and by this period seems to be used to indicate the entire Mosaic law (i.e., the covenant itself).[6]

---

1. See Baldwin, *Haggai, Zechariah, Malachi*, 245; Glazier-McDonald, *Malachi*, 173.

2. Verhoef, *Haggai and Malachi*, 297. JB takes it as a strong disjunctive, "No"; cf. J. M. P. Smith, *Haggai, Zechariah, Malachi*, 66, "but."

3. Waltke-O'Connor, §16.3.1b; 16.3.3c. The second pronoun is also introduced by the disjunctive conjunction "but" (ibid., §39.2).

4. The Heb. *bānîm* has several levels of meaning. On the literal, biological level it can mean "male descendants of the next generation" (e.g., Gen. 49:8), "male descendants several generations removed" (2 Chron. 22:9), or "descendants several generations removed without gender specification" (e.g., "the children of Israel"). The latter is the use in this verse.

5. See Verhoef, *Haggai and Malachi*, 297; Petersen, *Zechariah 9–14 and Malachi*, 212.

6. Hill, *Malachi*, 299.

Israel's relationship to the law has two aspects. (1) She has, in an act of commission, "turned away." Indicating departing from a known road or path (Ex. 3:3–4; Jer. 15:5), the verb used here (*sûr*) is metaphorical, morally straying from God's course in blatant, mutinous disregard for their obligations (Jer. 5:23; 6:28). The priests previously departed from the teaching of God (*sûr* in Mal. 2:8). As a natural consequence, the people, who were supposed to receive instruction from them, cannot help but stray themselves. (2) As a act of omission, they do not "keep" or obey (cf. 2:9; 3:14) the laws.[7] Priestly laxity in keeping/preserving knowledge of God (2:7) results here also in the people naturally following their lead.

This has been going on for a long time, from the period of their "forefathers." "Ever since the time of" is only used in one other Scripture passage (2 Kings 19:25), referring to a time long ago. While this may refer here to the immediately preceding generation of miscreants exiled to Babylon (Ezra 9:7), it more likely refers to a much earlier period, that of the straying Exodus generation (cf. Ps. 95:9)[8] or even of the patriarchs themselves (Deut. 4:37; 10:15). If the latter, Israel and its ancestors have been straying from God ever since the initial promises to the covenant were given to Abram in Genesis 12:1–3.

Hope is not lost, however, since God makes an offer to his people: Mutual restoration is possible if only they return to him. Rather than using a conditional verbal form, "if you return" (so REB), the writer uses an imperative, highlighting a desired immediate response. "Return" (*šûb*) is a covenant term, indicating a return to a previously established relationship.[9] If the offending party, Israel, returns to the relationship originally established by the covenant, the other party, Yahweh, will reciprocate. The second use of *šûb*, with God as subject, is from the point of view of the people, since God, as covenant keeper, has not moved away from his people; rather, they have departed from him. It is also conditional, since from the perspective of the people, they will not experience the blessings of Yahweh's return (3:10–12) until they make the first move themselves. The restored, postexilic community heard this plea for repentance on several occasions (almost word for word in Zech.

---

7. Hill (ibid., 300) suggests that the two verbs serve as a hendiadys, a form representing "two aspects of a complex situation." Both verbs highlight the act of purposefully ignoring the covenantal laws.

8. Glazier-McDonald, *Malachi*, 181–82, suggests that the covenant-profaning intermarriages condemned by Malachi in 2:10 harked back to earlier mentions of undesirable relationships outside of the covenant community (Ex. 34:10–14; Deut 7:16). See also where they are said to have strayed (Deut. 9:12).

9. W. L. Holladay, *The Root ŠUBH in the Old Testament* (Leiden: Brill, 1958), 120.

1:3; cf. Hag. 1:12–14; Zech. 8:14–17). His return is assured by the use of the messenger formula ("says the LORD Almighty").

Not learning from their previous attempts, the people again enter into dispute with God (see outline, p. 212), using a form similar to that opening the book (1:2). Their question regards the means of their return ("how?" "in what [way]?"). This could be an honest act of repentance in which the people, convicted of the error of their ways, ask for instruction on the restorative steps they must follow. More likely in the context of their previous responses and of God's following rebuttal, however, this is a sarcastic protest of innocence: "What do you mean, we need to return? We haven't done anything wrong!"

Yahweh answers this question by posing a question of his own (3:8), helping the people see the need for their repentance. The question opens with an interrogative particle used of questions demanding a "yes/no" answer (though it could also be exclamatory, expressing surprise). God is astonished that anyone could possibly wish to rob him.[10] This verb (*qbᶜ*) occurs four times in this section and in Proverbs 22:23, where it is in synonymous parallelism with "rob." It appears here to have been a play on the name "Jacob" (Mal. 3:6), which consists of the same root letters in different order (ᶜqb). As the Jacobites are in name, so they are in nature, since God asserts that they are robbers. An independent pronoun ("you") specifically indicates the transgressing party in contrast to the party wronged, also explicitly indicated by a pronoun ("me"), making a stark contrast between the two parties: What Israel implicitly denies, Yahweh strongly affirms.

Israel brings a counterrebuttal, again asking "how?" (cf. 1:2, 6, 7, 17; 3:7). They seek a recent example of the charge, using a perfect form ("we have robbed you") rather than a present, ongoing participle ("are we robbing," NIV, NRSV). Yahweh counters with specifics: "In tithes and offerings." "Tithes" are the tenth part (Ezek. 45:11, 14) of the land's produce set aside as an obligation to God for the use of the Levites (Lev. 27:30–32; Num. 18:21) and, every three years, for others who were not self-sufficient (Deut. 14:28; 26:12). "Offerings" are either voluntary (Deut. 12:6) or mandatory (Ex. 25:2; 29:27–28; Ezek. 20:40) gifts to God. Israel has been neglecting the provisions necessary for the ongoing operation of the temple cult.

---

10. *ʾādām*, the subject of the verb, connotes the more generic "human, person" (NJB, NRSV, NLT; see D. J. A. Clines, "אדם, the Hebrew for 'Human, Humanity': A Response to James Barr," *VT* 53 [2003]: 297–310) rather than an engendered "man, male person" (most English translations, using the ambiguously unengendered "man"; see J. Barr, "One Man, or All Humanity?" in A. Brenner and J. van Henten, ed., *Recycling Biblical Figures* [Leiderdorp: Deo Publishing, 1999], 3–21).

The results to Israel ("you," v. 9; cf. vv. 6, 8) of repeatedly robbing God are severe: They are "cursed." The verbal root (ʾrr) occurs previously in the prophecy for those defrauding him in their sacrifices (1:14) and as a warning to unresponsive priests (2:2[2x]). This has now come to fruition, since none heeded God's earlier call. Previously having warned about punishment through a curse (2:2; cf. Deut. 28:20, 27) on the miscreants, now the verbal form indicates the middle voice, with the curse inexorably coming on its own, without mention of any verbal subject bringing it about. What God warned or promised has now taken place. This apparently refers to the gamut of socioeconomic hardships that the postexilic Hebrew community is facing, reflecting the promises/warnings of Deuteronomy 28:15–68, difficulties detailed in both history (Ezra–Nehemiah) and prophecy (Haggai, Zechariah, Daniel).

The cause of the curse is again reiterated: robbery. The word order heightens the impact of the charge, since Hebrew organizes the sentence with direct object ("me"), subject ("you"), and verb ("ones robbing"). The attention is directed less to the action than to the One against whom it is being perpetuated ("do you realize that it is me!"), with secondary emphasis on the perpetrators ("you, of all people!"). They are singled out yet again in the last phrase, since all are involved, with emphasis shown in the NIV by the layout of the phrase "the whole nation of you." God's people are here identified by the term "nation," a word that elsewhere in Malachi refers to their pagan neighbors (1:11, 14; 3:12)—ironically the ones who treat Yahweh as he should be treated. As the people are united in paternity (2:10), they are now united in perfidy.

In verse 10, the prophet provides a remedy for Israelite wrongdoings: Present the tithe, the subject of their previous robbery (v. 8). Earlier the subject was raised in a minimal fashion, but now it is expanded. The "whole" of it is highlighted, picking up on "all" the people who have strayed (v. 9). This word suggests that the problem is not one of completely avoiding this obligation, but rather of responding only half-heartedly. The destination for the tithes is the "storehouse" ("house of the treasury"), a phrase used elsewhere in the context of the tithe (Neh. 10:38–39; cf. Dan. 1:2). This is the facility associated with the temple that kept the supplies of the priests and Levites, whose needs were provided from the public coffer (2 Chron. 8:15; Neh. 12:44; 13:12), as well as goods for royal use (1 Kings 14:26). The consequence or purpose ("[so] that") of bringing the tithes is food or provisions for the house of God. This is needed to provide for the priestly attendants of the temple (Num. 18:21–32, esp. v. 31), called here "my house."

God then directs a second command toward Israel, to "test" or examine him "in this" (i.e., the resumption of tithes and offerings). The verb *bḥn* is often used of God's examining others (Jer. 9:6; Zech. 13:9), checking for purity and adherence to his laws. God as direct object of the verb is much rarer. Israel's "fathers" (Mal. 1:6; 2:10; 3:7) of the Exodus generation tried his patience at Meribah (Ps. 95:9; cf. Ex. 17:7, where a different Heb. word for "test" is used). God challenges the Israelites, who have repeatedly failed their own tests and broken their covenant obligations, to test him, their covenant partner. Adding an emphatic particle (w^e) to the imperative intensifies the command ("be sure to test me").

The criteria by which the people might judge whether God passes the test follow. They begin with the particle ("if") and a negative ("not") plus the verb "I will open" (*ptḥ*), all functioning as a kind of double negative. Stating that "I fail the test if I don't do something" is equivalent to saying that I am sure to do that thing ("You just see if I don't!"). The same form is used in oaths, where a negative sounding statement ("[May God strike me dead] if I do not do X"; cf. 1 Sam. 3:17; 14:44) is in fact a positive promise ("I will surely do X").

God promises to open the heavenly floodgates, in contrast to when he did so in the Flood story (Gen. 7:11; 8:2). There the results were catastrophic and judgmental, whereas here that is reversed, because unimaginable blessings (cf. Joel 2:14) will fall. The rain provides the blessing of foodstuffs, associated with "openings" in other passages as well (2 Kings 7:1–2, 19). These heavenly openings for rain were heretofore closed because of the people's neglect of the things of God (cf. Deut. 28:22; Hag. 1:11). Rather than a drought of withheld rain, blessing waters pours out (Eccl. 11:3) like oil (Zech. 4:12).

A unique phrase quantifies the divine blessing ("that you will not have room enough for it"; lit., "until the ending of its sufficiency"; cf. Ps. 72:7). Numerous interpretations are proposed, but the context makes it clear that Malachi envisions a superabundance of produce enabled by the saturating rain. Rather than questioning and disputing with God, the people must trust him.

God then promises to address the blights hindering the land's fruitfulness (v. 11): things that consume the fruit before it can be harvested and plants that do not carry their fruit to useful maturity. He will do so by "preventing" (*gʿr*) these scourges, just as he previously "rebuked" (*gʿr*) the priests and their descendants for leading the people away from a fruitful relationship with him (2:3). This will be for the benefit of Judah ("for you," occurring three times in 3:11).

The first problem addressed is "the eater" or, in a context where voracious eating is detrimental, the devourer (Job 20:21; Ezek. 36:13). The previous use of the same root (*ʾkl*; 1:12) saw the priests despising the food offered to God, and now those for whom it is not intended are consuming the very sustenance of life that the food offerings represent. It is commonly understood that this refers to insect infestation, akin to that of the locusts found in Joel (Joel 2:5; NRSV; cf. NIV, "pests"), which fits better than seeing the verbal subject as human (cf., e.g., Lev. 26:16), since no human oppressor is evident in the book. God's intervention halts any further ruination (cf. Jer. 11:19) of the crops, even though the priests saw fit to sacrifice "ruined" ("blemished," 1:14) animals and ruin the covenant (2:8; "violated") by perverting their duties.

Second, God stops the fruit producers (here, the grape vines) from casting, or prematurely losing, their fruit. The same root (*škl*) describes the premature loss of a fetus (Gen. 31:38; Ex. 23:26). If either descendants or sustenance is in jeopardy, so is the nation's continuing existence. The grapes are described as being "in the field," a cultivated crop (cf. Isa. 32:12) from the context, though the term is also used of wild grapes (2 Kings 4:39). God emphasizes his promise through the messenger formula ("says the LORD Almighty," cf. 1:2, 4, etc.).

The opening grammatical form of verse 12 indicates sequential action ("then"), a further, subsequent result spreading beyond Judah to her neighbors, the nations. They will recognize the true, honored position of God, even though his own people have earlier denied his power (1:11, 14). They will verbally acknowledge the divine blessing coming to Judah (cf. Gen. 30:13), something that Judah itself has been slow to do. The reason for this is specified: Judah ("you," emphatically indicated by the independent personal pronoun) will become (lit.) a "land of delight." Where previously God was not delighted ("pleased," Mal. 1:10) with useless sacrifices brought by unrepentant disputants, now that the correct covenant relationship is restored, delight and acceptance are restored as well. The repeated messenger formula (cf. 3:11) drives home the seriousness of the need for repentance after a serious lapse of covenant relationship.

UNCHANGEABLE GOD. In the context of a coming judgment on Judah, Yahweh states his unchangeableness (3:6). Is this a theologically universal statement regarding God's immutability, or is it something else? This is important in the world of the Old Testament since the gods of Israel's neighbors could and did change their minds. A most famous example of this occurred when the Assyrian gods created humanity to serve them, only to turn around and seek to wipe these same creatures out.[11] It was theologically important for Israel as well, since their

---

11. See COS, 1:450–51.

very existence as a people depended on whether their God showed this same kind of fickleness.

The context speaks of a contrast painted between an unchangeable God on the one hand, and the Israelites who repeatedly abandoned God's decrees from the very start of their existence as a chosen people on the other. This change regarding the decrees is thus the key element, making the focus of the discussion the relationship between the signatory parties to the covenant that God established with the patriarchs and Israel (Gen. 15; 17; Ex. 19–24).

The possibility of Israel's departing from her covenantal stipulations was clear from the outset, since the covenant included curses, that is, punishments that would befall them if they did so (e.g., Deut. 28:15–68; Josh. 24:20). The fact that she, and those who lead her, repeatedly did so during their life as a nation is the subject of concern in the records of her history (see the paradigmatic statement of Israel's cycle of history in Judg. 2:10–23) as well as the words of her prophets (e.g., Hos. 4:1–2, 6b, 10–13; Amos 2:4). God, by contrast, is "not a human being" (Hos. 11:9). He cannot change the promises he has made (Ps. 110:4, quoted in Heb. 7:21), so his promised blessings are sure (James 1:17–18).

In Hosea, God compares his own response to one of anger and destruction, a natural, human reaction following the abandonment of the covenant. This is not a response possible to God since he is God. While Israel might turn their back on the covenant and God himself, "decovenanting" themselves if you like, God cannot do so since it goes against his very nature. God cannot change his relationship with his people even when they act as if they are no longer his people. For this reason, the covenant with Abraham and his descendants is a permanent one (e.g., Gen. 17:7, 13, 19), not because it will not be breached by Israel but because God will not let it come to an end.

In the context of Malachi, therefore, God's immutability relates *to the covenant;* it is not a universal statement regarding his character. This is not to either deny or affirm his universal immutability, which is in itself an important and fraught question, but is outside the scope of a discussion of Malachi.[12]

Returning to God. Malachi calls the people to return to him and his covenant (3:7). In the world of the Old Testament, covenants or treaties were

---

12. This is part of the debate concerning the openness of God. For a discussion of this wider issue, see, e.g., C. H. Pinnock et al., *The Openness of God: A Biblical Challenge to the Traditional Understanding of God* (Downers Grove, Ill.: InterVarsity Press, 1994); J. Sanders, *The God Who Risks* (Downers Grove, Ill.: InterVarsity Press, 1998); B. A. Ware, *God's Lesser Glory: The Diminished God of Open Theism* (Wheaton, Ill.: Crossway, 2000); C. H. Pinnock, *Most Moved Mover: A Theology of God's Openness* (Grand Rapids: Baker, 2001); N. Geisler and H. W. House, *The Battle for God: Responding to the Challenge of Neotheism* (Grand Rapids: Kregel, 2001).

common forms of international relations (see Bridging Contexts section of 2:1–9). An integral part of these treaties was a section of blessings and curses that applied to the signatories if they kept the covenant stipulations or if they broke them. These are also part of several Old Testament covenantal sections, most notably the book of Deuteronomy, which is argued to be in the form of a covenant document. It shows a common ratio between the blessings and the curses, with the latter given much more prominence (28:15–68) than the former (28:1–14). This indicates either that there was much more chance of someone breaking the covenant, or else that keeping the covenant was intrinsically more rewarding, so needing less supplemental support.

As well as being in a covenantal relationship with her God, Israel and Judah were allied with Assyria and Babylonia as their vassals or subject, owing them at least begrudged allegiance as well as tribute (e.g., 2 Kings 15:19–20; 16:7–8; 17:2–3). To stop providing the latter indicated that the former no longer existed, that the vassal was in rebellion. This customarily called for a military response to force the recalcitrant vassal back into the fold (e.g., 2 Kings 15:28–29; 17:3–6). If this restoration appeared unlikely, more drastic steps were taken, with the rebel vassal leaders either killed or taken into exile, and new people from other vassal states resettled in the land (e.g., 2 Kings 17:7–41; 18:9–12; 24:1–2, 10–16; 25:1–21; 1 Chron. 5:26).[13]

Israel's covenant with Yahweh included punishments that could be, and were, meted out when Israel broke it (see, e.g., Amos 3:11 referring to Deut. 28:25; Amos 4:6 to Deut. 28:36–42; Amos 4:7 to Deut. 28:23–24; Amos 4:9 to Deut. 28:22; cf. 2 Kings 6:29 to Deut. 28:53–57). What is unique among ancient Near Eastern covenant elements was a provision like that found in Deuteronomy 30, where forgiveness and restoration were offered. Blessings and curses came, including the promised exile. But even this seemingly irreversible step could be rectified if Israel would only turn back to their covenant relationship (30:2–3). If they returned to God, he would return to them (cf. Mal. 3:7). While God is a God of justice and righteousness, holding wrongdoers responsible for their willfulness, he is also a God of grace, showing forgiveness toward those who repent.[14] Malachi is thus continuing this tradition of preaching the gospel of grace even in the Old Testament.

---

13. The capture of the Judean city of Lachish (2 Kings 18:13–15), the cruel death of its leaders, and the exile of its people can be seen on the wall reliefs of the palace of the Assyrian king Sennacherib in Nineveh (see J. B. Pritchard, *The Ancient Near East*, vol. 1, *An Anthology of Texts and Pictures* [Princeton: Princeton Univ. Press, 1958], fig. 101; also found at http://www.blueletterbible.org/images/bible_images/History/lachish.html.

14. Forgiveness is an important theological theme running throughout Scripture, e.g., Ex. 34:7, 9; Num. 14:18–19; 2 Chron. 6:21, 25, 27, 30; 7:13; Neh. 9:17; Ps. 79:9; 86:5; 98:8; 103:3; 130:4; Matt. 6:12; 26:28; Mark 2:7–10; 11:25; Eph. 1:7; 1 John 1:9.

TESTING THE LORD. Malachi 3:10 has become the linchpin for a stream within the charismatic movement called variously the "faith movement," "health-and-wealth gospel," "prosperity theology," or "name it and claim it." The movement has flourished over the past four decades and is mainly associated with such names as Kenneth Hagin and his son, Kenneth Hagin Jr., Kenneth and Gloria Copeland, Joyce Meyer, Benny Hinn, Robert Tilton, and Marilyn Hickey.[15] Among its teachings is the claim that what one confesses or claims from God will become a reality. It is a form of forcing God's hand by human activity, taking the unchangeable covenant promises of God and misapplying them. One area in which this is to be done is in one's tithe. According to their reading of Malachi 3:10, "In tithing, you are laying the foundation for financial security and abundance. You are establishing deposits with God which can be used when you need them."[16]

While it is good to remind the church of neglected scriptural texts, including those about giving and the power of God to bless and transform lives, it is important to read them in context and using a proper hermeneutic. A record of God's acting in a certain way, or even requiring that something be done, does not necessarily make that action or requirement a universal principle. While much of Scripture is applicable to numerous times and places, much of it is also historically and contextually specific. For example, even though Jesus commanded travelers to take only a staff on a journey, none of us ever leave on a trip with only a staff (Mark 6:8). Moreover, just because Paul survived the bite of a poisonous snake (Acts 28:3–6) does not mean that we should expect God will always spare us in the same way.[17] This is not to deny God's power to provide and to preserve if he so chooses, but it does deny our ability to manipulate him because we have misread the text.

The context of Malachi 3 is important in this regard. The message is specifically to the priests in Judah who are robbing God and experiencing drought and blight as a result. The blessing promised if they follow the regulations concerning their obligations is of literal showers, breaking the drought and subsequent famine. There is nothing of finances envisioned

---

15. For discussions of the movement, see B. Barron, *The Health and Wealth Gospel* (Downers Grove, Ill.: InterVarsity Press, 1987); C. E. Hummel, *The Prosperity Gospel* (Downers Grove, Ill.: InterVarsity Press, 1991).

16. K. Copeland, *The Laws of Prosperity* (Forth Worth: Kenneth Copeland, 1974), 72.

17. This is especially true if one in reality is putting God to the test, trying to force him to respond in the desired way based on a reading of Mark 16:18, which itself is suspect on text-critical grounds.

here, which is how the prosperity group reads this passage. The call here is not so much to put God to the test, since he previously promised covenant keepers abundance and blessing, even in terms of an opened heaven (Deut. 28:12). The test is rather of the priests and Levites: Will they fulfill their obligations so God can then respond through blessing? A question that such faith teachers might better take to heart as they are urging followers to send their financial resources to them for their own use is, "Will a man rob God? Yet you rob me" (Mal. 3:8).

There is also a wider issue beyond this particular passage. God's promises do not change, but neither do their recipients. God pledges blessings (Deut. 28:3–14), but they are conditional. The recipients of God's blessings are those who "fully obey the LORD your God and carefully follow all his commands.... All these blessings will come upon you and accompany you if you obey the LORD your God" (28:1–2). When some in Israel abandon the covenant, God does not change either his promises or their recipients. The latter are the same, but Israel is no longer among them. God doesn't change, they do. It thus appears, rather than a "name it and claim it" approach to God, to be more appropriate to have a "live it" theology: Act as a child of God and you will be treated as one.

Malachi 3:13–4:6 [3:24]

"**Y**OU HAVE SAID harsh things against me," says the LORD. "Yet you ask, 'What have we said against you?' ¹⁴"You have said, 'It is futile to serve God. What did we gain by carrying out his requirements and going about like mourners before the LORD Almighty? ¹⁵But now we call the arrogant blessed. Certainly the evildoers prosper, and even those who challenge God escape.'"

¹⁶Then those who feared the LORD talked with each other, and the LORD listened and heard. A scroll of remembrance was written in his presence concerning those who feared the LORD and honored his name.

¹⁷"They will be mine," says the LORD Almighty, "in the day when I make up my treasured possession. I will spare them, just as in compassion a man spares his son who serves him. ¹⁸And you will again see the distinction between the righteous and the wicked, between those who serve God and those who do not.

⁴:¹"Surely the day is coming; it will burn like a furnace. All the arrogant and every evildoer will be stubble, and that day that is coming will set them on fire," says the LORD Almighty. "Not a root or a branch will be left to them. ²But for you who revere my name, the sun of righteousness will rise with healing in its wings. And you will go out and leap like calves released from the stall. ³Then you will trample down the wicked; they will be ashes under the soles of your feet on the day when I do these things," says the LORD Almighty.

⁴"Remember the law of my servant Moses, the decrees and laws I gave him at Horeb for all Israel.

⁵"See, I will send you the prophet Elijah before that great and dreadful day of the LORD comes. ⁶He will turn the hearts of the fathers to their children, and the hearts of the children to their fathers; or else I will come and strike the land with a curse."

IN SPITE OF God's reassuring words in the previous section, Judah continues with one more disputation (3:13–15). The genre changes, however, with a historical note of repentance and response to God's pleas (v. 16), to which God responds with promises of restoration. He also looks beyond the present, postexilic situation of Judah to the nation's future. In an eschatological passage, and in almost apocalyptic terms, God promises judgment (4:1, 3) and blessing (4:2) to his foes and friends, respectively. The book closes with a reminder of the covenant and the obligations it places on both parties—Israel to keep its stipulations (4:4), and God to allow and effect restoration and reconciliation (4:5–6).

A Final Disputation (3:13–15)

FOR THE LAST time, Malachi's hearers dispute a divine claim. In this case, it is a dispute about words rather than actions: Israel's words are "harsh, severe" against Yahweh. Israel has no authority to overturn her God, but she acts as if she does, actively speaking against his demands and desires. Elsewhere, Israel is exhorted to be strong in the face of opposition (Josh. 1:6; Hag. 2:4), but now, ironically, she can only be strong in opposition to the one ("me") who seeks her good. The words of opposition against God are probably those of Malachi 2:17, where Israel perverted God's perspective on right and wrong. Going beyond the weariness caused in that earlier context, God now takes active steps of judgment.

The hearers ("you") respond with a characteristic disputational interrogative, turning the accusation back as a question, "what, how [NRSV]?" (cf. 1:2, 6, 7; 2:14, 17; 3:7, 8, 14). The disputers ask how they are speaking (*dbr*) in a harsh way. The Niphal verbal stem used here in 3:13, 16) is rare with the verb *dbr*, only occurring twice outside of Malachi (Ps. 119:23; Ezek. 33:30). In those two contexts there is dialogue, with people speaking together, which some take to be the understanding here as well ("how have we conversed together against you?" (NJPS; cf. 3:16, NIV). The verb is neutral, but the preposition *ʿal* gives it an oppositional character.

Yahweh responds in verse 14 by quoting statements that the people have previously made. They are impugning the worth of following and serving God. In this context, divine service involves correctly observing cultic and covenantal regulations, the validity of which priest and people have repeatedly disputed in this prophecy. Here they do so again, characterizing this service as "futile," something not producing intended or promised results (cf. Job 15:31; Isa. 1:13; Jer. 2:30; 4:30; 6:29; 46:11).

They then ask the related question of whether there is any "gain" in following God (having apparently forgotten those benefits listed in 3:10–12). "Gain" is neutral, sometimes indicating things ill-gotten (e.g., Ex. 18:21; 1 Sam. 8:3; Isa. 33:15; 57:17), but at other times showing no stigma attached to its acquisition (e.g., Judg. 5:19; Ps. 30:10; Mic. 4:13). Here there is no obviously negative connotation to the word, though the writer may well have in mind the negative nuances of many passages in which the term is used.

Two clauses describe possible sources for gain. The first concerns keeping ("carrying out"; cf. 2:7, 9, 15, 16; 3:7) a "requirement," a noun deriving from the same root as the verb (*šāmar mišmeret*, lit., "keeping a kept thing"). This combination generally refers to duties owed to God (e.g., Gen. 26:5; Deut. 11:1; Zech. 3:7), which obligation is being challenged.

The second clause refers to going about (*hlk*) in a dark, black manner (*qᵉdōranît*), an adverb used only here in the Old Testament but deriving from a verbal root indicating being dark, black (Joel 2:10; 5:15), with the extended meaning of being in mourning (Jer. 8:21; 14:2). This may refer to penitence the people displayed outwardly but did not find efficacious, perhaps because it was not real, heartfelt remorse.[1] The people went around in this state in the presence of the Almighty himself (1:4), but the outward act of contrition did not seem to have the expected results, since it was insincere.

Judah's reported speech continues with a new thought, introduced by the temporal adverb "now" (cf. 1:9; 2:1), raising the stakes from simply expressing doubt concerning the efficacy of serving God to denying and reversing his ethical norms. Those accused as "you" in verse 13 are now condemned by their own words ("we"), emphasizing their identity through the independent personal pronoun opening the clause. Judah blesses the arrogant (4:1), those who take pride in their sin and independence from God (Ps. 19:13; Isa. 13:11; Jer. 43:2). There is an unexpected reversal, since the earlier use of the verb had the pagans blessing Judah because of the God's evident grace, while here God's own people pervert this by lauding those who deny the standards of the source of blessing.

The coordinating adverb "certainly" (*gam*) heads both of the next two clauses and is best understood as heightening their emphasis ("certainly ... and even" [NIV]; "indeed," NAB, NJPS). They concern "evildoers," a further description of the previously mentioned "arrogant." These people serve grammatically as the subject of the next three clauses.[2] (1) The first verb (*bnh*) deals

---

1. See Hill, *Malachi*, 334.

2. The NIV obscures the existence of three separate clauses by rendering the second verb as a participle ("those who challenge") rather than the finite verbal form of the Hebrew ("they challenged").

with being "built [up]," used of places and things physically erected (e.g., cities and temples; Num. 13:22; Zech. 1:16; 8:9), but also referring to continuing a family line through the birth of children to those previously barren (e.g., Gen. 16:2; 30:3). Here this verb has a positive connotation, often translated as "prosper" (NIV, NRSV), though the writer points out that those who are so materially blessed in the eyes of the recalcitrant Judeans are not those whom God himself blesses in other, more relational and covenantal ways.

(2) They have also "tested" (*bḥn* ; NIV, "challenge") God. This is a term of opposition or provocation (e.g., Ps. 95:9; a meaning more commonly associated with the verb *nsh*; Num. 14:22; Ps. 106:14) rather than the positive, affirming action earlier called for by God (Mal. 3:10).

(3) Finally, these arrogant evildoers are able to avoid what they deserve for their actions ("escape," like those fleeing destruction; Gen. 19:17; Joel 2:32). Through this quotation, the speakers are overturning God's perspective regarding what is acceptable and what is not. This involves not simply a debate about words, but a reversal of truth (cf. Gen. 3:4).

Repentance and Restoration (3:16–18)

VERSE 16 BEGINS with a temporal adverb (*ʾāz*) that also has logical connotations ("then"), indicating a new point of narrative focus. This also shows the more acceptable response of others in the prophet's audience in contrast to those who have made such a poor showing in the previous verse. This group is made up of God fearers (mentioned twice in this verse), those showing appropriate awe and reverence for God and his ways (cf. 1:6, 14; 2:5; 3:5). They speak together,[3] with the mutual interaction on a positive, supportive note between intimates rather than the contentious relationship found earlier in the book (2:10).

Yahweh himself attentively hears this discussion and responds by memorializing those who fear him. For this he uses a "scroll of remembrance," an instrument only mentioned again in Esther 6:1 as a Persian record of events and people important in the history of the kingdom (a royal diary). Those in correct relationship with God are honored by being inscribed herein (cf. Ps. 69:29; Ezek. 13:9), contrasting to those whose negative acts are recorded in less permanent media (cf. Jer. 17:13).

This record is kept for God's use, like the Persian record kept for royal consultation. The subjects of the record, in addition to fearing God, are also described as honoring or highly regarding his name, representing Yahweh himself (cf. Isa. 33:8; 53:3). Ironically, this high regard for the person of God

---

3. The root *dbr* in the Niphal, exhibiting the reflexive use of the verbal stem; note the following phrase, "with each other" (lit., "a person with his friend").

is like that of the surrounding pagans (Mal. 1:11, 14) but unlike that of the Israelite priests, who show it contempt (1:6).

God goes on to claim as his own those who rightly regard him (3:17), just as he does the Levites (cf. Num. 3:12; 8:14) and as he promises to his reestablished covenant community (Jer. 24:7; 32:38; Ezek. 11:20; 14:11; 37:23; Zech. 8:8), and indeed to other nations who follow him (Zech. 2:15). He seals this promise by repeating the messenger formula ("says the LORD Almighty").

The fulfillment receives a time designation: "in the day" (lit., "during the day"), perhaps referring to his coming day, a time of judgment for apostates (3:2) but here a day of blessing for the righteous (cf. 4:1). This is a day when God ("I") acts, something the righteous have hoped for (3:16). Through the use of a participle, indicating an ongoing activity, God indicates he is making these people a "treasured possession" (*segullâ*). This term does not occur in other prophets, but elsewhere it designates a rare possession of God, select from among all others (Ex. 19:5; Deut. 7:6; 14:2; 26:18; Ps. 135:4), or some special object of a king (1 Chron. 29:3; Eccl. 2:8). These people, who through their actions place themselves farther from a relationship with God than their pagan neighbors (cf. 1:11, 14), now are restored to him by his actions.

God continues to declare his actions, sparing the people in his pity, compassion, and grace from the punishment that is their due as covenant breakers. Though they de facto have denied the father-son covenant relationship between themselves and God through not rendering to him honor (cf. 1:6; 3:6) or service (cf. 3:18, 22), God's "compassion" compares to that of a loving father (cf. 4:6) toward his obedient child. At least one of the parties of the covenant relationship remains aware of the affiliation and the obligations it entails.

The sequence of future events started in verse 17 continues in verse 18 with actions undertaken by Israel, the second covenant partner. Israel will (lit.) "return and see," a construction in which the first verb functions as an adverb, modifying the second as an action that is done "again" (i.e., "you will again see"). "Seeing" here denotes cognition ("know, understand"; cf. English, "I *see* what you mean") rather than physical vision (1:5). Israel's insight extends to the ability to discriminate between the righteous and the wicked (4:3), a distinction between moral good and evil that they previously denied (2:17; 3:15). The nature of these descriptions is elucidated in the comparison between "those who serve God and those who do not" (3:17). Morality is here indicated by action.

A Look to the Future (4:1–3 [3:19–21])

THE COMING DAY in which God acts (3:2, 17) now receives greater definition. Verse 1 begins with the emphatic/logical adverb (*kî* "for, indeed") plus an emphatic particle (*hinnēh*), indicating the immediacy of an event (see comment on 3:1). This combination, coupled with the following participle ("is coming"), join to indicate that "the day" is just around the corner (Zech. 2:10; 3:9; 11:16; cf. Amos 4:2). This day, referring back to that mentioned in 3:17, is more fully identified as "the day of the LORD" (4:5, called elsewhere "that day"), a day of judgment (e.g., Zeph. 1:9, 10) but also of blessing (e.g., Joel 4:18; Amos 9:11; Mic. 4:6; Zeph. 3:11; Zech. 2:11), though in this case the former aspect dominates.

A characteristic of this day is indicated by the participle *bō'ēr*, functioning adjectivally to describe how it comes: "burning" (cf. Joel 1:19) "like a furnace" (NIV) or oven (NRSV; Ex. 8:3; Lev. 2:4). The connotation is not positive, such as with kitchen cooking, but negative, indicating heat such as that from a destructive blast furnace (Ps. 21:9; Isa. 9:17; 10:17). Those subject to the heat are the "evildoers" of 3:15. Israel condones these folk, but God condemns them, treating them as "chaff" or "stubble," the remainders of grain husks and stalk after harvest (Ex. 5:12). Since grain cannot be harvested wet, the chaff is tinder dry and ignites easily.

Burning chaff is often a biblical metaphor for judgment (Isa. 5:24; 33:11; 47:14; Joel 2:5; Obad. 18), which God brings by having the coming day itself "set [the chaff of the wicked] on fire," a verb used elsewhere in such a context (*lht*; Deut. 32:22; Isa. 42:25; Ps. 97:3; 106:18; cf. Gen. 3:24; Ps. 104:4). God's consuming, judgmental fire burning the chaff of Israel reverses Obadiah 18, where Israel is itself the fire burning Edom's chaff in judgment against them, a similar judgment that God says he will bring in Malachi 1:2–4.

Usually a fire leaves something behind after it dies down, but God's fiery judgment is so fierce that nothing remains. Continuing the vegetation metaphor, Israel is destroyed "root and branch," a merism in which the two extremes stood for the entire object. This highlights the totality of the coming destruction, with its completeness made more evident through the burning even of the roots, which ordinarily do not succumb to a flash fire, being protected by the earth. New life can shoot up from a remaining root (Job 14:8–9; Isa. 11:1; 37:31). On that coming day, the people who asked for justice (2:17) will see it, and it will befall them.

Judgment is not the final word for all of Judah, however (4:2), only for the wicked. Others revere God's name, as is done among the nations (1:14), with Levi (2:5), and with some of Israel (3:16). Such reverence is lacking among the Israelite wrongdoers (3:5), but since all such evildoers are to be destroyed, the remaining faithful are blessed. This blessing is explained in terms of a metaphor of a rising sun. The sun is ambiguous in its metaphorical use, sometimes indicating harmful, scorching heat (Ps. 121:6; Isa. 49:10; Jonah 4:8), which a first-time reader could see as continuing the theme of judgment of the last verse. There is a metaphorical reversal here, however, since this sun is associated with both "righteousness" and "healing."

The "sun of righteousness" is a unique construct/genitive phrase, with the second noun modifying the first, though the nature of the modification is unclear (just as, in English, "of" linking two nouns has multiple possible connotations). The second noun could modify the first as an attributive adjective ("a righteous sun"), with the sun being characterized by righteousness. This has been understood as referring to God himself, a divine title with messianic overtones (cf. Jer. 23:5–6; 33:15). Many English translations allude to this by making the phrase definite, "the sun of righteousness" (KJV, which also capitalizes "Sun"; NASB, NIV, NRSV), even though the Hebrew is indefinite. It also seems to have been an interpretation from the time of Jesus, as shown by the words of Zechariah (Luke 1:76–79, in combination with Isa. 9:2).[4] The same verb (*zrḥ*, "shine") is also used of the appearing of God himself in all of his glory in a theophany (Deut. 33:2; Isa. 60:2). In ancient Egypt and Mesopotamia deities, including those represented by the sun, are at times depicted with wings.[5]

But "sun of righteousness" could also be an objective genitive, where the righteousness is produced or caused by the sun. The NJPS seems to take this view in translating as "a sun of victory," though "victory" is not generally associated with this Hebrew term. Also the interpretation stumbles on suggesting that God brings about the righteousness, where the passage's structure seems to contrast the wickedness done by some in Israel with the righteousness, covenant faithfulness of others among the people.

Whatever interpretation is adopted, the sun is a fitting evidence of a new day that dawns (cf. 1:11), a day of healing rather than of the oppression and deprivation that was there heretofore (3:5). Healing is needed from physical ailment or wounds (cf. 2 Chron. 21:18; Jer. 33:6) or apostasy (2 Chron. 36:16). It is contrasted to trouble, terror, disaster, and brokenness (Prov. 6:15; 13:17; 29:1; Jer. 8:15; 14:19) and compared to sweet honey, life, and true peace from God (Prov. 4:22; 16:24; Jer. 33:6). Rather than the fire of judgment, the balm of healing arrives by means of the "wings" of the sun of God, or, using an opposite metaphor, providing the protective shadow of God's wings (cf. Ps. 17:8; 36:7; 57:1; 63:7).

---

4. See Kaiser, *Malachi*, 105.

5. O. Keel, *The Symbolism of the Biblical World: Ancient Near Eastern Iconography and the Book of Psalms* (Winona Lake, Ind.: Eisenbrauns, 1997), 27–28, 215–17; O. Keel and C. Uehlinger, *Gods, Goddesses, and Images of God in Ancient Israel* (Minneapolis: Fortress, 1996), 389.

The metaphor changes from birds to calves that are penned up and getting fat (1 Sam. 28:24; Jer. 46:21; Amos 6:4; cf. the promised blessings of Mal. 3:10). When released from captivity, Israel from her sinful fellows and calves from their pen, they gambol around in exuberance (Jer. 50:11).

God acts in bringing the day and its judgment, but Judah has a part in it as well (4:3). The verb describing their action (ʿss) only occurs here in the Old Testament, but apparently meant "to crush, pummel" (cf. "newly trodden wine" from the same root; Joel 1:5; 4:18; Amos 9:13). The righteous of Judah will trample the wicked underfoot like so much dust, the residue of a fierce destruction (Ezek. 28:18). The metaphor may also indicate the complete subjugation of the wicked by the faithful (Deut. 11:24). Those repeatedly defying and challenging God will be put in their place by those faithful to him and loved by him (Mal. 1:2).

The hearers can be sure that this message is true because of its originator, Yahweh himself ("says the LORD Almighty"). He is also the One identified at the beginning of the description of this day (4:1), so that this little subsection opens and closes on the same note.

A Closing Covenant Reminder (4:4–6 [3:22–24])

THE PROPHECY CLOSES with two further addresses to "you," in the context of the book's being for those who fear God (4:2). Many commentators see these as two secondary additions. They change form from the previous sections, since they are not disputations but rather a command (4:4) and a prophetic curse along with identifying the messenger of 3:1 (4:5–6). It should be noted that the LXX reverses the order of verses 4 and 5–6, possibly indicating that they were added at two different times, or else as a matter of sensitivity, not wanting to end a book (whether Malachi, the book of the Twelve, or the entire prophetic corpus)[6] on a negative note.

In 4:4, the audience is commanded, using an imperative form, to "remember" and act upon the Mosaic law, just as God himself remembers his covenant with Israel and acts according to it, saving Israel from Egyptian captivity (cf. Ex. 2:24; 6:5). In the biblical notion of remembering, cognition is not sufficient; it also requires faithful obedience. It is directed here to an unidentified "you," most likely—at least in the present, canonical shape of the book—the righteous of the previous verse.

The object of their obedience is identified by three nouns: law, decree, and judgment. "Law" (tôrâ) is the true path (2:6) that the priests should follow (2:7), but instead the wayward priests have perverted it to the destruction

---

6. W. Rudolph, *Haggai–Sacharja–Maleachi* (KAT 13/4; Gütersloh: Mohn, 1976), 7.

of others (2:8–9). These laws must again be remembered and kept. The law is associated with "Moses" (cf. Josh. 23:6; 1 Kings 2:3; 2 Kings 14:6; 23:25; 2 Chron. 23:18; Ezra 3:2; 7:6; Neh. 8:1), described as God's "servant." Mosaic law and servanthood are joined together in several other passages (Josh. 8:31–32; Dan. 9:11, cf. v. 13). Note especially Joshua 1:13, where Israel is commanded to "remember the command that Moses the servant of the LORD gave you," a command associated with rest and land, the same thing that is threatened if covenant obedience is not delivered (Mal. 4:6). This law was given on Mount "Horeb," an alternative name for Mount Sinai (Ex. 33:6; Deut. 1:19), and it is directed to "all" Israelites, who have the option of being righteous if they just remember the laws.

The other terms for the law, "decrees" (*ḥoq*) and "judgments" (*mišpaṭ*; NIV "laws"), occur regularly together, especially in Deuteronomy (e.g., Deut. 4:5, 8, 14; 5:1; 6:1; 7:11). Judah, already condemned for not complying with God's decrees (Mal. 3:7) and for denying judgment to God (2:17; cf. 3:5), is now reminded of their validity and necessity.

This book closes with a two-verse promise of events soon to take place. The opening particle *hinnēh* ("see"; cf. comments on 4:1), especially when accompanied by a participle, as here, indicates immediacy—something that has just (e.g., Gen. 37:9; Josh. 2:2; 1 Kings 3:21) or soon would (Mal. 2:3) happen. In Malachi, the majority of uses of this particle are in conjunction with the imminent coming of the Day (3:1[2x]; 4:1), which holds in this verse as well. Before that Day arrives, however, another event deriving from God himself will precede it. He is about to send a messenger (cf. 3:1) to Judah ("you") in the person of Elijah. The most frequent use in this book of the preposition + pronoun suffix combination "to you" are in contexts of blessing befalling faithful Judah (3:10[2x], 11[3x]; 4:2). This may indicate that the messenger has potential for good here as well.

Elijah's name occurs in two forms in the Old Testament, a shorter form such as occurs here (*ʾēliyyâ*; 2 Kings 1:3, 4, 8, 12), and a longer form (*ʾēliyyāhû*; over eighty times between 1 Kings 17 and 2 Kings 10). Elijah was the prophet who successfully stood against the growing influence of Baal worship in Israel and now stands against another form of burgeoning apostasy, neglect of the law. His mysterious disappearance, with no mention of his death (2 Kings 2:11–12), leaves open the possibility of his reappearing and continuing his prophetic ministry.

In Malachi, this ministry becomes associated eschatologically with the coming Day of Yahweh (cf. 3:1–2), which can be either a day of salvation or judgment (see "Bridging Contexts" section). Here both elements are at least potential. This day is described as "great and dreadful." God's arrival on that day is a momentous event ("great") and awesome, inspiring dread. These two words occur together in several passages describing the vast and terrifying expanse of the desert facing the newly freed Israelites (Deut. 1:19), as well as the eschatological Day of the Lord with its cataclysmic natural phenomena (Joel 2:30–31, see comments), and even the nature of the God behind this day (Dan. 9:4; Neh. 4:14). The nature of the Day is ambiguous, based on this description; it can bring either weal or woe.

Verse 5 has strong linguistic parallels with Joel 2:31. There the coming day is preceded by the sun and moon turning to darkness and blood, respectively, just as Elijah precedes it here, and it also has the potential of either blessing for those who call on (remember) God, or hardship for those who do not.

Elijah's ministry will be one of restoration and repentance (*šûb* in Hiphil, "cause to return"; cf. 2:6), something God desires (3:7, 18; cf. Deut. 4:30; 30:2–3; Hos. 14:1–2; Lam. 3:40). "Heart" (cf. Mal. 2:2) is not used elsewhere as the object of this verb. The heart is the seat of the emotions, desires, and resolve, much like the combination in today's metaphorical language of the heart and mind. The restoration will be mutual (lit., fathers to sons and sons to fathers), though neither term is used here with gender exclusivity (cf. 2:10; 3:17, where God is metaphorically father to Israel, consisting of males and females designated as "sons"). The term "fathers" can also be the Judean ancestors, the forefathers who earlier entered into covenant with God (cf. Zech. 1:2–4), so this may be yet another form of the exhortation to obedience (Mal. 4:4). The result is a complete contrast to Ezekiel's vision of cannibalism as part of the punishment necessitated by apostasy, fathers and sons eating each other (Ezek. 5:10).

If there is no restoration ("or else, lest," indicating a contingency), a curse results. Repentance is urged for fear that, if it does not occur, dire consequences will follow. The ominous event is expressed with two verbs. The first ("I will come") indicates that the coming Day of the Lord (cf. 4:1) is in fact a theophany, with God himself making an appearance. While the concept of God's coming is neutral, since it can be for either blessing (Deut. 33:2–5; Hos. 6:3; Hab. 3:3) or punishment (Isa. 3:14; 13:5; 19:1), here it is negative, as indicated by the second verb, "to strike."

If God does come, he will strike the land, a verb used elsewhere of God's striking Egypt through the plagues (Ex. 3:20; cf. 12:12; Jer. 21:6, where Israel also suffers plague) and punishing Israel for her sins (Lev. 26:24; cf. Amos 3:15). It is also one of the punishments for breach of covenant (Deut. 28:22), which is appropriate here, a fulfillment of the punishment if the covenant is abandoned. Here God's punishment falls on "the land," the territory (cf. Gen. 15:18–21) of his covenant people, Judah, who are being called to respond to their covenant obligations. The word "land" can also have a broader meaning, the entire earth (cf. Gen. 1:1). The potential danger of the eschatological coming of the Lord and his Day can thus be cosmic, as it is in other prophetic contexts (e.g., Isa. 24:1–13; Joel 2:30–31; Obad. 15).

The nature of the judgment and the means by which God strikes is "with a curse" (*ḥērem*), elsewhere used of things banned for anything other than divine use, things that are completely destroyed (e.g., Deut. 7:26; Josh. 6:17; 7:12; 22:20). Even Israel and Judah are subject to such destruction because of their forefathers' sins (Isa. 43:27–28). Wishing this fate on someone is a high form of curse (e.g., Josh. 7; Job 31:30; 2 Kings 2:24; Matt. 25:41), that they be totally and permanently destroyed.

DAY OF THE LORD. The motif closing Malachi is a rich motif in other prophets as well. The Day of the Lord is like a coin, having two faces, one positive and the other negative (see also comments in the introduction to Joel). This is seen in Amos, the first to mention the topic:

> Woe to you who long
> > for the day of the LORD!
> Why do you long for the day of the LORD?
> > That day will be darkness, not light. (Amos 5:18)

Based on this verse, the popular Israelite view was of a day of light and blessing, one benefiting them as God's chosen people. Yahweh paints a different picture, however, one of darkness and judgment. From Amos's immediate context, the cause of misunderstanding this Day becomes clear. The prophet continues:

> I hate, I despise your religious feasts;
> > I cannot stand your assemblies.
> Even though you bring me burnt offerings and grain offerings,
> > I will not accept them.
> Though you bring choice fellowship offerings,
> > I will have no regard for them.
> Away with the noise of your songs!
> > I will not listen to the music of your harps. (Amos 5:21–23)

These rituals, established initially by God,[7] take the place of a true relationship with God, which is not to be marked by outward ritual observance

---

7. See Lev. 23 for a discussion of the religious feasts and assemblies, Lev. 1–3 for the burnt, grain, and fellowship offerings, and several mentions of Yahweh's music (e.g., 1 Chron. 6:16–17; 2 Chron. 5:12–13; 29:27–28).

but by ethical actions toward one's fellow Israelites. Amos's following positive command shows this: "But let justice roll on like a river, righteousness like a never-failing stream!" (Amos 5:24). God says that a true Israelite is a covenant keeper, involving sociopolitical action as well as ritual action.

Without a correct horizontal relationship with one's fellow humans, a vertical relationship with God is impossible. If one does not embody the covenant obligations, one is not a member of God's people, even if one can say, "I am a child of Abraham." A family tree does not make someone an Israelite; rather, it is a faithful heart. It is not the Israelite's view of the Day of the Lord that is wrong; it is in fact very correct. The Day is blessing to the true members of God's people, and judgment for those who are not. Israel's misunderstanding concerns what constitutes a true member of God's people.

Unfortunately for Israel, the Day is most often described as a day of judgment (e.g., Ezek. 13:5; Joel 1:15; 2:1, 11, 31; Zeph. 1:7–18; Zech. 14:1) rather than one of blessing (e.g., Isa. 11:11; Joel 3:18; Zech. 14:6–11). The same judgment holds for other nations as well, who will experience God and his Day in the same way (e.g., Babylon, Isa. 13:6; Egypt and her African neighbors, Ezek. 30; the entire world, Isa. 13:9; Joel 3:14; Obad. 15; Acts 2:20; 2 Peter 3:10).

In the New Testament, both positive and negative elements continue, and the Lord of the Day becomes associated with Jesus. For example, 1 Corinthians 5:5 describes the destruction of the sinful nature (that which is not fit for God's kingdom), but the salvation of the spirit (that which is fit for the covenant community) "on the day of the Lord." Paul develops the idea of the Day as a positive time (e.g., 2 Cor. 1:14), though it still has judgment elements for those outside the covenant kingdom (e.g., 1 Thess. 5:2; 2 Thess. 2:1–12, where the Day is associated with Jesus [2:1], and destruction is of the lawless [2:7], those outside the covenant community).

Malachi picks up two elements of the Judgment Day from previous texts. (1) It is coming, and quickly (e.g., Isa. 13:6, 9; Ezek. 30:3; Joel 1:16; 2:1; Obad. 15; Zeph. 1:7, 14). (2) At least part of the judgment comes in the form of fire (e.g., Ezek. 30:14, 16; Joel 1:19–20; 2:3, 30; Obad. 18; Zeph. 1:18). Fire also has two sides: It is destructive (e.g., Deut. 32:22; Ps. 21:9; 50:3; Mal. 4:1), but also refines and purifies (e.g., Jer. 6:29; Ezek. 24:11–12; Zech. 13:9; Mal. 3:2; 1 Cor. 3:13; 1 Peter 1:7; Rev. 3:18). The impact of the Day is thus relative in both Testaments: It brings good to God's own, but ill to his enemies, no matter their ethnic background. Theology (and more specifically ethics, how one lives), not genealogy, determines how one will experience the Day.

The prophecies, covering several centuries, show the importance of the Day of the Lord for God's people. It has several different manifestations, not all referring to a single, cataclysmic Day. It drew the hearers' attention to judgment against Judah through an actual plague of locusts (Joel), against Edom (Obadiah), or against Judah through the fall of Jerusalem in 586 B.C. (Amos). It also points ahead to an eschatological Day, when the world will be affected in a mighty way (Isa. 13; Zech. 14; Matt. 24; Mark 13; Rom. 2:5–10; 2 Peter 3). It can well be envisioned like the Allies' attacks on mainland Europe during World War II. While there were smaller raids on various parts of the continent during the course of the war, it was June 6, 1944, which was D-Day. So there are numerous judgments of God on his people and the nations, but there will also be a final D-Day of the Lord, in which he will reestablish his rule over the earth through judgment, but followed by blessing.[8]

Elijah. Moses is the figure most associated with the Old Testament law (Mal. 4:4), while Elijah is a key figure in the growth of Israelite prophecy and other elements of the history of Israel. He prophesied during the troubled times of Ahab (mid-ninth century B.C.). Because of his marriage to Jezebel, Ahab allowed Canaanite worship, especially that of Baal, to gain a strong footing in the land (1 Kings 16:30–33). Most of Elijah's recorded ministry involved standing against this departure from Israel's covenant with God (cf. Ex. 20:3).[9] Even though only from a small town in Transjordan and not even owning his own land (1 Kings 17:1), he is, through his faithfulness, given recognition as a "man of God" (17:18, 24) and a "prophet" (18:22, 36). Because of his courageous stand, even in the face of death (19:2), he stemmed the tide of encroaching paganism, protecting Israelite religion and culture in much the same way Greek culture was preserved from domination by the Persians through the stand the Greeks made in the Battle of Marathon (490 B.C.).

Beside his heroism, Elijah is also a tantalizing figure because, according to the biblical record, he did not die. He was instead carried up into heaven in a whirlwind, which his successor, Elisha, saw as the very chariots of Yahweh himself (2 Kings 2:11–12). Since he did not die in a way similar to most human experience, tradition arose about his possible bodily return. These two elements—his possible return and his heroic stand for God at a crucial time in Israel's history—led to his mention by Malachi.

Both elements are also picked up in the New Testament. When Jesus asks what the people might be saying about his own identity, Peter states that some take him to be the returned Elijah (Matt. 16:14; Mark 6:15; 8:28). Jesus

---

8. For further discussion on the Day of the Lord, see, e.g., J. D. Nogalski, "The Day(s) of Yahweh in the Book of the Twelve," in *Thematic Threads in the Book of the Twelve* (BZAW 325; Berlin: de Gruyter, 2003), 192–213.

9. L. L. Bronner, *The Stories of Elijah and Elisha as Polemics against Baal Worship* (Leiden: Brill, 1968).

himself earlier said that this role is rather played by John the Baptist (Matt. 11:14), since he also played a key role in Israel's history, being the one who heralded the arrival of the kingdom of God through the appearance of God the Son (11:12). John too, according to the prophecy revealed to his father, Zechariah, was the one to bring Malachi's prophecy to completion by restoring family relationships (Luke 1:17; cf. Mal. 4:6). Zechariah also mentioned a second role, to return "the disobedient to the wisdom of the righteous— to make ready a people prepared for the Lord." This is apparently what is implied, though not stated with the same terminology, in Malachi 4:4, where the hearers are commanded to remember, and act upon, the Mosaic law.

On the Mount of Transfiguration (Matt. 17:1–13; Mark 9:2–13), Elijah physically appeared beside Jesus, along with Moses. Moses represents the covenantal law and Elijah the prophets, those charged to call the people and their rulers back to covenant faithfulness. These figures, concluding both the prophetic word in the Old Testament and the Protestant canon, direct the readers' attention to the canon in its entirety, the Law and the Prophets. Their eschatological position in relation to God is determined by a return to the historical relationship on which Israel as a nation was established and to which she had been repeatedly called back.

Contemporary Significance

BASIS FOR MORALITY. Malachi draws a contrast between those whose actions align themselves with the will of God (those who fear him, 3:16) and others, including the priests and Levites, whose actions do not (1:6–3:15). Using terms already noted, Malachi notes that there are those for whom the coming Day will be a blessing and those for whom it will be a time of pain. What is the difference between these two groups—or perhaps bringing the discussion closer to home, what makes the difference in whether we choose between doing right or wrong? This is an important question because it asks how our ethics (i.e., what we do) relates to our theology (i.e., what we believe). We must ask this because we do not face the same situations as those facing Malachi's generation, but we still face decisions regarding aligning faith and practice today.

Jesus saw the all-too-common disconnect between the theology and ethics when he asked: "Why do you call me, 'Lord, Lord,'[a theological statement] and do not do what I say [an ethical practice]?" (Luke 6:46). Knowledge is not sufficient, and Jesus commanded that knowledge and correct response to that knowledge be wedded when he said, as part of the Great Commission, to *teach* people *to obey* everything he commanded (Matt. 28:20). James also said that a strictly theological religion, no matter how correct that theology is, is insufficient in itself; it must be enfleshed ("Religion that God our Father accepts as pure and faultless is this: to look after orphans and widows in their distress," James 1:27).

One aspect of decision making is not the topic of discussion here, namely, what is commonly called "guidance," seeking a pathway through life looking to the long-term horizon (itself an important topic in its own right).[10] The interest here is rather on individual choices made when facing everyday options, looking to the next step rather than the journey's end.

Classically, there have been two approaches to making such ethical decisions, identified by the technical terms *deontology* and *teleology*. Deontology describes a decision-making process based on following certain rules. It is externally motivated by duty, for example of a child toward the parent. It has the advantage of knowing exactly what one is expected to do since it is extremely task-oriented. *Teleology* looks to the goals, asking what the desired outcome is so one may base decisions on what best leads to that outcome. It has the advantage of knowing where one is headed, which is not the case for a deontological approach.

Both of these approaches have their faults, however. One is that there is no complete list of rules; one can never be completely certain of the duty in any given situation. One's parents will not always be around. Moreover, Paul states that the rules themselves, the law, can actually inspire sin by pushing rebellion against those rules (Rom. 5:20; 7:7–8). He also indicates that this kind of rule-book decision-making is simply supervisory until we outgrow it (Gal. 3:24–25). The Levites condemned by Malachi illustrate another problem with decisions completely made according to rules. They see how close they can come to fulfilling the letter of the law without crossing over the line either to disobedience or to full-fledged commitment. They take a minimalist approach to obedience: What's the least I can get away with? They bring sacrifice, but try to do so at the least cost to themselves (Mal. 1:12–14).

A goal-directed ethic, by contrast, has a problem in that some goals are not attainable and so can lead to despair. More troubling is an attitude that says that the goal justifies the means. The focus can often not be on the people involved but simply on the task to be accomplished.

A third, more biblical approach to ethical decision-making concerns character or virtue. It flows from who we are as human beings, including

---

10. See, e.g., D. Willard, *Hearing God: Developing a Conversational Relationship with God* (Downers Grove, Ill.: InterVarsity Press, 1999); G. L. Sittser, *The Will of God as a Way of Life: Finding and Following the Will of God* (Grand Rapids: Zondervan, 2000); B. Waltke, *Finding the Will of God: A Pagan Notion?* (Grand Rapids: Eerdmans, 2002).

our upbringing, our traditions, and the values we have inculcated. Goals are also an important part of how we decide since they are part of who we are, but they do not completely make up our character. The New Testament describes the inner motivation as deriving from the Holy Spirit (Rom. 7:6; 8:4) who transforms the fallen human nature that is the directing force before conversion (7:4–6), giving us a new ability to make right decisions as part of our very being (2:15) since we are a new creation (2 Cor. 5:17). Paul in so many words advocates this character ethics as against duty ethics in Galatians 6:15: "Neither circumcision nor uncircumcision [the rules] means anything; what counts is a new creation [a new character]." Ethical decision-making thus becomes part of our spiritual DNA.[11]

This relates to the issue of integrity, where the question is often framed as: What do you do when you are alone? In such a case, there is no one to enforce any external rules or to know whether an action leads to any desired goal. All that compels an action is the content of one's character.[12] In the view of Malachi, those who fear the Lord are those whose character is shaped through walking with him and whose very thoughts are of him (Mal. 3:16). The priests and Levites, however, ask, "What's in it for me; how can I maximize my own gain?"

Unfortunately, these distinctions are still evident within the church. We are all aware of pastors who are more concerned with the number of people in the pews than they are for the amount of Christlikeness that is in the hearts, including their own. Our eye is too often on statistics rather than sanctification, duty rather than discipleship, and, unfortunately, words (including our own name) on a page rather than the Word in a heart. Do our actions put us, as either individuals or as a church, on the wrong side of the anticipated Day of the Lord?

Remembering. Malachi charged his hearers to remember the laws of God (Mal. 4:4). The church is also being commanded to remember. When instituting communion or the Eucharist, Jesus indicates that the bread symbolizes his body and the wine his blood. He said, "Do this in

---

11. For fairly recent uses of character ethics, see S. Hauerwas, *Character and the Christian Life: A Study in Theological Ethics* (San Antonio: Trinity Univ. Press, 1975); with C. Pinches, *Christians among the Virtues: Theological Conversations with Ancient and Modern Ethics* (Notre Dame: Univ. of Notre Dame Press, 1997); cf. R. S. Smith, *Virtue Ethics and Moral Knowledge: Philosophy of Language after MacIntyre and Hauerwas* (Burlington, Vt.: Ashgate, 2003); M. J. Dawn, *Sexual Character: Beyond Technique to Intimacy* (Grand Rapids: Eerdmans, 1993); *Unfettered Hope: A Call to Faithful Living in an Affluent Society* (Louisville: Westminster John Knox, 2003).

12. Borrowing from the title of a book by S. Steele, *The Content of Our Character: A New Vision of Race in America* (New York: St. Martins, 1990).

remembrance of me" (1 Cor. 11:24–25). This is not just to be a cerebral enterprise, reminiscing about old times, but a commitment to action (*"Do this"*).

What does this command refer to? How did the disciples understand these words? The Jews were well versed not only in Scripture but also in their national history, so when they heard Jesus using the words, "This is the cup of the new covenant in my blood" (1 Cor. 11:25), they would have picked up on the intended reference. The "new" covenant presupposes an "old" one, which is described in Exodus 24, the story of Israel ratifying the Mosaic covenant. As part of the ceremony, Moses read the law he had just received from God on Mount Sinai, and the people agreed to it: "We will do everything the LORD has said; we will obey" (Ex. 24:7). Then Moses sprinkled sacrificial blood on all of the people, describing it to them: "This is the blood of the covenant that the LORD has made with you." Entering into an agreement to obey was their covenant with God, an occasion marked by eating and drinking by the leaders (24:11), a covenant meal celebrating the successful completion of an agreement.

Jews today remember not only the covenant blessings of God but also Elijah in their celebration of Passover. This spring festival (Ex. 12; Num. 28:16–25) is a reminder of God's liberation of their ancestors from slavery in Egypt at the start of their journey to Sinai, the place where they became God's covenant people. At the table during the Passover meal a place remains empty, and the door is opened to welcome an awaited guest. They look for Elijah, anticipating him as the harbinger of the Messiah (Mal. 4:5).

Christian communion is also a covenant meal, linked chronologically and theologically to the Passover (Luke 22:7–13). The meal is a reminder of the great sacrificial work of Christ on the cross and also that, in eating, we make a covenant commitment to God, sacrificially offering ourselves (Rom. 12:1) in obedience to his expressed wishes, promising to fulfill our own work. We join Israel in saying, "We will do everything the LORD has said." Remembering without responding is actually forgetting.

Remembering also has eschatological ramifications. It directs us first of all to the initial, close relationship between God and humanity as established in creation (Gen. 1–2) and the subsequent separation between God and humanity because of rebellion and disobedience (Gen. 3). The rest of Scripture is a reminder of how God made provision to restore the original relationship, first through the superintendence of the law of Moses (e.g., Gal. 3:25) and then through the fulfilling of that law by Jesus Christ

(Matt. 5:17), the Messiah of whom John the Baptist, fulfilling Elijah's role (Matt. 11:14), was the herald.[13]

This directs one's attention to the coming Day when creation will be restored (Rom. 8:19–23), with humanity restored to a new heaven and earth (Rev. 21:1–8), a new and eschatological Eden when human-divine relationship will be restored not by human effort but by divine sacrifice. Marred human relationships will also be restored, with family harmony (Mal. 4:6) replacing fratricide (Gen. 4:8).

---

13. For a moving look at the theology of Elijah in the events of the Passion, see N. T. Wright, *The Crown and the Cross: Meditations on the Cross and the Life of the Spirit* (Grand Rapids: Eerdmans, 1992), 41–45.

Scripture Index

Scripture Index

Scripture Index

Subject Index

Bring ancient truth to modern life with the

NIV Application Commentary series

Covering both the Old and New Testaments, the **NIV Application Commentary** series is a staple reference for pastors seeking to bring the Bible's timeless message into a modern context. It explains not only what the Bible means but also how that meaning impacts the lives of believers today.

Genesis

This commentary demonstrates how the text charts a course of theological affirmation that results in a simple but majestic account of an ordered, purposeful cosmos with God at the helm, masterfully guiding it, and what this means to us today.

John H. Walton ISBN: 0-310-206170

Exodus

The truth of Christ's resurrection and its resulting impact on our lives mean that to Christians, the application of Exodus is less about how to act than it is about what God has done and what it means to be his children.

Peter Enns ISBN: 0-310-20607-3

Leviticus, Numbers

Roy Gane's commentary on Leviticus and Numbers helps readers understand how the message of these two books, which are replete with what seem to be archaic laws, can have a powerful impact on Christians today.

Roy Gane ISBN: 0-310-21088-7

Judges, Ruth

This commentary helps readers learn how the messages of Judges and Ruth can have the same powerful impact today that they did when they were first written. Judges reveals a God who employs very human deliverers but refuses to gloss over their sins and the consequences of those sins. Ruth demonstrates the far-reaching impact of a righteous character.

K. Lawson Younger Jr. ISBN: 0-310-20636-7

1&2 Samuel

In Samuel, we meet Saul, David, Goliath, Jonathan, Bathsheba, the witch of Endor, and other unforgettable characters. And we encounter ourselves. For while the culture and conditions of Israel under its first kings are vastly different from our own, the basic issues of humans in relation to God, the Great King, have not changed. Sin, repentance, forgiveness, adversity, prayer, faith, and the promises of God—these continue to play out in our lives today.

Bill T. Arnold   ISBN: 0-310-21086-0

1&2 Chronicles

First and Second Chronicles are a narrative steeped in the best and worst of the human heart—but they are also a revelation of Yahweh at work, forwarding his purposes in the midst of fallible people, but a people who trust in the Lord and his word through the prophets. God has a plan to which he is committed.

Andrew E. Hill   ISBN: 0-310-20610-3

Esther

Karen H. Jobes shows what a biblical narrative that never mentions God tells Christians about him today.

Karen H. Jobes   ISBN: 0-310-20672-3

Psalms Volume 1

Gerald Wilson examines Books 1 and 2 of the Psalter. His seminal work on the shaping of the Hebrew Psalter has opened a new avenue of psalms research by shifting focus from exclusive attention to individual psalms to the arrangement of the psalms into groups.

Gerald H. Wilson   ISBN: 0-310-20635-9

Proverbs

Few people can remember when they last heard a sermon from Proverbs or looked together at its chapters. In this NIV Application Commentary on Proverbs, Paul Koptak gives numerous aids to pastors and church leaders on how to study, reflect on, and apply this book on biblical wisdom as part of the educational ministry of their churches.

Paul Koptak   ISBN: 0-310-21852-7

Ecclesiastes, Song of Songs

Ecclesiastes and Songs of Songs have always presented particular challenges to their readers, especially if those readers are seeking to understand them as part of Christian Scripture. Revealing the links between the Scriptures and our own times, Iain Provan shows how these wisdom books speak to us today with relevance and conviction.

Iain Provan   ISBN: 0-310-21372-X

Isaiah

Isaiah wrestles with the realities of people who are not convicted by the truth but actually hardened by it, and with a God whose actions sometimes seem unintelligible, or even worse, appears to be absent. Yet Isaiah penetrates beyond these experiences to an even greater reality. Isaiah sees God's rule over history and his capacity to take the worst of human actions and use it for good. He declares the truth that even in the darkest hours, the Holy One of Israel is infinitely trustworthy.

John N. Oswalt   ISBN: 0-310-20613-8

Jeremiah/Lamentations

These two books cannot be separated from the political conditions of ancient Judah. Beginning with the time of King Josiah, who introduced religious reform, Jeremiah reflects the close link between spiritual and political prosperity or disaster for the nation as a whole.

J. Andrew Dearman   ISBN: 0-310-20616-2

Ezekiel

Discover how, properly understood, this mysterious book with its obscure images offers profound comfort to us today.

Iain M. Duguid   ISBN: 0-310-21047-X

Daniel

Tremper Longman III reveals how the practical stories and spellbinding apocalyptic imagery of Daniel contain principles that are as relevant now as they were in the days of the Babylonian Captivity.

Tremper Longman III   ISBN: 0-310-20608-1

Hosea, Amos, Micah

Scratch beneath the surface of today's culture and you'll find we're not so different from ancient Israel. Revealing the links between Israel eight centuries B.C. and our own times, Gary V. Smith shows how the prophetic writings of Hosea, Amos, and Micah speak to us today with relevance and conviction.

Gary V. Smith

ISBN: 0-310-20614-6

Jonah, Nahum, Habakkuk, Zephaniah

James Bruckner shows how the messages of these four Old Testament prophets, who lived during some of Israel and Judah's most turbulent times, are as powerful in today's turbulent times as when first written.

James Bruckner

ISBN: 0-310-20637-5

Haggai, Zechariah

This commentary on Haggai and Zechariah helps readers learn how the message of these two prophets who challenged and encouraged the people of God after the return from Babylon can have the same powerful impact on the community of faith today.

Mark J. Boda

ISBN: 0-310-20615-4

Matthew

Matthew helps readers learn how the message of Matthew's gospel can have the same powerful impact today that it did when the author first wrote it.

Michael J. Wilkins

ISBN: 0-310-49310-2

Mark

Learn how the challenging gospel of Mark can leave recipients with the same powerful questions and answers it did when it was written.

David E. Garland

ISBN: 0-310-49350-1

Luke
Focus on the most important application of all: "the person of Jesus and the nature of God's work through him to deliver humanity."

Darrell L. Bock   ISBN: 0-310-49330-7

John
Learn both halves of the interpretive task. Gary M. Burge shows readers how to bring the ancient message of John into a modern context. He also explains not only what the book of John meant to its original readers but also how it can speak powerfully today.

Gary M. Burge   ISBN: 0-310-49750-7

Acts
Study the first portraits of the church in action around the world with someone whose ministry mirrors many of the events in Acts. Biblical scholar and worldwide evangelist Ajith Fernando applies the story of the church's early development to the global mission of believers today.

Ajith Fernando   ISBN: 0-310-49410-9

Romans
Paul's letter to the Romans remains one of the most important expressions of Christian truth ever written. Douglas Moo comments on the text and then explores issues in Paul's culture and in ours that help us understand the ultimate meaning of each paragraph.

Douglas J. Moo   ISBN: 0-310-49400-1

1 Corinthians
Is your church struggling with the problem of divisiveness and fragmentation? See the solution Paul gave the Corinthian Christians over 2,000 years ago. It still works today!

Craig Blomberg   ISBN: 0-310-48490-1

2 Corinthians
Often recognized as the most difficult of Paul's letters to understand, 2 Corinthians can have the same powerful impact today that it did when it was first written.

Scott J. Hafemann

ISBN: 0-310-49420-6

Galatians
A pastor's message is true not because of his preaching or people-management skills, but because of Christ. Learn how to apply Paul's example of visionary church leadership to your own congregation.

Scot McKnight

ISBN: 0-310-48470-7

Ephesians
Explore what the author calls "a surprisingly comprehensive statement about God and his work, about Christ and the gospel, about life with God's Spirit, and about the right way to live."

Klyne Snodgrass

ISBN: 0-310-49340-4

Philippians
The best lesson Philippians provides is how to encourage people who actually are doing quite well. Learn why not all the New Testament letters are reactions to theological crises.

Frank Thielman

ISBN: 0-310-49300-5

Colossians/Philemon
The temptation to trust in the wrong things has always been strong. Use this commentary to learn the importance of trusting only in Jesus, God's Son, in whom all the fullness of God lives. No message is more important for our postmodern culture.

David E. Garland

ISBN: 0-310-48480-4

1&2 Thessalonians

Paul's letters to the Thessalonians say as much to us today about Christ's return and our resurrection as they did in the early church. This volume skillfully reveals Paul's answers to these questions and how they address the needs of contemporary Christians.

Michael W. Holmes   ISBN: 0-310-49380-3

1&2 Timothy, Titus

Reveals the context and meanings of Paul's letters to two leaders in the early Christian Church and explores their present-day implications to help you to accurately apply the principles they contain to contemporary issues.

Walter L. Liefeld   ISBN: 0-310-50110-5

Hebrews

The message of Hebrews can be summed up in a single phrase: "God speaks effectively to us through Jesus." Unpack the theological meaning of those seven words and learn why the gospel still demands a hearing today.

George H. Guthrie   ISBN: 0-310-49390-0

James

Give your church the best antidote for a culture of people who say they believe one thing but act in ways that either ignore or contradict their belief. More than just saying, "Practice what you preach," James gives solid reasons why faith and action must coexist.

David P. Nystrom   ISBN: 0-310-49360-9

1 Peter

The issue of the church's relationship to the state hits the news media in some form nearly every day. Learn how Peter answered the question for Christians surviving under Roman rule and how it applies similarly to believers living amid the secular institutions of the modern world.

Scot McKnight   ISBN: 0-310-49290-4

2 Peter, Jude

Introduce your modern audience to letters they may not be familiar with and show why they'll want to get to know them.

Douglas J. Moo

ISBN: 0-310-20104-7

Letters of John

Like the community in John's time, which faced disputes over erroneous "secret knowledge," today's church needs discernment in affirming new ideas supported by Scripture and weeding out harmful notions. This volume will help you show today's Christians how to use John's example.

Gary M. Burge

ISBN: 0-310-48620-3

Revelation

Craig Keener offers a "new" approach to the book of Revelation by focusing on the "old." He stresses the need for believers to prepare for the possibility of suffering for the sake of Jesus.

Craig S. Keener

ISBN: 0-310-23192-2

Praise for the NIV Application Commentary Series

This series promises to become an indispensable tool for every pastor and teacher who seeks to make the Bible's timeless message speak to this generation."

—Billy Graham

"It is encouraging to find a commentary that is not only biblically trustworthy but also contemporary in its application. **The NIV Application Commentary** series will prove to be a helpful tool in the pastor's sermon preparation. I use it and recommend it."

—Charles F. Stanley, Pastor, First Baptist Church of Atlanta

"**The NIV Application Commentary** is an outstanding resource for pastors and anyone else who is serious about developing 'doers of the Word.'"

—Rick Warren, Pastor, Saddleback Community Church, Author, *The Purpose-Driven Church*

"**The NIV Application Commentary** series shares the same goal that has been the passion of my own ministry—communicating God's Word to a contemporary audience so that they feel the full impact of its message."

—Bill Hybels, Willow Creek Community Church

"**The NIV Application Commentary** series helps pastors and other Bible teachers with one of the most neglected elements in good preaching—accurate, useful application. Most commentaries tell you a few things that are helpful and much that you do not need to know. By dealing with the original meaning and contemporary significance of each passage, **The NIV Application Commentary** series promises to be helpful all the way around."

—Dr. James Montgomery Boice, Tenth Presbyterian Church

"If you want to avoid hanging applicational elephants from interpretive threads, then **The NIV Application Commentary** is for you! This series excels at both original meaning and contemporary signficance. I support it 100 percent."

—Howard G. Hendricks, Dallas Theological Seminary

"**The NIV Application Commentary** series doesn't fool around: It gets right down to business, bringing this ancient and powerful Word of God into the present so that it can be heard and delivered with all the freshness of a new day, with all the immediacy of a friend's embrace."

—Eugene H. Peterson, Regent College

"This series dares to go where few scholars have gone before—into the real world of biblical application faced by pastors and teachers every day. This is everything a good commentary series should be."

—Leith Anderson, Pastor, Wooddale Church

"This is THE pulpit commentary for the 21st century."

—George K. Brushaber, President, Bethel College & Seminary

"Here, at last, is a commentary that makes the proper circuit from the biblical world to main street. **The NIV Application Commentary** is a magnificent gift to the church."

—R. Kent Hughes, Pastor, College Church, Wheaton, IL

Look for the NIV Application Commentary *at your local Christian bookstore*

"Academically well informed ... this series helps the contemporary reader hear God's Word and consider its implications; scholarship in the service of the Church."

—Arthur Rowe, Spurgeon's College

"The NIV Application Commentary series promises to be of very great service to all who preach and teach the Word of God."

—J. I. Packer, Regent College

"The NIV Application Commentary series will be a great help for readers who want to understand what the Bible means, how it applies, and what they should do in response."

—Stuart Briscoe, Pastor, Elmbrook Church

"The NIV Application Commentary meets the urgent need for an exhaustive and authoritative commentary based on the New International Version. This series will soon be found in libraries and studies throughout the evangelical community."

—Dr. James Kennedy, Ph.D., Senior Minister,
Coral Ridge Presbyterian Church

"... for readers who want a reliable synthesis with a strong emphasis on application.... [Provides a] freshness that can benefit students, teachers, and (especially) church leaders ... makes good devotional reading, precisely because it emphasizes the contemporary application.... This approach refreshes and challenges the reader, and would make helpful material for sermon-preparation or Bible study.... At a time when many pastors are deeply in need of inspiration and encouragement, these volumes ... would be a good investment for congregations, even if it means adding a line to the annual budget."

—*Christianity Today*

"This commentary needs to be given full marks for what it is attempting to do. This is to provide a commentary for the English reader that takes exegesis seriously and still has space left for considerations of what the text is saying in today's world.... One will understand everything that one reads. May its tribe increase!"

—*Journal of the Evangelical Theological Society*

"... a useful, nontechnical commentary.... In the application section are illustrations, which, to pastors seeking a fresh approach, are worth the price of the book.... Other useful features include same-page footnotes; Greek words transliterated in the text of the commentary; and an attractive, user-friendly layout. Pastors and Bible teachers who want to emphasize contemporary application will find this commentary a useful tool."

—*Bookstore Journal*

"... one of the most helpful commentary sets from recent years."

—Alabama Southern Baptist Convention

"Some commentaries build walls that isolate you back in the ancient world. The NIV Application Commentary builds bridges that make the Bible come alive with meaning for contemporary life—and the series does so concisely, clearly and accurately. No wasted words or academic detours—just solid help and practical truth!"

—Warren Wiersbe

Look for the NIV Application Commentary at your local Christian bookstore

We want to hear from you. Please send your comments about this book to us in care of zreview@zondervan.com. Thank you.

ZONDERVAN.com/
AUTHORTRACKER
follow your favorite authors